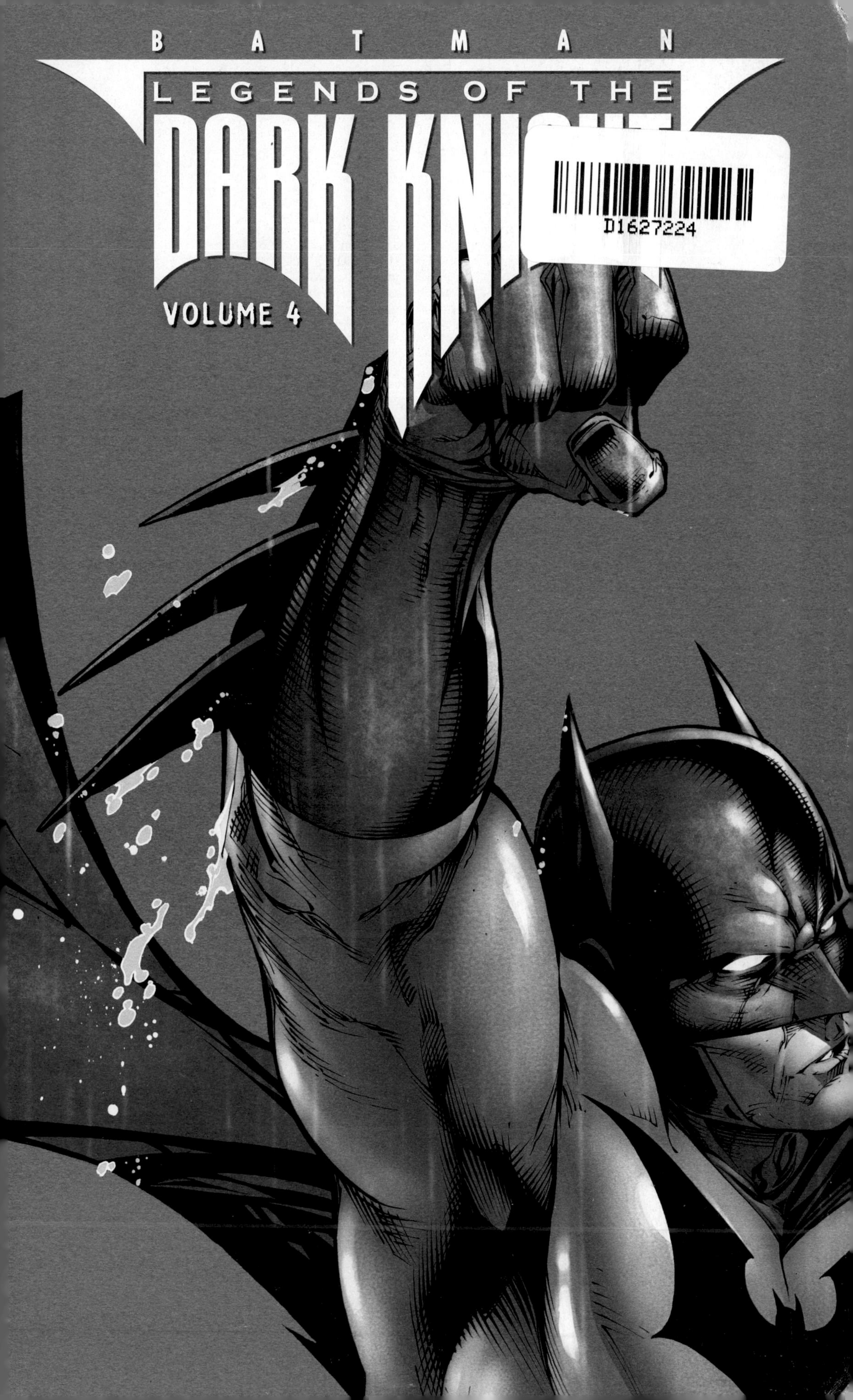
BATMAN
LEGENDS OF THE
DARK KNI
VOLUME 4

HANK KANALZ KRISTY QUINN MIKE MARTS EDITORS - ORIGINAL SERIES
JESSICA CHEN ASSISTANT EDITOR - ORIGINAL SERIES
LIZ ERICKSON EDITOR
ROBBIN BROSTERMAN DESIGN DIRECTOR - BOOKS
DAMIAN RYLAND PUBLICATION DESIGN

HANK KANALZ SENIOR VP - VERTIGO & INTEGRATED PUBLISHING

DIANE NELSON PRESIDENT
DAN DIDIO and JIM LEE CO-PUBLISHERS
GEOFF JOHNS CHIEF CREATIVE OFFICER
AMIT DESAI SENIOR VP - MARKETING & FRANCHISE MANAGEMENT
AMY GENKINS SENIOR VP - BUSINESS & LEGAL AFFAIRS
NAIRI GARDINER SENIOR VP - FINANCE
JEFF BOISON VP - PUBLISHING PLANNING
MARK CHIARELLO VP - ART DIRECTION & DESIGN
JOHN CUNNINGHAM VP - MARKETING
TERRI CUNNINGHAM VP - EDITORIAL ADMINISTRATION
LARRY GANEM VP - TALENT RELATIONS & SERVICES
ALISON GILL SENIOR VP - MANUFACTURING & OPERATIONS
JAY KOGAN VP-BUSINESS & LEGAL AFFAIRS, PUBLISHING
JACK MAHAN VP - BUSINESS AFFAIRS, TALENT
NICK NAPOLITANO VP - MANUFACTURING ADMINISTRATION
SUE POHJA VP - BOOK SALES
FRED RUIZ VP - MANUFACTURING OPERATIONS
COURTNEY SIMMONS SENIOR VP - PUBLICITY
BOB WAYNE SENIOR VP - SALES

BATMAN: LEGENDS OF THE DARK KNIGHT VOLUME 4

DC COMICS, 4000 WARNER BLVD., BURBANK, CA 91522
A WARNER BROS. ENTERTAINMENT COMPANY.
PRINTED BY RR DONNELLEY, SALEM, VA, USA. 4/24/2015.
FIRST PRINTING. ISBN: 978-1-4012-5467-4

LIBRARY OF CONGRESS CATALOGING-IN-PUBLICATION DATA

BATMAN : LEGENDS OF THE DARK KNIGHT. VOLUME 4 / CHARLES SOULE, SHANE DAVIS, DENNIS CALERO.
PAGES CM
ISBN 978-1-4012-5467-4 (PAPERBACK)
1. GRAPHIC NOVELS. I. SOULE CHARLES. II. DAVIS, SHANE. III. CALERO, DENNIS.

PN6728.B36B4247 2014
741.5'973--DC23

2014027356

SUSTAINABLE FORESTRY INITIATIVE
Certified Chain of Custody
20% Certified Forest Content, 80% Certified Sourcing
www.sfiprogram.org
SFI-01042
APPLIES TO TEXT STOCK ONLY

BATMAN
LEGENDS OF THE
DARK KNIGHT

VOLUME 4

Joshua WILLIAMSON · Charles SOULE · Frank HANNAH
Derek FRIDOLFS · Kenneth Elliott JONES · Shane DAVIS
Brandon MONTCLARE · Mike W. BARR · Jim KREUGER
WRITERS

WES CRAIG · DENNIS CALERO · MARCO TURINI
DREW EDWARD JOHNSON · DEXTER SOY · JASON SHAWN ALEXANDER
TOM LYLE · TOM RANEY · SHANE DAVIS
SANDRA HOPE · MICHELLE DELECKI
ARTISTS

LEE LOUGHRIDGE · DENNIS CALERO · LEO PACIAROTTI · KATHRYN LAYNO
DEXTER SOY · SHERARD JACKSON · WENDY BROOME · SEBASTIEN LAMIRAND
COLORISTS

Saida TEMOFONTE · DERON BENNETT
LETTERERS

Ed BENES with Kathryn LAYNO
COLLECTION COVER ARTISTS

BATMAN created by BOB KANE

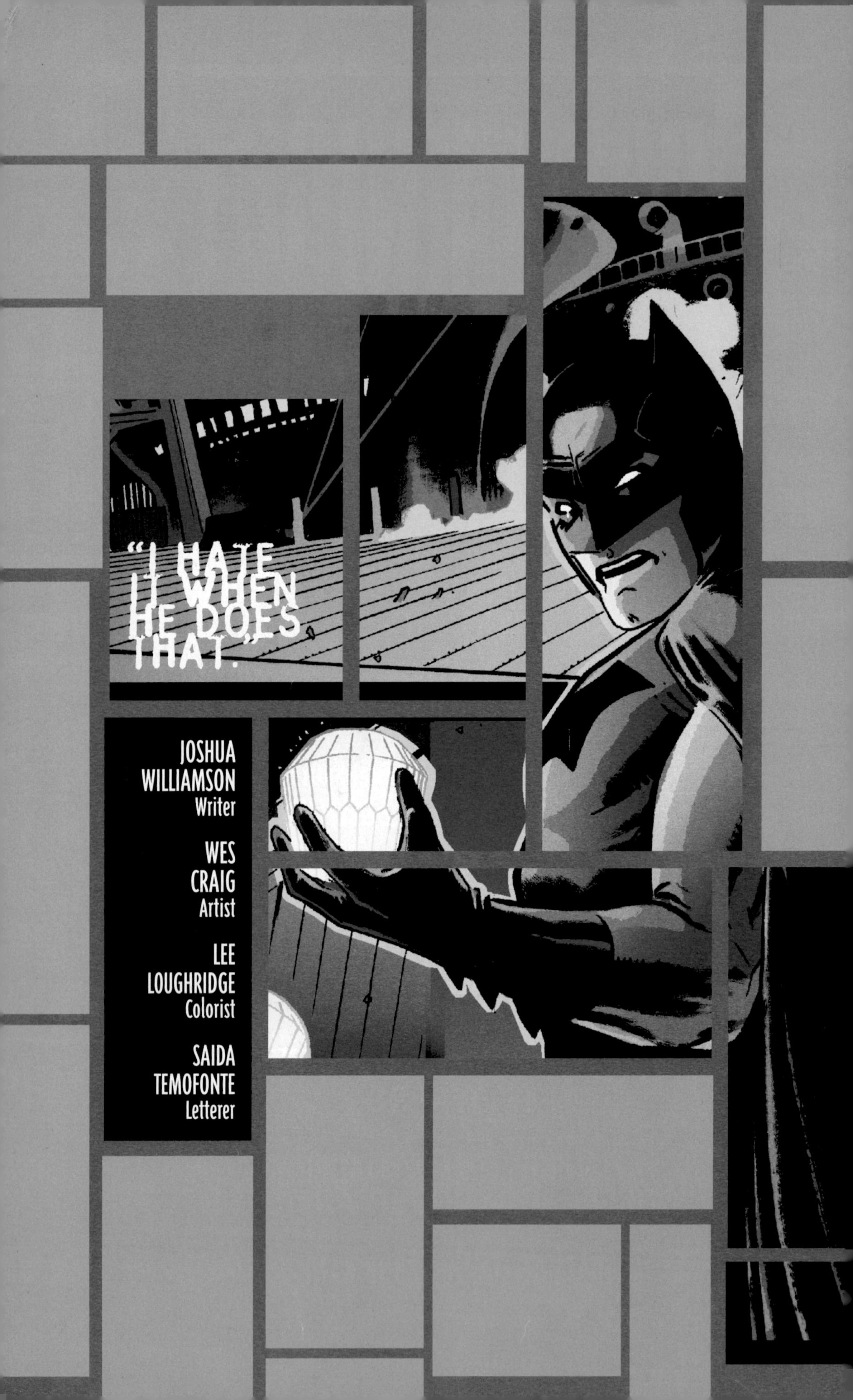
"I HATE IT WHEN HE DOES THAT."

JOSHUA WILLIAMSON
Writer

WES CRAIG
Artist

LEE LOUGHRIDGE
Colorist

SAIDA TEMOFONTE
Letterer

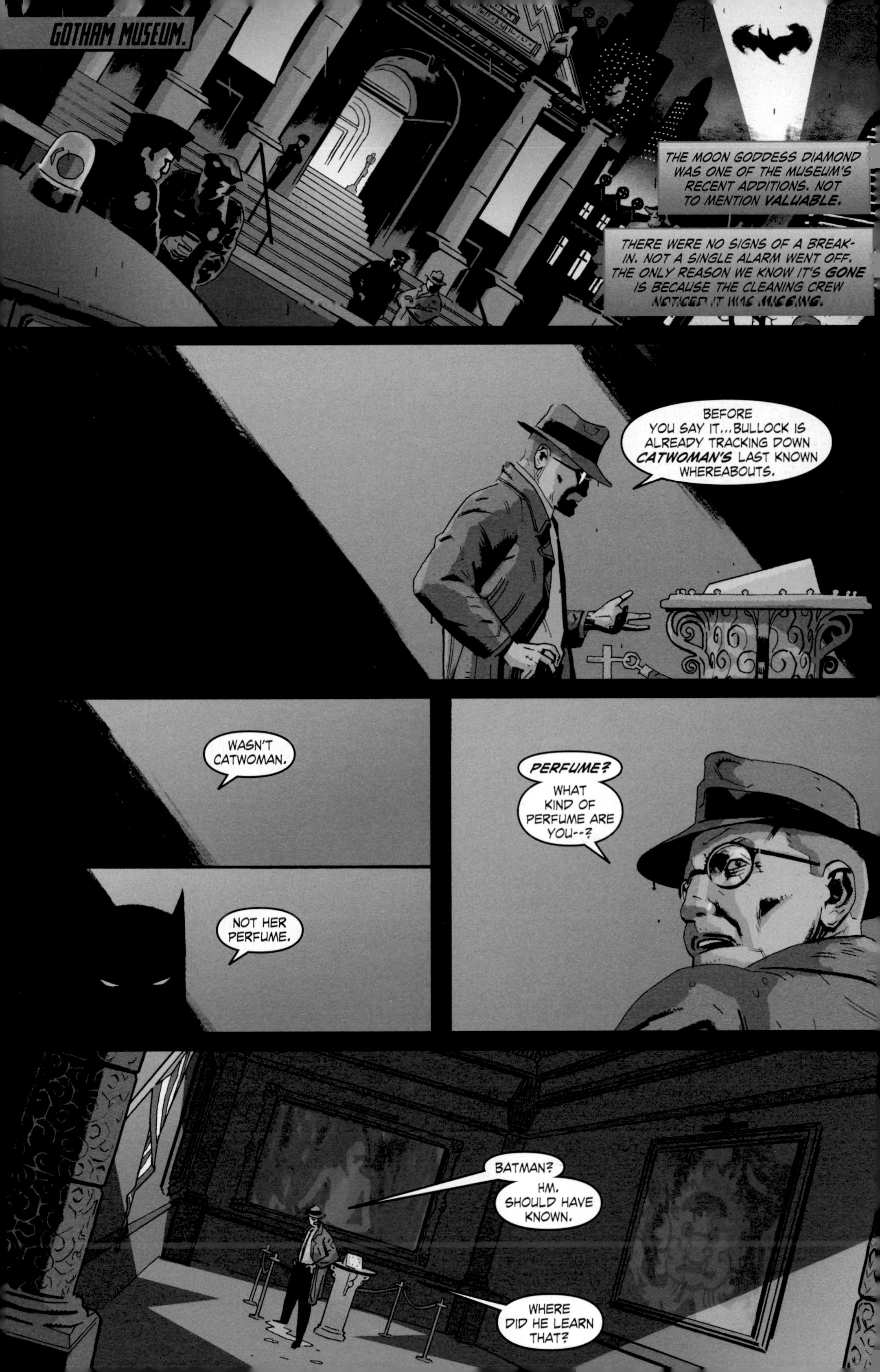
GOTHAM MUSEUM.
THE MOON GODDESS DIAMOND WAS ONE OF THE MUSEUM'S RECENT ADDITIONS. NOT TO MENTION VALUABLE.
THERE WERE NO SIGNS OF A BREAK-IN. NOT A SINGLE ALARM WENT OFF. THE ONLY REASON WE KNOW IT'S GONE IS BECAUSE THE CLEANING CREW NOTICED IT WAS MISSING.
BEFORE YOU SAY IT...BULLOCK IS ALREADY TRACKING DOWN CATWOMAN'S LAST KNOWN WHEREABOUTS.
WASN'T CATWOMAN.
NOT HER PERFUME.
PERFUME? WHAT KIND OF PERFUME ARE YOU--?
BATMAN?
HM. SHOULD HAVE KNOWN.
WHERE DID HE LEARN THAT?

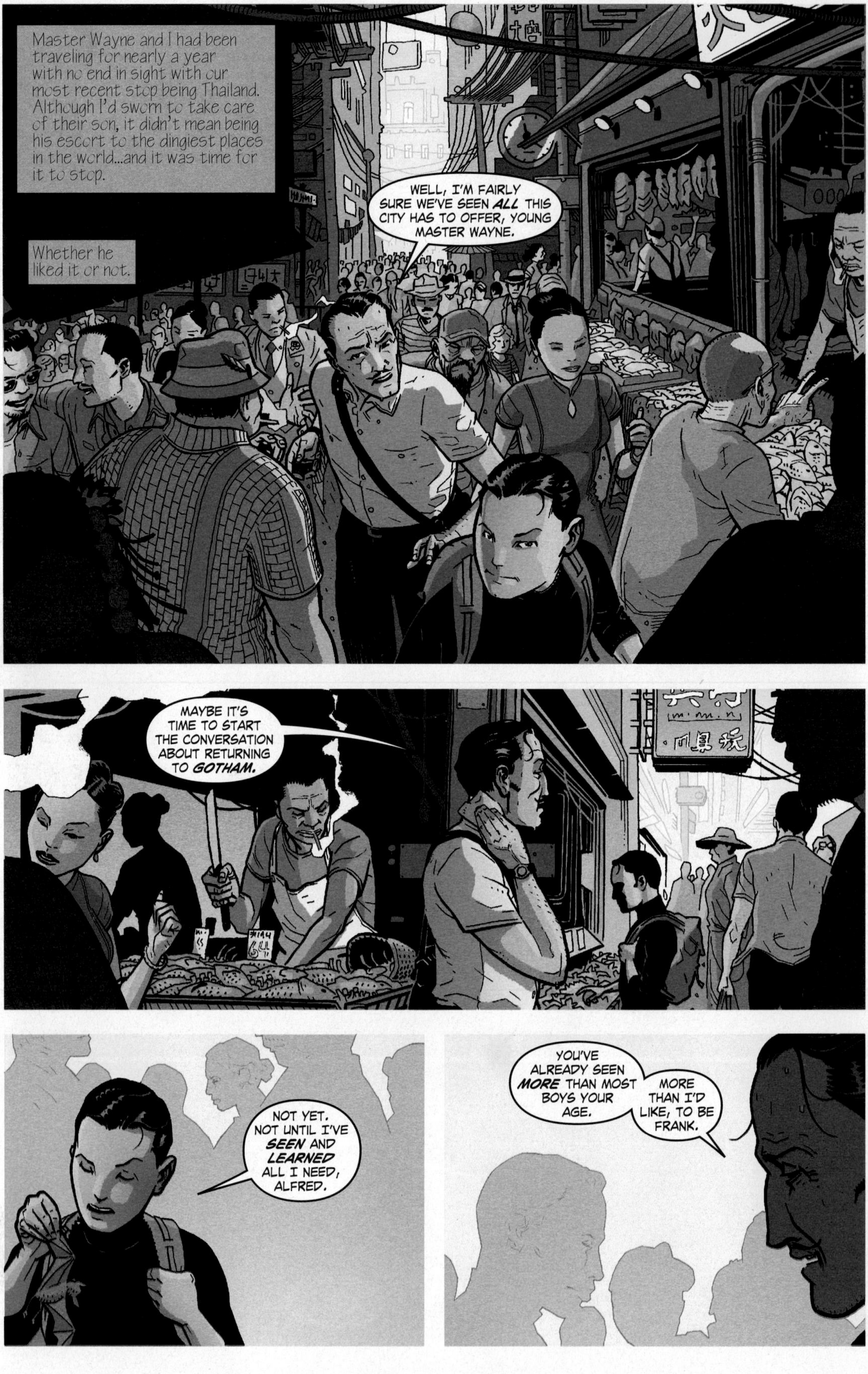
Master Wayne and I had been traveling for nearly a year with no end in sight with our most recent stop being Thailand. Although I'd sworn to take care of their son, it didn't mean being his escort to the dingiest places in the world...and it was time for it to stop.
WELL, I'M FAIRLY SURE WE'VE SEEN ALL THIS CITY HAS TO OFFER, YOUNG MASTER WAYNE.
Whether he liked it or not.
MAYBE IT'S TIME TO START THE CONVERSATION ABOUT RETURNING TO GOTHAM.
NOT YET. NOT UNTIL I'VE SEEN AND LEARNED ALL I NEED, ALFRED.
YOU'VE ALREADY SEEN MORE THAN MOST BOYS YOUR AGE.
MORE THAN I'D LIKE, TO BE FRANK.

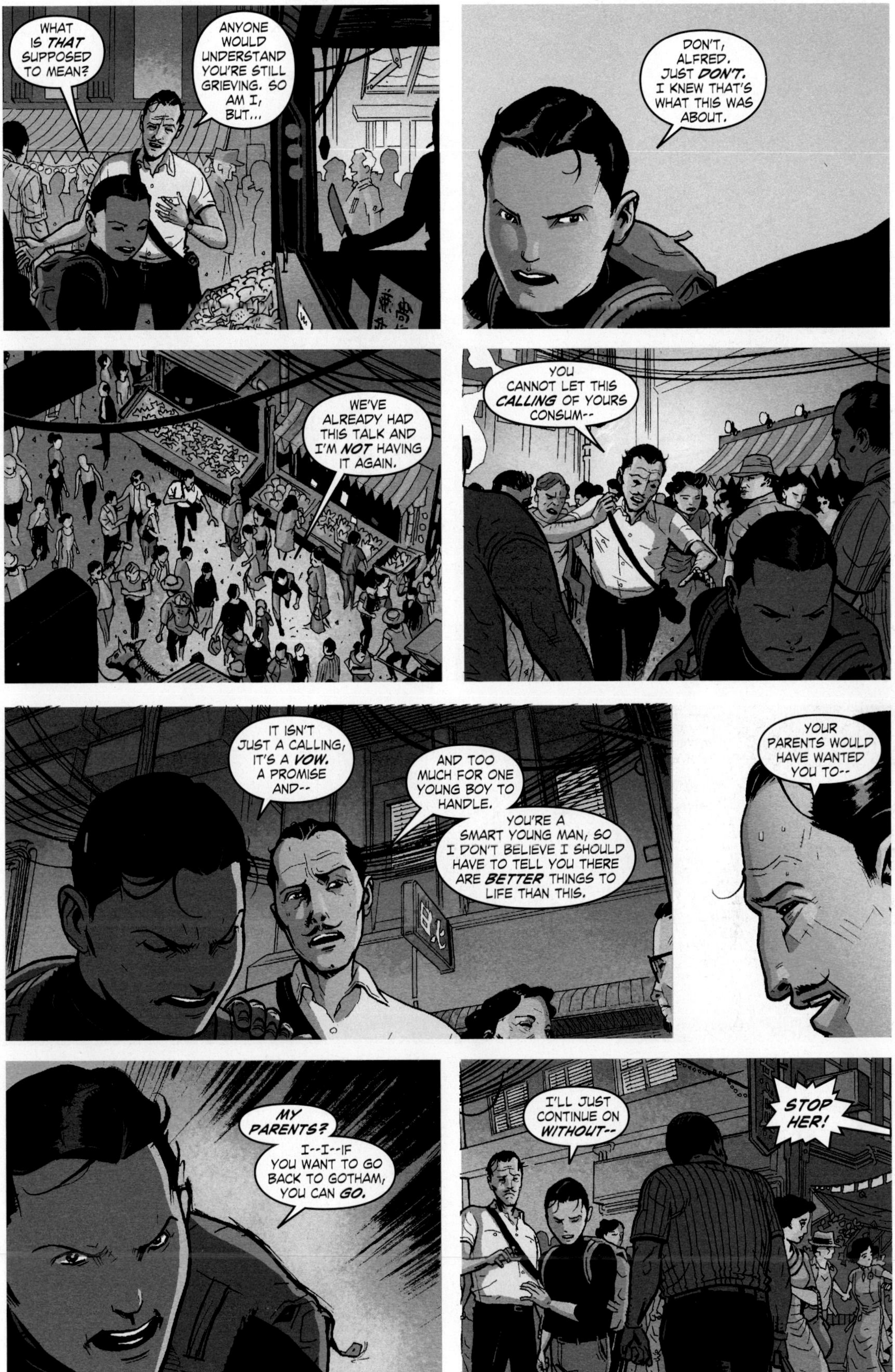
WHAT IS THAT SUPPOSED TO MEAN?
ANYONE WOULD UNDERSTAND YOU'RE STILL GRIEVING. SO AM I, BUT...
DON'T, ALFRED. JUST DON'T. I KNEW THAT'S WHAT THIS WAS ABOUT.
WE'VE ALREADY HAD THIS TALK AND I'M NOT HAVING IT AGAIN.
YOU CANNOT LET THIS CALLING OF YOURS CONSUM--
IT ISN'T JUST A CALLING, IT'S A VOW. A PROMISE AND--
AND TOO MUCH FOR ONE YOUNG BOY TO HANDLE.
YOU'RE A SMART YOUNG MAN, SO I DON'T BELIEVE I SHOULD HAVE TO TELL YOU THERE ARE BETTER THINGS TO LIFE THAN THIS.
YOUR PARENTS WOULD HAVE WANTED YOU TO--
MY PARENTS?
I--I--IF YOU WANT TO GO BACK TO GOTHAM, YOU CAN GO.
I'LL JUST CONTINUE ON WITHOUT--
STOP HER!

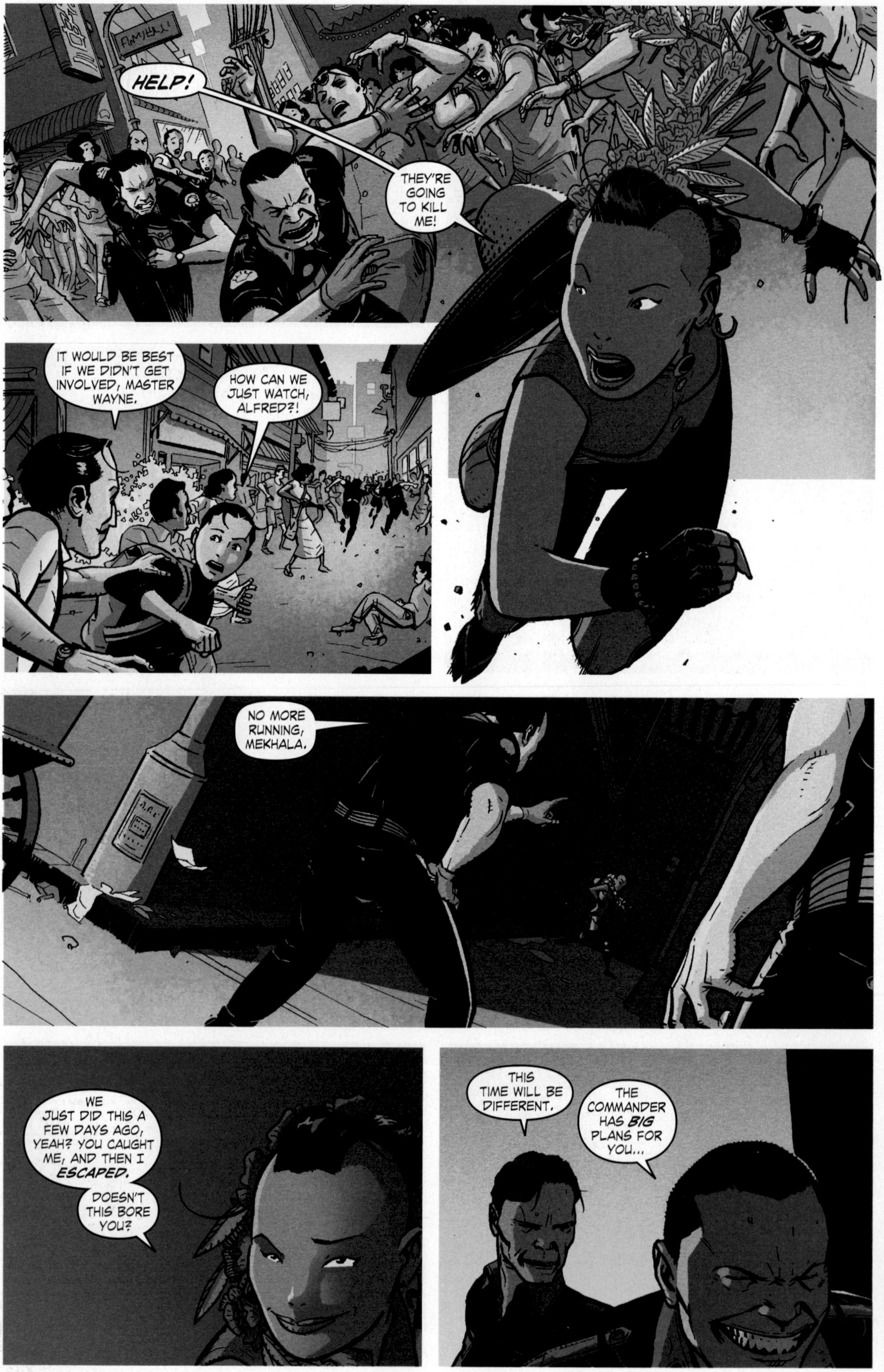
HELP!
THEY'RE GOING TO KILL ME!
IT WOULD BE BEST IF WE DIDN'T GET INVOLVED, MASTER WAYNE.
HOW CAN WE JUST WATCH, ALFRED?!
NO MORE RUNNING, MEKHALA.
WE JUST DID THIS A FEW DAYS AGO, YEAH? YOU CAUGHT ME, AND THEN I ESCAPED.
DOESN'T THIS BORE YOU?
THIS TIME WILL BE DIFFERENT.
THE COMMANDER HAS BIG PLANS FOR YOU...

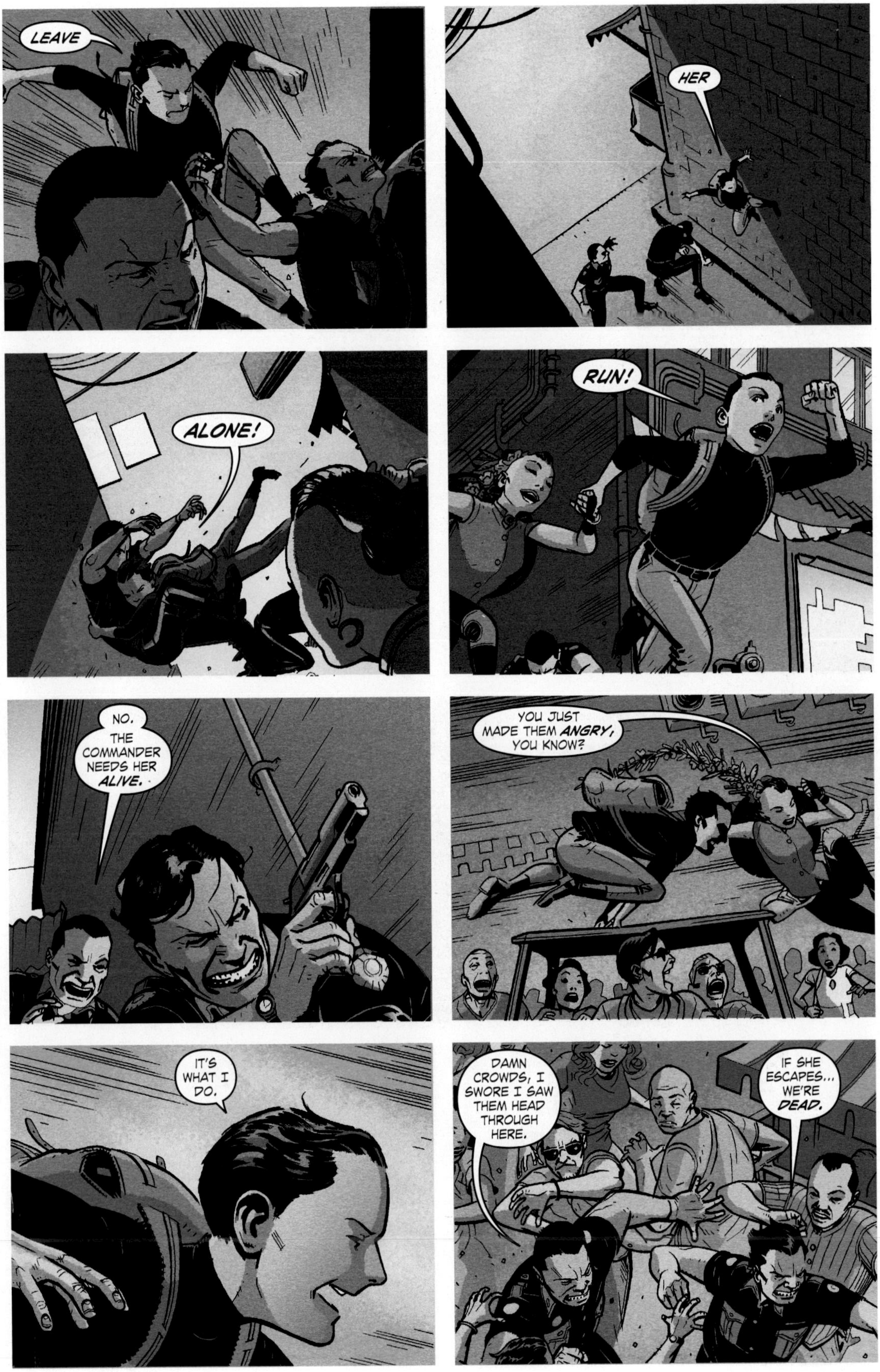
LEAVE
HER
ALONE!
RUN!
NO. THE COMMANDER NEEDS HER ALIVE.
YOU JUST MADE THEM ANGRY, YOU KNOW?
IT'S WHAT I DO.
DAMN CROWDS, I SWORE I SAW THEM HEAD THROUGH HERE.
IF SHE ESCAPES... WE'RE DEAD.

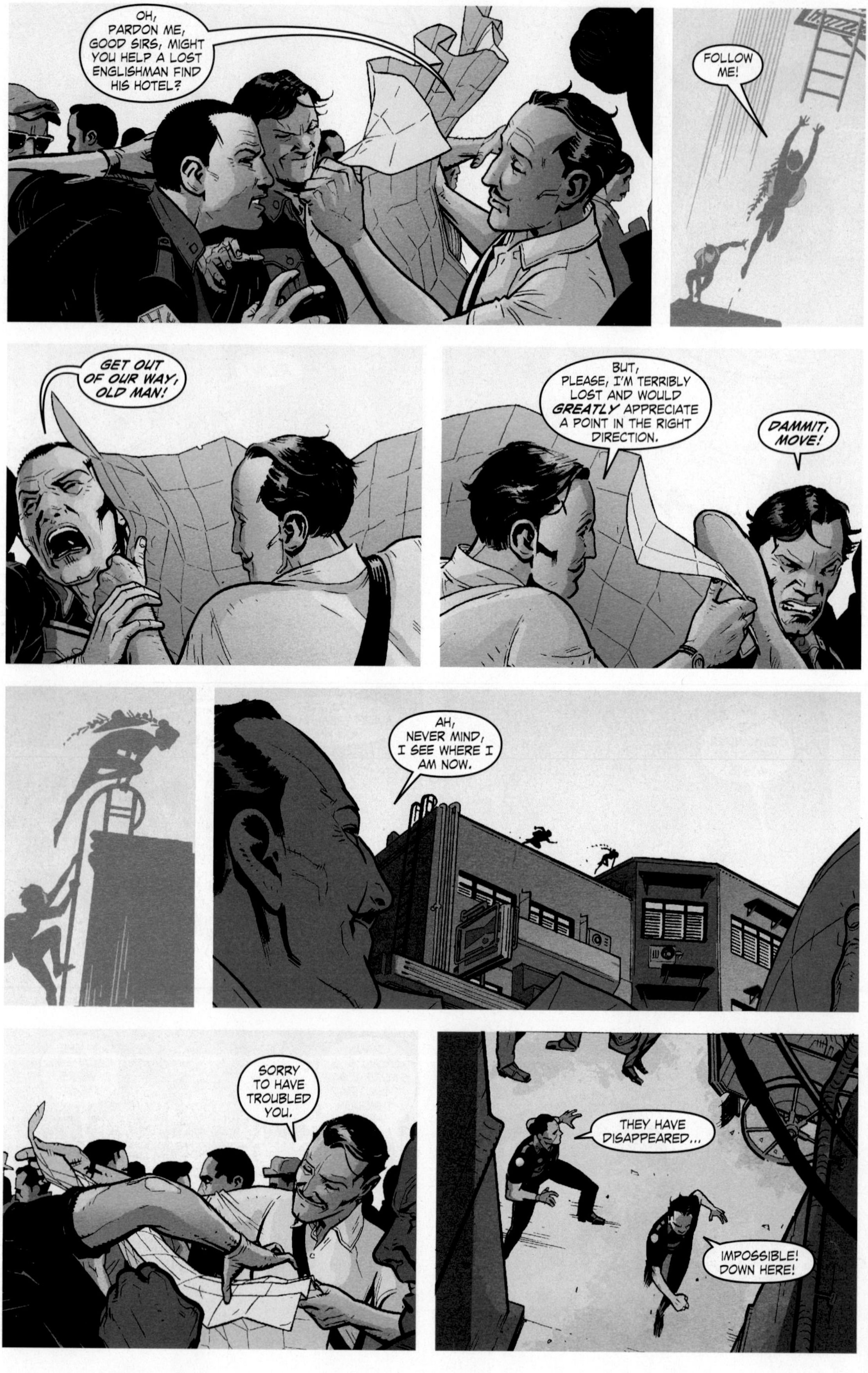
OH, PARDON ME, GOOD SIRS, MIGHT YOU HELP A LOST ENGLISHMAN FIND HIS HOTEL?
FOLLOW ME!
GET OUT OF OUR WAY, OLD MAN!
BUT, PLEASE, I'M TERRIBLY LOST AND WOULD GREATLY APPRECIATE A POINT IN THE RIGHT DIRECTION.
DAMMIT, MOVE!
AH, NEVER MIND, I SEE WHERE I AM NOW.
SORRY TO HAVE TROUBLED YOU.
THEY HAVE DISAPPEARED...
IMPOSSIBLE! DOWN HERE!

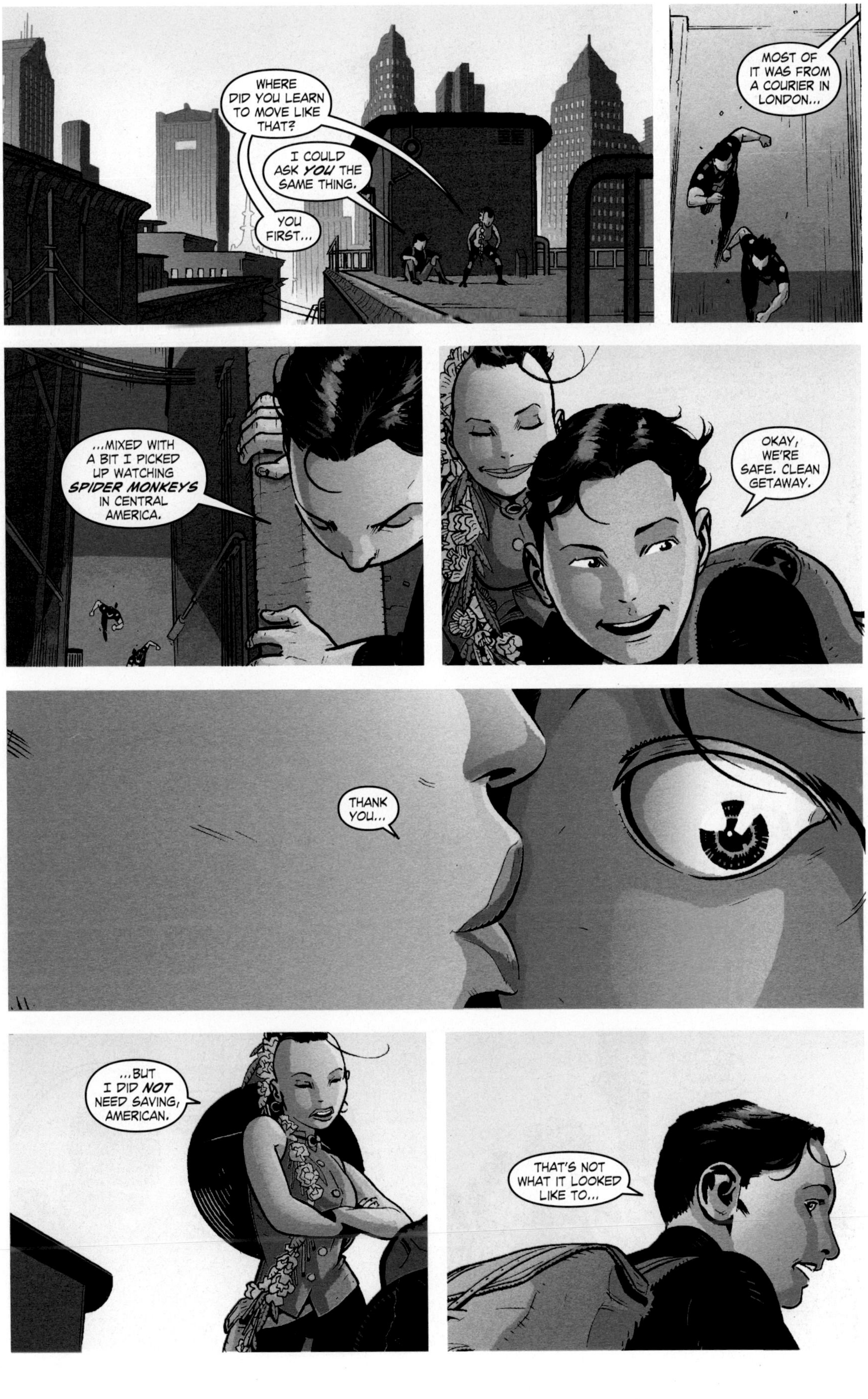
WHERE DID YOU LEARN TO MOVE LIKE THAT?
I COULD ASK YOU THE SAME THING.
YOU FIRST...
MOST OF IT WAS FROM A COURIER IN LONDON...
...MIXED WITH A BIT I PICKED UP WATCHING SPIDER MONKEYS IN CENTRAL AMERICA.
OKAY, WE'RE SAFE. CLEAN GETAWAY.
THANK YOU...
...BUT I DID NOT NEED SAVING, AMERICAN.
THAT'S NOT WHAT IT LOOKED LIKE TO...

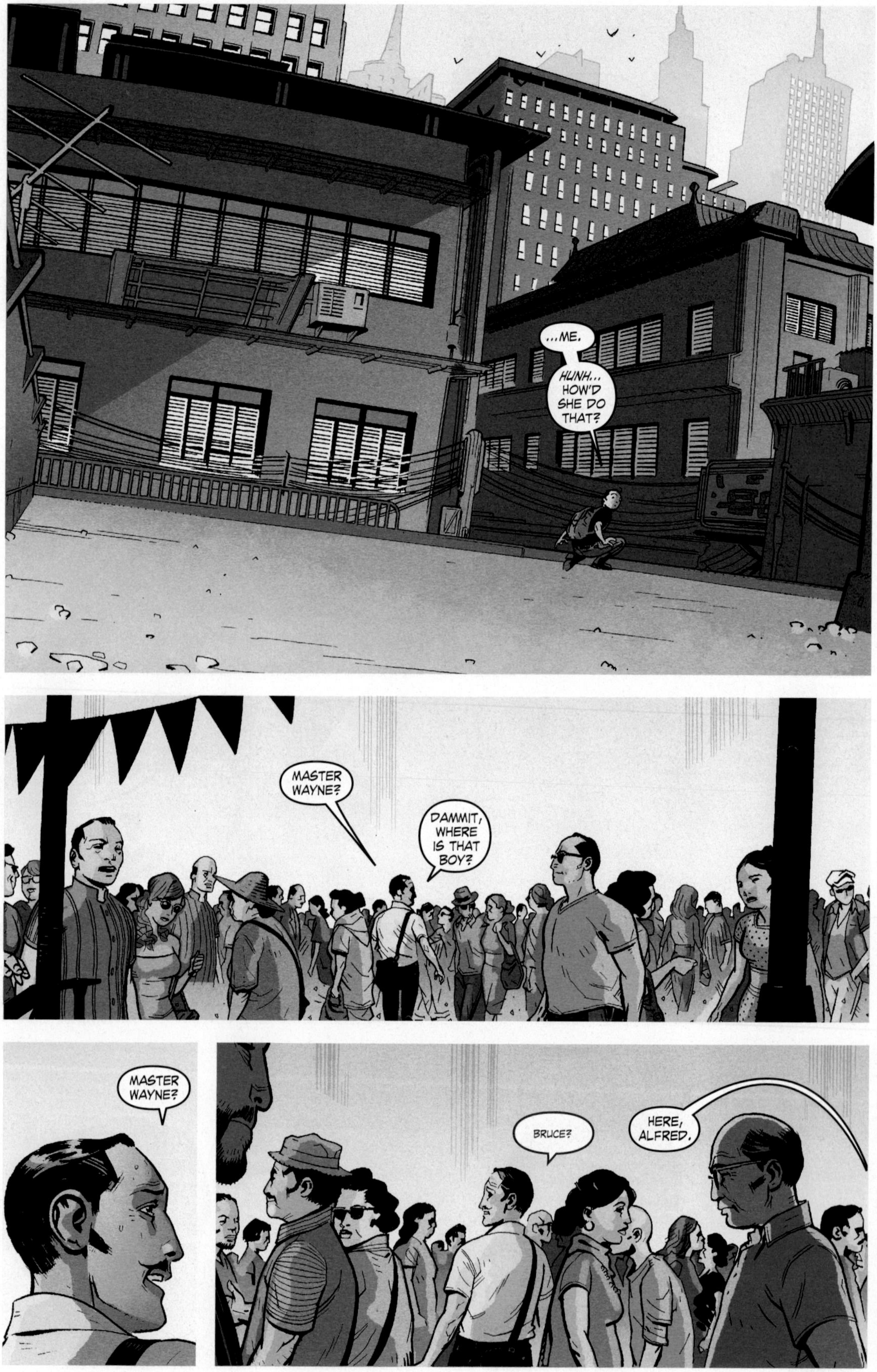

...ME.
HUNH... HOW'D SHE DO THAT?
MASTER WAYNE?
DAMMIT, WHERE IS THAT BOY?
MASTER WAYNE?
BRUCE?
HERE, ALFRED.

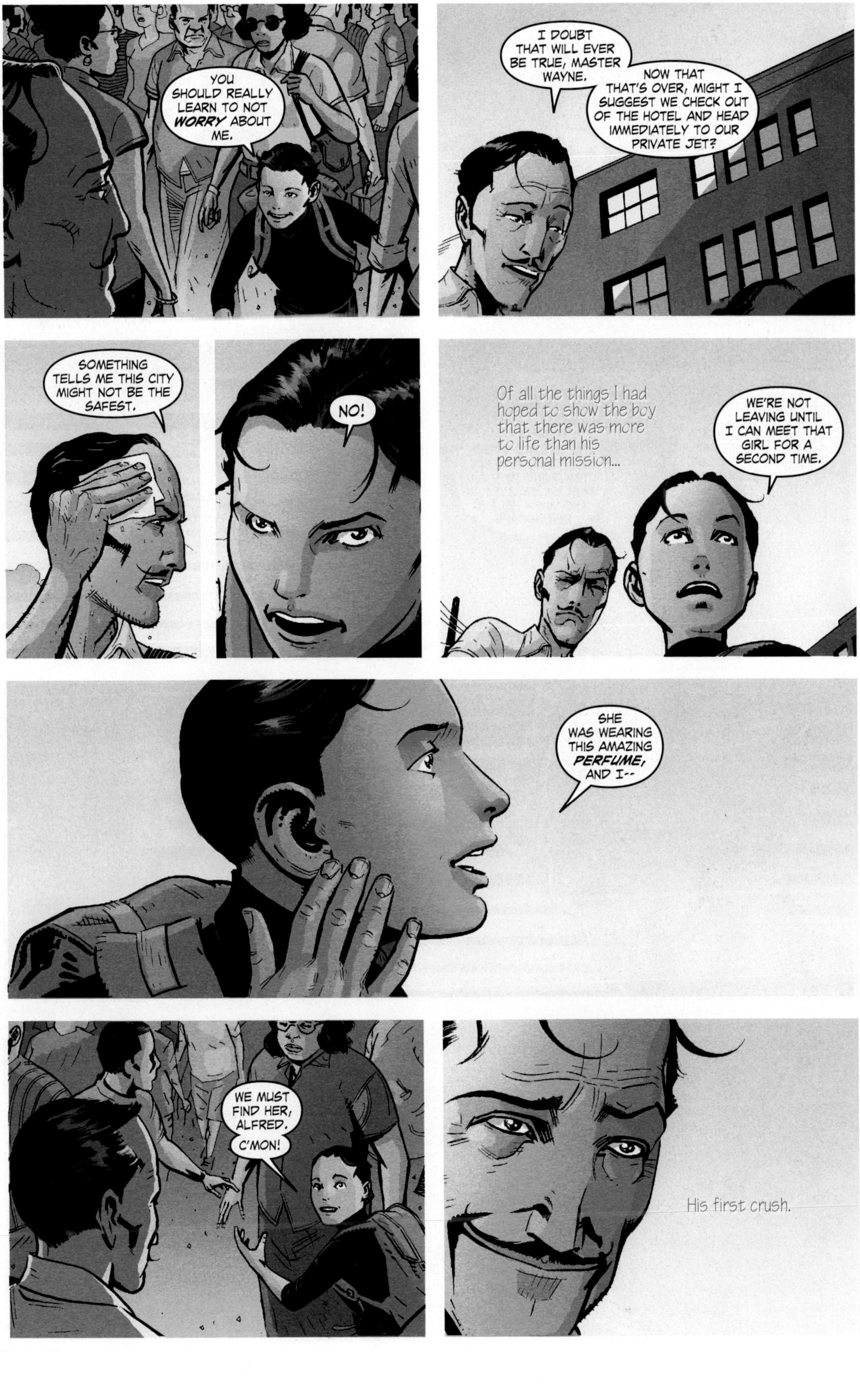
YOU SHOULD REALLY LEARN TO NOT WORRY ABOUT ME.
I DOUBT THAT WILL EVER BE TRUE, MASTER WAYNE.
NOW THAT THAT'S OVER, MIGHT I SUGGEST WE CHECK OUT OF THE HOTEL AND HEAD IMMEDIATELY TO OUR PRIVATE JET?
SOMETHING TELLS ME THIS CITY MIGHT NOT BE THE SAFEST.
NO!
Of all the things I had hoped to show the boy that there was more to life than his personal mission...
WE'RE NOT LEAVING UNTIL I CAN MEET THAT GIRL FOR A SECOND TIME.
SHE WAS WEARING THIS AMAZING PERFUME, AND I--
WE MUST FIND HER, ALFRED.
C'MON!
His first crush.

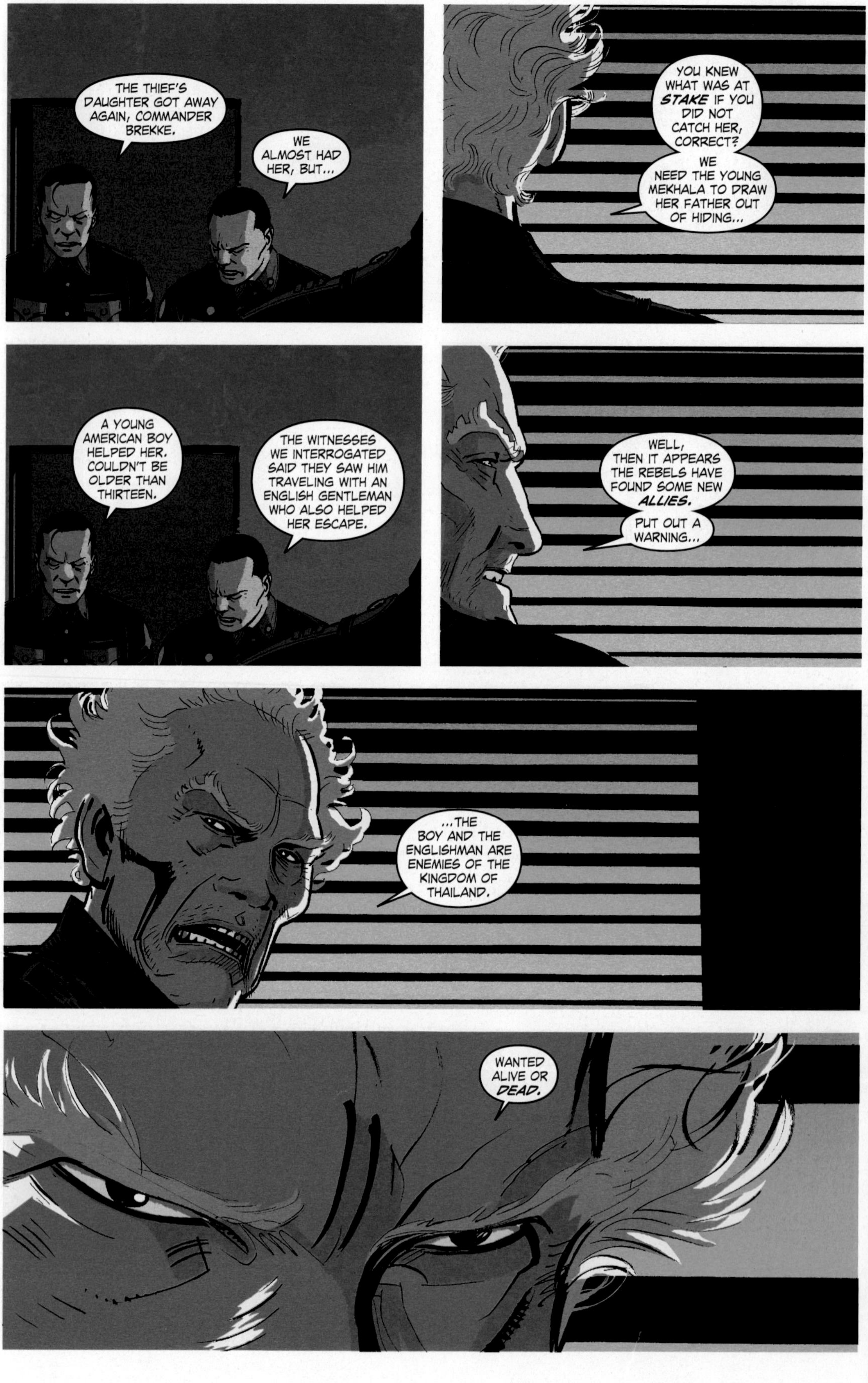
THE THIEF'S DAUGHTER GOT AWAY AGAIN, COMMANDER BREKKE.
WE ALMOST HAD HER, BUT...
YOU KNEW WHAT WAS AT STAKE IF YOU DID NOT CATCH HER, CORRECT?
WE NEED THE YOUNG MEKHALA TO DRAW HER FATHER OUT OF HIDING...
A YOUNG AMERICAN BOY HELPED HER. COULDN'T BE OLDER THAN THIRTEEN.
THE WITNESSES WE INTERROGATED SAID THEY SAW HIM TRAVELING WITH AN ENGLISH GENTLEMAN WHO ALSO HELPED HER ESCAPE.
WELL, THEN IT APPEARS THE REBELS HAVE FOUND SOME NEW ALLIES.
PUT OUT A WARNING...
...THE BOY AND THE ENGLISHMAN ARE ENEMIES OF THE KINGDOM OF THAILAND.
WANTED ALIVE OR DEAD.

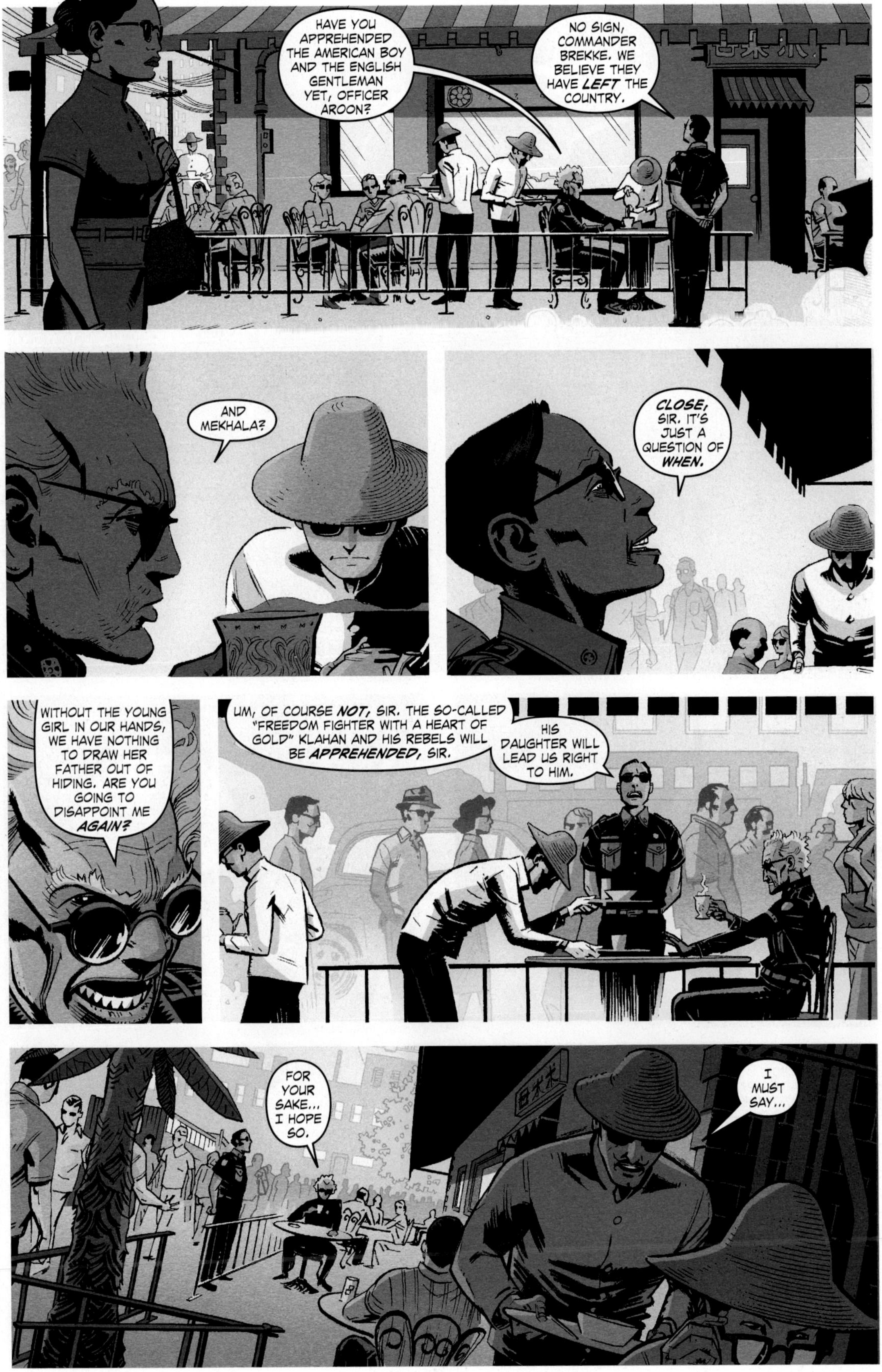
HAVE YOU APPREHENDED THE AMERICAN BOY AND THE ENGLISH GENTLEMAN YET, OFFICER AROON?
NO SIGN, COMMANDER BREKKE. WE BELIEVE THEY HAVE LEFT THE COUNTRY.
AND MEKHALA?
CLOSE, SIR. IT'S JUST A QUESTION OF WHEN.
WITHOUT THE YOUNG GIRL IN OUR HANDS, WE HAVE NOTHING TO DRAW HER FATHER OUT OF HIDING. ARE YOU GOING TO DISAPPOINT ME AGAIN?
UM, OF COURSE NOT, SIR. THE SO-CALLED "FREEDOM FIGHTER WITH A HEART OF GOLD" KLAHAN AND HIS REBELS WILL BE APPREHENDED, SIR.
HIS DAUGHTER WILL LEAD US RIGHT TO HIM.
FOR YOUR SAKE... I HOPE SO.
I MUST SAY...

...I NEVER THOUGHT I'D USE MY YEARS OF STAGECRAFT FOR SOMETHING LIKE *THAT*.

HER NAME IS MEKHALA...

IT'S A *LOVELY* NAME, MASTER WAYNE, BUT I FEEL LIKE WE'VE INDULGED YOUR CURIOSITY *ENOUGH* AND IT'S TIME WE TAKE OUR *LEAVE*.

DIDN'T YOU HEAR THEM, ALFRED? SHE DIDN'T DO ANYTHING *WRONG*, THEY'RE TRYING TO USE HER TO CATCH HER *FATHER*.

AND I'D RATHER WE NOT GET CAUGHT BETWEEN A *CORRUPT* POLICE FORCE AND TEAM OF ROBIN HOODS, IF YOU DON'T MIND.

BUT THAT'S *NOT* WHAT THIS IS ABOUT.

WHAT *IS* THIS ABOUT, THEN?

I JUST-- I'D LIKE TO SEE HER AGAIN, AND... NOW...

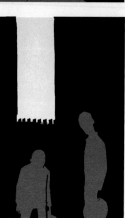

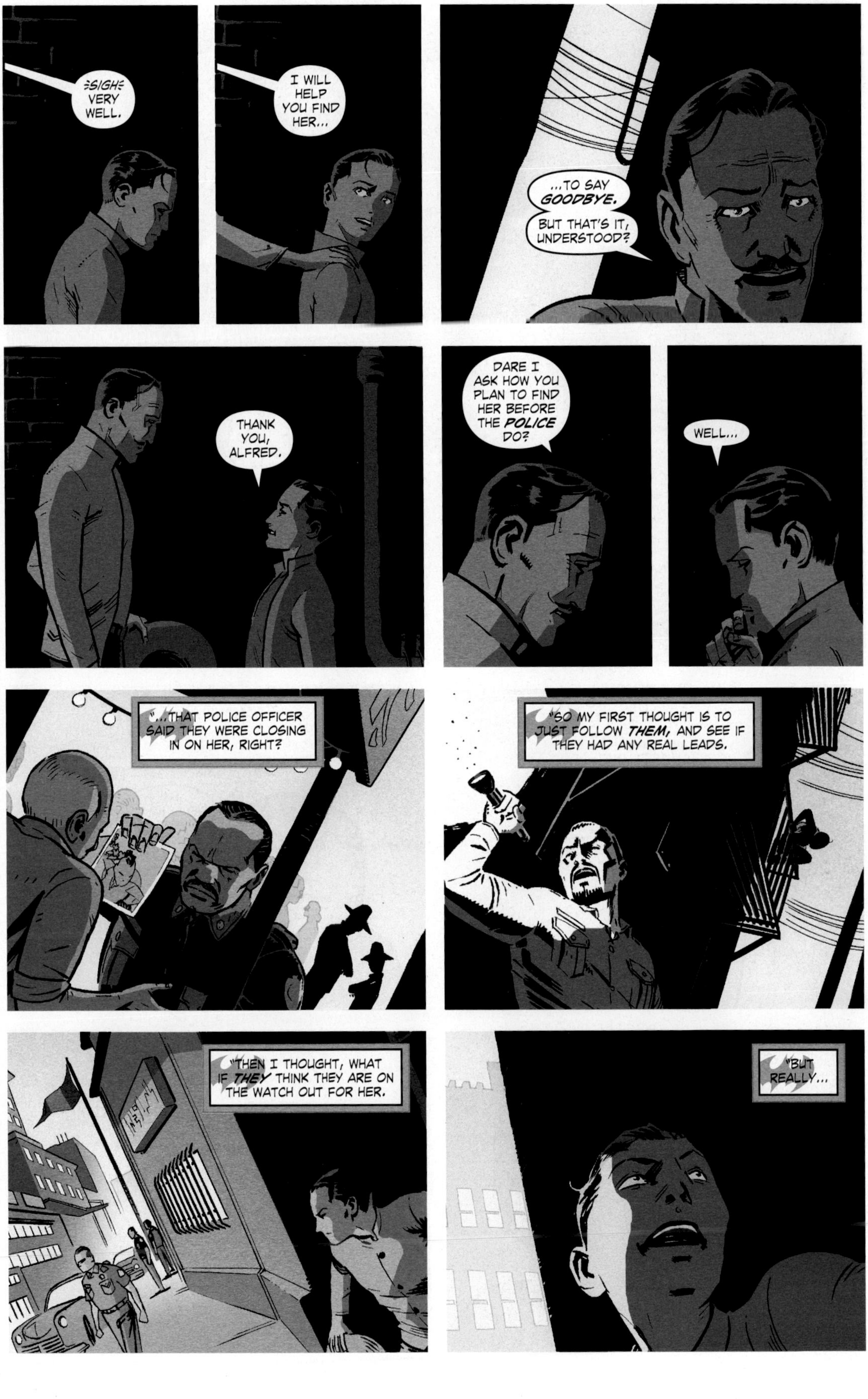

≈SIGH≈ VERY WELL.
I WILL HELP YOU FIND HER...
...TO SAY GOODBYE.
BUT THAT'S IT, UNDERSTOOD?
THANK YOU, ALFRED.
DARE I ASK HOW YOU PLAN TO FIND HER BEFORE THE POLICE DO?
WELL...
"...THAT POLICE OFFICER SAID THEY WERE CLOSING IN ON HER, RIGHT?
"SO MY FIRST THOUGHT IS TO JUST FOLLOW THEM, AND SEE IF THEY HAD ANY REAL LEADS.
"THEN I THOUGHT, WHAT IF THEY THINK THEY ARE ON THE WATCH OUT FOR HER.
"BUT REALLY...

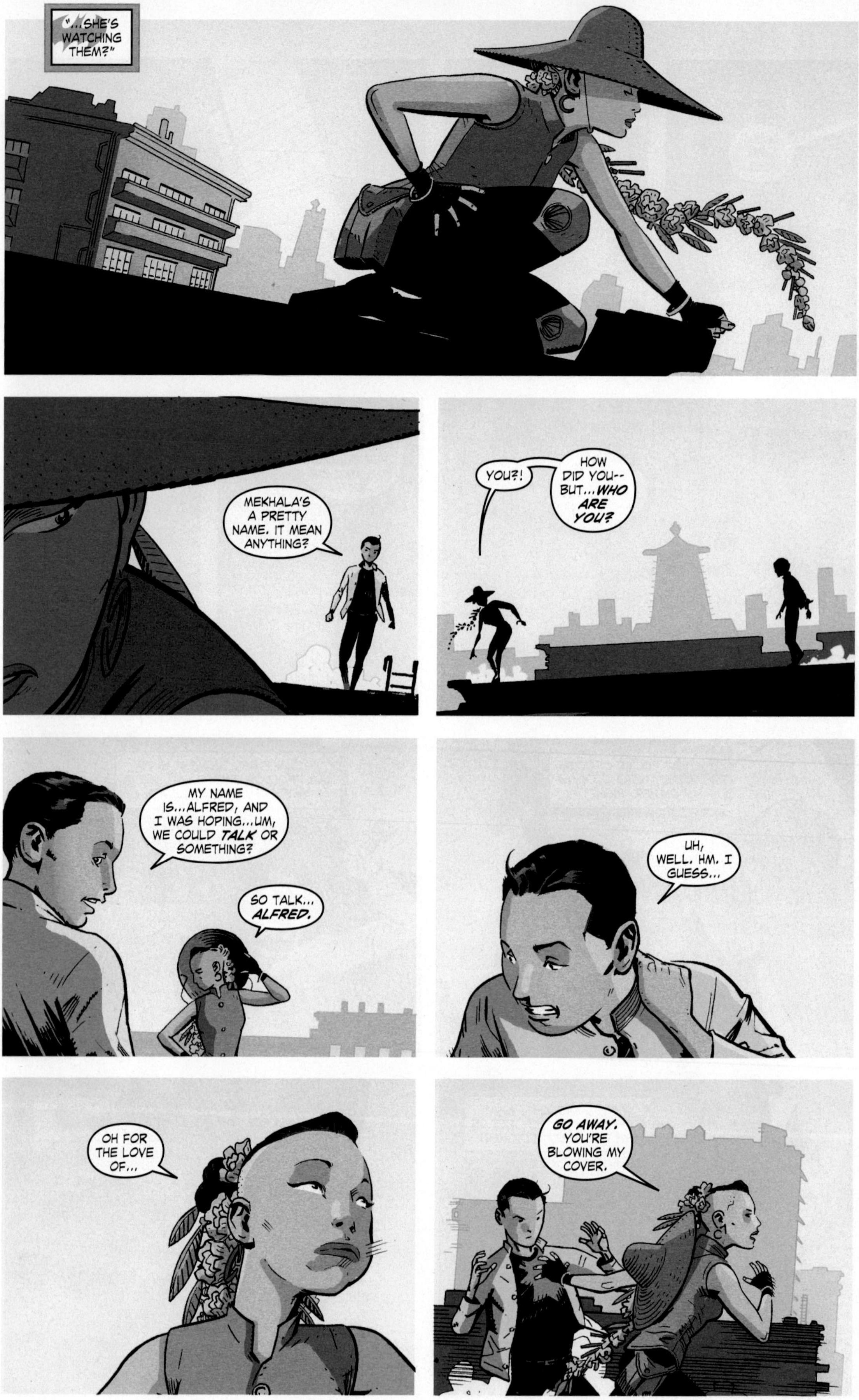
"...SHE'S WATCHING THEM?"
MEKHALA'S A PRETTY NAME. IT MEAN ANYTHING?
YOU?!
HOW DID YOU-- BUT...WHO ARE YOU?
MY NAME IS...ALFRED, AND I WAS HOPING...UM, WE COULD TALK OR SOMETHING?
SO TALK... ALFRED.
UH, WELL. HM. I GUESS...
OH FOR THE LOVE OF...
GO AWAY. YOU'RE BLOWING MY COVER.

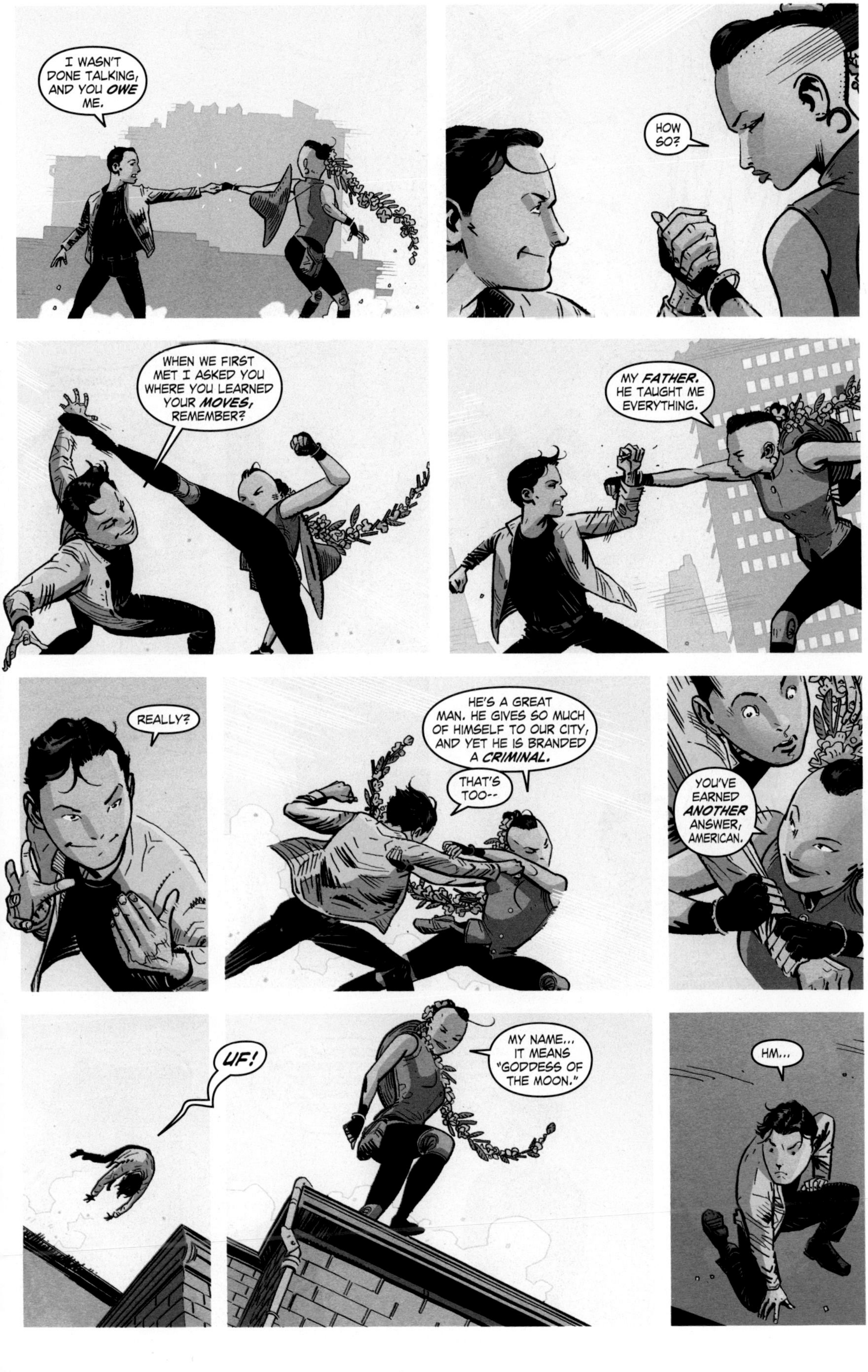
I WASN'T DONE TALKING, AND YOU OWE ME.
HOW SO?
WHEN WE FIRST MET I ASKED YOU WHERE YOU LEARNED YOUR MOVES, REMEMBER?
MY FATHER. HE TAUGHT ME EVERYTHING.
REALLY?
HE'S A GREAT MAN. HE GIVES SO MUCH OF HIMSELF TO OUR CITY, AND YET HE IS BRANDED A CRIMINAL.
THAT'S TOO--
YOU'VE EARNED ANOTHER ANSWER, AMERICAN.
UF!
MY NAME... IT MEANS "GODDESS OF THE MOON."
HM...

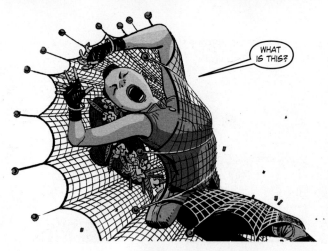

WHAT IS THIS?

YOU'RE OURS NOW, GIRL!

HOLD HER DOWN!

MEKHA--!

NO.

LET ME GO, YOU IMBECILES!

YOU KNOW I WILL NEVER LEAD YOU TO MY FATHER!

STAY STILL. THIS IS TOO DANGEROUS FOR US NOW.

WE DON'T EXPECT YOU TO, MY DEAR.

YOUR FATHER HAS SPENT ENOUGH TIME IN OUR PRISONS THAT WE KNOW HE'D NEVER LET HIS DAUGHTER STAY IN ONE.

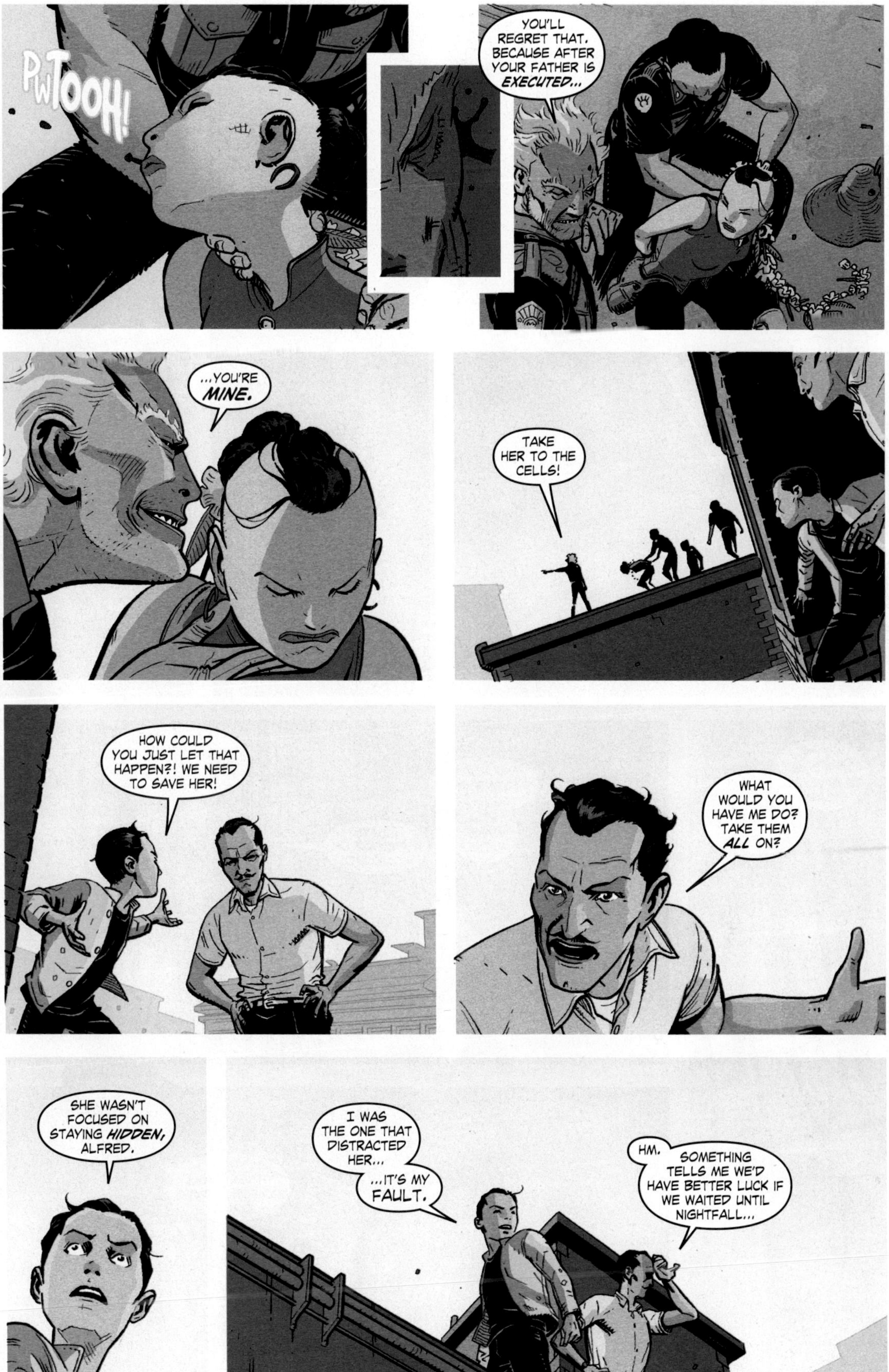
PWTOOH!
YOU'LL REGRET THAT. BECAUSE AFTER YOUR FATHER IS EXECUTED...
...YOU'RE MINE.
TAKE HER TO THE CELLS!
HOW COULD YOU JUST LET THAT HAPPEN?! WE NEED TO SAVE HER!
WHAT WOULD YOU HAVE ME DO? TAKE THEM ALL ON?
SHE WASN'T FOCUSED ON STAYING HIDDEN, ALFRED.
I WAS THE ONE THAT DISTRACTED HER...
...IT'S MY FAULT.
HM.
SOMETHING TELLS ME WE'D HAVE BETTER LUCK IF WE WAITED UNTIL NIGHTFALL...

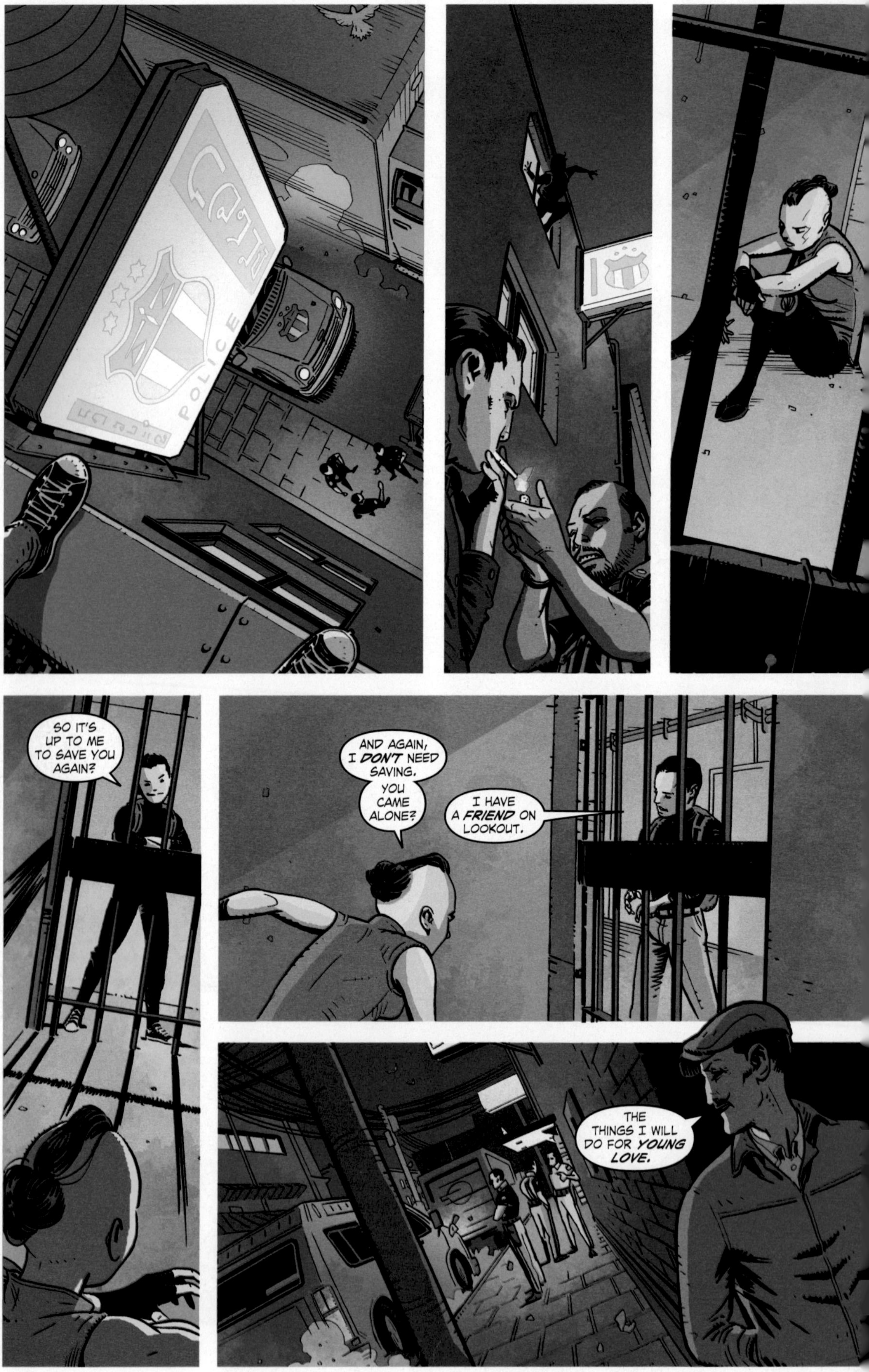
POLICE
SO IT'S UP TO ME TO SAVE YOU AGAIN?
AND AGAIN, I DON'T NEED SAVING. YOU CAME ALONE?
I HAVE A FRIEND ON LOOKOUT.
THE THINGS I WILL DO FOR YOUNG LOVE.

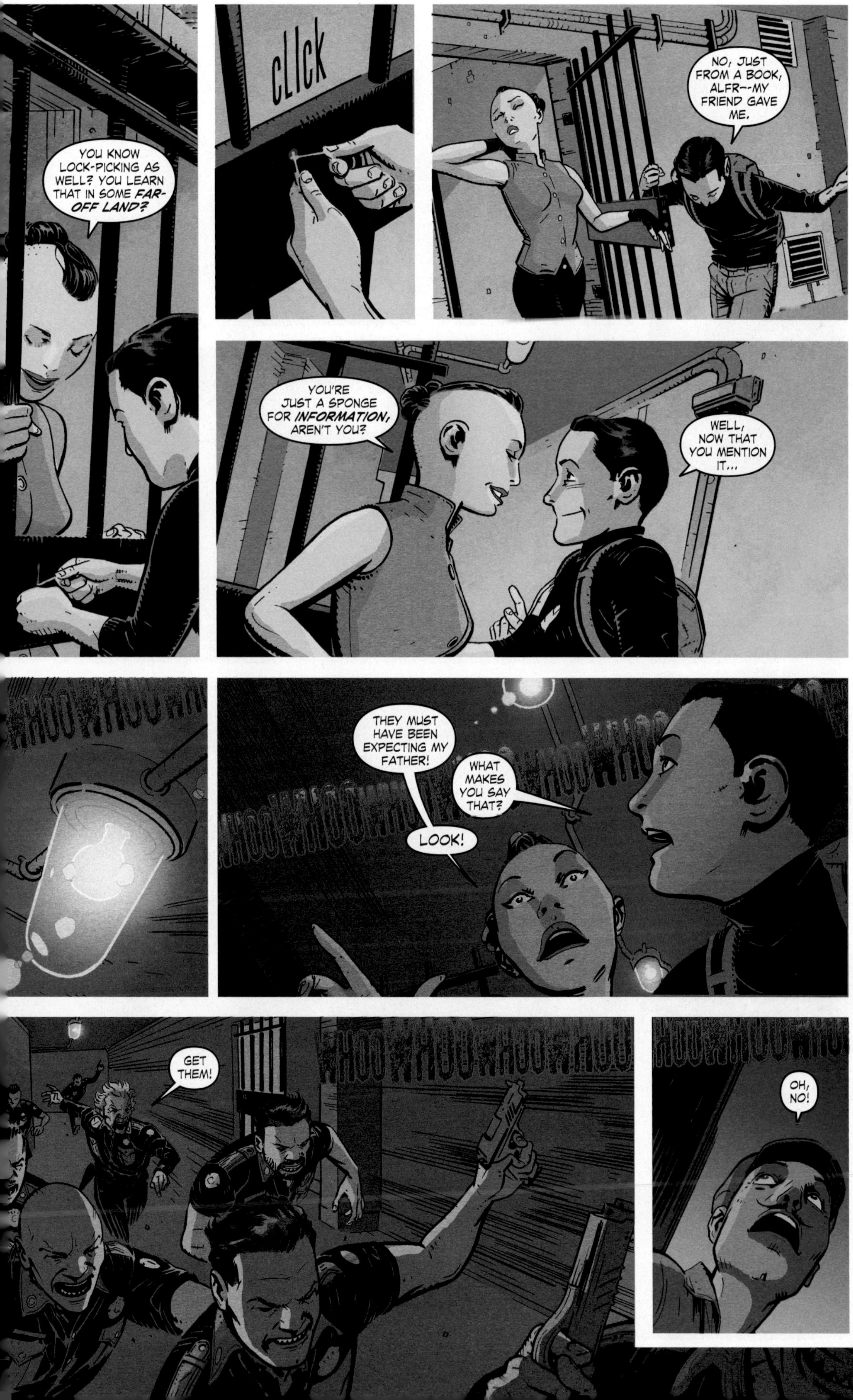
YOU KNOW LOCK-PICKING AS WELL? YOU LEARN THAT IN SOME FAR-OFF LAND?
cLIck
NO, JUST FROM A BOOK, ALFR--MY FRIEND GAVE ME.
YOU'RE JUST A SPONGE FOR INFORMATION, AREN'T YOU?
WELL, NOW THAT YOU MENTION IT...
THEY MUST HAVE BEEN EXPECTING MY FATHER!
WHAT MAKES YOU SAY THAT?
LOOK!
GET THEM!
OH, NO!

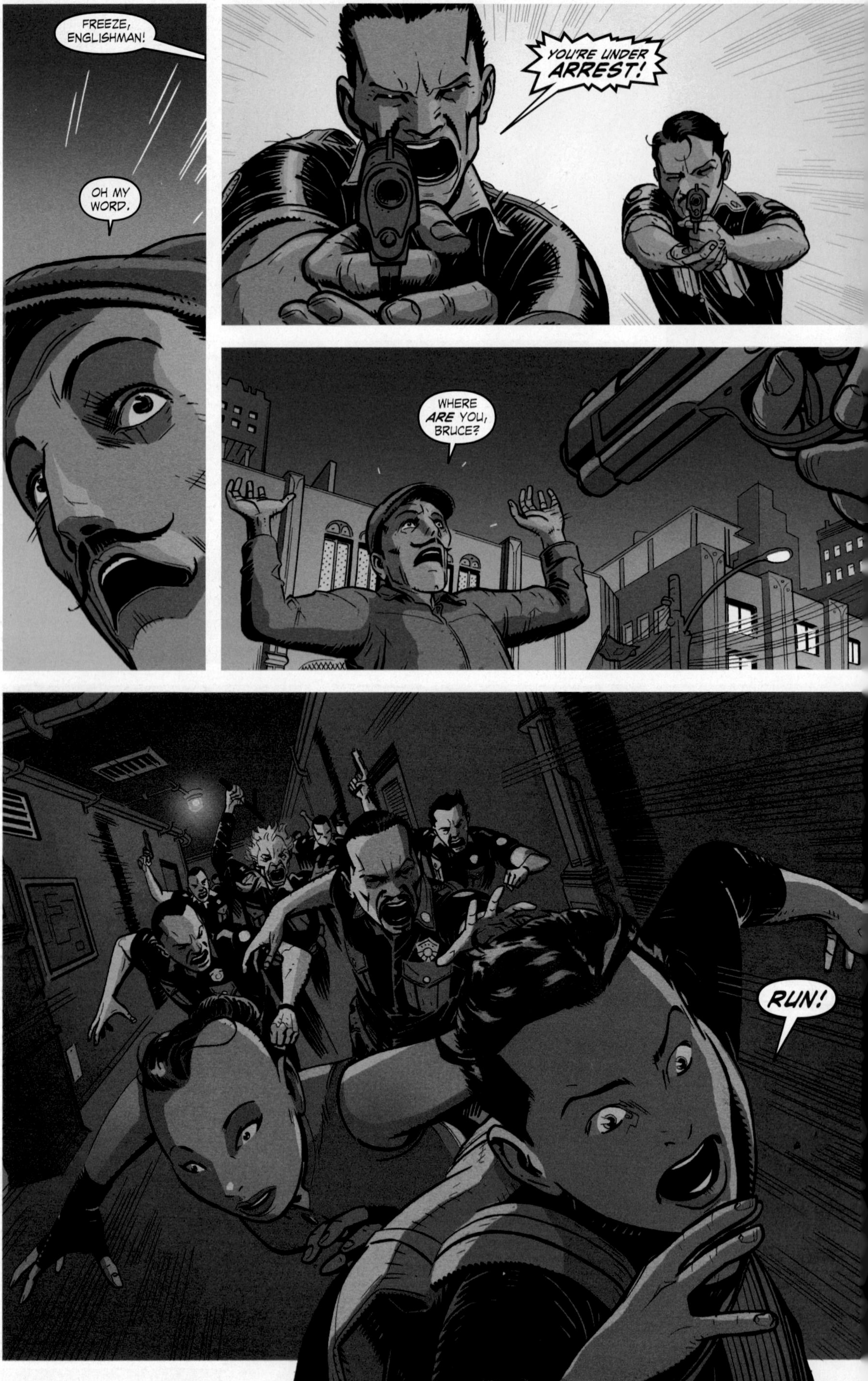
FREEZE, ENGLISHMAN!
YOU'RE UNDER ARREST!
OH MY WORD.
WHERE ARE YOU, BRUCE?
RUN!

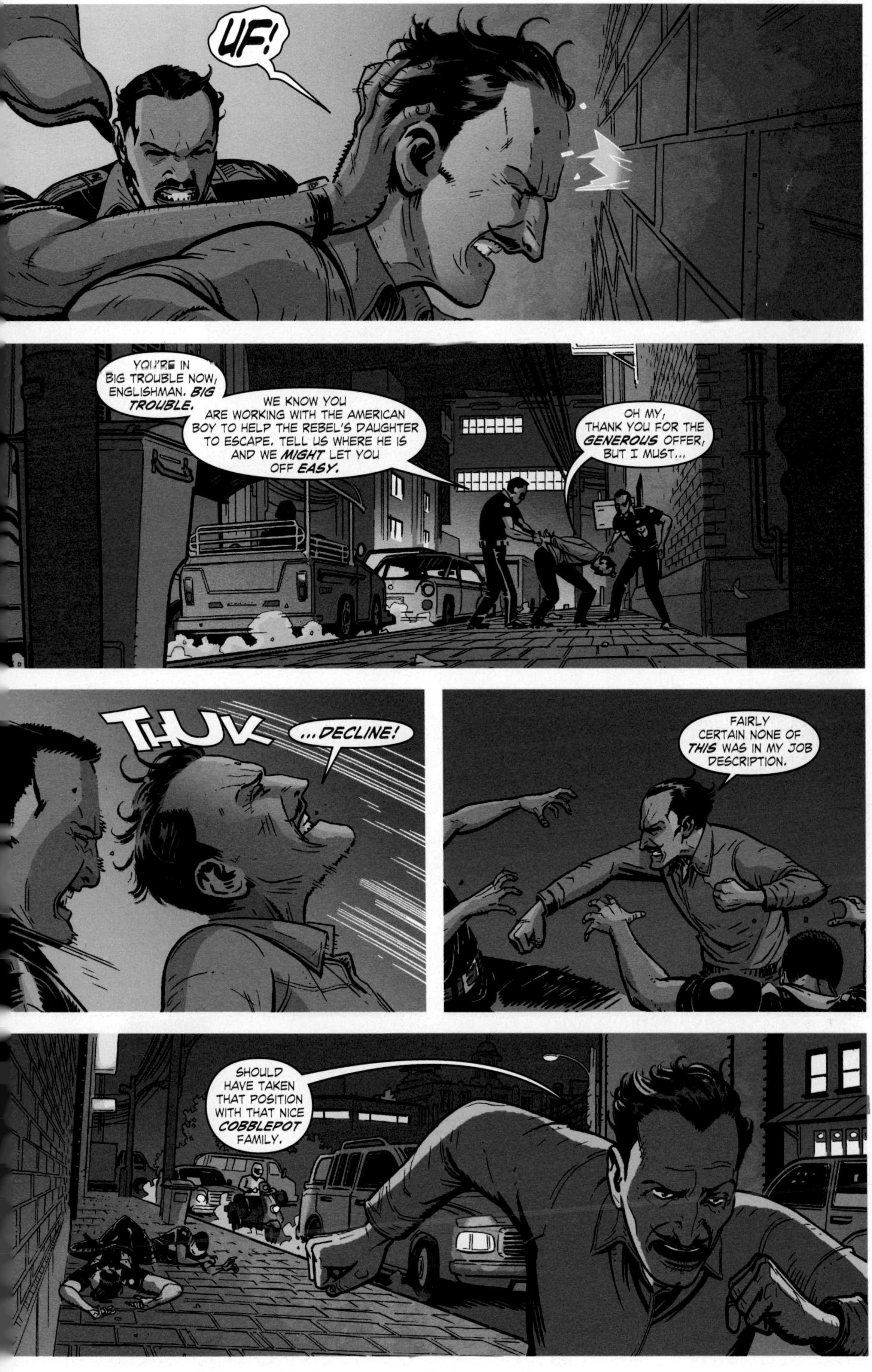
UF!
YOU'RE IN BIG TROUBLE NOW, ENGLISHMAN. BIG TROUBLE.
WE KNOW YOU ARE WORKING WITH THE AMERICAN BOY TO HELP THE REBEL'S DAUGHTER TO ESCAPE. TELL US WHERE HE IS AND WE MIGHT LET YOU OFF EASY.
OH MY, THANK YOU FOR THE GENEROUS OFFER, BUT I MUST...
THUK
...DECLINE!
FAIRLY CERTAIN NONE OF THIS WAS IN MY JOB DESCRIPTION.
SHOULD HAVE TAKEN THAT POSITION WITH THAT NICE COBBLEPOT FAMILY.

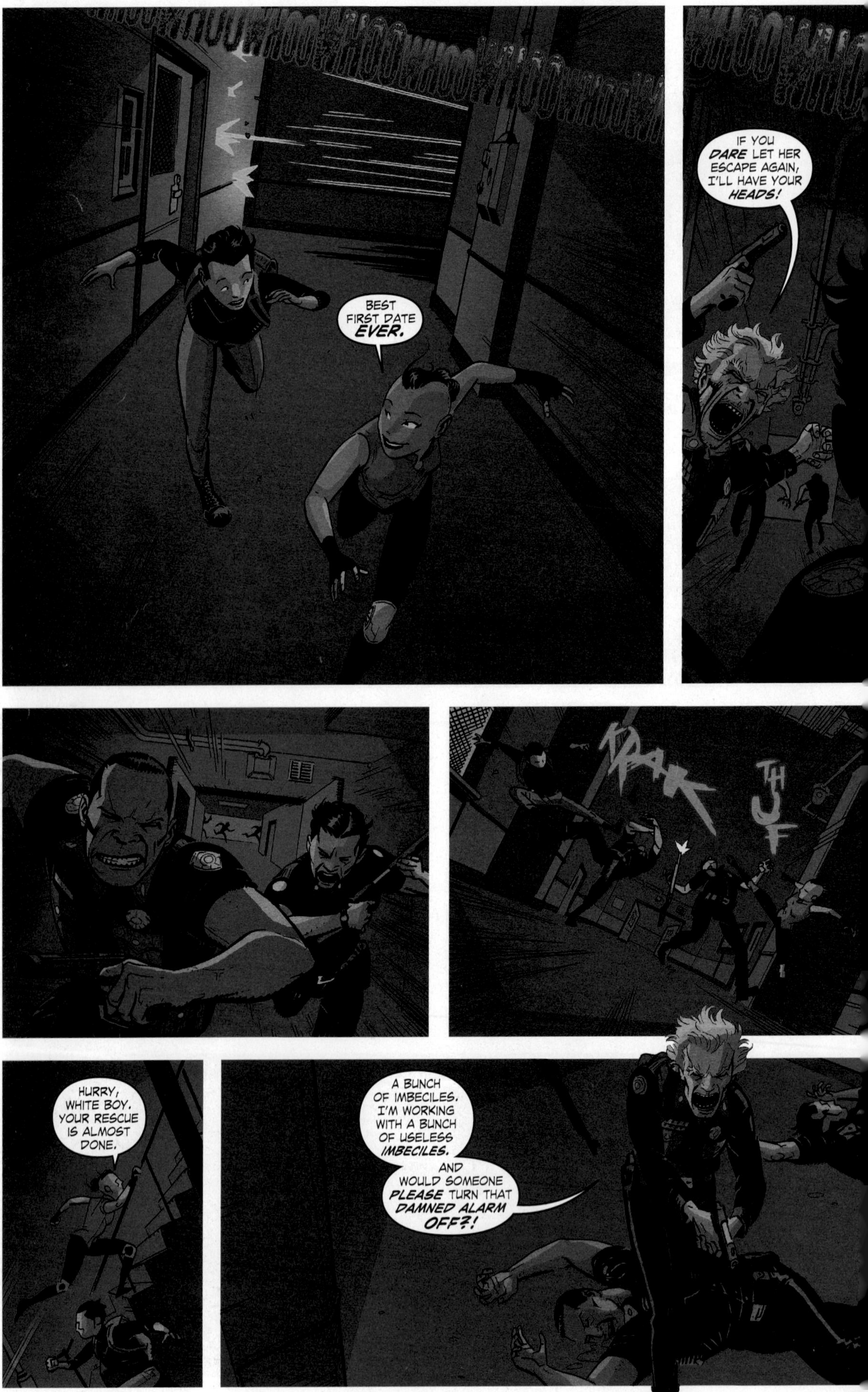
WHOOWHOOWHOOWHOOWHOOWHOOWHOO
BEST FIRST DATE EVER.
WHOOWHOOWHOO
IF YOU DARE LET HER ESCAPE AGAIN, I'LL HAVE YOUR HEADS!
KRAK
THJF
HURRY, WHITE BOY. YOUR RESCUE IS ALMOST DONE.
A BUNCH OF IMBECILES. I'M WORKING WITH A BUNCH OF USELESS IMBECILES.
AND WOULD SOMEONE PLEASE TURN THAT DAMNED ALARM OFF?!

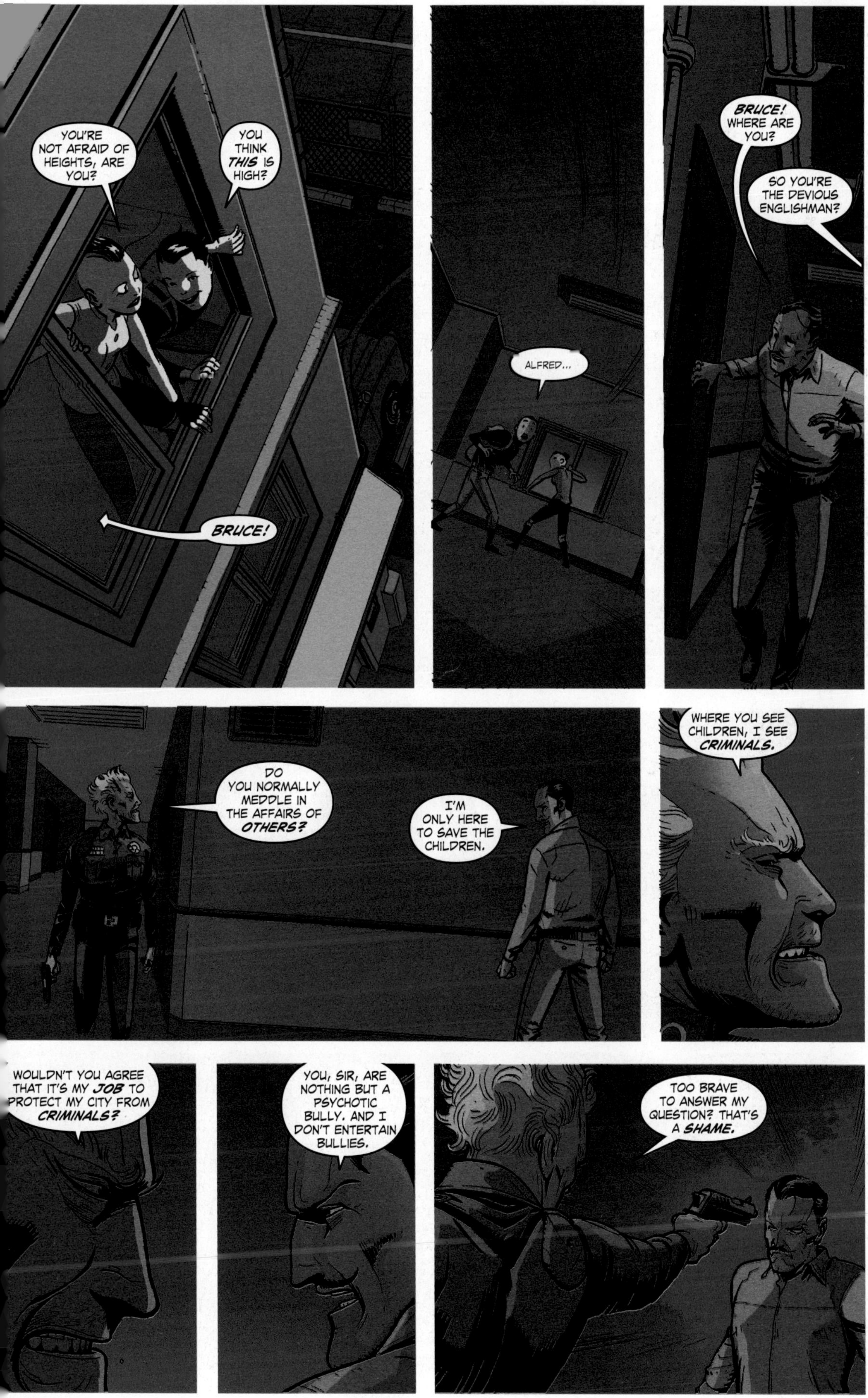
YOU'RE NOT AFRAID OF HEIGHTS, ARE YOU?
YOU THINK THIS IS HIGH?
BRUCE!
ALFRED...
BRUCE! WHERE ARE YOU?
SO YOU'RE THE DEVIOUS ENGLISHMAN?
DO YOU NORMALLY MEDDLE IN THE AFFAIRS OF OTHERS?
I'M ONLY HERE TO SAVE THE CHILDREN.
WHERE YOU SEE CHILDREN, I SEE CRIMINALS.
WOULDN'T YOU AGREE THAT IT'S MY JOB TO PROTECT MY CITY FROM CRIMINALS?
YOU, SIR, ARE NOTHING BUT A PSYCHOTIC BULLY. AND I DON'T ENTERTAIN BULLIES.
TOO BRAVE TO ANSWER MY QUESTION? THAT'S A SHAME.

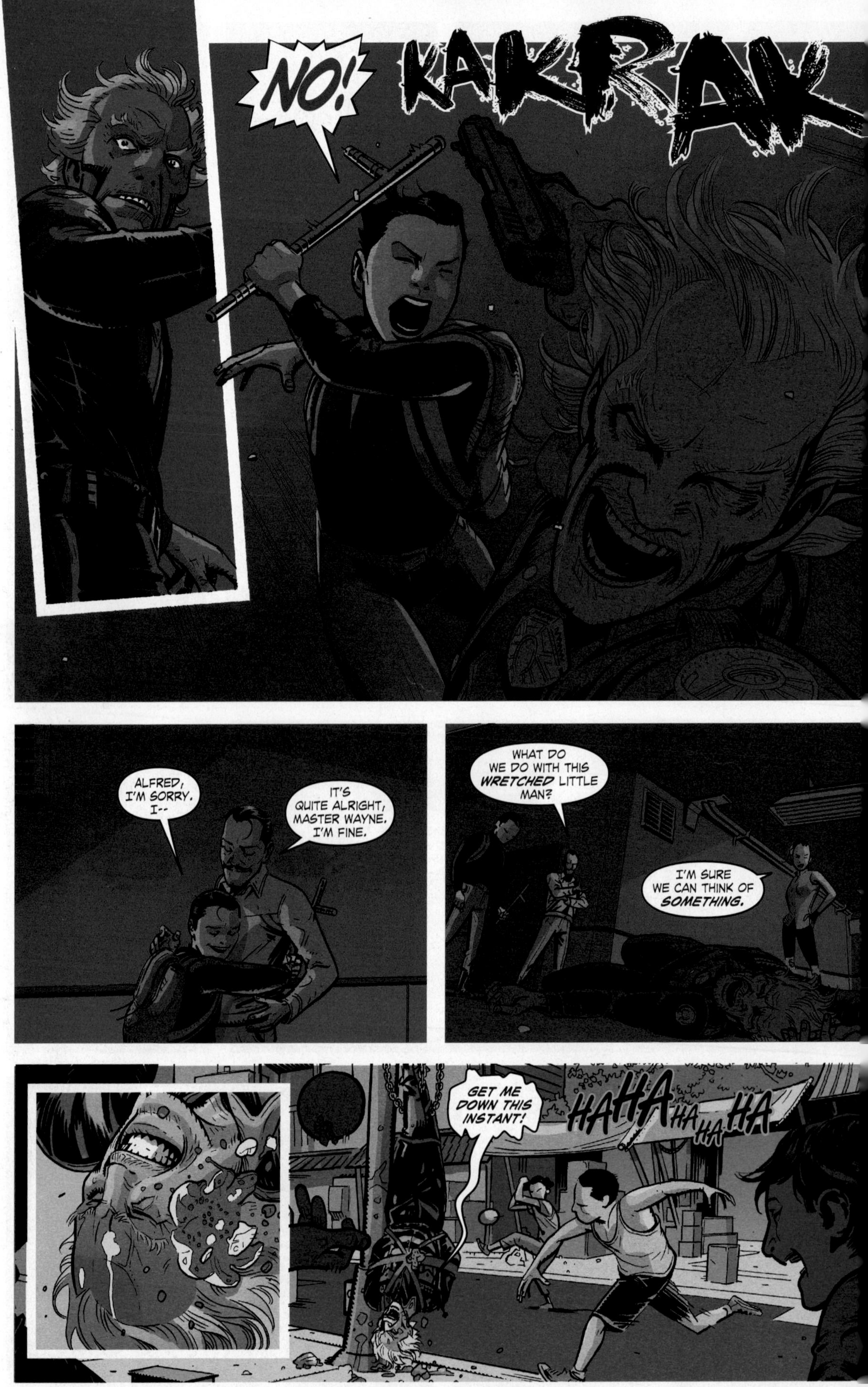
NO!
KAKRAK
ALFRED, I'M SORRY. I--
IT'S QUITE ALRIGHT, MASTER WAYNE. I'M FINE.
WHAT DO WE DO WITH THIS *WRETCHED* LITTLE MAN?
I'M SURE WE CAN THINK OF *SOMETHING.*
GET ME DOWN THIS INSTANT!
HAHAHAHAHA

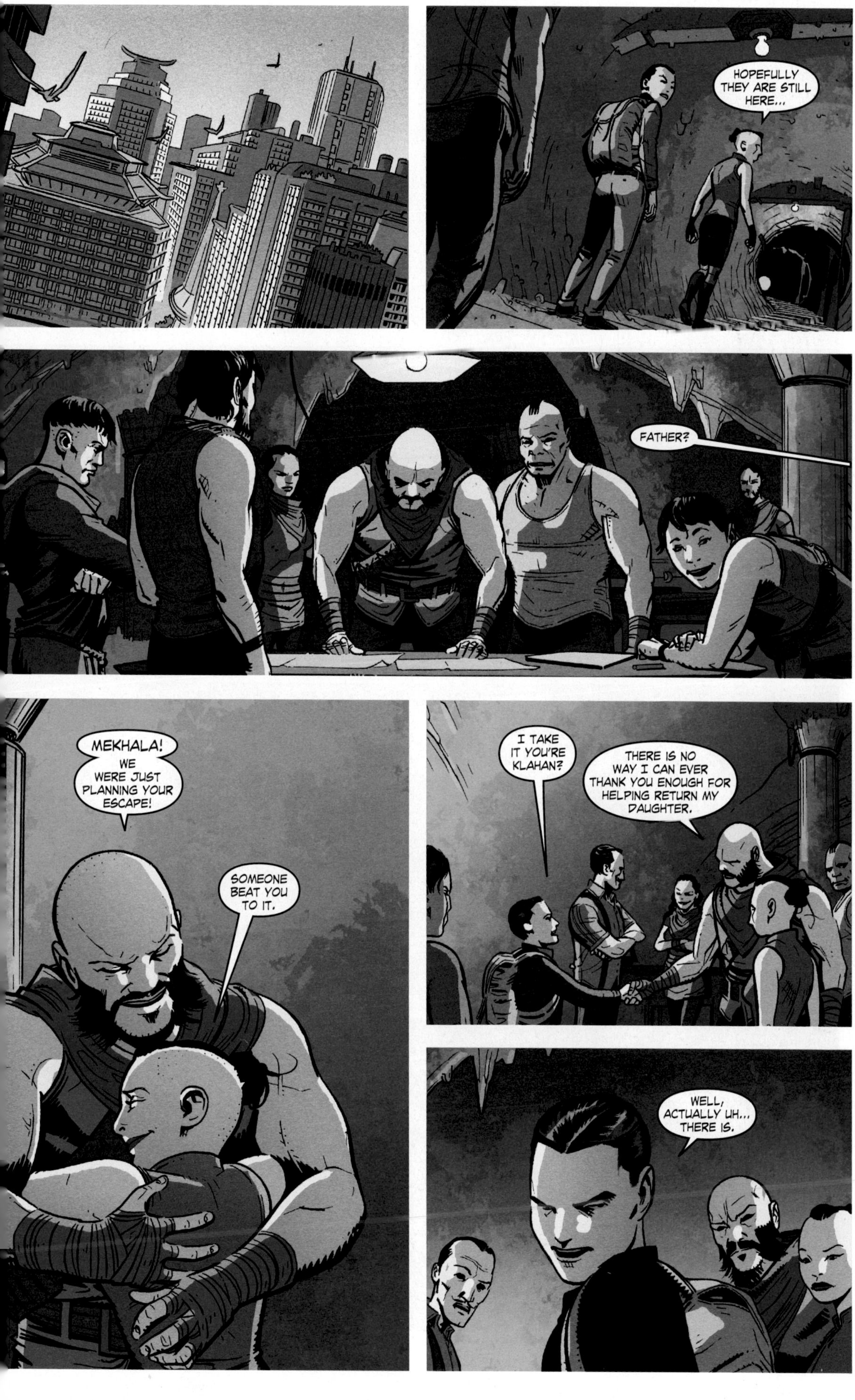
HOPEFULLY THEY ARE STILL HERE...
FATHER?
MEKHALA! WE WERE JUST PLANNING YOUR ESCAPE!
SOMEONE BEAT YOU TO IT.
I TAKE IT YOU'RE KLAHAN?
THERE IS NO WAY I CAN EVER THANK YOU ENOUGH FOR HELPING RETURN MY DAUGHTER.
WELL, ACTUALLY UH... THERE IS.

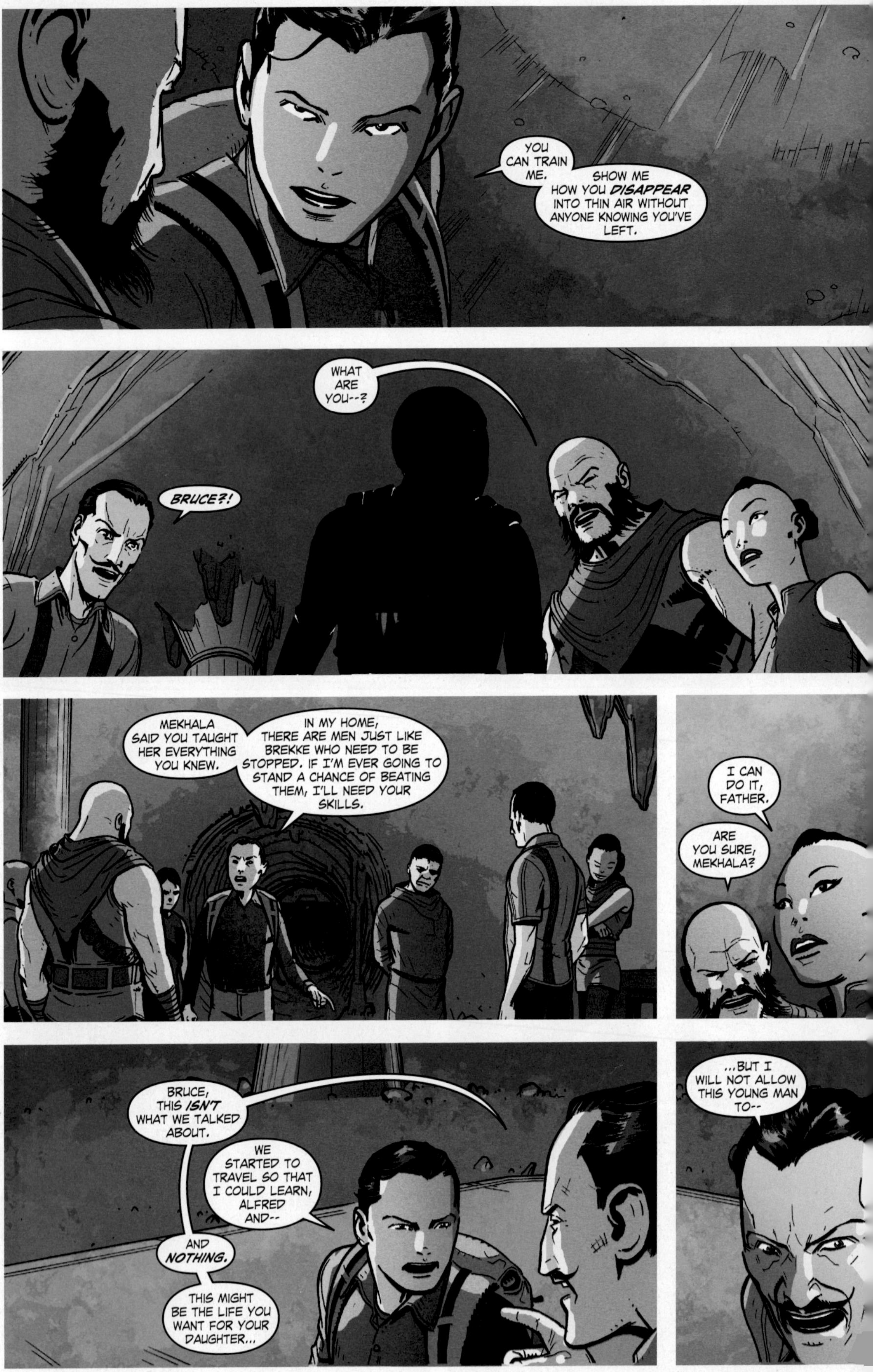
YOU CAN TRAIN ME.
SHOW ME HOW YOU DISAPPEAR INTO THIN AIR WITHOUT ANYONE KNOWING YOU'VE LEFT.
WHAT ARE YOU--?
BRUCE?!
MEKHALA SAID YOU TAUGHT HER EVERYTHING YOU KNEW.
IN MY HOME, THERE ARE MEN JUST LIKE BREKKE WHO NEED TO BE STOPPED. IF I'M EVER GOING TO STAND A CHANCE OF BEATING THEM, I'LL NEED YOUR SKILLS.
I CAN DO IT, FATHER.
ARE YOU SURE, MEKHALA?
BRUCE, THIS ISN'T WHAT WE TALKED ABOUT.
WE STARTED TO TRAVEL SO THAT I COULD LEARN, ALFRED AND--
AND NOTHING.
THIS MIGHT BE THE LIFE YOU WANT FOR YOUR DAUGHTER...
...BUT I WILL NOT ALLOW THIS YOUNG MAN TO--

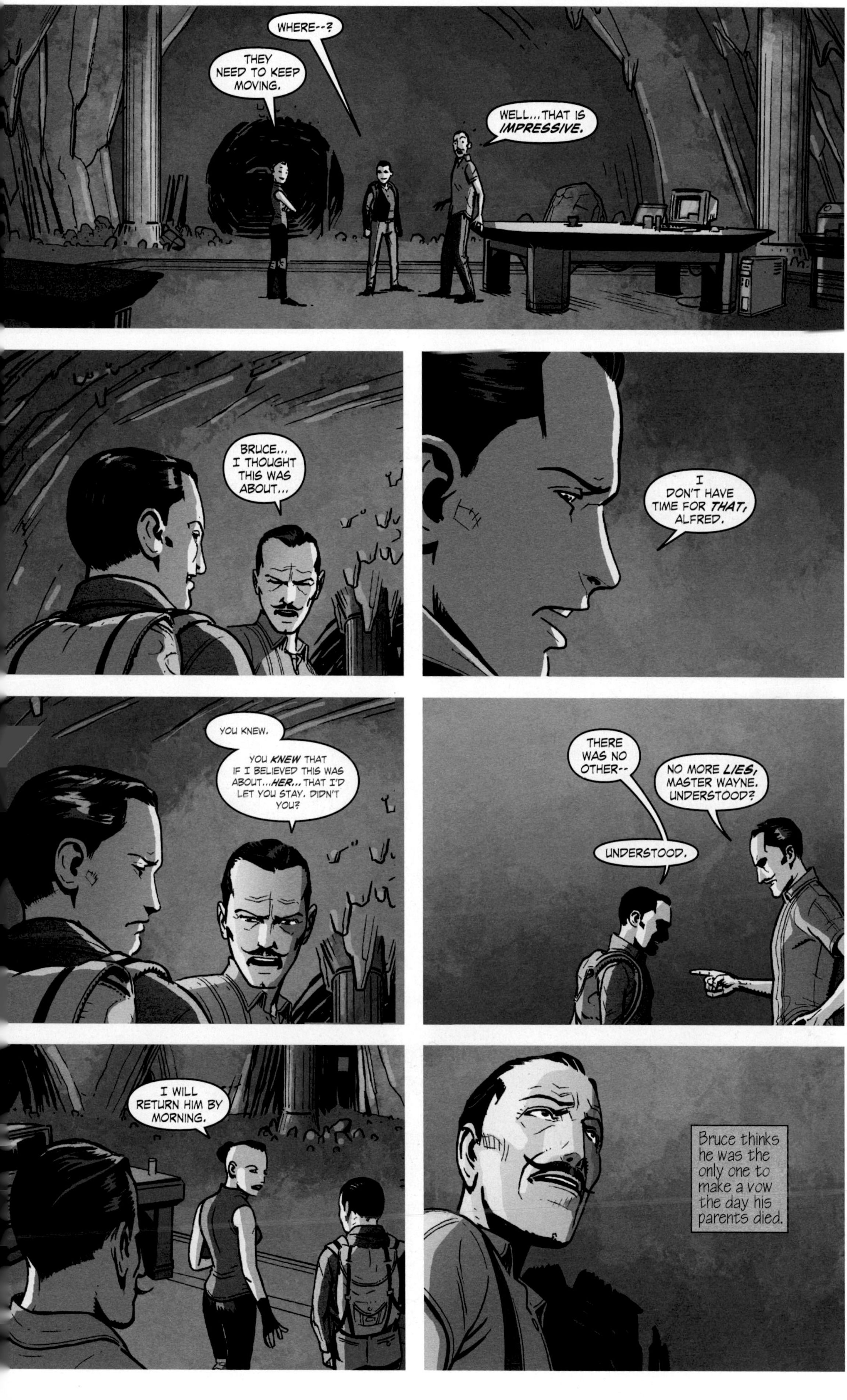

THEY NEED TO KEEP MOVING.
WHERE--?
WELL...THAT IS IMPRESSIVE.
BRUCE... I THOUGHT THIS WAS ABOUT...
I DON'T HAVE TIME FOR THAT, ALFRED.
YOU KNEW.
YOU KNEW THAT IF I BELIEVED THIS WAS ABOUT...HER... THAT I'D LET YOU STAY. DIDN'T YOU?
THERE WAS NO OTHER--
NO MORE LIES, MASTER WAYNE. UNDERSTOOD?
UNDERSTOOD.
I WILL RETURN HIM BY MORNING.
Bruce thinks he was the only one to make a vow the day his parents died.

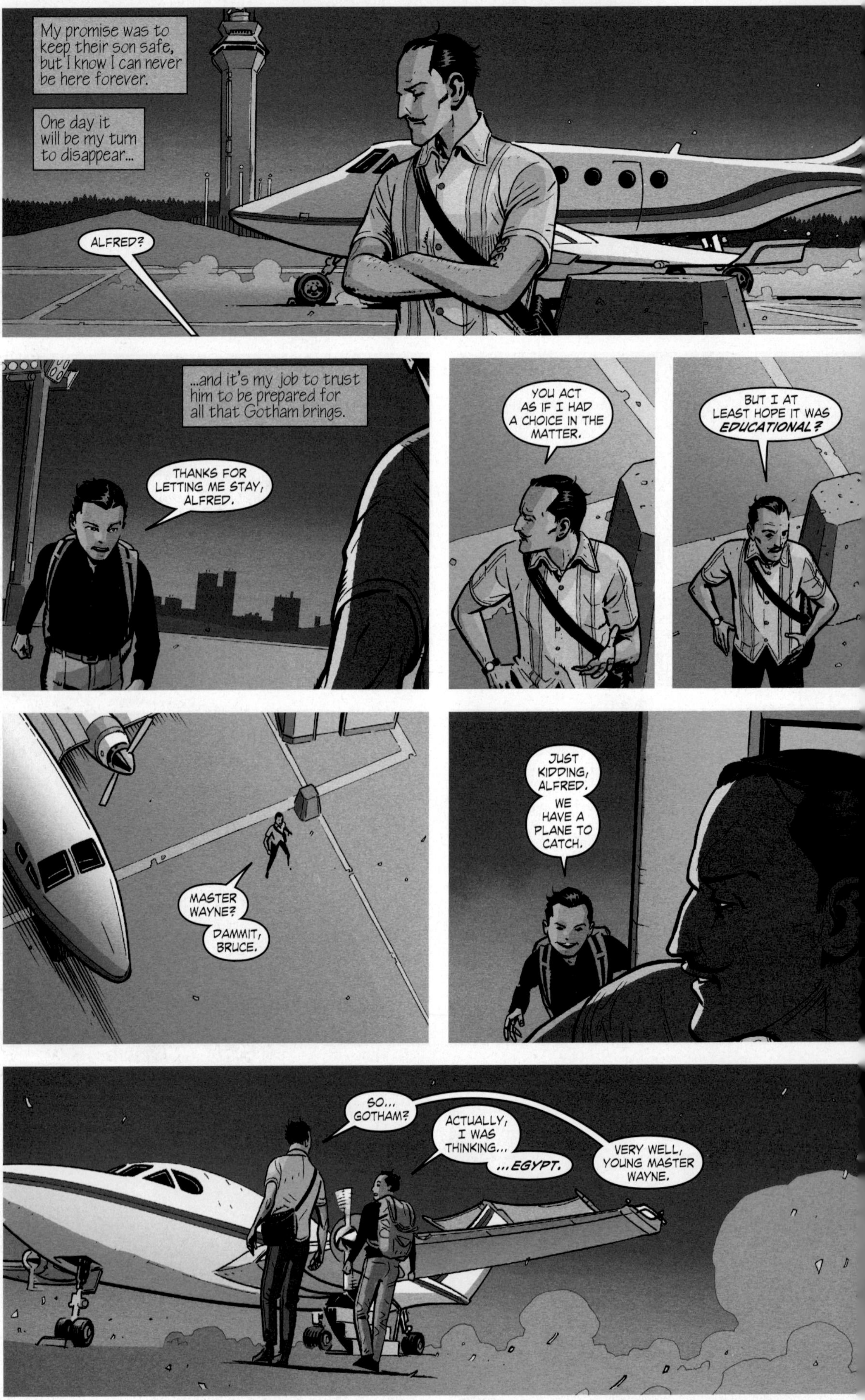
My promise was to keep their son safe, but I know I can never be here forever.
One day it will be my turn to disappear...
ALFRED?
...and it's my job to trust him to be prepared for all that Gotham brings.
THANKS FOR LETTING ME STAY, ALFRED.
YOU ACT AS IF I HAD A CHOICE IN THE MATTER.
BUT I AT LEAST HOPE IT WAS EDUCATIONAL?
MASTER WAYNE?
DAMMIT, BRUCE.
JUST KIDDING, ALFRED.
WE HAVE A PLANE TO CATCH.
SO... GOTHAM?
ACTUALLY, I WAS THINKING...
...EGYPT.
VERY WELL, YOUNG MASTER WAYNE.

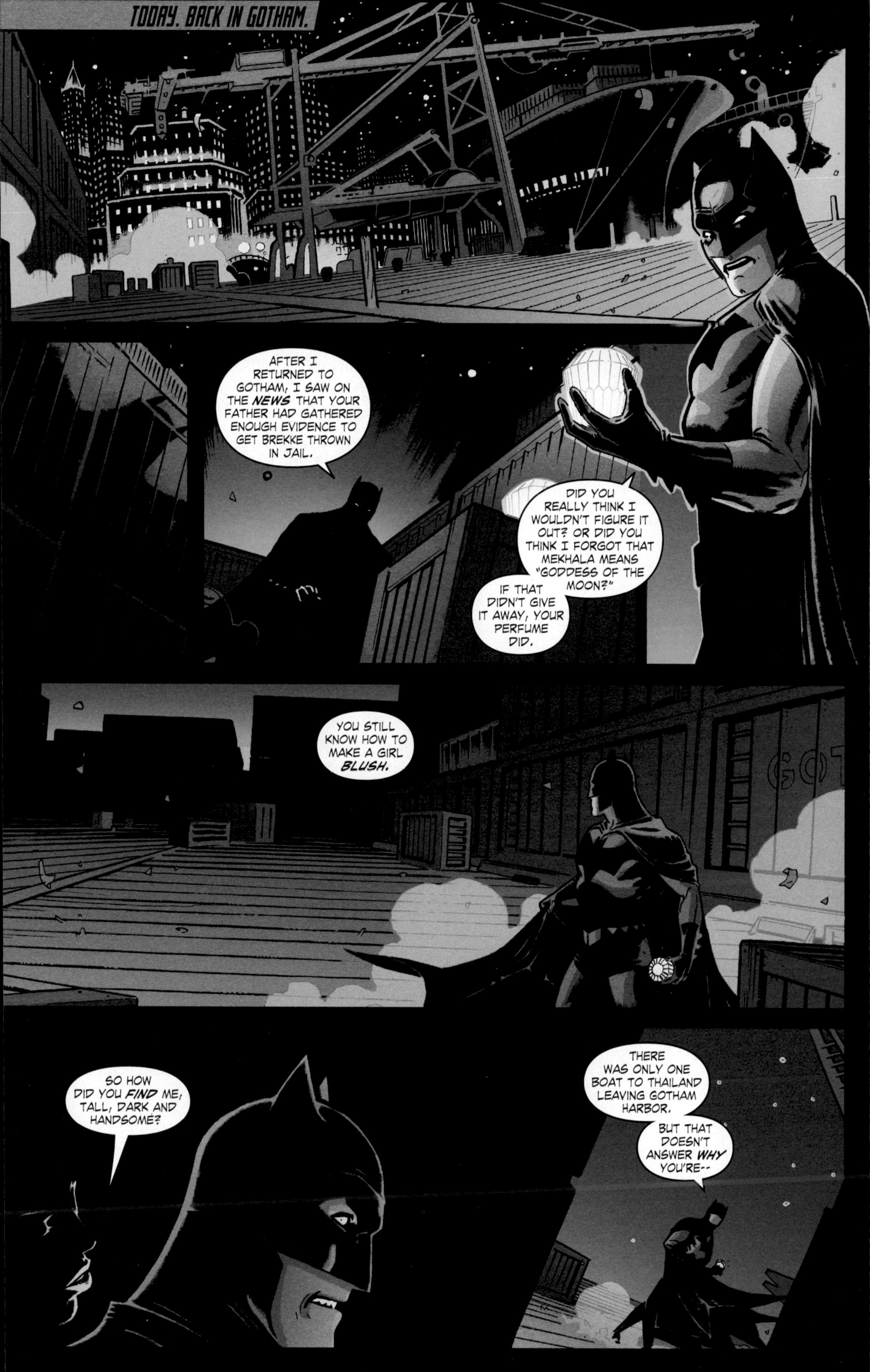
TODAY. BACK IN GOTHAM.
AFTER I RETURNED TO GOTHAM, I SAW ON THE NEWS THAT YOUR FATHER HAD GATHERED ENOUGH EVIDENCE TO GET BREKKE THROWN IN JAIL.
DID YOU REALLY THINK I WOULDN'T FIGURE IT OUT? OR DID YOU THINK I FORGOT THAT MEKHALA MEANS "GODDESS OF THE MOON?"
IF THAT DIDN'T GIVE IT AWAY, YOUR PERFUME DID.
YOU STILL KNOW HOW TO MAKE A GIRL BLUSH.
SO HOW DID YOU FIND ME, TALL, DARK AND HANDSOME?
THERE WAS ONLY ONE BOAT TO THAILAND LEAVING GOTHAM HARBOR.
BUT THAT DOESN'T ANSWER WHY YOU'RE--

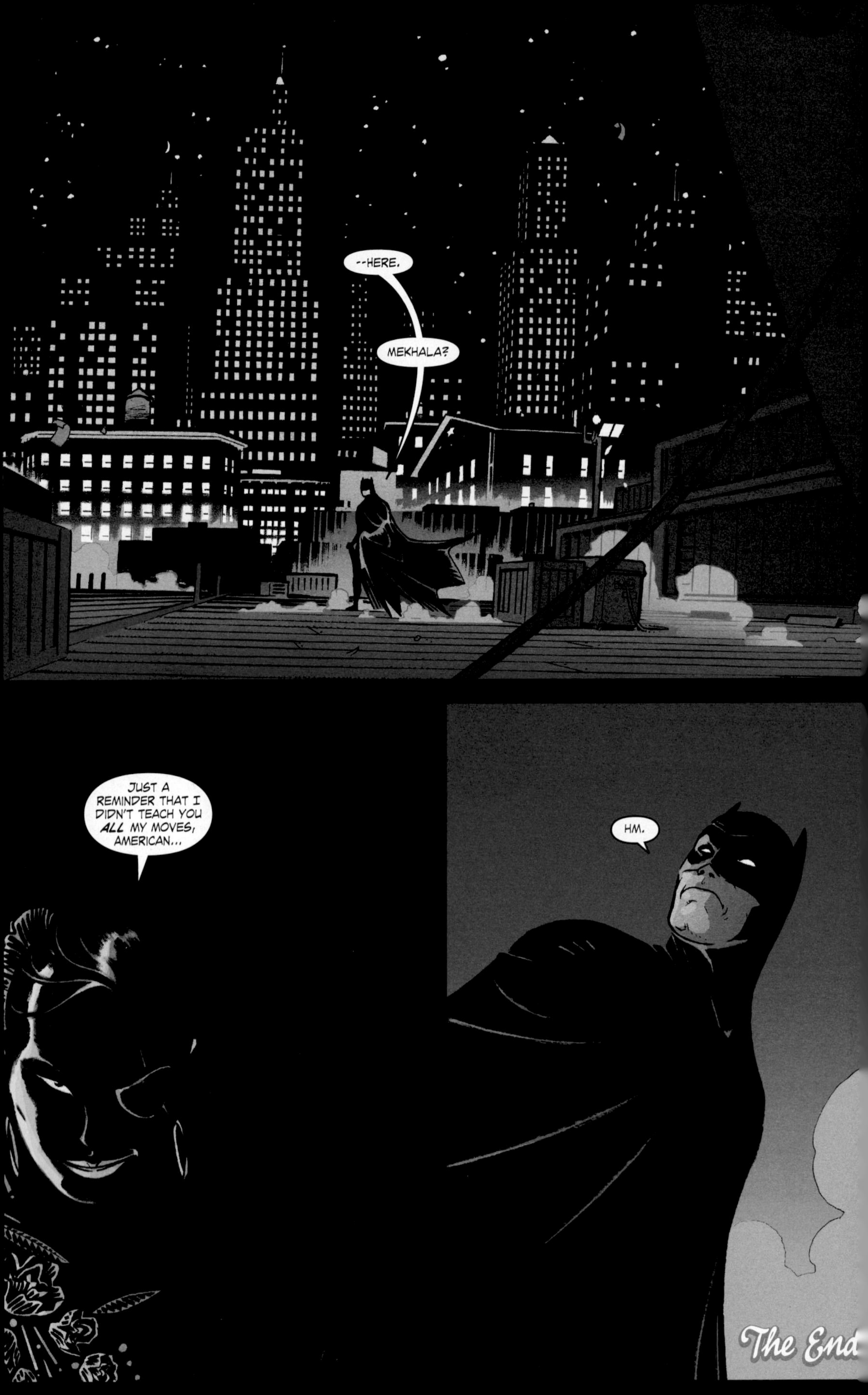
--HERE.
MEKHALA?
JUST A REMINDER THAT I DIDN'T TEACH YOU ALL MY MOVES, AMERICAN...
HM.
The End

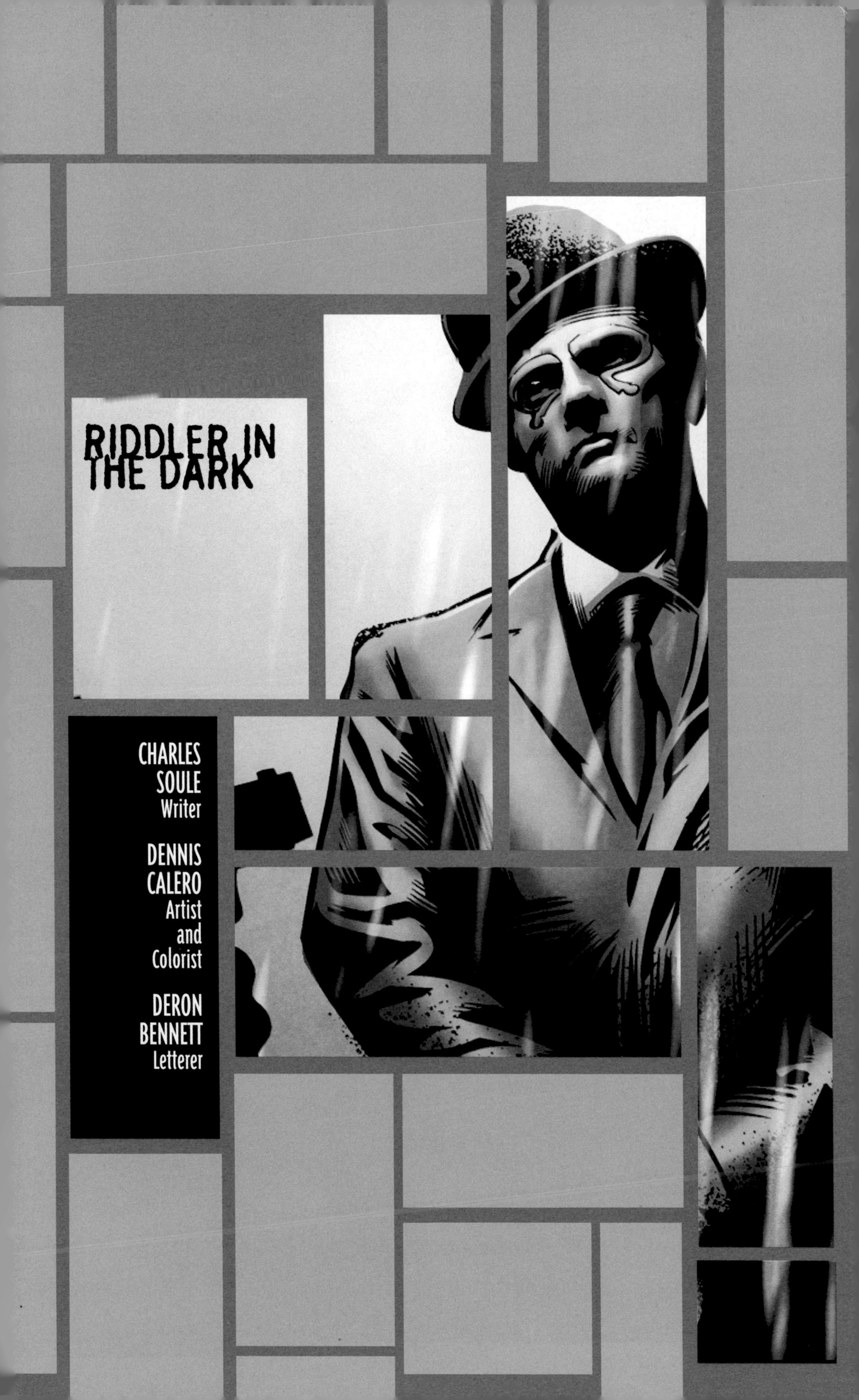
RIDDLER IN THE DARK
CHARLES SOULE Writer
DENNIS CALERO Artist and Colorist
DERON BENNETT Letterer

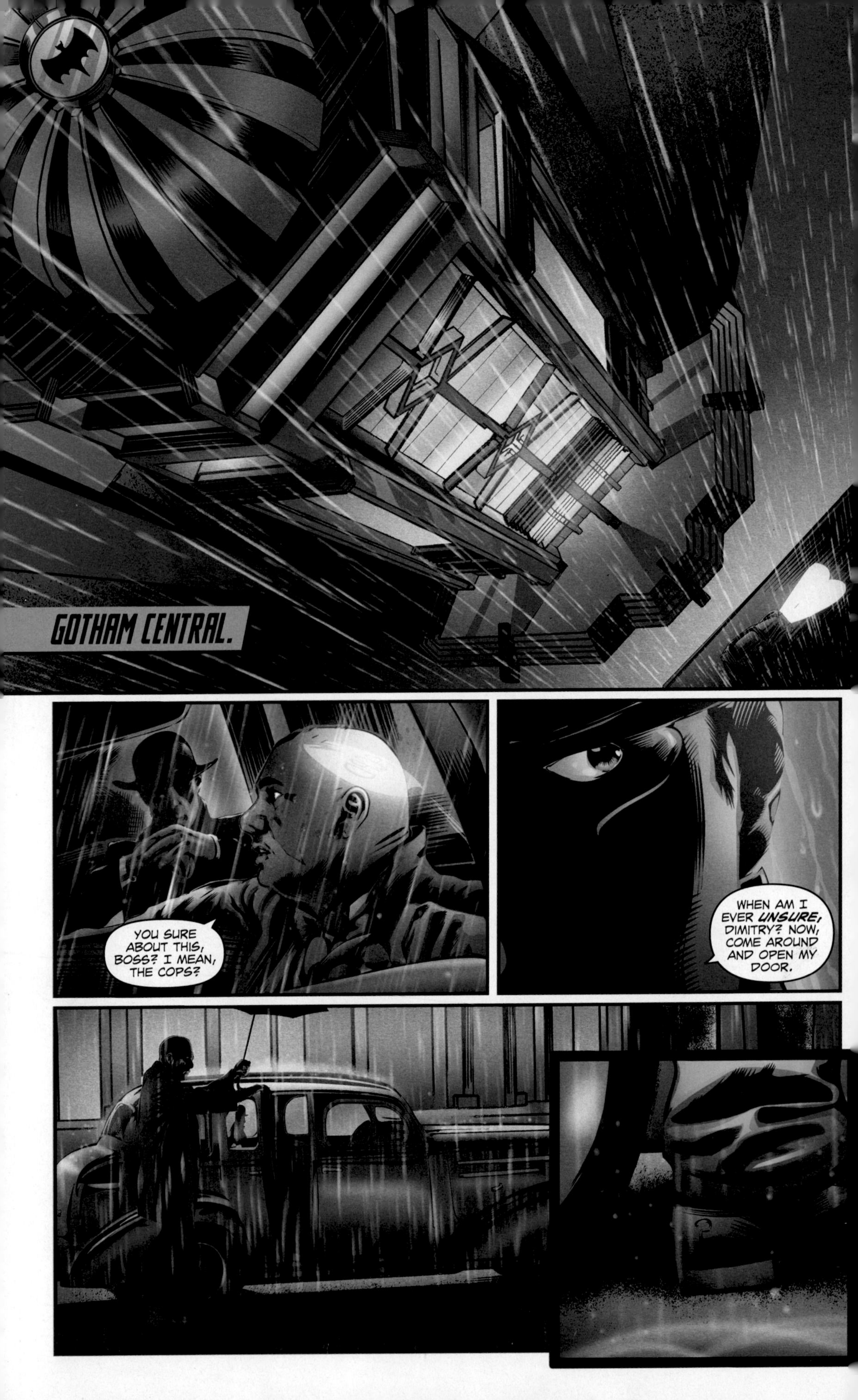
GOTHAM CENTRAL.
YOU SURE ABOUT THIS, BOSS? I MEAN, THE COPS?
WHEN AM I EVER UNSURE, DIMITRY? NOW, COME AROUND AND OPEN MY DOOR.

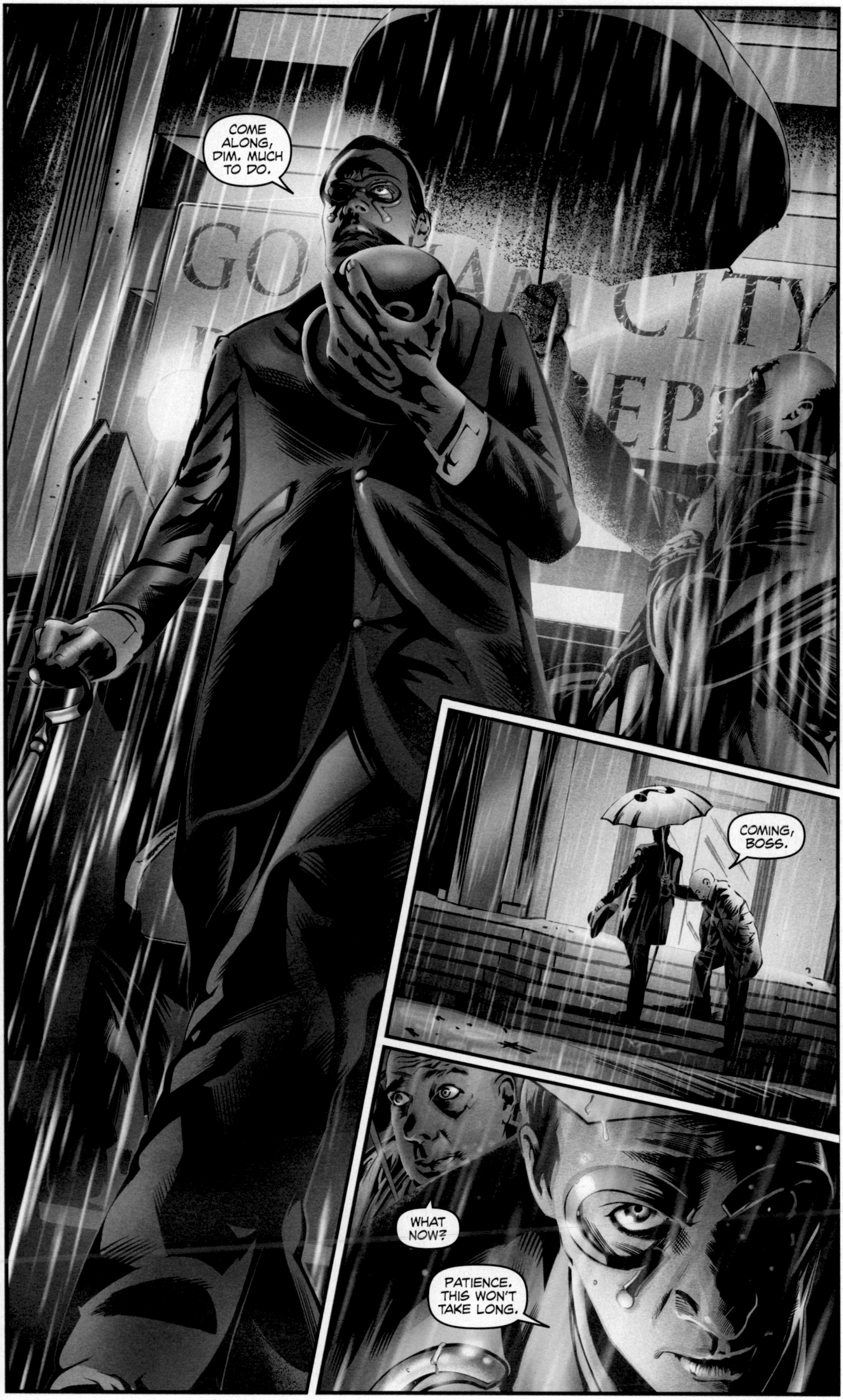
COME ALONG, DIM. MUCH TO DO.
GOTHAM CITY
DEPT
COMING, BOSS.
WHAT NOW?
PATIENCE. THIS WON'T TAKE LONG.

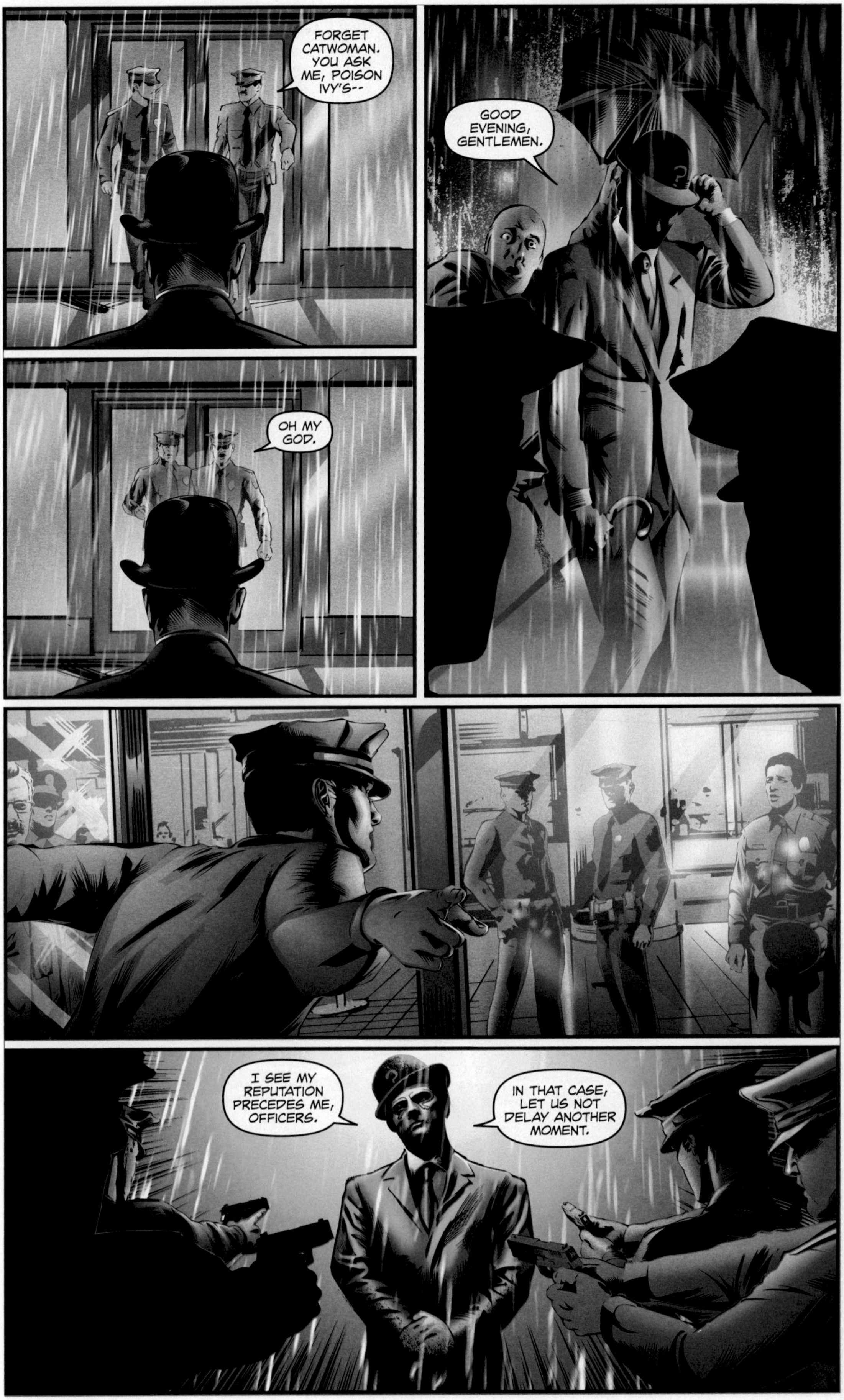
FORGET CATWOMAN. YOU ASK ME, POISON IVY'S--
GOOD EVENING, GENTLEMEN.
OH MY GOD.
I SEE MY REPUTATION PRECEDES ME, OFFICERS.
IN THAT CASE, LET US NOT DELAY ANOTHER MOMENT.

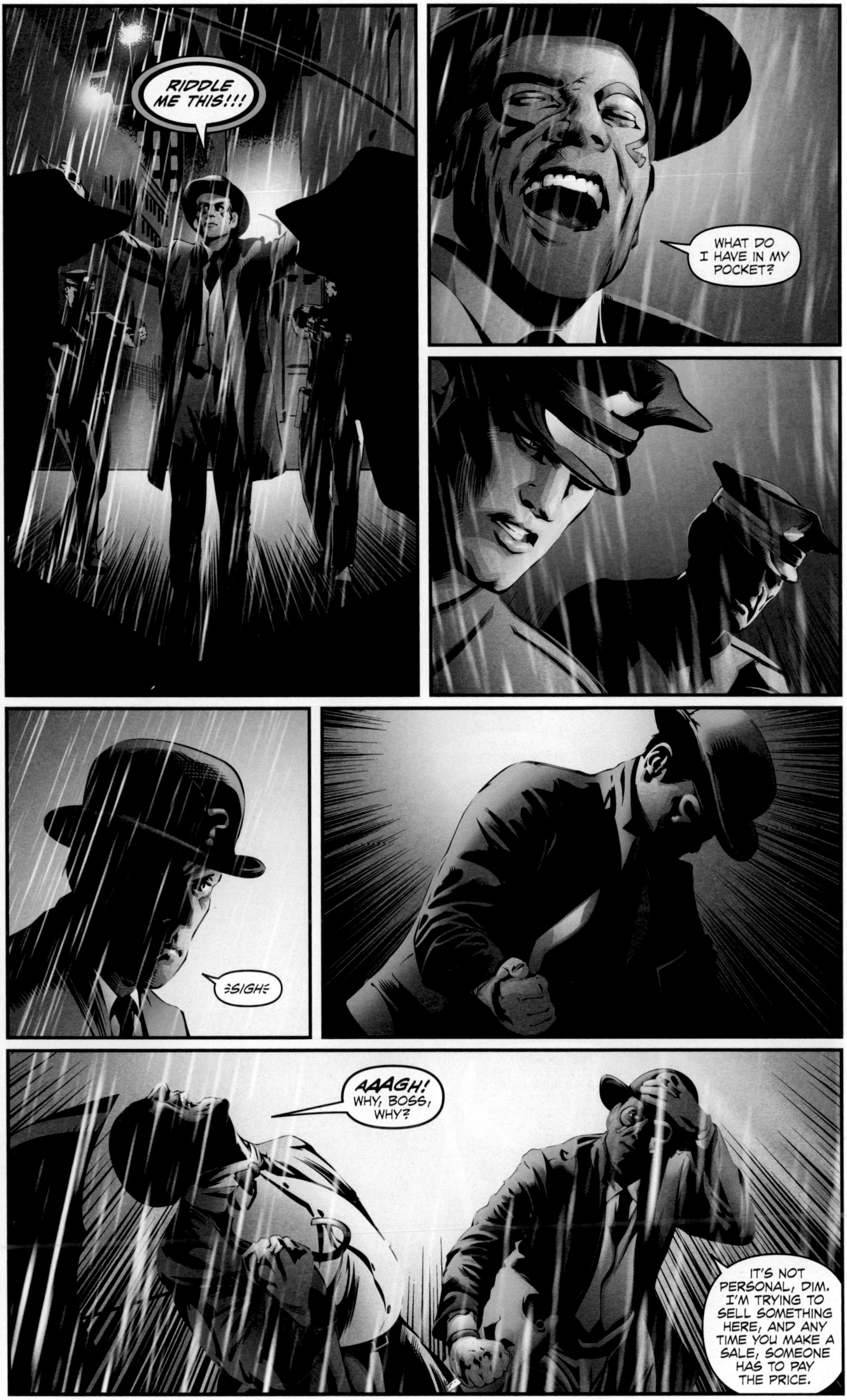
RIDDLE ME THIS!!!
WHAT DO I HAVE IN MY POCKET?
SIGH
AAAGH! WHY, BOSS, WHY?
IT'S NOT PERSONAL, DIM. I'M TRYING TO SELL SOMETHING HERE, AND ANY TIME YOU MAKE A SALE, SOMEONE HAS TO PAY THE PRICE.

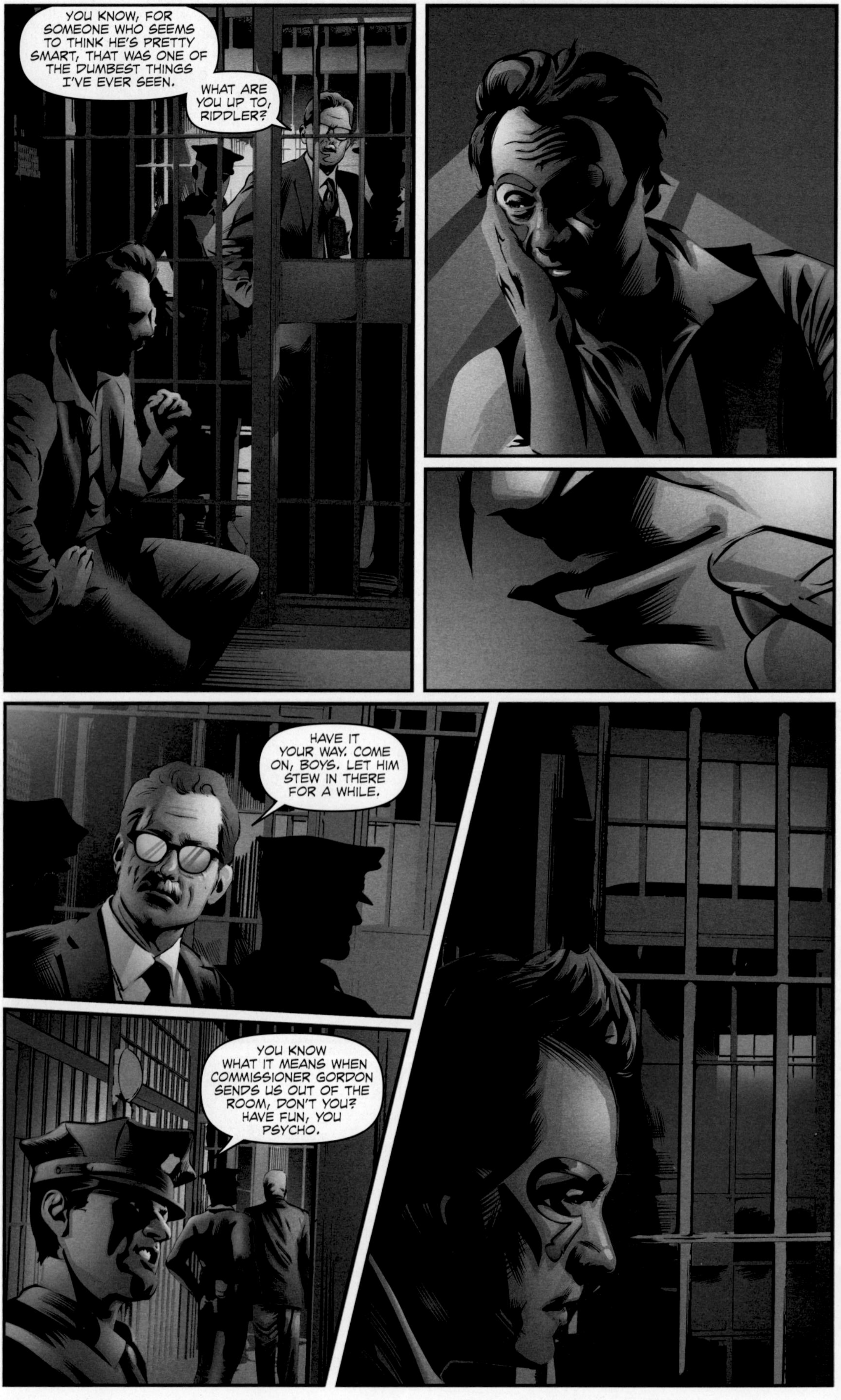
YOU KNOW, FOR SOMEONE WHO SEEMS TO THINK HE'S PRETTY SMART, THAT WAS ONE OF THE DUMBEST THINGS I'VE EVER SEEN.
WHAT ARE YOU UP TO, RIDDLER?
HAVE IT YOUR WAY. COME ON, BOYS. LET HIM STEW IN THERE FOR A WHILE.
YOU KNOW WHAT IT MEANS WHEN COMMISSIONER GORDON SENDS US OUT OF THE ROOM, DON'T YOU? HAVE FUN, YOU PSYCHO.

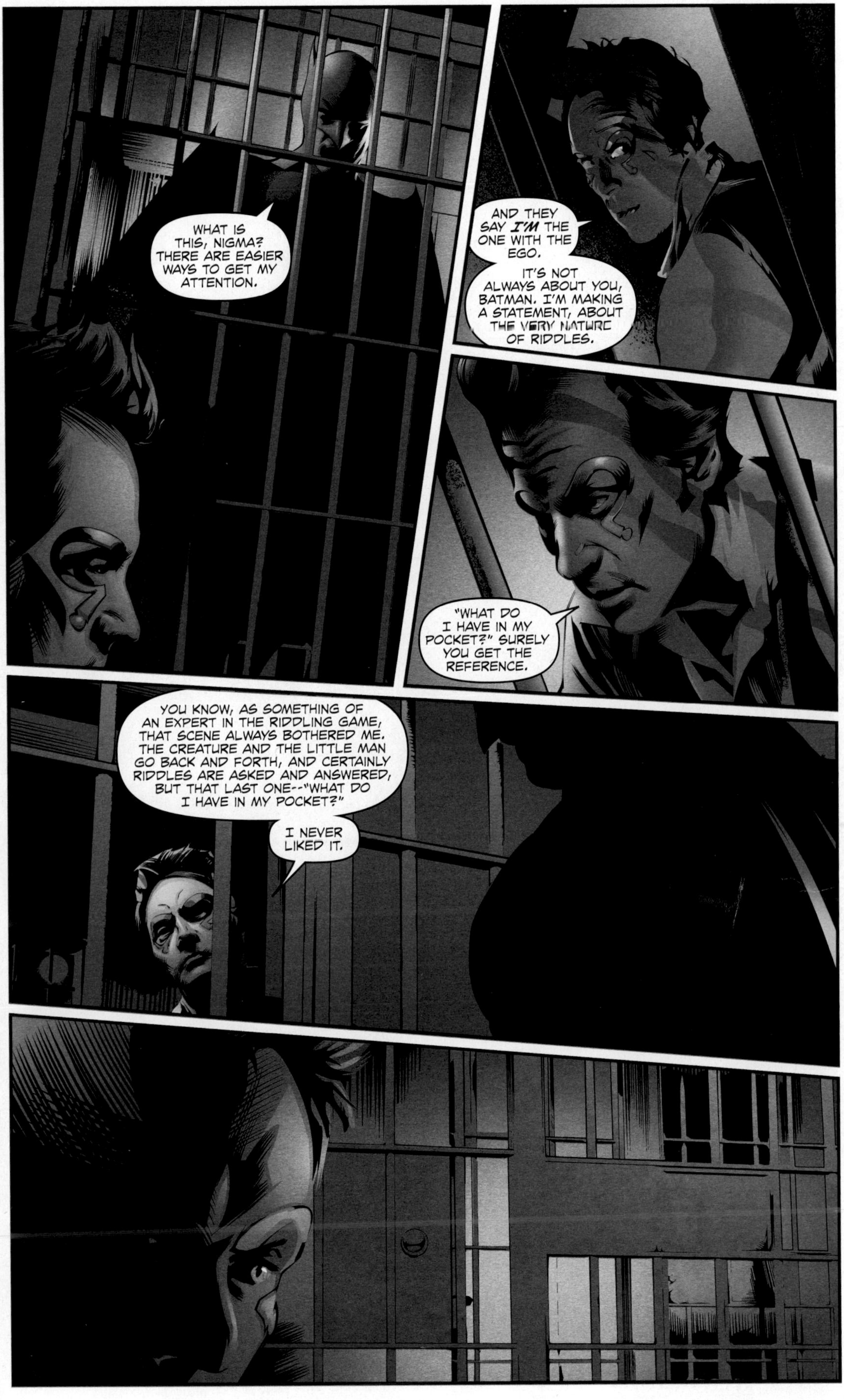
WHAT IS THIS, NIGMA? THERE ARE EASIER WAYS TO GET MY ATTENTION.
AND THEY SAY *I'M* THE ONE WITH THE EGO.
IT'S NOT ALWAYS ABOUT YOU, BATMAN. I'M MAKING A STATEMENT, ABOUT THE VERY NATURE OF RIDDLES.
"WHAT DO I HAVE IN MY POCKET?" SURELY YOU GET THE REFERENCE.
YOU KNOW, AS SOMETHING OF AN EXPERT IN THE RIDDLING GAME, THAT SCENE ALWAYS BOTHERED ME. THE CREATURE AND THE LITTLE MAN GO BACK AND FORTH, AND CERTAINLY RIDDLES ARE ASKED AND ANSWERED, BUT THAT LAST ONE--"WHAT DO I HAVE IN MY POCKET?"
I NEVER LIKED IT.

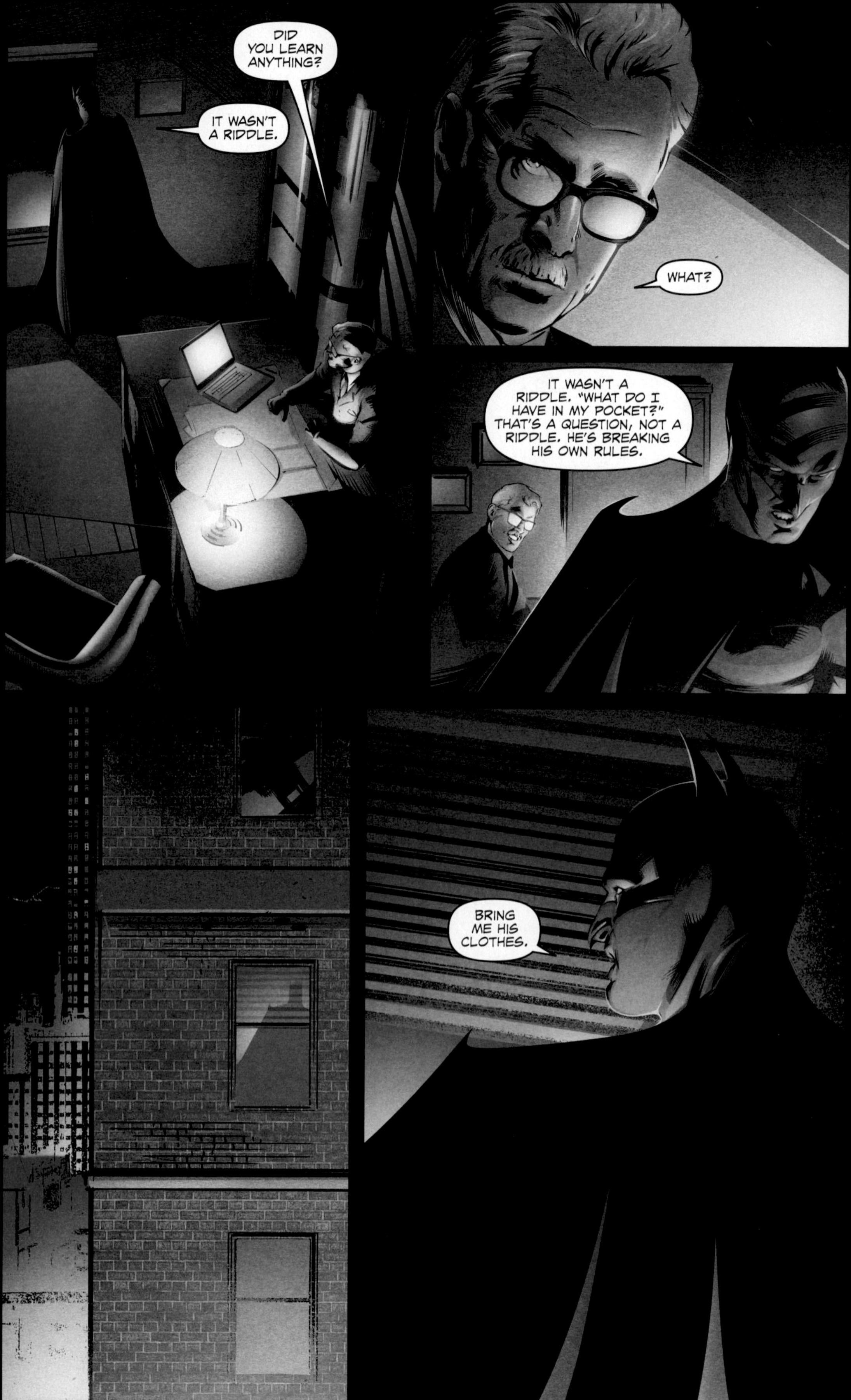
DID YOU LEARN ANYTHING?
IT WASN'T A RIDDLE.
WHAT?
IT WASN'T A RIDDLE. "WHAT DO I HAVE IN MY POCKET?" THAT'S A QUESTION, NOT A RIDDLE. HE'S BREAKING HIS OWN RULES.
BRING ME HIS CLOTHES.

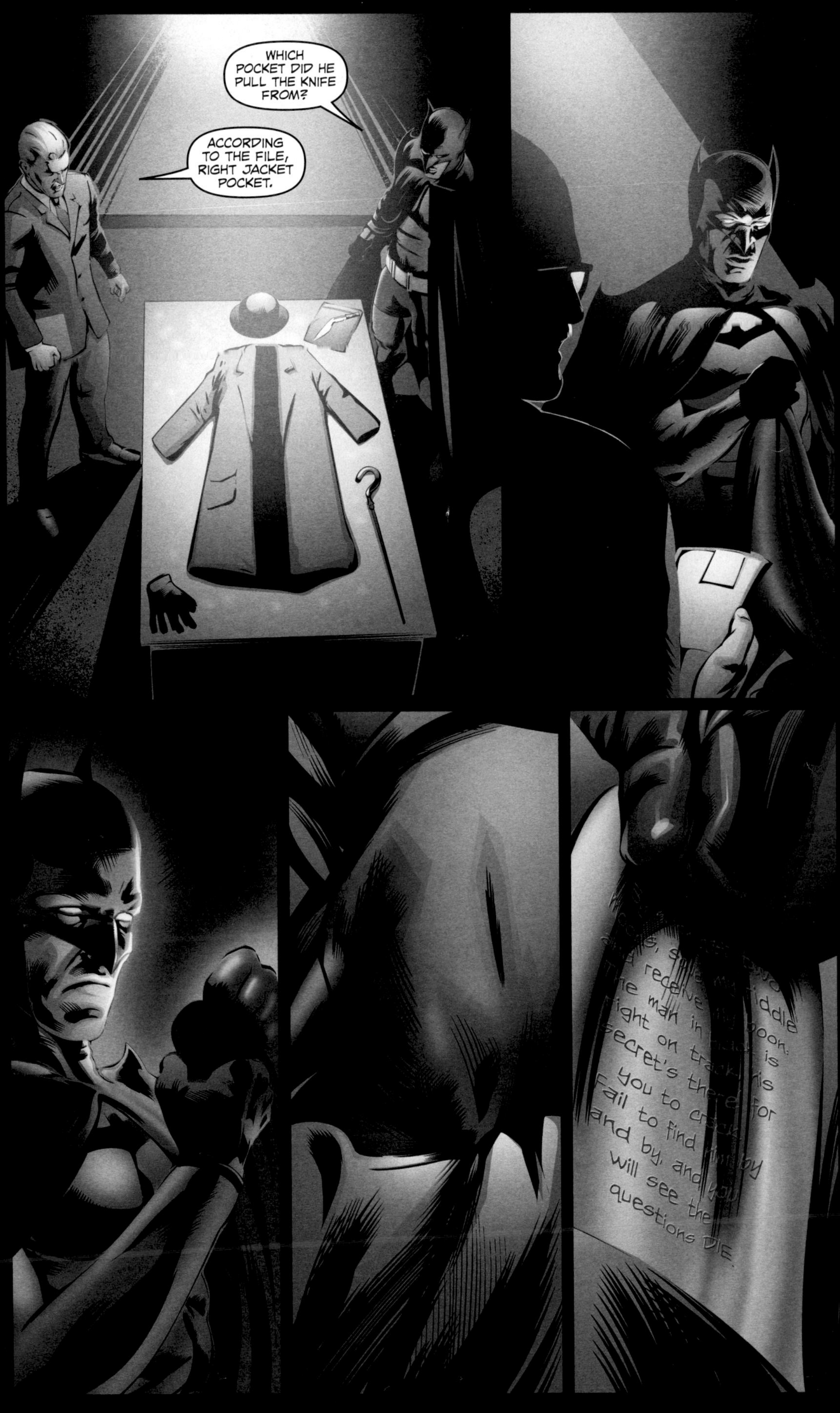
WHICH POCKET DID HE PULL THE KNIFE FROM?
ACCORDING TO THE FILE, RIGHT JACKET POCKET.
receive
man in
is
right on
secret's
for
you to
fail to find
and by, and
will see the
questions DIE.

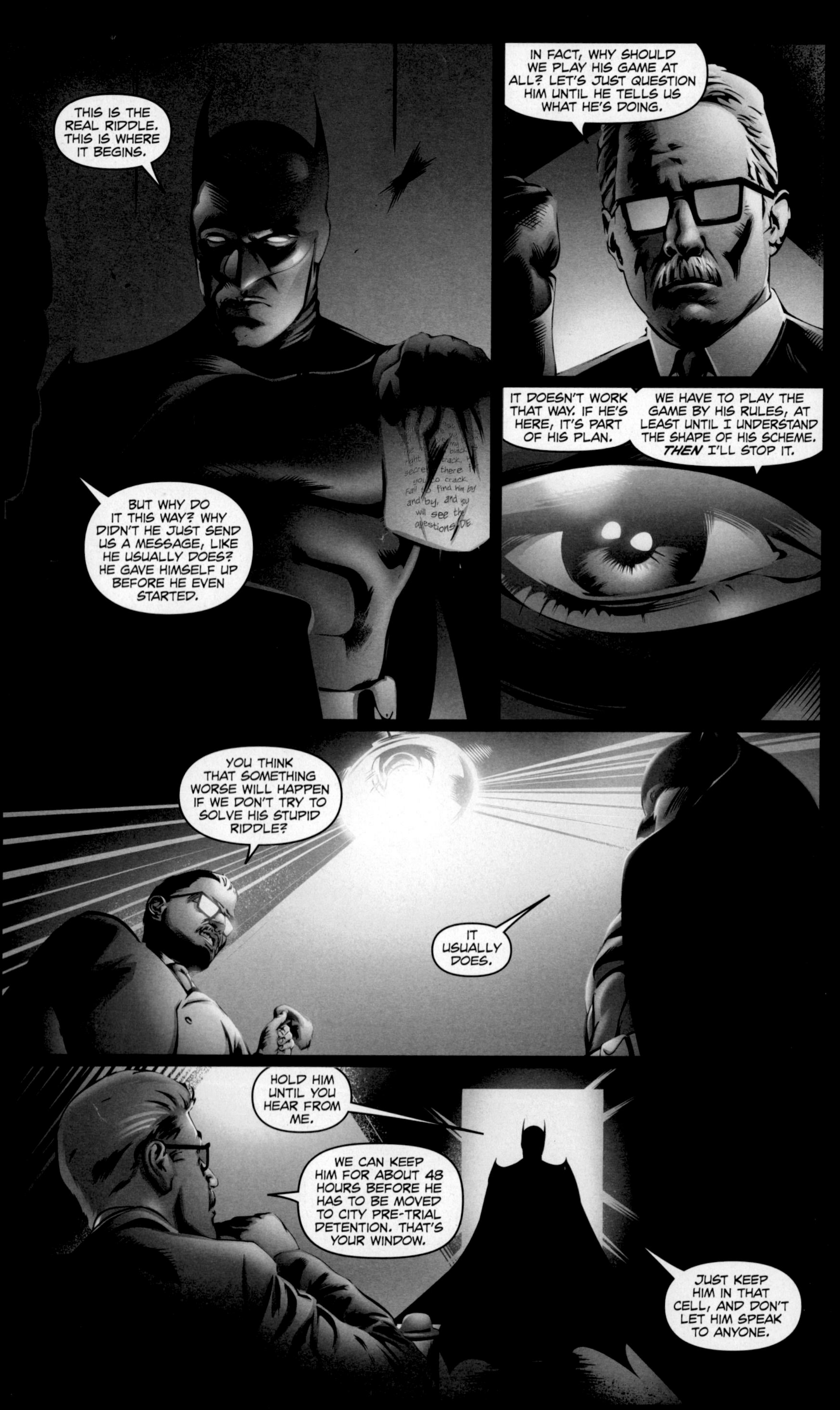
THIS IS THE REAL RIDDLE. THIS IS WHERE IT BEGINS.
BUT WHY DO IT THIS WAY? WHY DIDN'T HE JUST SEND US A MESSAGE, LIKE HE USUALLY DOES? HE GAVE HIMSELF UP BEFORE HE EVEN STARTED.
IN FACT, WHY SHOULD WE PLAY HIS GAME AT ALL? LET'S JUST QUESTION HIM UNTIL HE TELLS US WHAT HE'S DOING.
IT DOESN'T WORK THAT WAY. IF HE'S HERE, IT'S PART OF HIS PLAN.
WE HAVE TO PLAY THE GAME BY HIS RULES, AT LEAST UNTIL I UNDERSTAND THE SHAPE OF HIS SCHEME. *THEN* I'LL STOP IT.
YOU THINK THAT SOMETHING WORSE WILL HAPPEN IF WE DON'T TRY TO SOLVE HIS STUPID RIDDLE?
IT USUALLY DOES.
HOLD HIM UNTIL YOU HEAR FROM ME.
WE CAN KEEP HIM FOR ABOUT 48 HOURS BEFORE HE HAS TO BE MOVED TO CITY PRE-TRIAL DETENTION. THAT'S YOUR WINDOW.
JUST KEEP HIM IN THAT CELL, AND DON'T LET HIM SPEAK TO ANYONE.

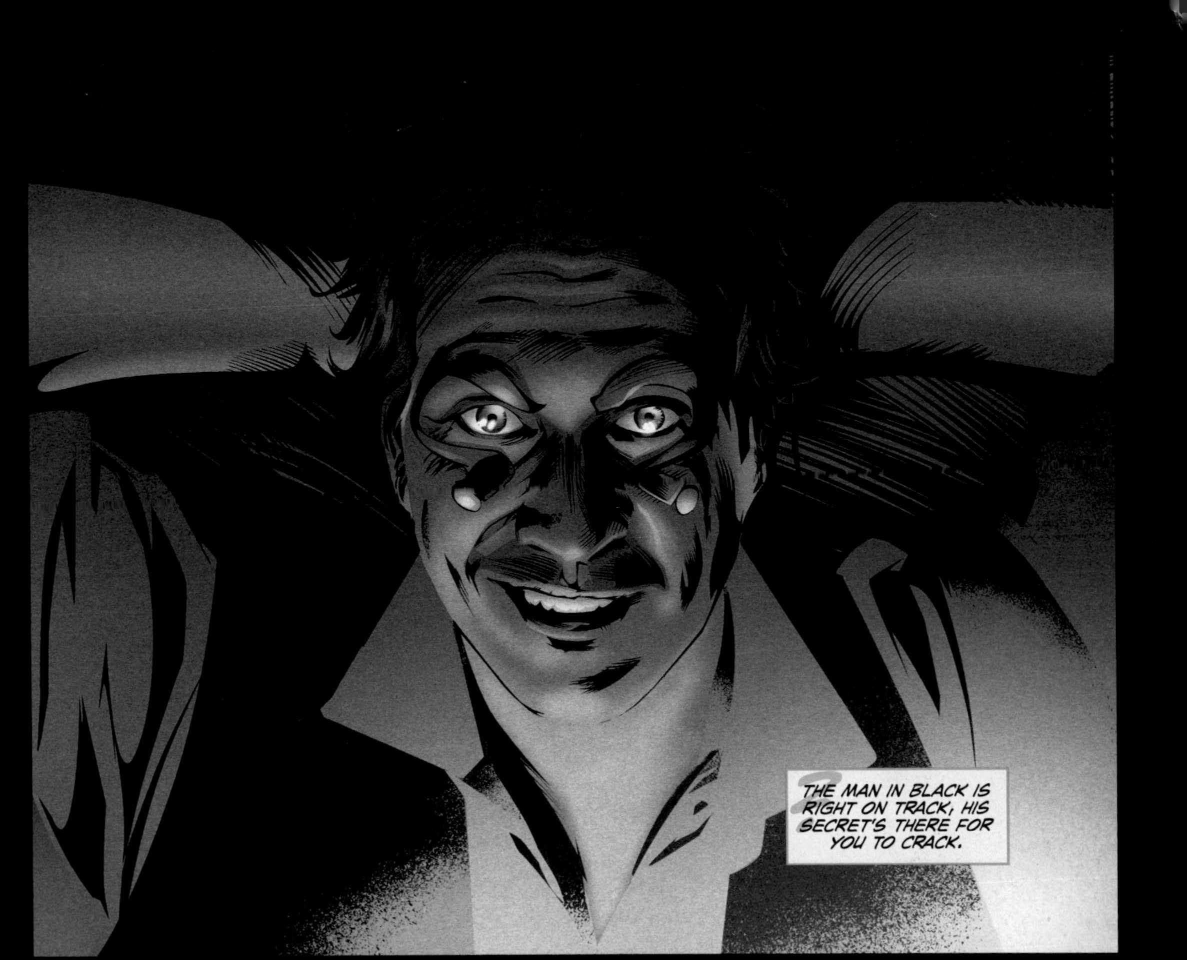
THE MAN IN BLACK IS RIGHT ON TRACK; HIS SECRET'S THERE FOR YOU TO CRACK.

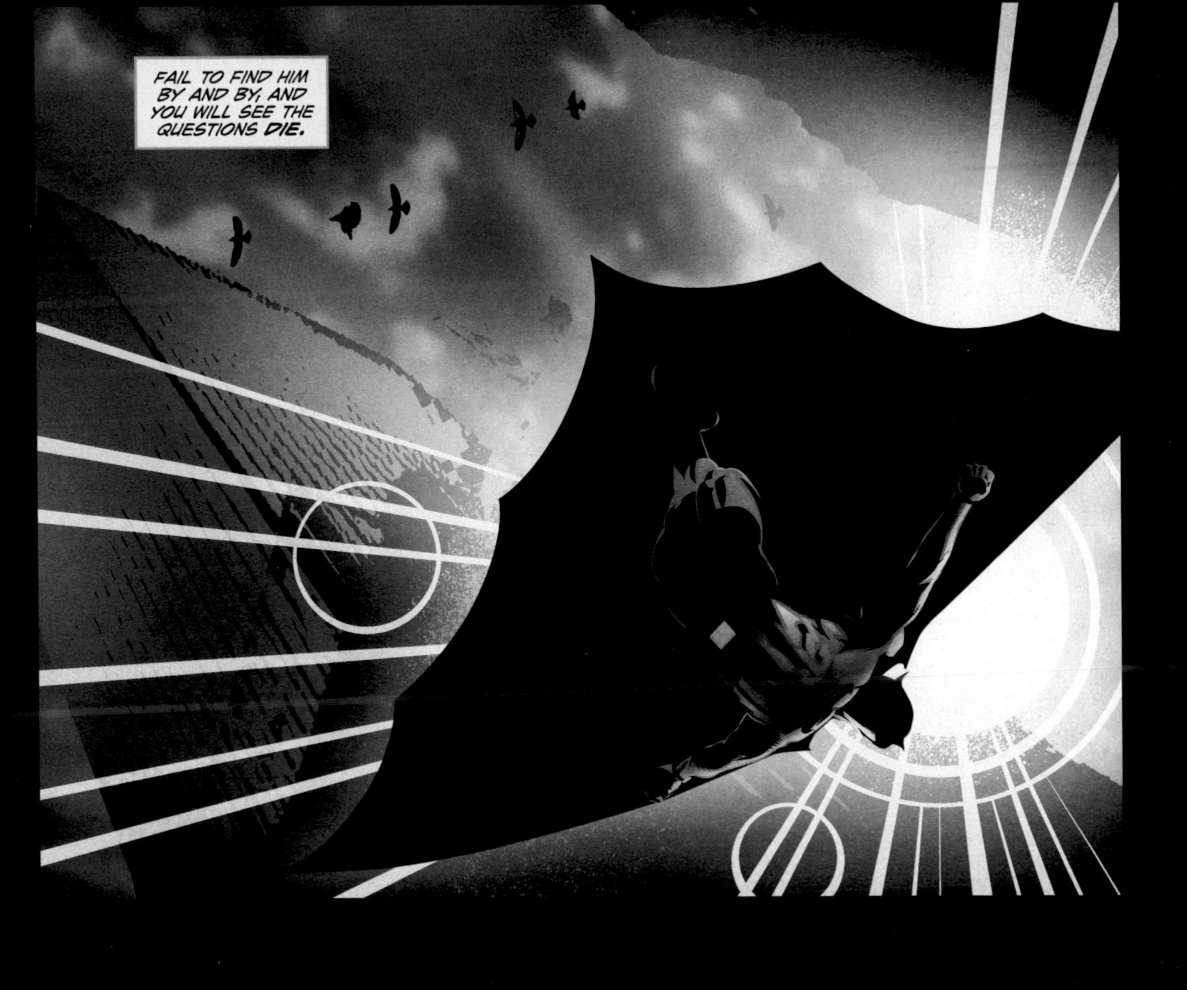
FAIL TO FIND HIM BY AND BY; AND YOU WILL SEE THE QUESTIONS DIE.

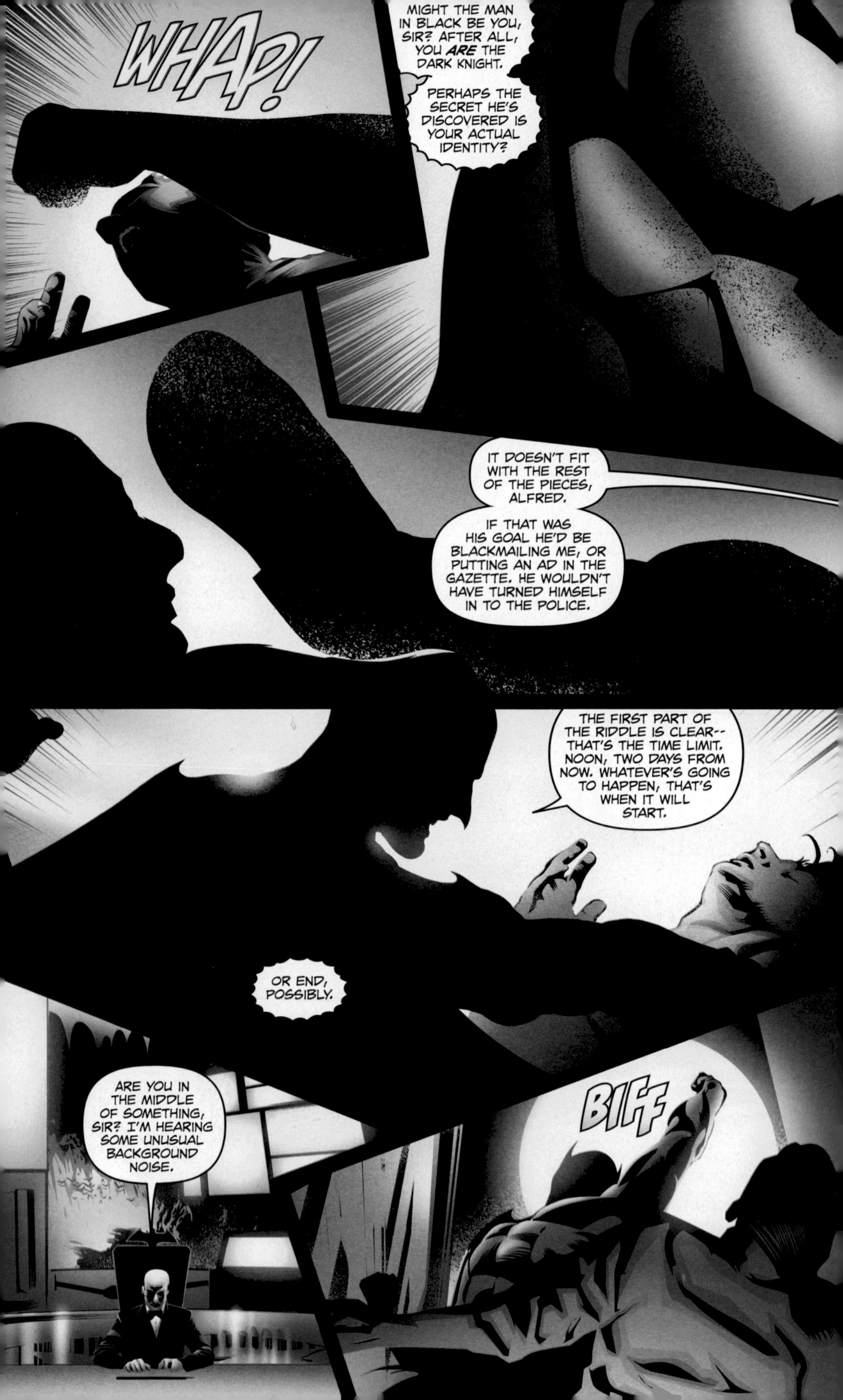
WHAP!
MIGHT THE MAN IN BLACK BE YOU, SIR? AFTER ALL, YOU *ARE* THE DARK KNIGHT.
PERHAPS THE SECRET HE'S DISCOVERED IS YOUR ACTUAL IDENTITY?
IT DOESN'T FIT WITH THE REST OF THE PIECES, ALFRED.
IF THAT WAS HIS GOAL HE'D BE BLACKMAILING ME, OR PUTTING AN AD IN THE GAZETTE. HE WOULDN'T HAVE TURNED HIMSELF IN TO THE POLICE.
THE FIRST PART OF THE RIDDLE IS CLEAR--THAT'S THE TIME LIMIT. NOON, TWO DAYS FROM NOW. WHATEVER'S GOING TO HAPPEN, THAT'S WHEN IT WILL START.
OR END, POSSIBLY.
ARE YOU IN THE MIDDLE OF SOMETHING, SIR? I'M HEARING SOME UNUSUAL BACKGROUND NOISE.
BIFF

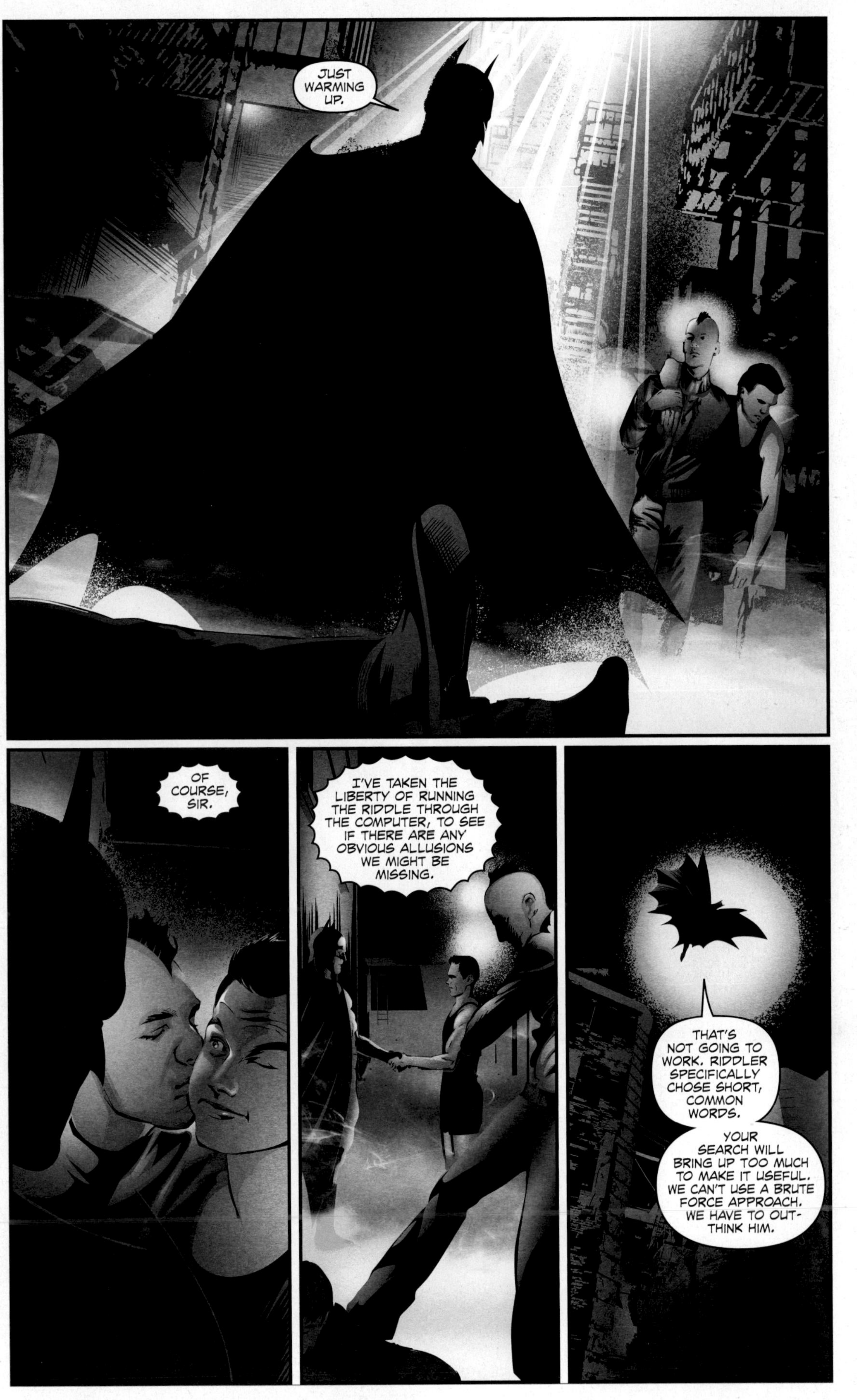
JUST WARMING UP.
OF COURSE, SIR.
I'VE TAKEN THE LIBERTY OF RUNNING THE RIDDLE THROUGH THE COMPUTER, TO SEE IF THERE ARE ANY OBVIOUS ALLUSIONS WE MIGHT BE MISSING.
THAT'S NOT GOING TO WORK. RIDDLER SPECIFICALLY CHOSE SHORT, COMMON WORDS.
YOUR SEARCH WILL BRING UP TOO MUCH TO MAKE IT USEFUL. WE CAN'T USE A BRUTE FORCE APPROACH. WE HAVE TO OUT-THINK HIM.

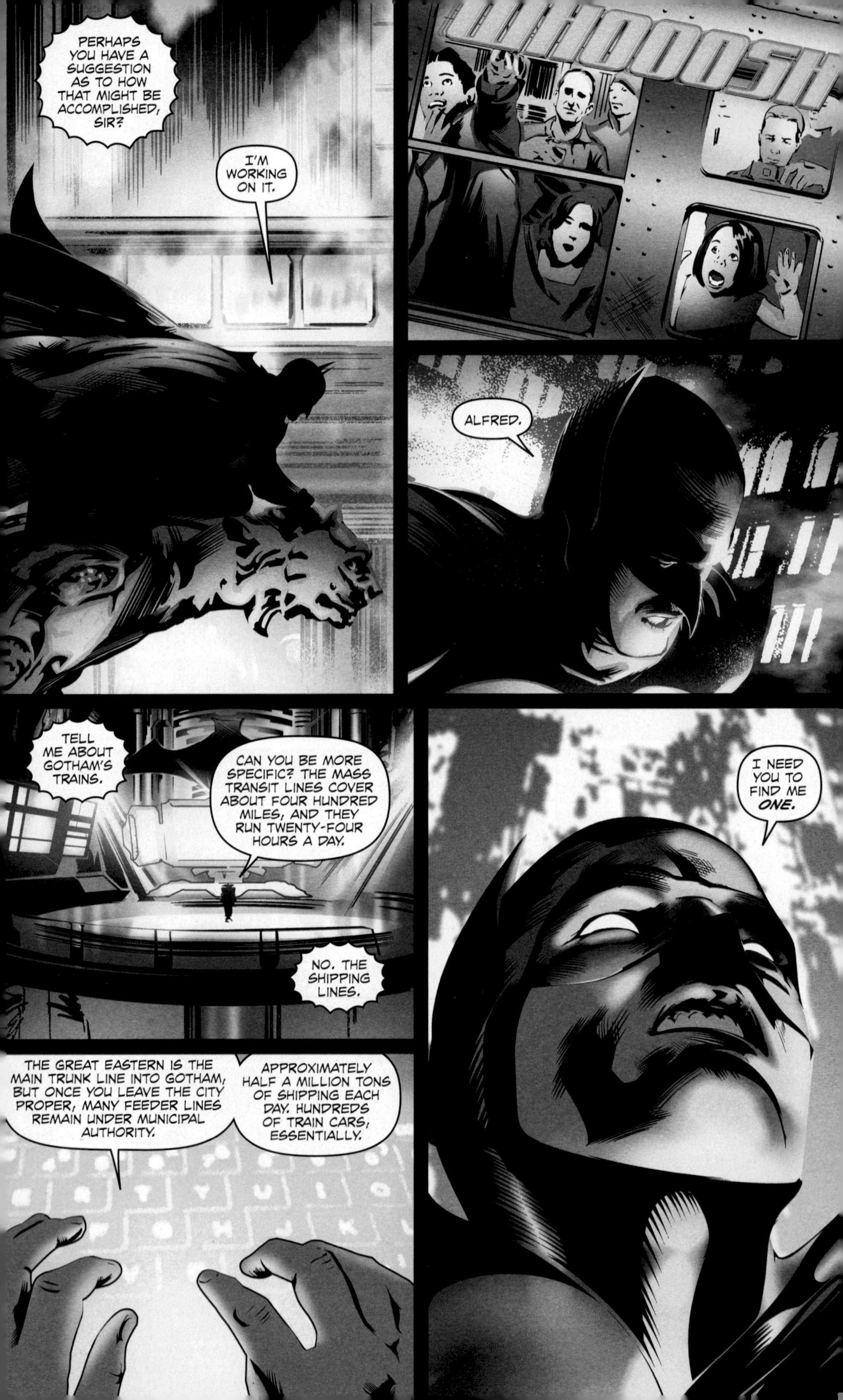

PERHAPS YOU HAVE A SUGGESTION AS TO HOW THAT MIGHT BE ACCOMPLISHED, SIR?
I'M WORKING ON IT.
WHOOOOSH
ALFRED.
TELL ME ABOUT GOTHAM'S TRAINS.
CAN YOU BE MORE SPECIFIC? THE MASS TRANSIT LINES COVER ABOUT FOUR HUNDRED MILES, AND THEY RUN TWENTY-FOUR HOURS A DAY.
NO. THE SHIPPING LINES.
THE GREAT EASTERN IS THE MAIN TRUNK LINE INTO GOTHAM, BUT ONCE YOU LEAVE THE CITY PROPER, MANY FEEDER LINES REMAIN UNDER MUNICIPAL AUTHORITY.
APPROXIMATELY HALF A MILLION TONS OF SHIPPING EACH DAY. HUNDREDS OF TRAIN CARS, ESSENTIALLY.
I NEED YOU TO FIND ME *ONE.*

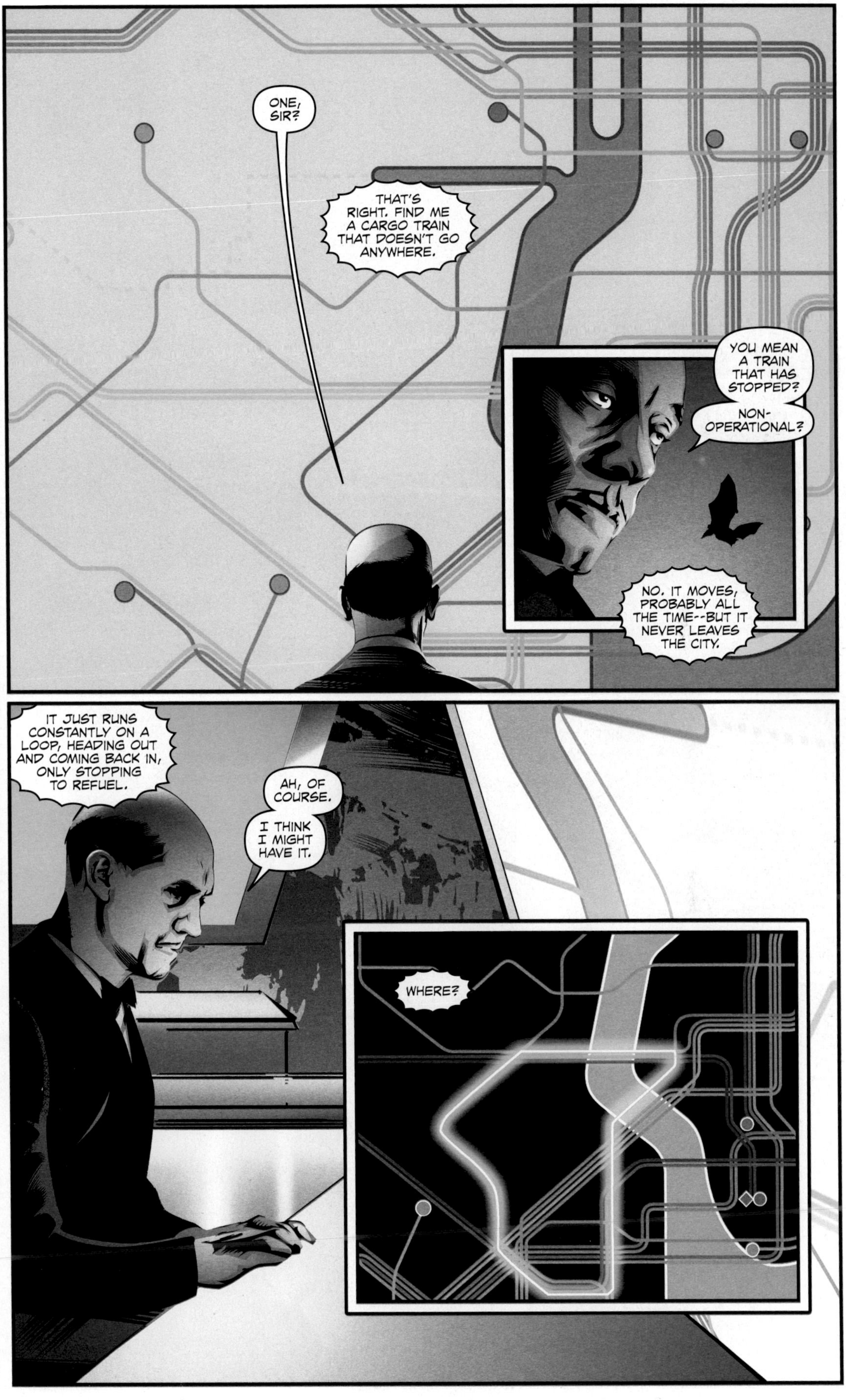
ONE, SIR?
THAT'S RIGHT. FIND ME A CARGO TRAIN THAT DOESN'T GO ANYWHERE.
YOU MEAN A TRAIN THAT HAS STOPPED?
NON-OPERATIONAL?
NO. IT MOVES, PROBABLY ALL THE TIME--BUT IT NEVER LEAVES THE CITY.
IT JUST RUNS CONSTANTLY ON A LOOP, HEADING OUT AND COMING BACK IN, ONLY STOPPING TO REFUEL.
AH, OF COURSE.
I THINK I MIGHT HAVE IT.
WHERE?

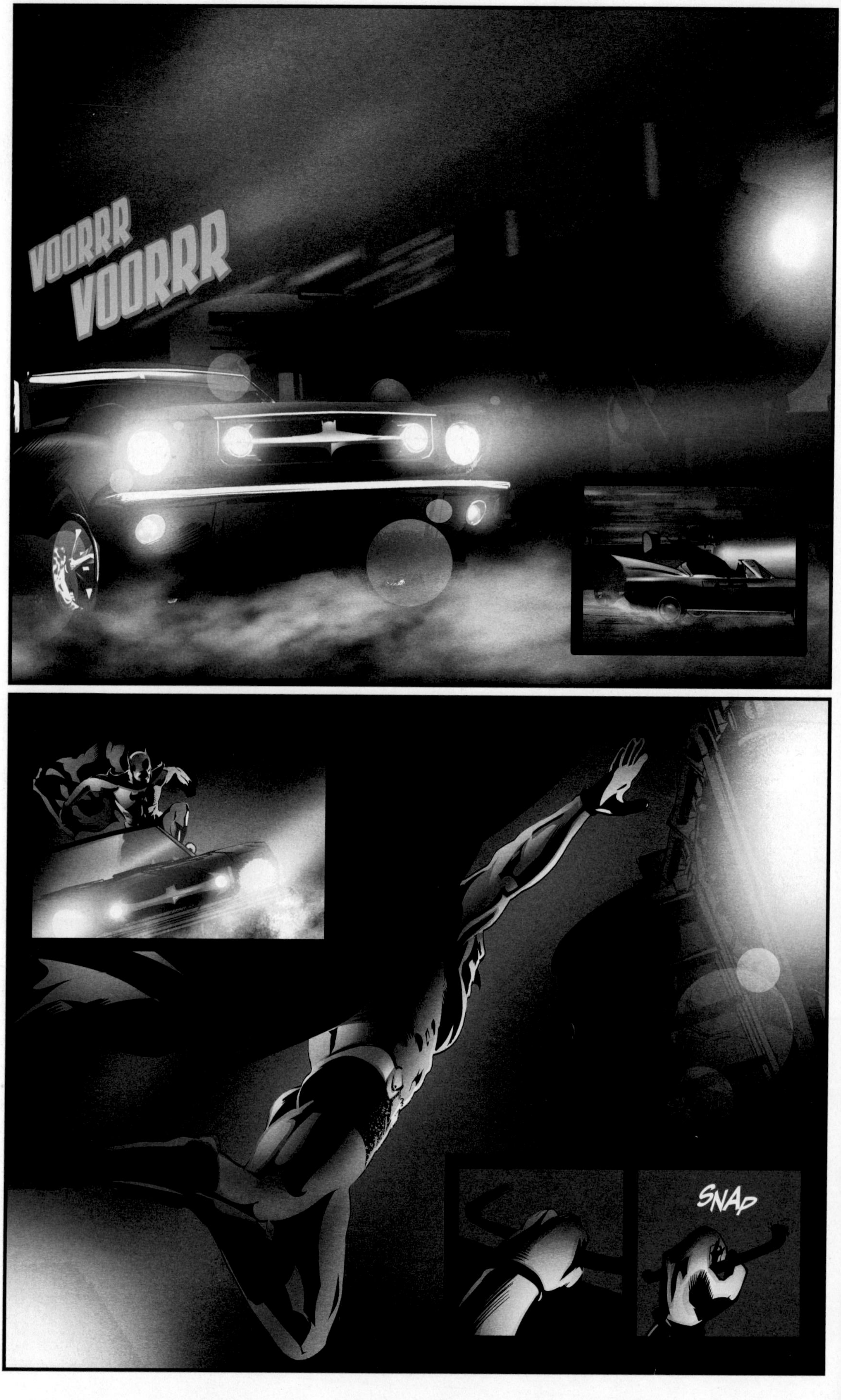
VOORRR
VOORRR
SNAP

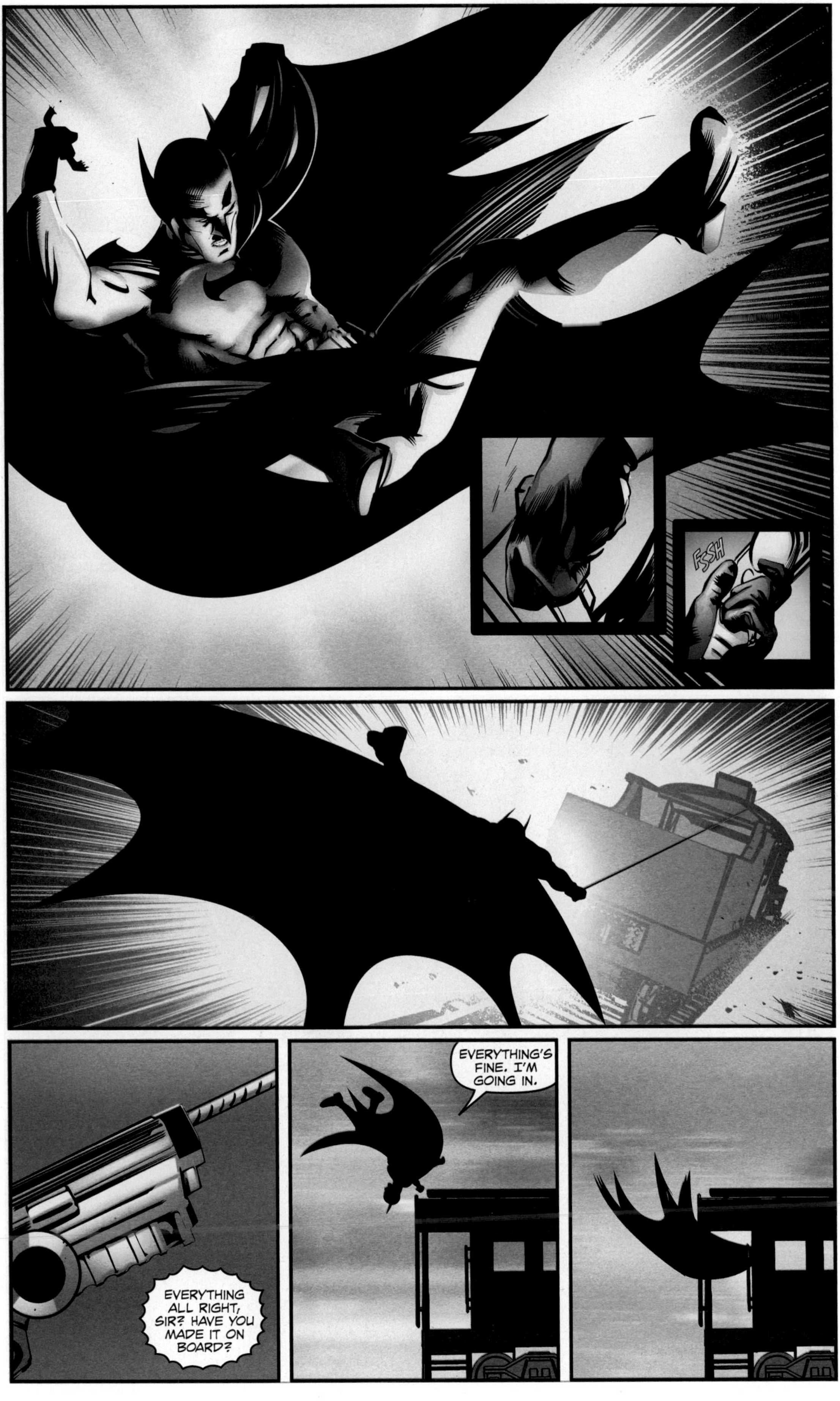
FSSH
EVERYTHING ALL RIGHT, SIR? HAVE YOU MADE IT ON BOARD?
EVERYTHING'S FINE. I'M GOING IN.

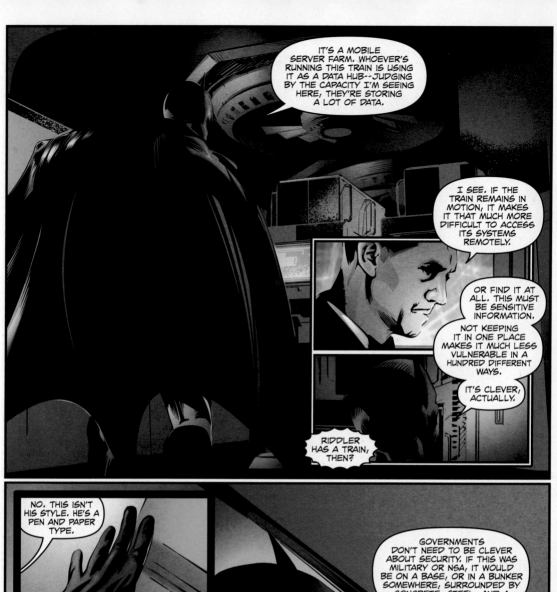

IT'S A MOBILE SERVER FARM. WHOEVER'S RUNNING THIS TRAIN IS USING IT AS A DATA HUB--JUDGING BY THE CAPACITY I'M SEEING HERE, THEY'RE STORING A LOT OF DATA.

I SEE. IF THE TRAIN REMAINS IN MOTION, IT MAKES IT THAT MUCH MORE DIFFICULT TO ACCESS ITS SYSTEMS REMOTELY.

OR FIND IT AT ALL. THIS MUST BE SENSITIVE INFORMATION.

NOT KEEPING IT IN ONE PLACE MAKES IT MUCH LESS VULNERABLE IN A HUNDRED DIFFERENT WAYS.

IT'S CLEVER, ACTUALLY.

RIDDLER HAS A TRAIN, THEN?

NO. THIS ISN'T HIS STYLE. HE'S A PEN AND PAPER TYPE.

GOVERNMENT, POSSIBLY?

GOVERNMENTS DON'T NEED TO BE CLEVER ABOUT SECURITY. IF THIS WAS MILITARY OR NSA, IT WOULD BE ON A BASE, OR IN A BUNKER SOMEWHERE, SURROUNDED BY CONCRETE, STEEL, AND A THOUSAND GUNS.

YOU HAVE ME STUMPED, THEN, SIR. WHOM DO YOU SUPPOSE...?

LET'S FIND OUT.

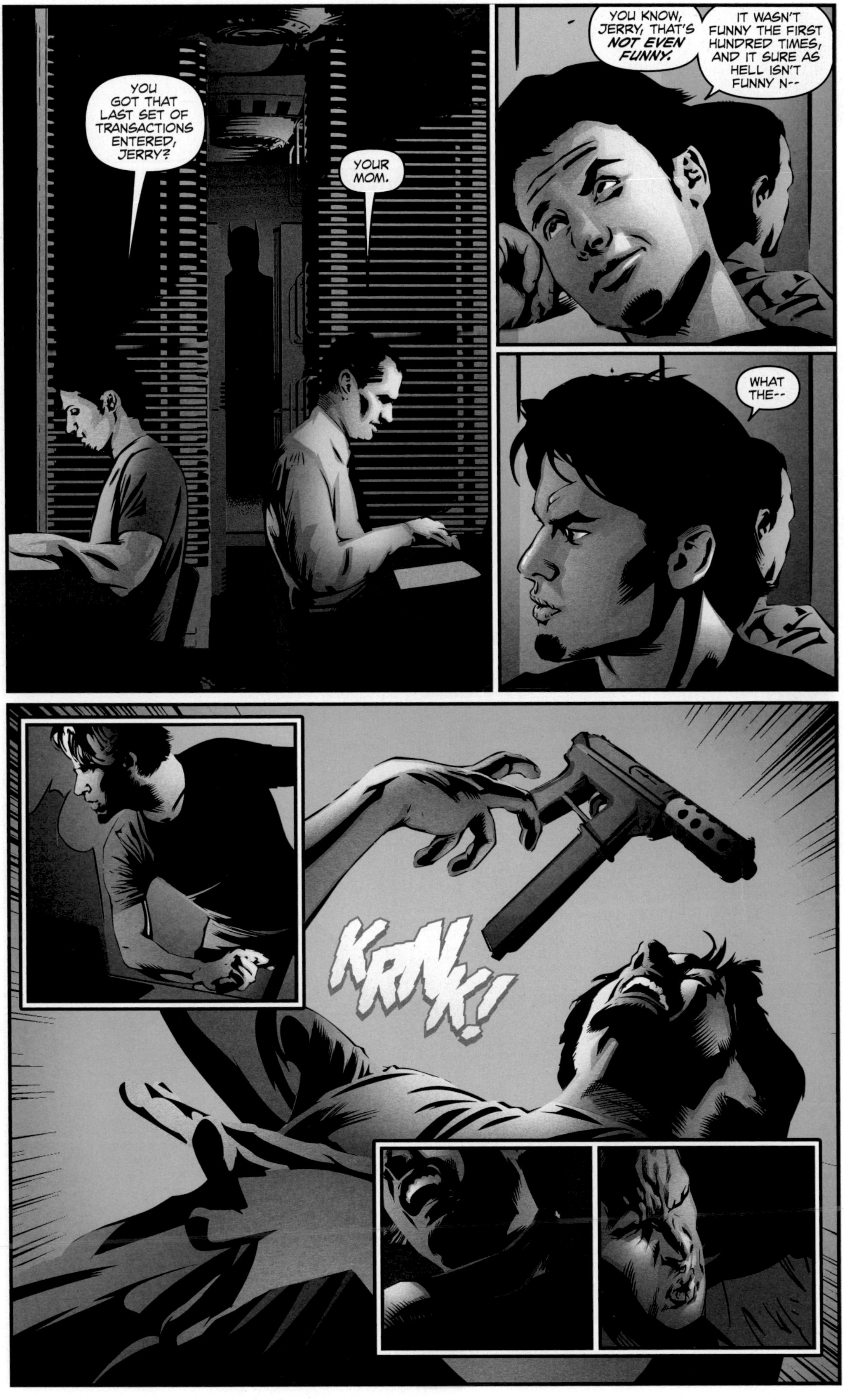
YOU GOT THAT LAST SET OF TRANSACTIONS ENTERED, JERRY?
YOUR MOM.
YOU KNOW, JERRY, THAT'S NOT EVEN FUNNY.
IT WASN'T FUNNY THE FIRST HUNDRED TIMES, AND IT SURE AS HELL ISN'T FUNNY N--
WHAT THE--
KRNK!

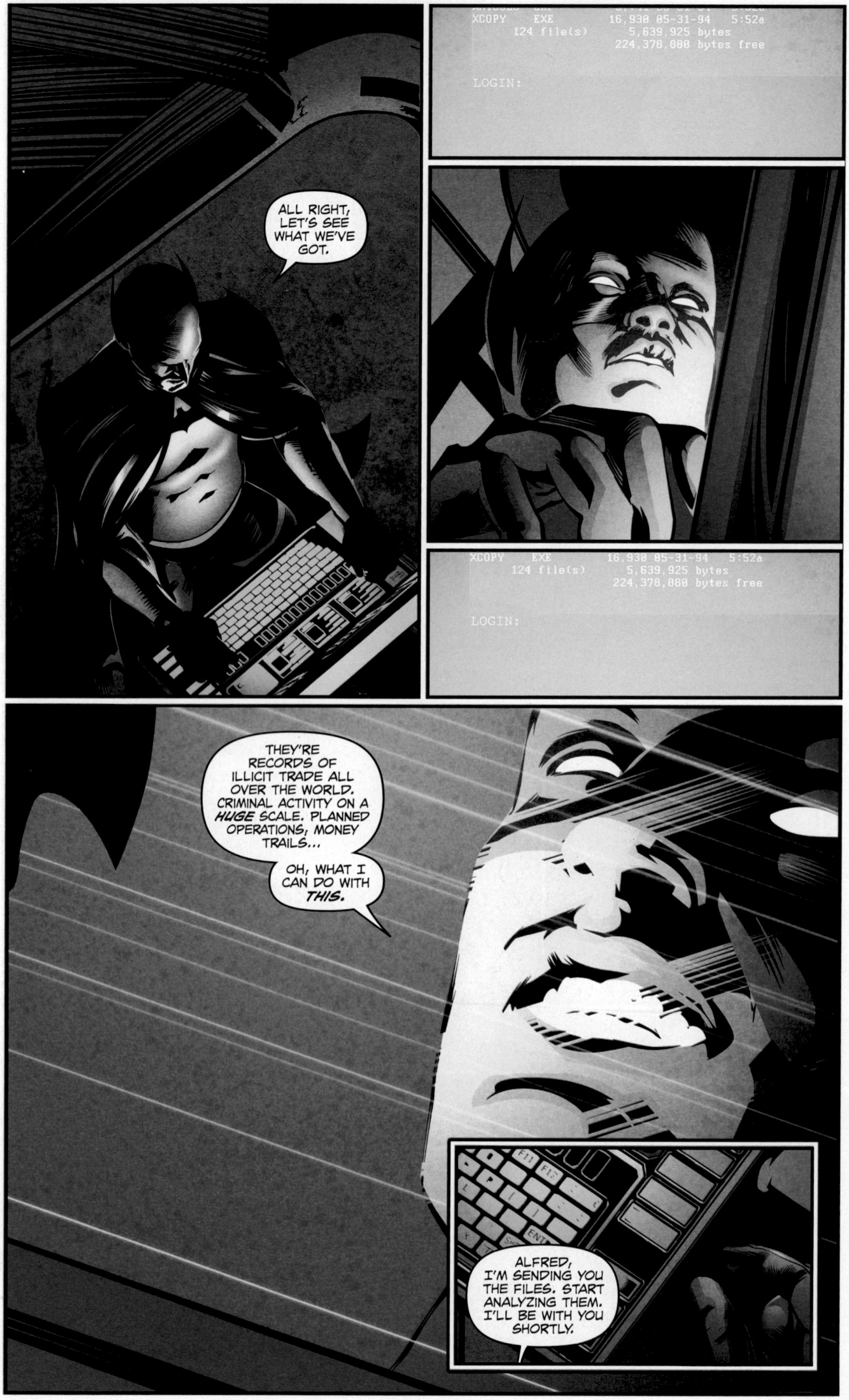

XCOPY EXE 16,930 05-31-94 5:52a
124 file(s) 5,639,925 bytes
224,378,880 bytes free
LOGIN:
ALL RIGHT, LET'S SEE WHAT WE'VE GOT.
XCOPY EXE 16,930 05-31-94 5:52a
124 file(s) 5,639,925 bytes
224,378,880 bytes free
LOGIN:
THEY'RE RECORDS OF ILLICIT TRADE ALL OVER THE WORLD. CRIMINAL ACTIVITY ON A *HUGE* SCALE. PLANNED OPERATIONS, MONEY TRAILS...
OH, WHAT I CAN DO WITH *THIS.*
ALFRED, I'M SENDING YOU THE FILES. START ANALYZING THEM. I'LL BE WITH YOU SHORTLY.

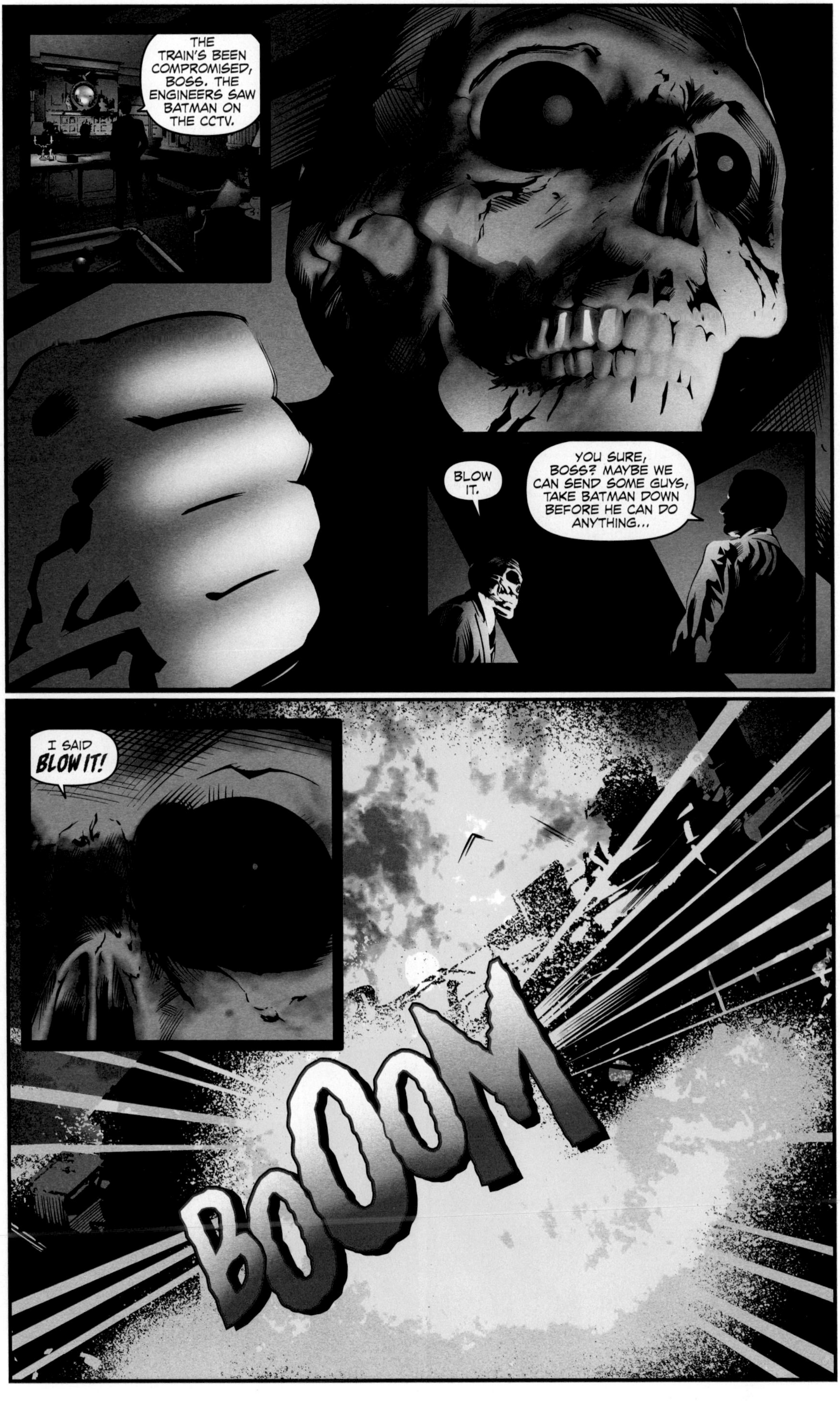
THE TRAIN'S BEEN COMPROMISED, BOSS. THE ENGINEERS SAW BATMAN ON THE CCTV.
YOU SURE, BOSS? MAYBE WE CAN SEND SOME GUYS, TAKE BATMAN DOWN BEFORE HE CAN DO ANYTHING...
BLOW IT.
I SAID BLOW IT!
BOOOOM

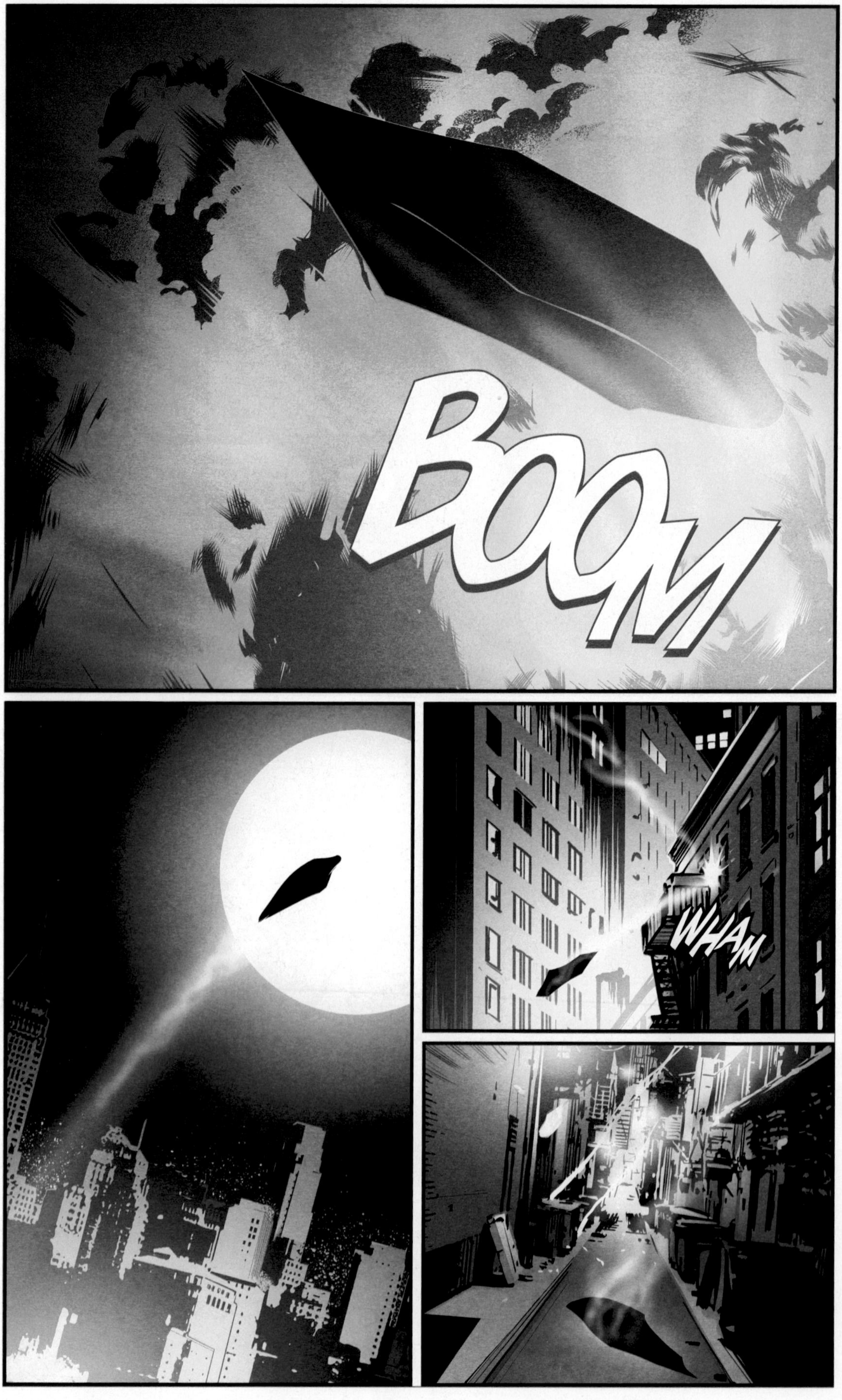
BOOM
WHAM

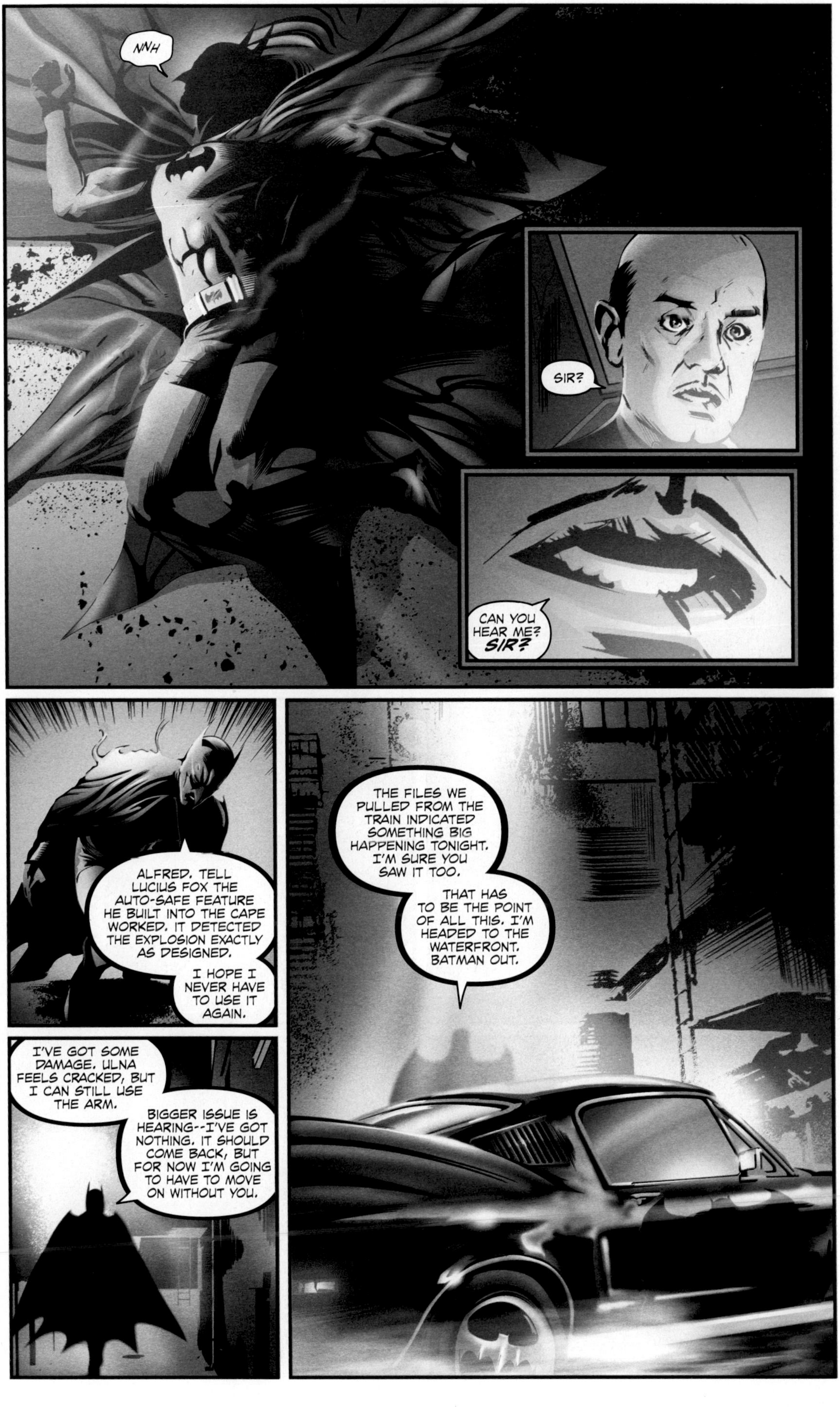
NNH
SIR?
CAN YOU HEAR ME? SIR?
ALFRED. TELL LUCIUS FOX THE AUTO-SAFE FEATURE HE BUILT INTO THE CAPE WORKED. IT DETECTED THE EXPLOSION EXACTLY AS DESIGNED.
I HOPE I NEVER HAVE TO USE IT AGAIN.
I'VE GOT SOME DAMAGE. ULNA FEELS CRACKED, BUT I CAN STILL USE THE ARM.
BIGGER ISSUE IS HEARING--I'VE GOT NOTHING. IT SHOULD COME BACK, BUT FOR NOW I'M GOING TO HAVE TO MOVE ON WITHOUT YOU.
THE FILES WE PULLED FROM THE TRAIN INDICATED SOMETHING BIG HAPPENING TONIGHT. I'M SURE YOU SAW IT TOO.
THAT HAS TO BE THE POINT OF ALL THIS. I'M HEADED TO THE WATERFRONT. BATMAN OUT.

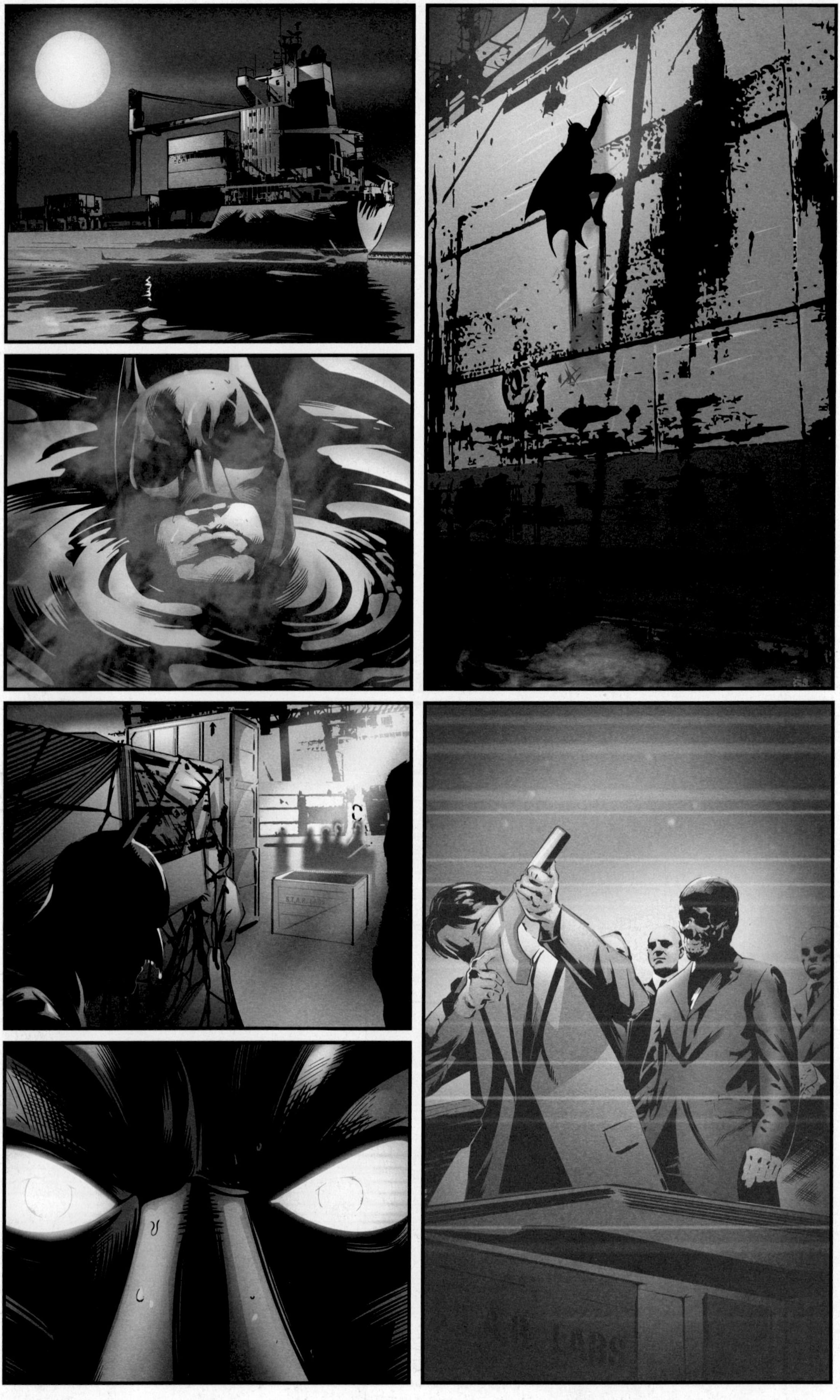

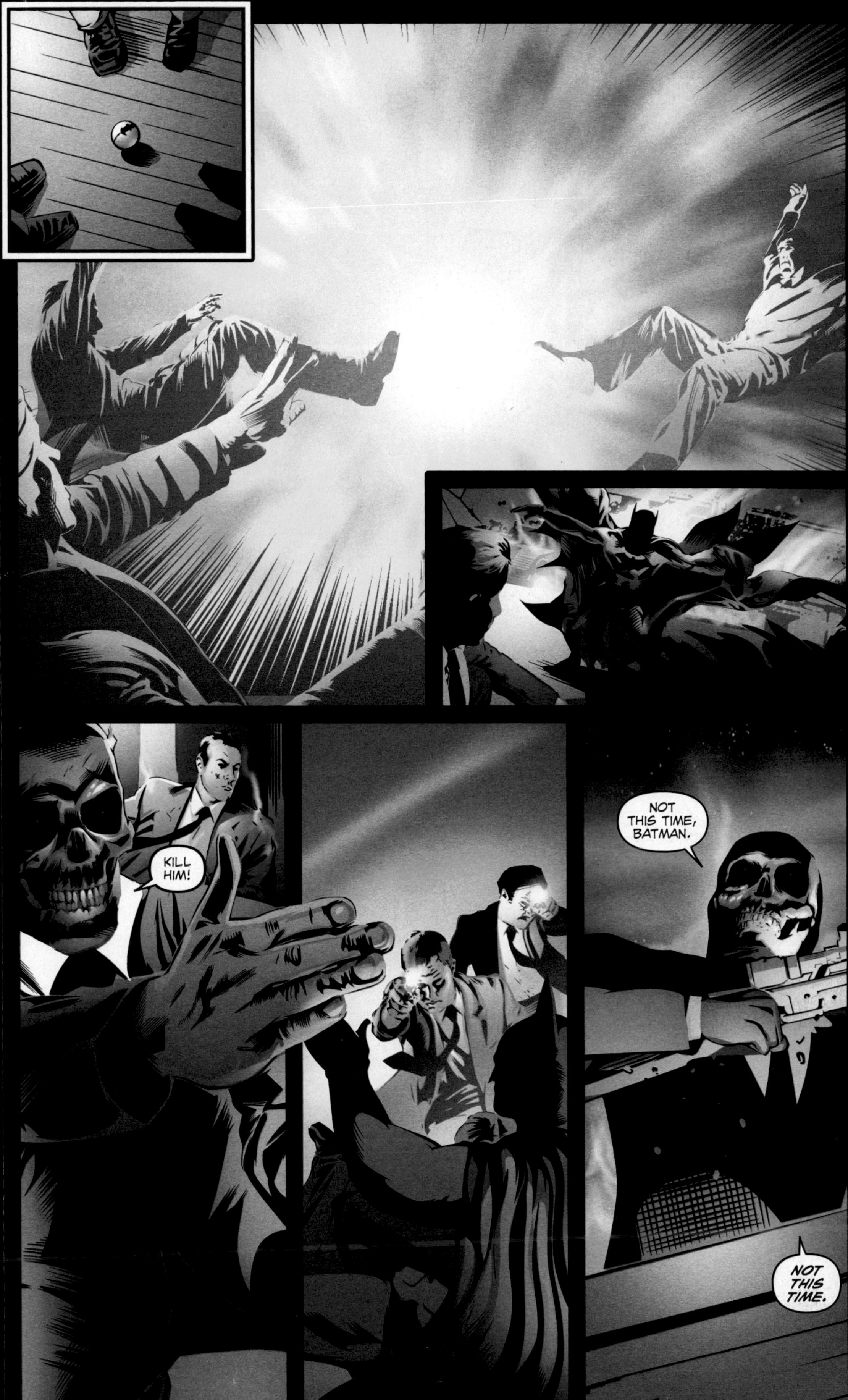
KILL HIM!
NOT THIS TIME, BATMAN.
NOT THIS TIME.

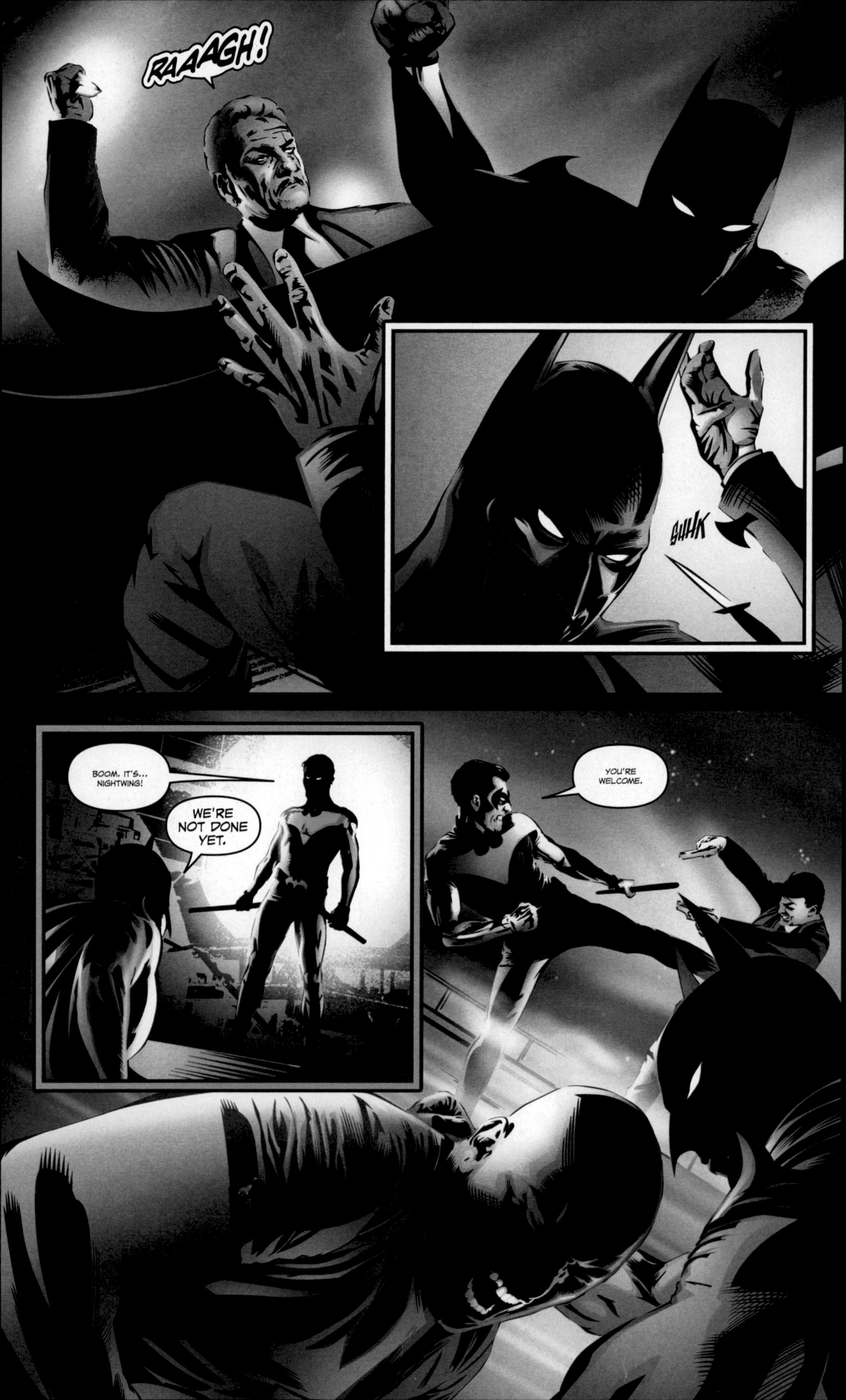
RAAAGH!
SHHK
BOOM. IT'S... NIGHTWING!
WE'RE NOT DONE YET.
YOU'RE WELCOME.

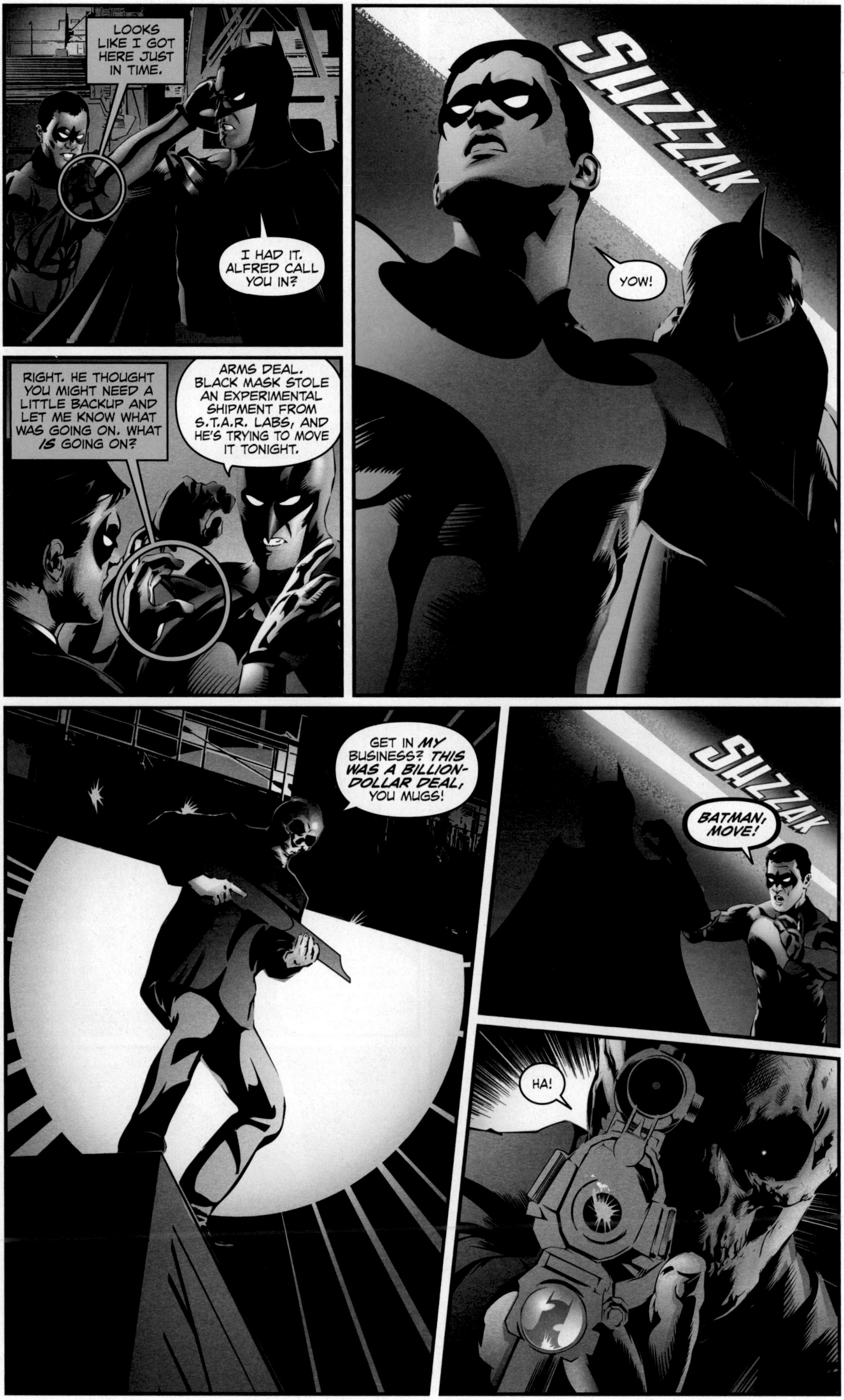
LOOKS LIKE I GOT HERE JUST IN TIME.
I HAD IT. ALFRED CALL YOU IN?
RIGHT. HE THOUGHT YOU MIGHT NEED A LITTLE BACKUP AND LET ME KNOW WHAT WAS GOING ON. WHAT *IS* GOING ON?
ARMS DEAL. BLACK MASK STOLE AN EXPERIMENTAL SHIPMENT FROM S.T.A.R. LABS, AND HE'S TRYING TO MOVE IT TONIGHT.
SHZZZAK
YOW!
GET IN *MY* BUSINESS? *THIS WAS A BILLION-DOLLAR DEAL,* YOU MUGS!
SHZZZAK
BATMAN, MOVE!
HA!

RELAX, NIGHTWING.

KZZZACK

HUH?

HOW'D I MISS THAT SHOT? THIS THING WAS ZEROED IN. PIECE OF JU--

THWOCK

OOF!

YOU CAN CUT OUT THE SIGN LANGUAGE, MY EARS ARE COMING BACK. I HEARD THE BATARANG HITTING BLACK MASK'S SKULL.

FANTASTIC.

I CAN'T BELIEVE HE MISSED--IS HE THAT BAD A SHOT?

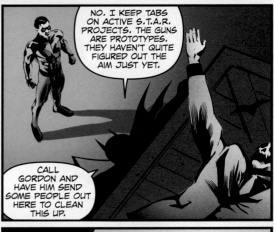

NO. I KEEP TABS ON ACTIVE S.T.A.R. PROJECTS. THE GUNS ARE PROTOTYPES. THEY HAVEN'T QUITE FIGURED OUT THE AIM JUST YET.

CALL GORDON AND HAVE HIM SEND SOME PEOPLE OUT HERE TO CLEAN THIS UP.

NOW.

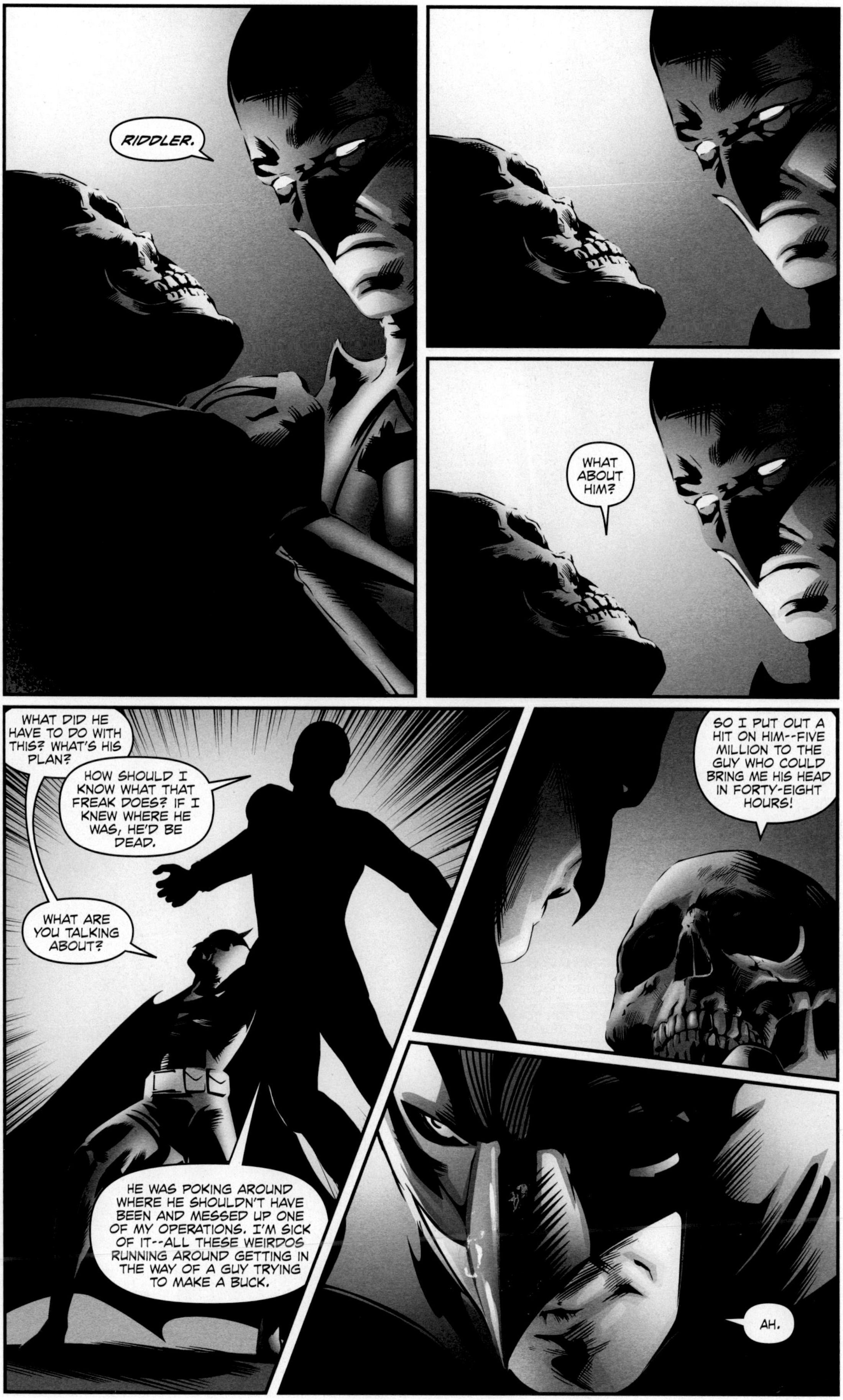
RIDDLER.
WHAT ABOUT HIM?
WHAT DID HE HAVE TO DO WITH THIS? WHAT'S HIS PLAN?
HOW SHOULD I KNOW WHAT THAT FREAK DOES? IF I KNEW WHERE HE WAS, HE'D BE DEAD.
WHAT ARE YOU TALKING ABOUT?
HE WAS POKING AROUND WHERE HE SHOULDN'T HAVE BEEN AND MESSED UP ONE OF MY OPERATIONS. I'M SICK OF IT--ALL THESE WEIRDOS RUNNING AROUND GETTING IN THE WAY OF A GUY TRYING TO MAKE A BUCK.
SO I PUT OUT A HIT ON HIM--FIVE MILLION TO THE GUY WHO COULD BRING ME HIS HEAD IN FORTY-EIGHT HOURS!
AH.

YOU KNOW, I ACTUALLY LIKED THIS ONE, NIGMA. THE RIDDLE WASN'T THE RIDDLE. *YOU* WERE THE RIDDLE.

OH?

IS THAT SO?

YOU SET ME ON BLACK MASK LIKE A TERRIER AFTER A RAT.

YOU KNEW I WOULDN'T BE ABLE TO RESIST THE INFORMATION ON THAT TRAIN, AND I'D GO AFTER BLACK MASK, TAKE HIM DOWN.

FROM THE BEGINNING, NONE OF THE PIECES FIT TOGETHER. NOT UNTIL I FOUND BLACK MASK.

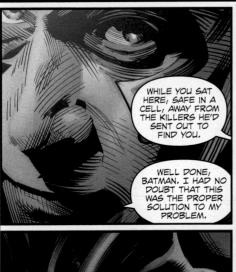

WHILE YOU SAT HERE, SAFE IN A CELL, AWAY FROM THE KILLERS HE'D SENT OUT TO FIND YOU.

WELL DONE, BATMAN. I HAD NO DOUBT THAT THIS WAS THE PROPER SOLUTION TO MY PROBLEM.

ACTUALLY, I SHOULD BE THANKING YOU. IT'S BEEN A GOOD NIGHT.

YOU KNOW, RIDDLER, THERE ARE EASIER WAYS. IT DOESN'T ALWAYS HAVE TO BE A RIDDLE.

FOR YOU, PERHAPS. NOT ME.

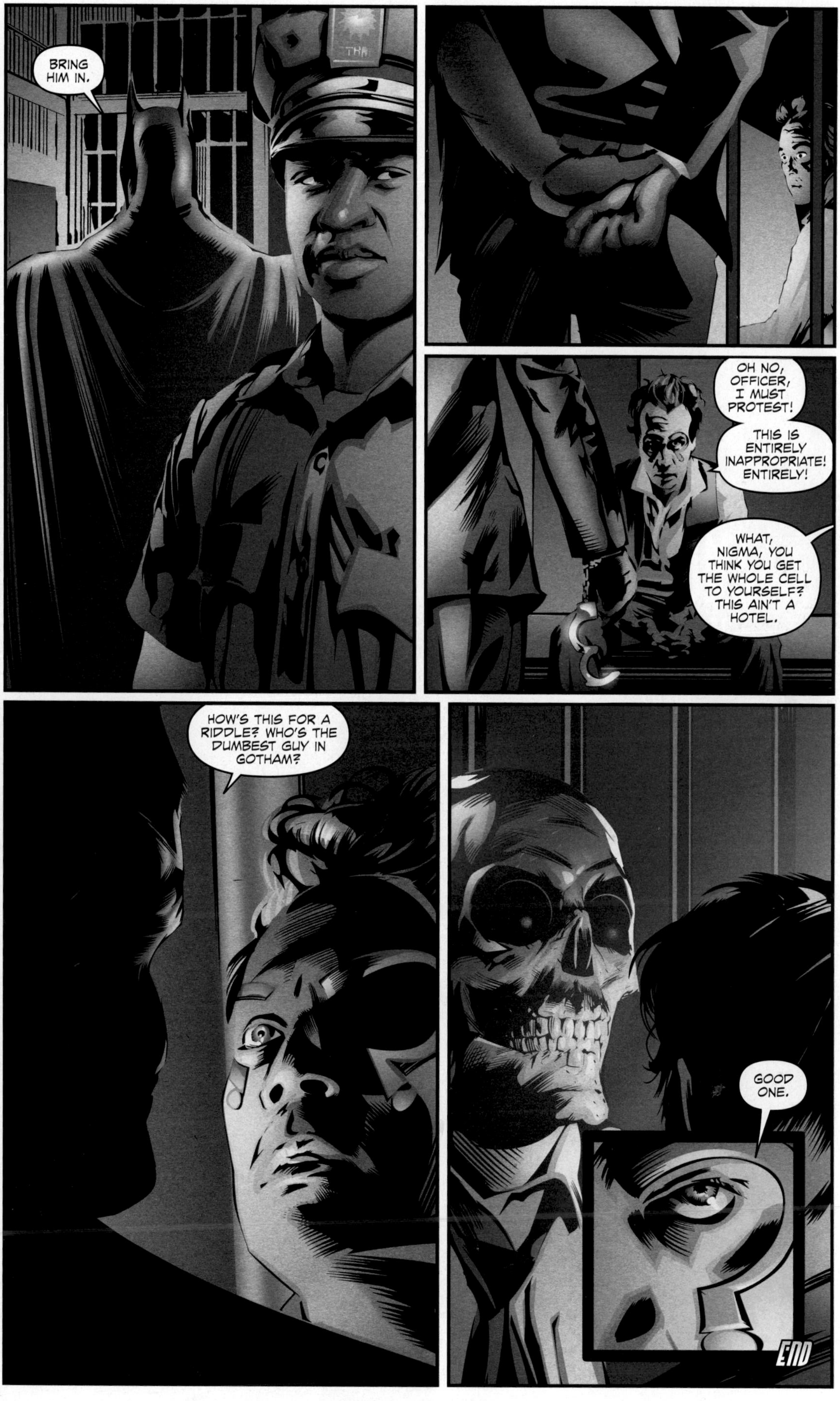
BRING HIM IN.
OH NO, OFFICER, I MUST PROTEST!
THIS IS ENTIRELY INAPPROPRIATE! ENTIRELY!
WHAT, NIGMA, YOU THINK YOU GET THE WHOLE CELL TO YOURSELF? THIS AIN'T A HOTEL.
HOW'S THIS FOR A RIDDLE? WHO'S THE DUMBEST GUY IN GOTHAM?
GOOD ONE.
END

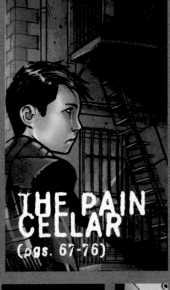

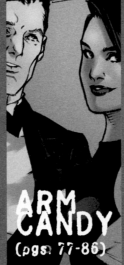

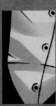

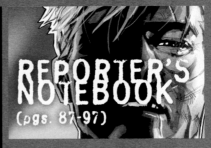

THE PAIN CELLAR
(pgs. 67-76)

FRANK HANNAH
Writer

MARCO TURINI
Artist

LEO PACIAROTTI
Colorist

SAIDA TEMOFONTE
Letterer

ARM CANDY
(pgs. 77-86)

FRANK HANNAH
Writer

DREW EDWARD JOHNSON
Artist

KATHRYN LAYNO
Colorist

SAIDA TEMOFONTE
Letterer

REPORTER'S NOTEBOOK
(pgs. 87-97)

FRANK HANNAH
Writer

DEXTER SOY
Artist and Colorist

SAIDA TEMOFONTE
Letterer

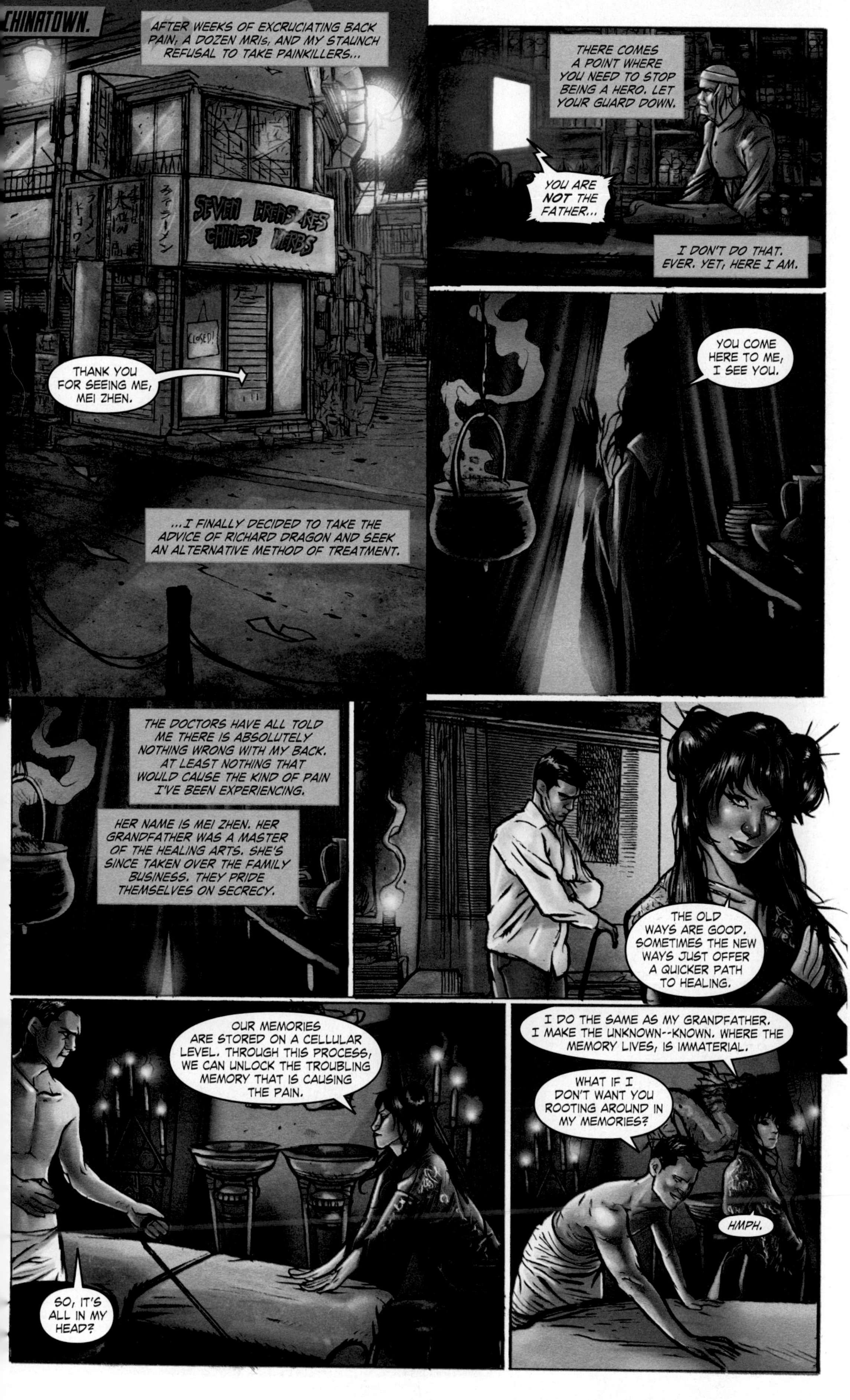
CHINATOWN.
AFTER WEEKS OF EXCRUCIATING BACK PAIN, A DOZEN MRIs, AND MY STAUNCH REFUSAL TO TAKE PAINKILLERS...
SEVEN TREASURES CHINESE HERBS
CLOSED!
THANK YOU FOR SEEING ME, MEI ZHEN.
...I FINALLY DECIDED TO TAKE THE ADVICE OF RICHARD DRAGON AND SEEK AN ALTERNATIVE METHOD OF TREATMENT.
THERE COMES A POINT WHERE YOU NEED TO STOP BEING A HERO. LET YOUR GUARD DOWN.
YOU ARE NOT THE FATHER...
I DON'T DO THAT. EVER. YET, HERE I AM.
YOU COME HERE TO ME, I SEE YOU.
THE DOCTORS HAVE ALL TOLD ME THERE IS ABSOLUTELY NOTHING WRONG WITH MY BACK. AT LEAST NOTHING THAT WOULD CAUSE THE KIND OF PAIN I'VE BEEN EXPERIENCING.
HER NAME IS MEI ZHEN. HER GRANDFATHER WAS A MASTER OF THE HEALING ARTS. SHE'S SINCE TAKEN OVER THE FAMILY BUSINESS. THEY PRIDE THEMSELVES ON SECRECY.
THE OLD WAYS ARE GOOD. SOMETIMES THE NEW WAYS JUST OFFER A QUICKER PATH TO HEALING.
OUR MEMORIES ARE STORED ON A CELLULAR LEVEL. THROUGH THIS PROCESS, WE CAN UNLOCK THE TROUBLING MEMORY THAT IS CAUSING THE PAIN.
SO, IT'S ALL IN MY HEAD?
I DO THE SAME AS MY GRANDFATHER. I MAKE THE UNKNOWN--KNOWN. WHERE THE MEMORY LIVES, IS IMMATERIAL.
WHAT IF I DON'T WANT YOU ROOTING AROUND IN MY MEMORIES?
HMPH.

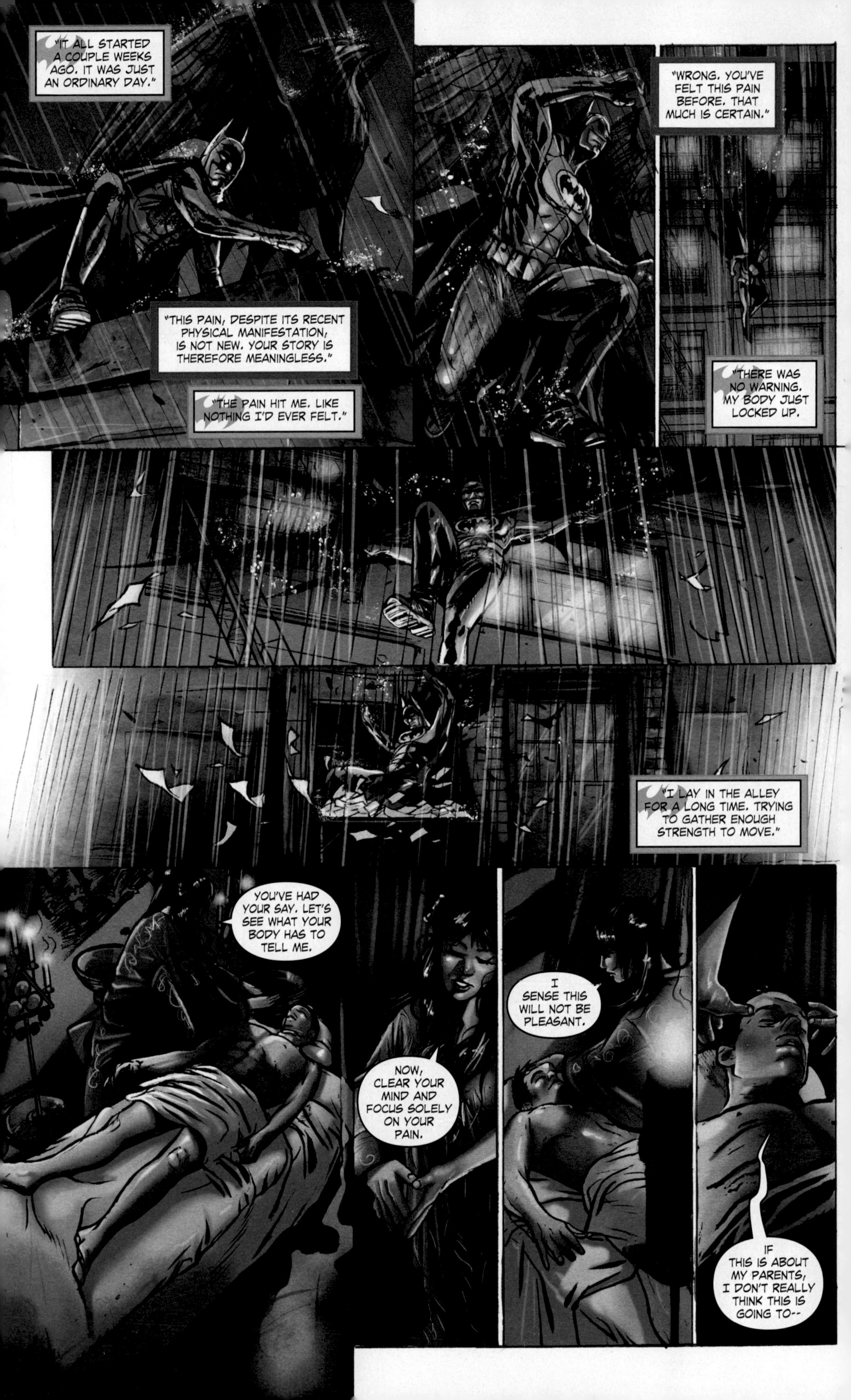
"IT ALL STARTED A COUPLE WEEKS AGO. IT WAS JUST AN ORDINARY DAY."
"THIS PAIN, DESPITE ITS RECENT PHYSICAL MANIFESTATION, IS NOT NEW. YOUR STORY IS THEREFORE MEANINGLESS."
"THE PAIN HIT ME. LIKE NOTHING I'D EVER FELT."
"WRONG. YOU'VE FELT THIS PAIN BEFORE. THAT MUCH IS CERTAIN."
"THERE WAS NO WARNING. MY BODY JUST LOCKED UP.
"I LAY IN THE ALLEY FOR A LONG TIME. TRYING TO GATHER ENOUGH STRENGTH TO MOVE."
YOU'VE HAD YOUR SAY. LET'S SEE WHAT YOUR BODY HAS TO TELL ME.
NOW, CLEAR YOUR MIND AND FOCUS SOLELY ON YOUR PAIN.
I SENSE THIS WILL NOT BE PLEASANT.
IF THIS IS ABOUT MY PARENTS, I DON'T REALLY THINK THIS IS GOING TO--

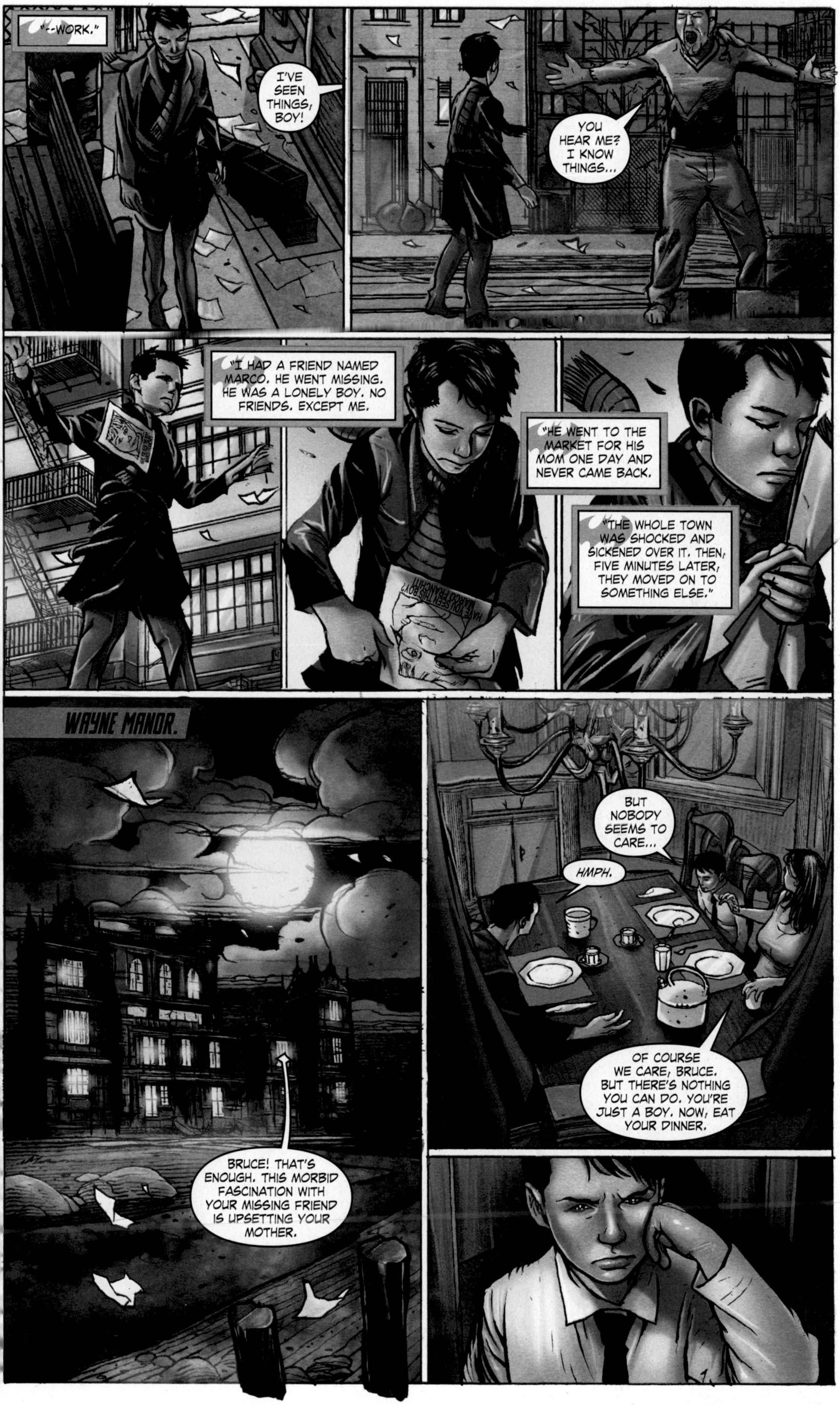
"--WORK."
I'VE SEEN THINGS, BOY!
YOU HEAR ME? I KNOW THINGS...
"I HAD A FRIEND NAMED MARCO. HE WENT MISSING. HE WAS A LONELY BOY. NO FRIENDS. EXCEPT ME.
"HE WENT TO THE MARKET FOR HIS MOM ONE DAY AND NEVER CAME BACK.
"THE WHOLE TOWN WAS SHOCKED AND SICKENED OVER IT. THEN, FIVE MINUTES LATER, THEY MOVED ON TO SOMETHING ELSE."
WAYNE MANOR.
BRUCE! THAT'S ENOUGH. THIS MORBID FASCINATION WITH YOUR MISSING FRIEND IS UPSETTING YOUR MOTHER.
BUT NOBODY SEEMS TO CARE...
HMPH.
OF COURSE WE CARE, BRUCE. BUT THERE'S NOTHING YOU CAN DO. YOU'RE JUST A BOY. NOW, EAT YOUR DINNER.

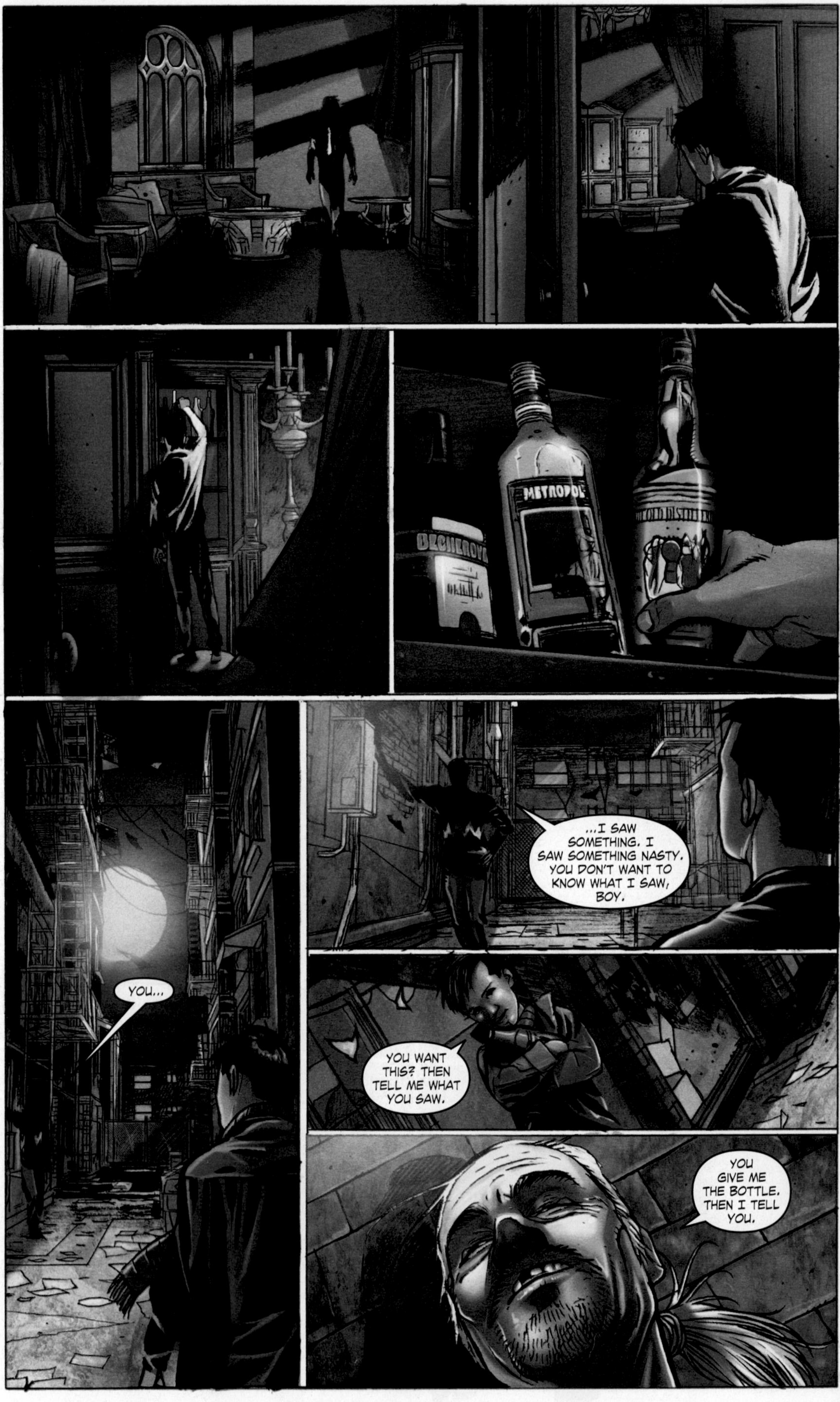
METROPOL
...I SAW SOMETHING. I SAW SOMETHING NASTY. YOU DON'T WANT TO KNOW WHAT I SAW, BOY.
YOU...
YOU WANT THIS? THEN TELL ME WHAT YOU SAW.
YOU GIVE ME THE BOTTLE. THEN I TELL YOU.

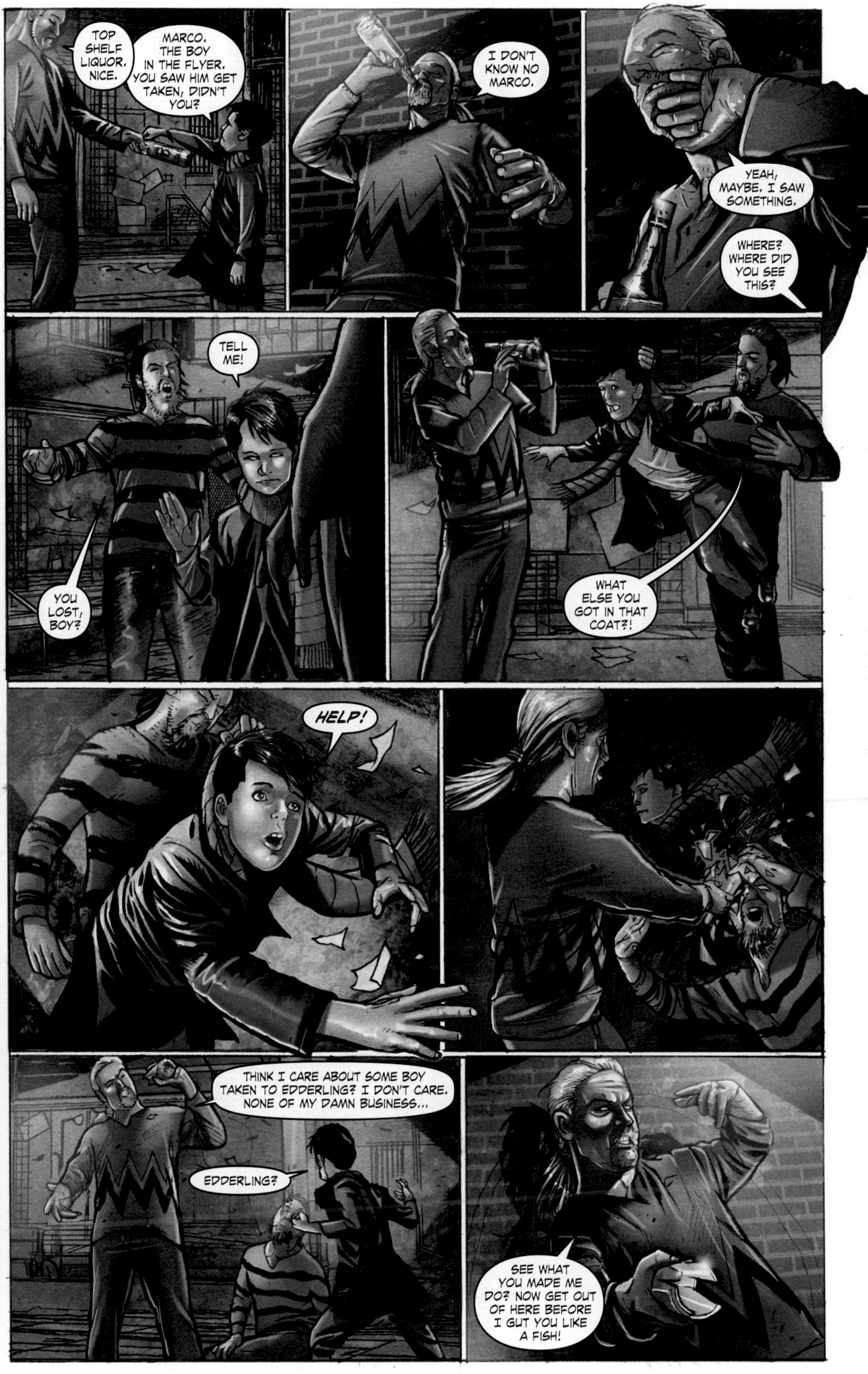
TOP SHELF LIQUOR. NICE.
MARCO. THE BOY IN THE FLYER. YOU SAW HIM GET TAKEN, DIDN'T YOU?
I DON'T KNOW NO MARCO.
YEAH, MAYBE. I SAW SOMETHING.
WHERE? WHERE DID YOU SEE THIS?
TELL ME!
YOU LOST, BOY?
WHAT ELSE YOU GOT IN THAT COAT?!
HELP!
THINK I CARE ABOUT SOME BOY TAKEN TO EDDERLING? I DON'T CARE. NONE OF MY DAMN BUSINESS...
EDDERLING?
SEE WHAT YOU MADE ME DO? NOW GET OUT OF HERE BEFORE I GUT YOU LIKE A FISH!

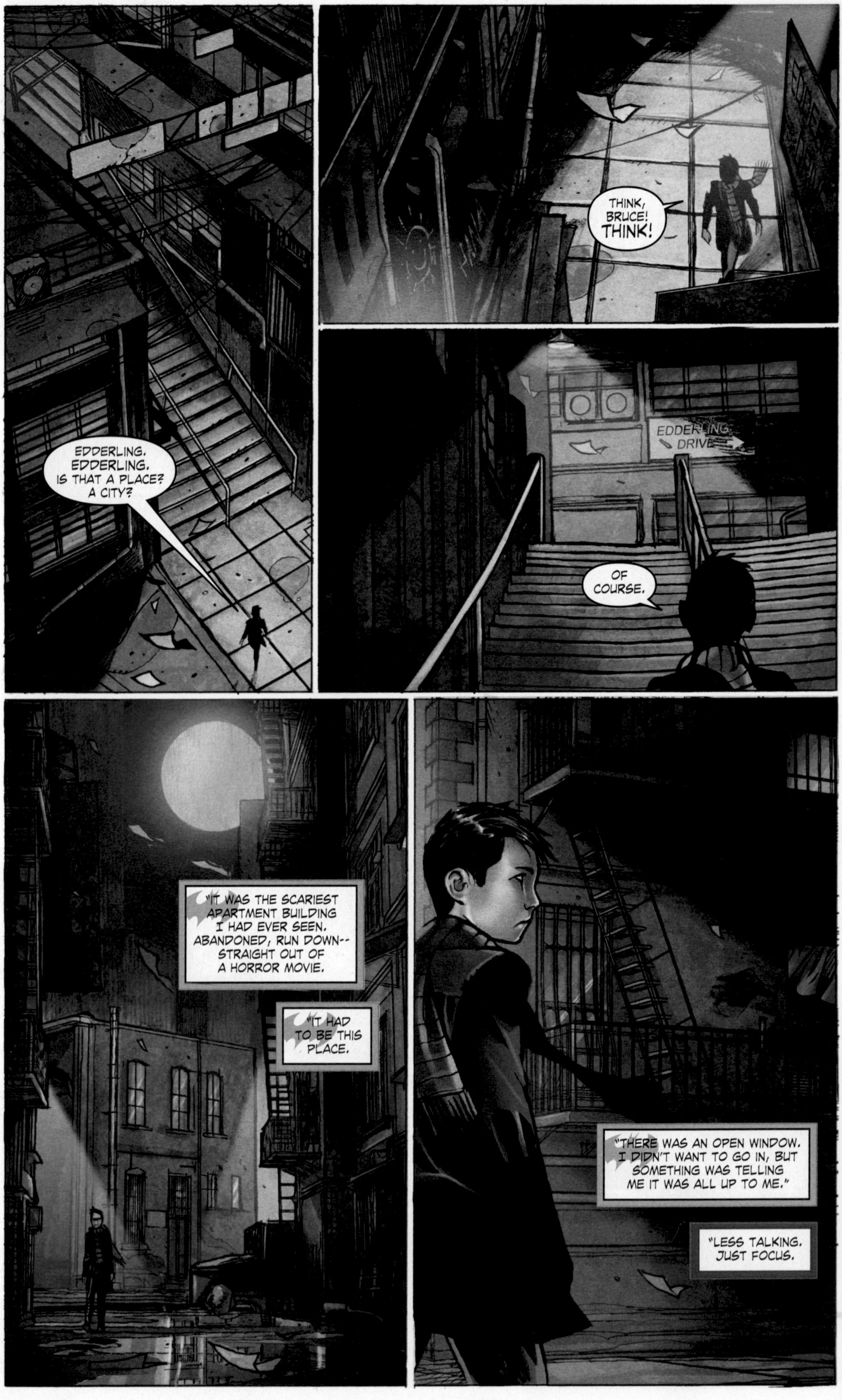
EDDERLING. EDDERLING. IS THAT A PLACE? A CITY?
THINK, BRUCE! THINK!
EDDERLING DRIVE
OF COURSE.
"IT WAS THE SCARIEST APARTMENT BUILDING I HAD EVER SEEN. ABANDONED, RUN DOWN--STRAIGHT OUT OF A HORROR MOVIE.
"IT HAD TO BE THIS PLACE.
"THERE WAS AN OPEN WINDOW. I DIDN'T WANT TO GO IN, BUT SOMETHING WAS TELLING ME IT WAS ALL UP TO ME."
"LESS TALKING. JUST FOCUS.

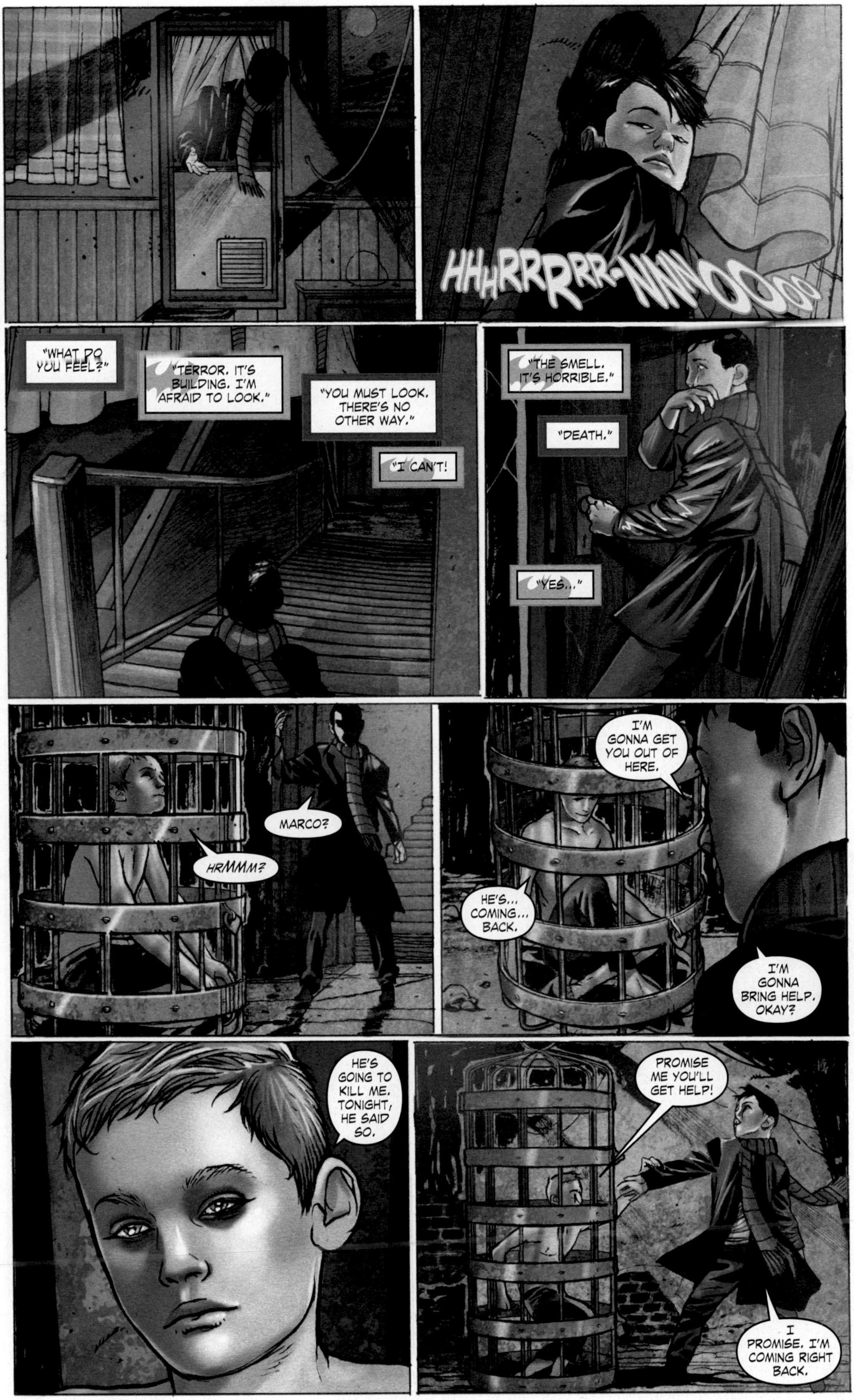
HHHRRRRR-NNNOOOO
"WHAT DO YOU FEEL?"
"TERROR. IT'S BUILDING. I'M AFRAID TO LOOK."
"YOU MUST LOOK. THERE'S NO OTHER WAY."
"I CAN'T!
"THE SMELL. IT'S HORRIBLE."
"DEATH."
"YES..."
MARCO?
HRMMM?
I'M GONNA GET YOU OUT OF HERE.
HE'S... COMING... BACK.
I'M GONNA BRING HELP. OKAY?
HE'S GOING TO KILL ME. TONIGHT, HE SAID SO.
PROMISE ME YOU'LL GET HELP!
I PROMISE. I'M COMING RIGHT BACK.

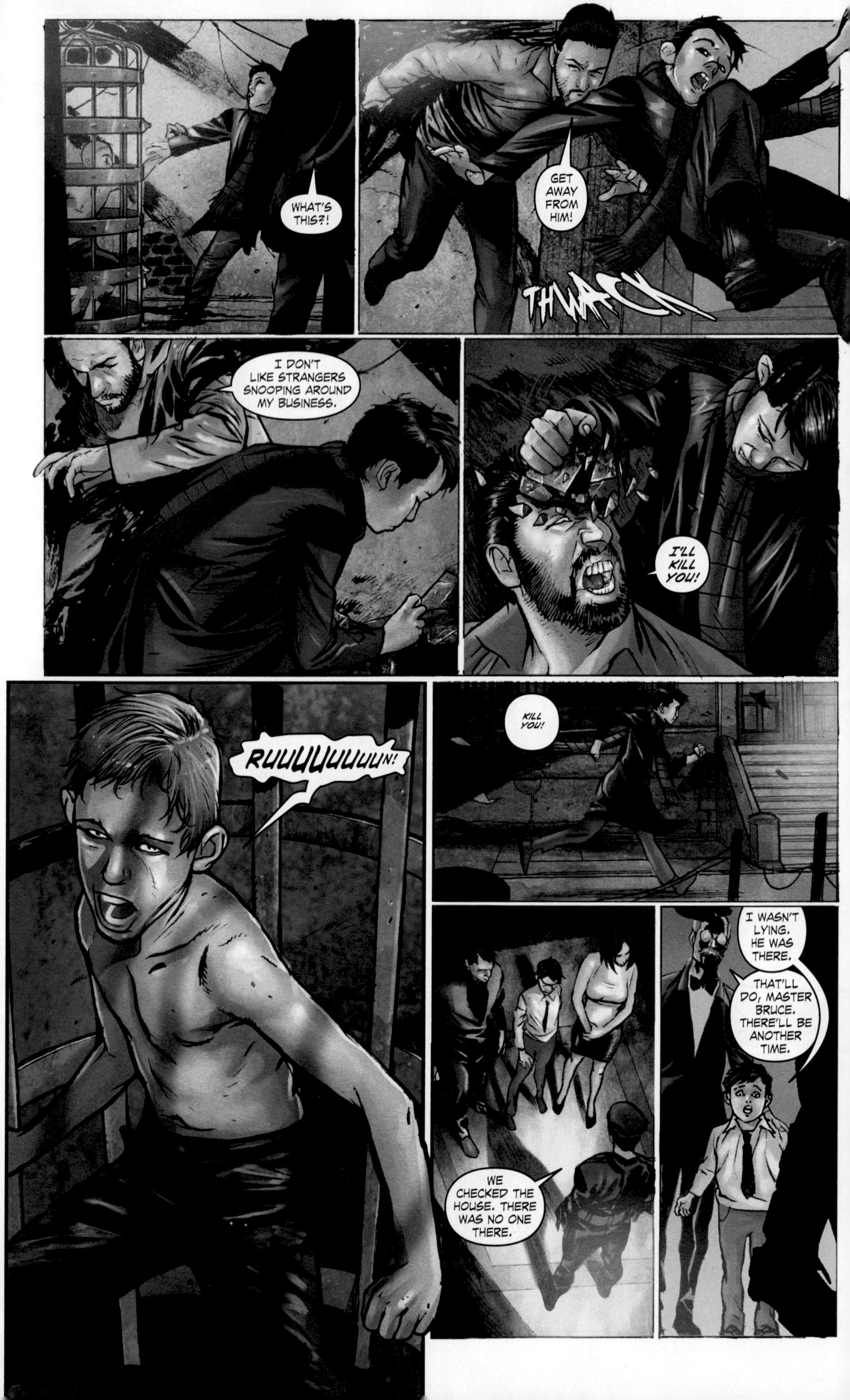
WHAT'S THIS?!
GET AWAY FROM HIM!
THWACK
I DON'T LIKE STRANGERS SNOOPING AROUND MY BUSINESS.
I'LL KILL YOU!
RUUUUUUUUUN!
KILL YOU!
WE CHECKED THE HOUSE. THERE WAS NO ONE THERE.
I WASN'T LYING. HE WAS THERE.
THAT'LL DO, MASTER BRUCE. THERE'LL BE ANOTHER TIME.

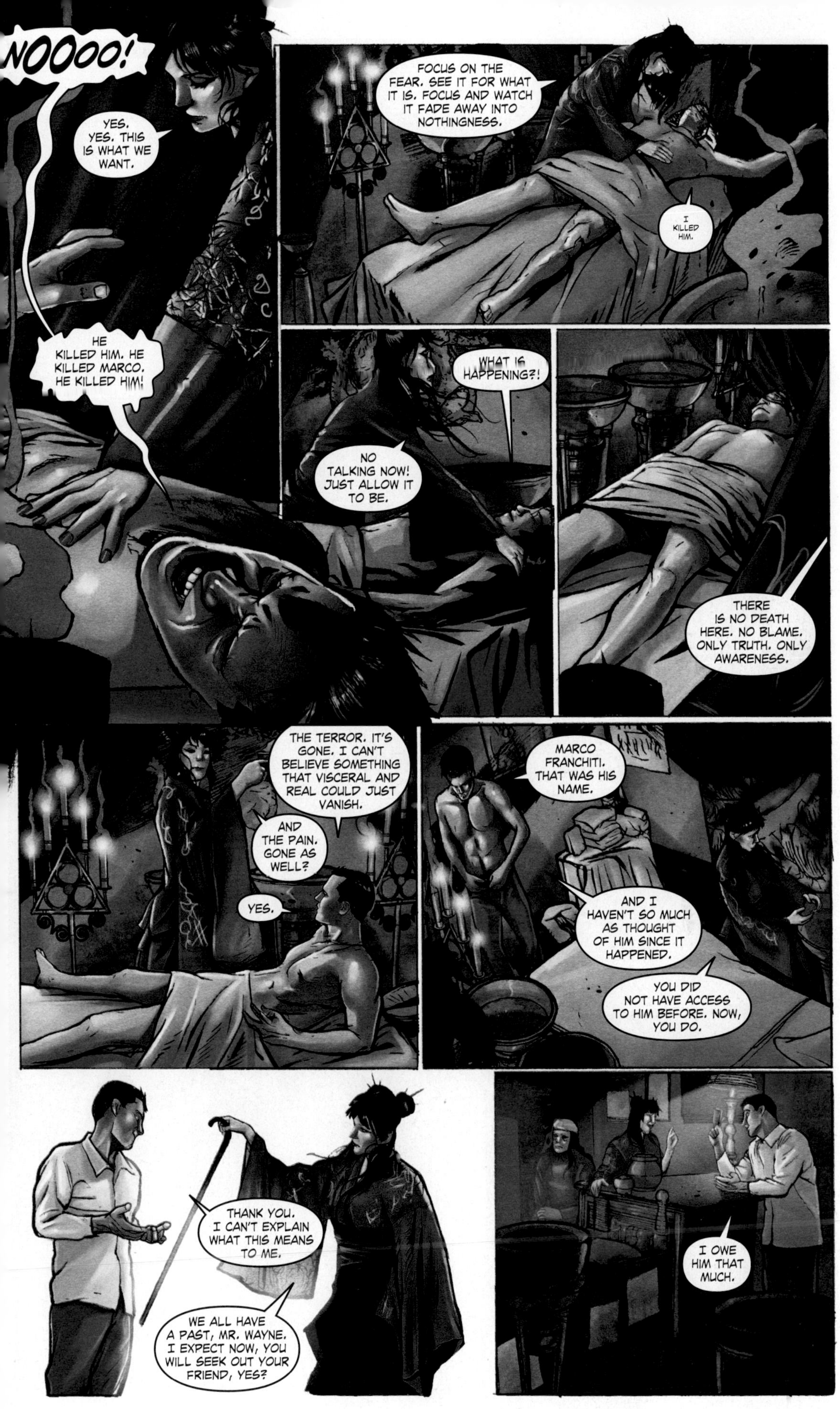
NOOOO!
YES. YES. THIS IS WHAT WE WANT.
HE KILLED HIM. HE KILLED MARCO. HE KILLED HIM!
FOCUS ON THE FEAR. SEE IT FOR WHAT IT IS. FOCUS AND WATCH IT FADE AWAY INTO NOTHINGNESS.
I KILLED HIM.
WHAT IS HAPPENING?!
NO TALKING NOW! JUST ALLOW IT TO BE.
THERE IS NO DEATH HERE. NO BLAME. ONLY TRUTH. ONLY AWARENESS.
THE TERROR. IT'S GONE. I CAN'T BELIEVE SOMETHING THAT VISCERAL AND REAL COULD JUST VANISH.
AND THE PAIN. GONE AS WELL?
YES.
MARCO FRANCHITI. THAT WAS HIS NAME.
AND I HAVEN'T SO MUCH AS THOUGHT OF HIM SINCE IT HAPPENED.
YOU DID NOT HAVE ACCESS TO HIM BEFORE. NOW, YOU DO.
THANK YOU. I CAN'T EXPLAIN WHAT THIS MEANS TO ME.
WE ALL HAVE A PAST, MR. WAYNE. I EXPECT NOW, YOU WILL SEEK OUT YOUR FRIEND, YES?
I OWE HIM THAT MUCH.

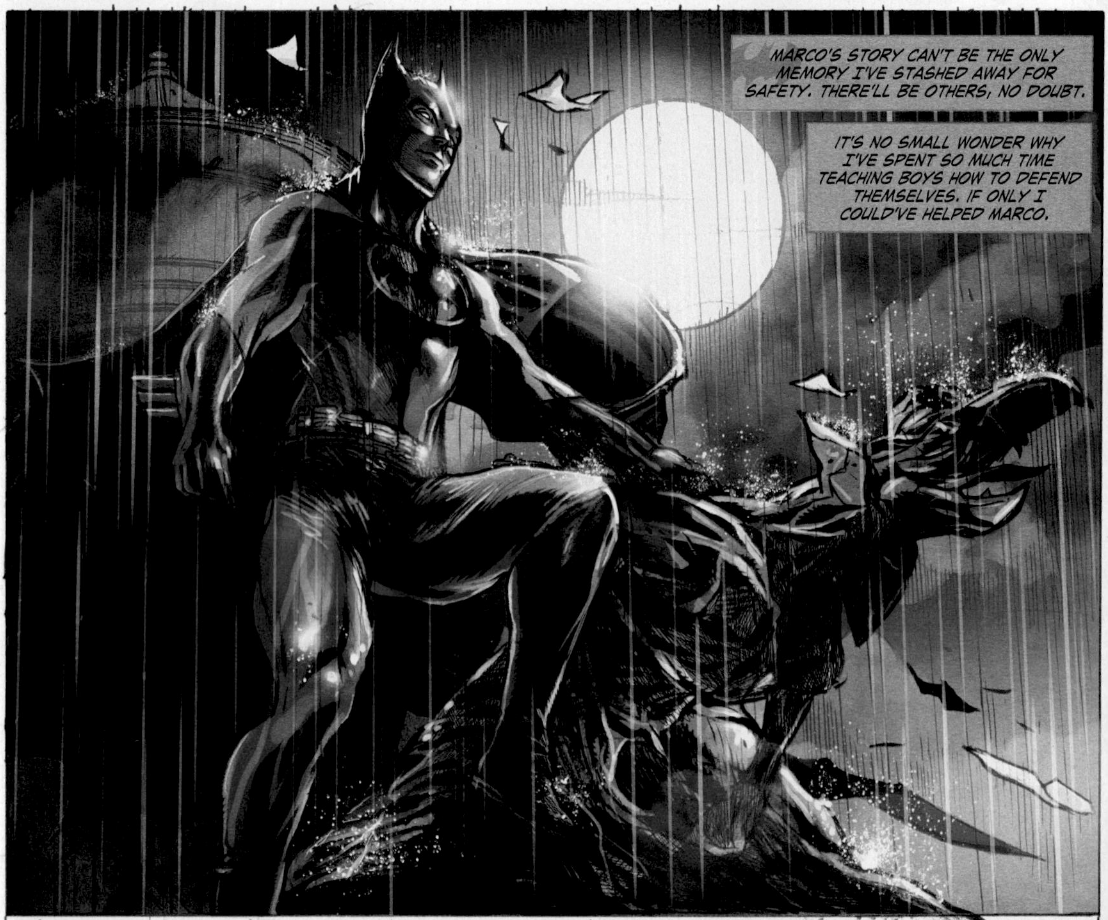
MARCO'S STORY CAN'T BE THE ONLY MEMORY I'VE STASHED AWAY FOR SAFETY. THERE'LL BE OTHERS, NO DOUBT.
IT'S NO SMALL WONDER WHY I'VE SPENT SO MUCH TIME TEACHING BOYS HOW TO DEFEND THEMSELVES. IF ONLY I COULD'VE HELPED MARCO.
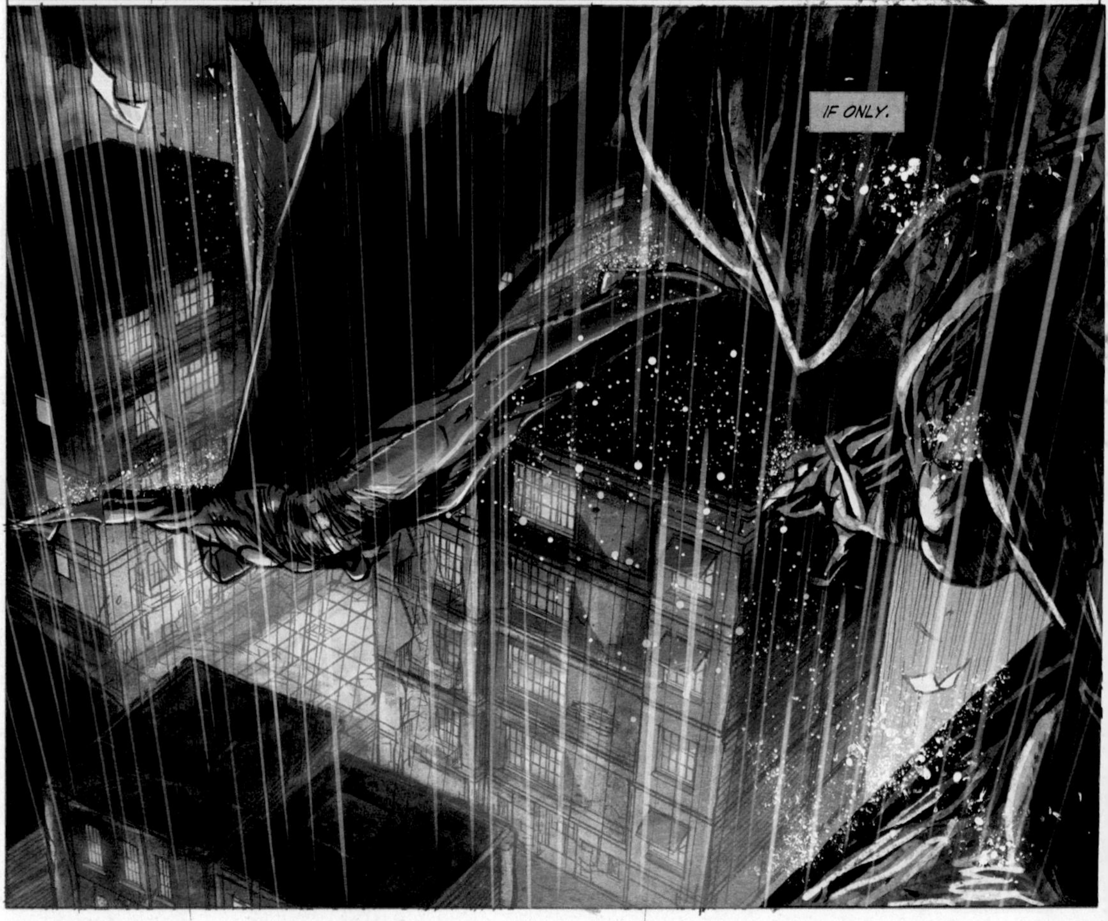
IF ONLY.

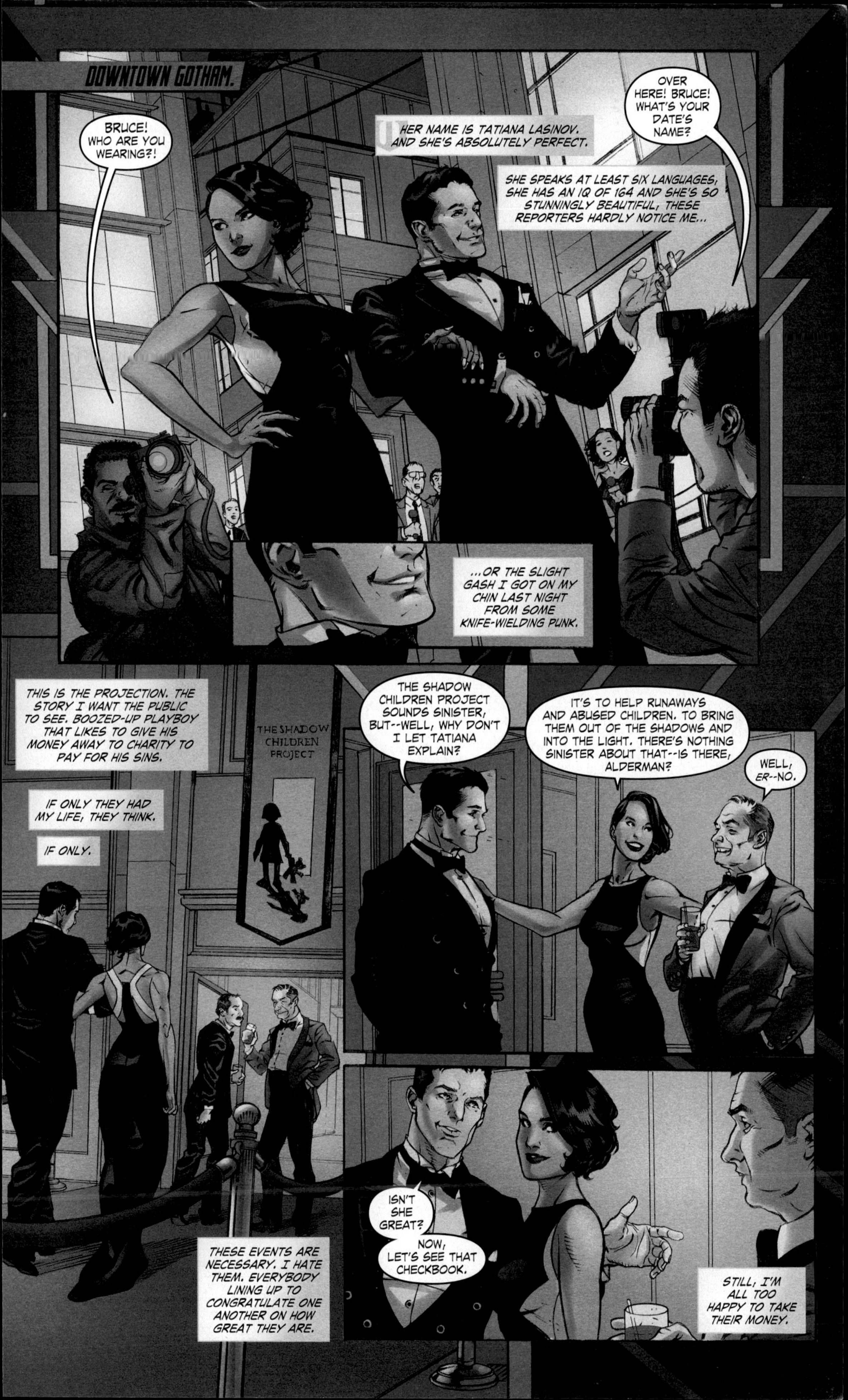
DOWNTOWN GOTHAM.
BRUCE! WHO ARE YOU WEARING?!
HER NAME IS TATIANA LASINOV. AND SHE'S ABSOLUTELY PERFECT.
OVER HERE! BRUCE! WHAT'S YOUR DATE'S NAME?
SHE SPEAKS AT LEAST SIX LANGUAGES, SHE HAS AN IQ OF 164 AND SHE'S SO STUNNINGLY BEAUTIFUL, THESE REPORTERS HARDLY NOTICE ME...
...OR THE SLIGHT GASH I GOT ON MY CHIN LAST NIGHT FROM SOME KNIFE-WIELDING PUNK.
THIS IS THE PROJECTION. THE STORY I WANT THE PUBLIC TO SEE. BOOZED-UP PLAYBOY THAT LIKES TO GIVE HIS MONEY AWAY TO CHARITY TO PAY FOR HIS SINS.
IF ONLY THEY HAD MY LIFE, THEY THINK.
IF ONLY.
THE SHADOW CHILDREN PROJECT
THE SHADOW CHILDREN PROJECT SOUNDS SINISTER, BUT--WELL, WHY DON'T I LET TATIANA EXPLAIN?
IT'S TO HELP RUNAWAYS AND ABUSED CHILDREN. TO BRING THEM OUT OF THE SHADOWS AND INTO THE LIGHT. THERE'S NOTHING SINISTER ABOUT THAT--IS THERE, ALDERMAN?
WELL, ER--NO.
ISN'T SHE GREAT?
NOW, LET'S SEE THAT CHECKBOOK.
THESE EVENTS ARE NECESSARY. I HATE THEM. EVERYBODY LINING UP TO CONGRATULATE ONE ANOTHER ON HOW GREAT THEY ARE.
STILL, I'M ALL TOO HAPPY TO TAKE THEIR MONEY.

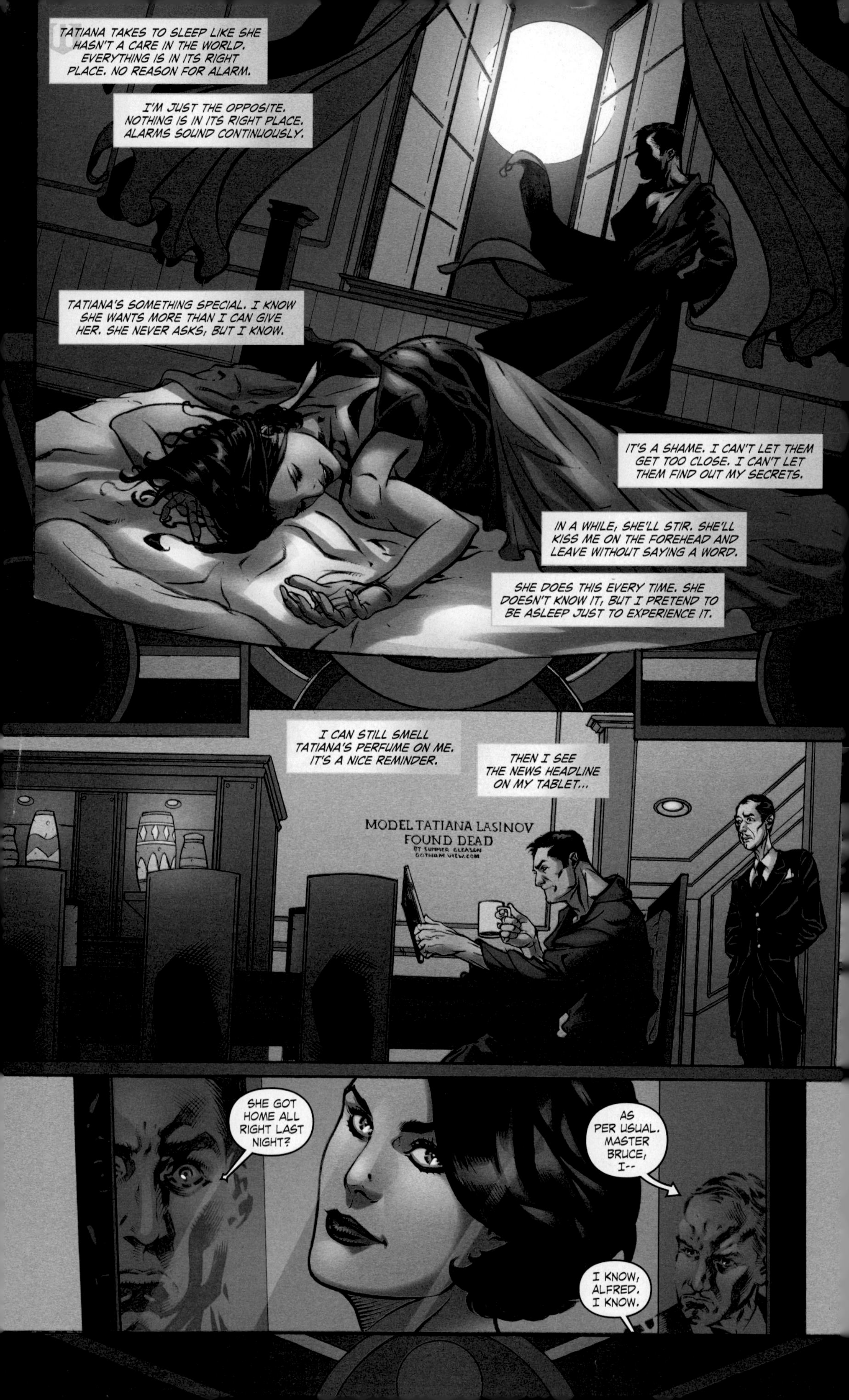
TATIANA TAKES TO SLEEP LIKE SHE HASN'T A CARE IN THE WORLD. EVERYTHING IS IN ITS RIGHT PLACE. NO REASON FOR ALARM.
I'M JUST THE OPPOSITE. NOTHING IS IN ITS RIGHT PLACE. ALARMS SOUND CONTINUOUSLY.
TATIANA'S SOMETHING SPECIAL. I KNOW SHE WANTS MORE THAN I CAN GIVE HER. SHE NEVER ASKS, BUT I KNOW.
IT'S A SHAME. I CAN'T LET THEM GET TOO CLOSE. I CAN'T LET THEM FIND OUT MY SECRETS.
IN A WHILE, SHE'LL STIR. SHE'LL KISS ME ON THE FOREHEAD AND LEAVE WITHOUT SAYING A WORD.
SHE DOES THIS EVERY TIME. SHE DOESN'T KNOW IT, BUT I PRETEND TO BE ASLEEP JUST TO EXPERIENCE IT.
I CAN STILL SMELL TATIANA'S PERFUME ON ME. IT'S A NICE REMINDER.
THEN I SEE THE NEWS HEADLINE ON MY TABLET...
MODEL TATIANA LASINOV FOUND DEAD
SHE GOT HOME ALL RIGHT LAST NIGHT?
AS PER USUAL. MASTER BRUCE, I--
I KNOW, ALFRED. I KNOW.

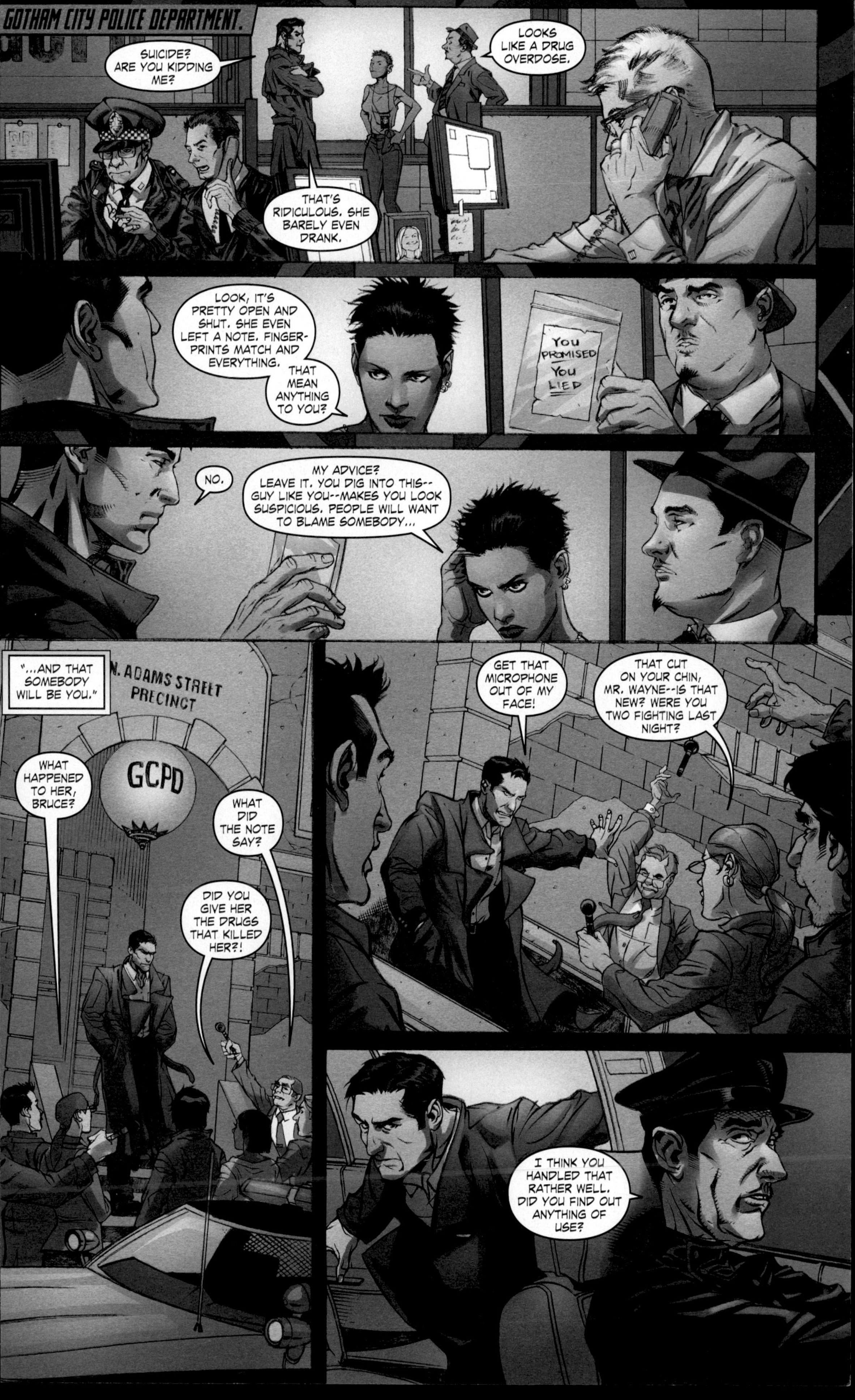
GOTHAM CITY POLICE DEPARTMENT.
SUICIDE? ARE YOU KIDDING ME?
LOOKS LIKE A DRUG OVERDOSE.
THAT'S RIDICULOUS. SHE BARELY EVEN DRANK.
LOOK, IT'S PRETTY OPEN AND SHUT. SHE EVEN LEFT A NOTE. FINGER-PRINTS MATCH AND EVERYTHING.
THAT MEAN ANYTHING TO YOU?
YOU PROMISED YOU LIED
NO.
MY ADVICE? LEAVE IT. YOU DIG INTO THIS-- GUY LIKE YOU--MAKES YOU LOOK SUSPICIOUS. PEOPLE WILL WANT TO BLAME SOMEBODY...
"...AND THAT SOMEBODY WILL BE YOU."
N. ADAMS STREET PRECINCT
GCPD
WHAT HAPPENED TO HER, BRUCE?
WHAT DID THE NOTE SAY?
DID YOU GIVE HER THE DRUGS THAT KILLED HER?!
GET THAT MICROPHONE OUT OF MY FACE!
THAT CUT ON YOUR CHIN, MR. WAYNE--IS THAT NEW? WERE YOU TWO FIGHTING LAST NIGHT?
I THINK YOU HANDLED THAT RATHER WELL. DID YOU FIND OUT ANYTHING OF USE?

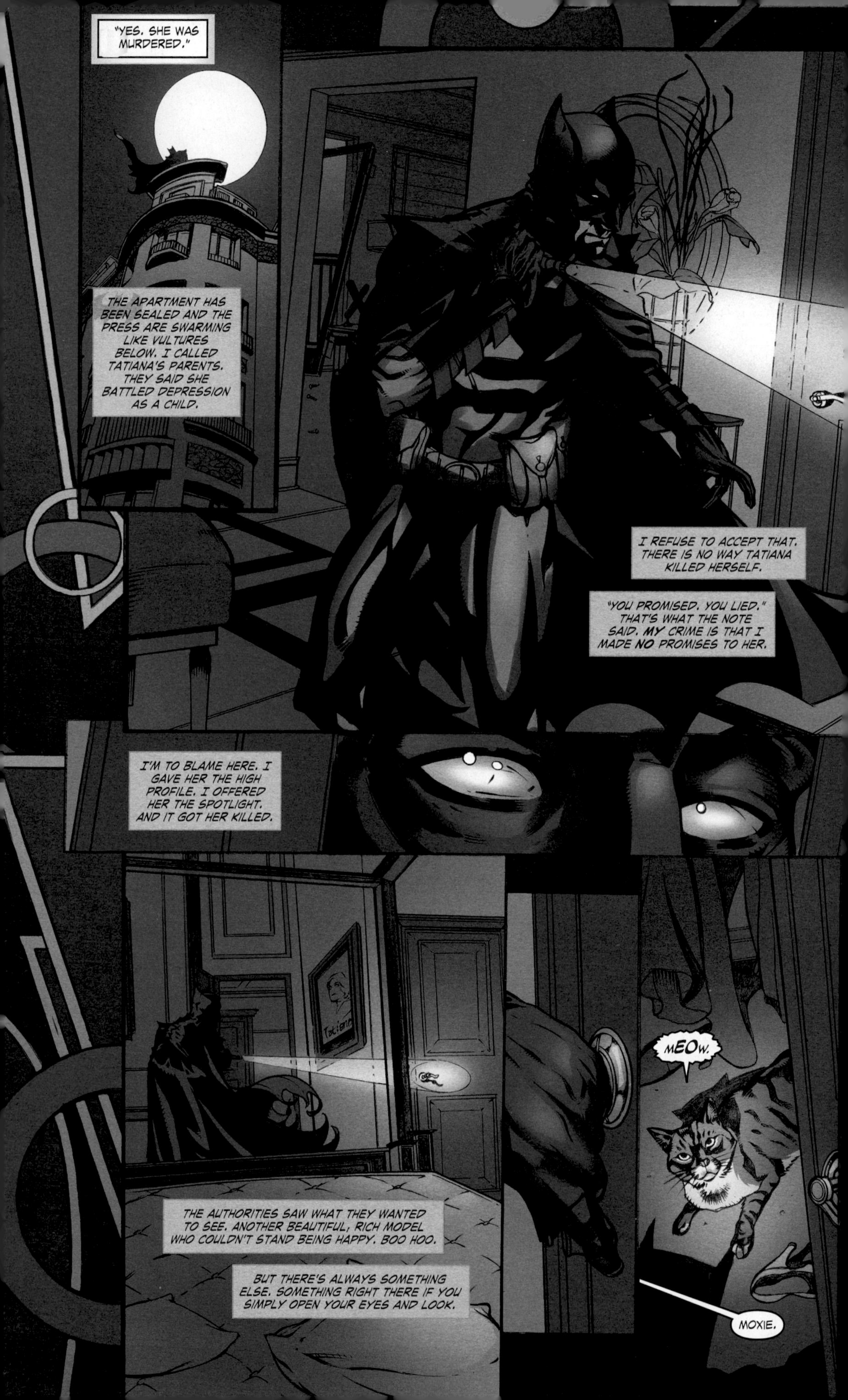
"YES. SHE WAS MURDERED."
THE APARTMENT HAS BEEN SEALED AND THE PRESS ARE SWARMING LIKE VULTURES BELOW. I CALLED TATIANA'S PARENTS. THEY SAID SHE BATTLED DEPRESSION AS A CHILD.
I REFUSE TO ACCEPT THAT. THERE IS NO WAY TATIANA KILLED HERSELF.
"YOU PROMISED. YOU LIED." THAT'S WHAT THE NOTE SAID. MY CRIME IS THAT I MADE NO PROMISES TO HER.
I'M TO BLAME HERE. I GAVE HER THE HIGH PROFILE. I OFFERED HER THE SPOTLIGHT. AND IT GOT HER KILLED.
THE AUTHORITIES SAW WHAT THEY WANTED TO SEE. ANOTHER BEAUTIFUL, RICH MODEL WHO COULDN'T STAND BEING HAPPY. BOO HOO.
BUT THERE'S ALWAYS SOMETHING ELSE. SOMETHING RIGHT THERE IF YOU SIMPLY OPEN YOUR EYES AND LOOK.
mEOw.
MOXIE.

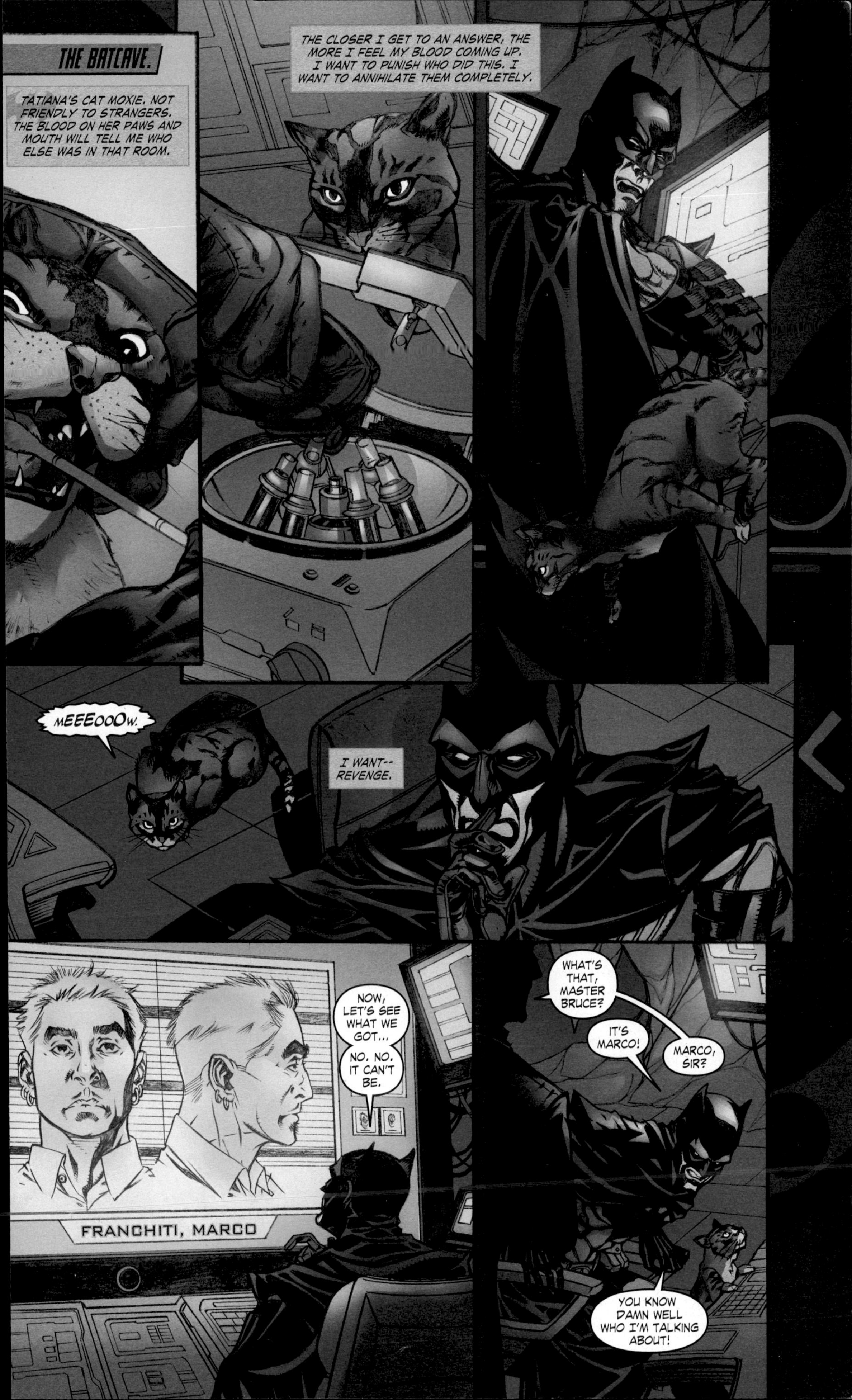
THE BATCAVE.
TATIANA'S CAT MOXIE. NOT FRIENDLY TO STRANGERS. THE BLOOD ON HER PAWS AND MOUTH WILL TELL ME WHO ELSE WAS IN THAT ROOM.
THE CLOSER I GET TO AN ANSWER, THE MORE I FEEL MY BLOOD COMING UP. I WANT TO PUNISH WHO DID THIS. I WANT TO ANNIHILATE THEM COMPLETELY.
mEEEoooW.
I WANT-- REVENGE.
FRANCHITI, MARCO
NOW, LET'S SEE WHAT WE GOT...
NO. NO. IT CAN'T BE.
WHAT'S THAT, MASTER BRUCE?
IT'S MARCO!
MARCO, SIR?
YOU KNOW DAMN WELL WHO I'M TALKING ABOUT!

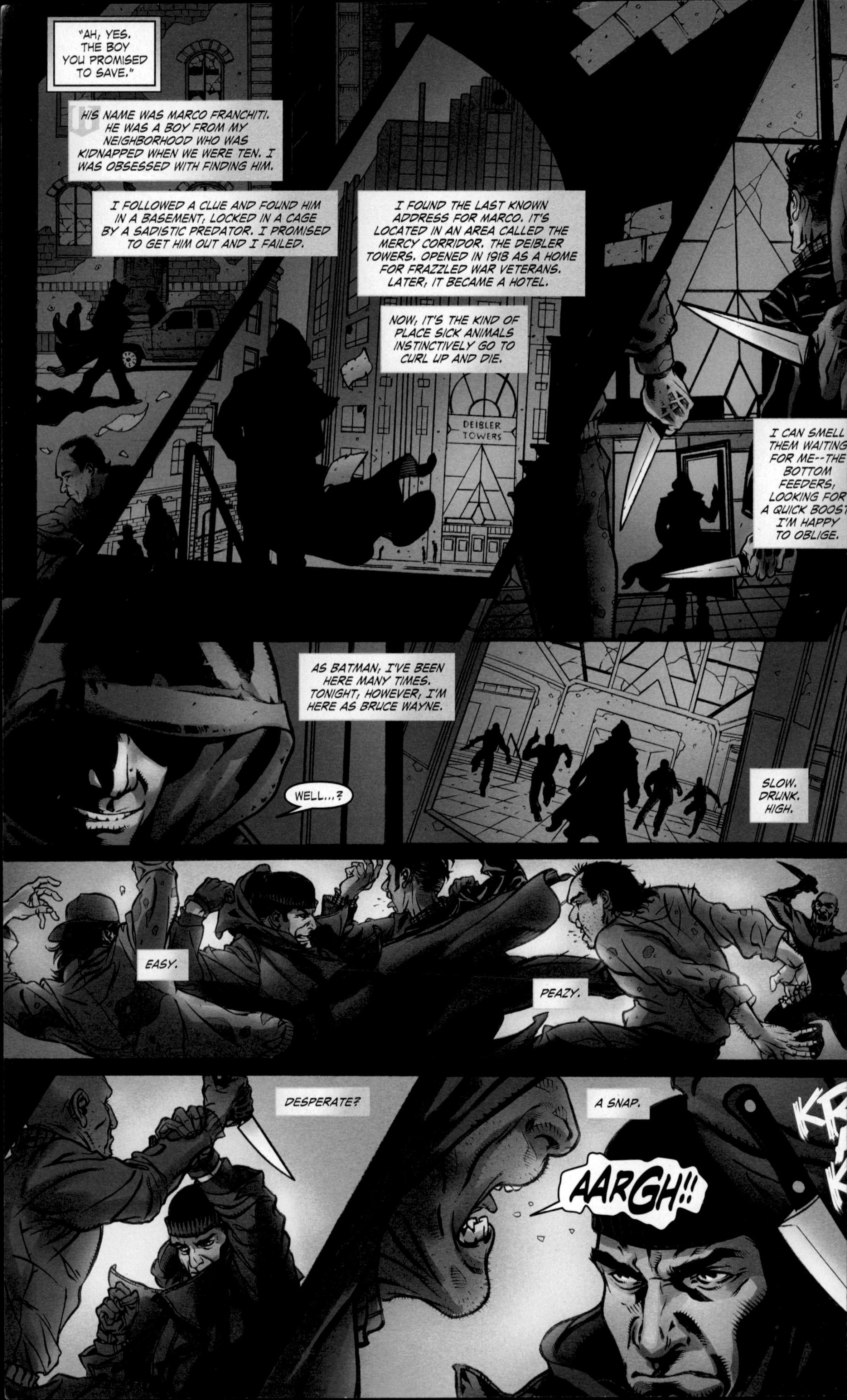
"AH, YES. THE BOY YOU PROMISED TO SAVE."
HIS NAME WAS MARCO FRANCHITI. HE WAS A BOY FROM MY NEIGHBORHOOD WHO WAS KIDNAPPED WHEN WE WERE TEN. I WAS OBSESSED WITH FINDING HIM.
I FOLLOWED A CLUE AND FOUND HIM IN A BASEMENT, LOCKED IN A CAGE BY A SADISTIC PREDATOR. I PROMISED TO GET HIM OUT AND I FAILED.
I FOUND THE LAST KNOWN ADDRESS FOR MARCO. IT'S LOCATED IN AN AREA CALLED THE MERCY CORRIDOR. THE DEIBLER TOWERS. OPENED IN 1918 AS A HOME FOR FRAZZLED WAR VETERANS. LATER, IT BECAME A HOTEL.
NOW, IT'S THE KIND OF PLACE SICK ANIMALS INSTINCTIVELY GO TO CURL UP AND DIE.
DEIBLER TOWERS
I CAN SMELL THEM WAITING FOR ME--THE BOTTOM FEEDERS, LOOKING FOR A QUICK BOOST. I'M HAPPY TO OBLIGE.
AS BATMAN, I'VE BEEN HERE MANY TIMES. TONIGHT, HOWEVER, I'M HERE AS BRUCE WAYNE.
WELL...?
SLOW. DRUNK. HIGH.
EASY.
PEAZY.
DESPERATE?
A SNAP.
AARGH!!

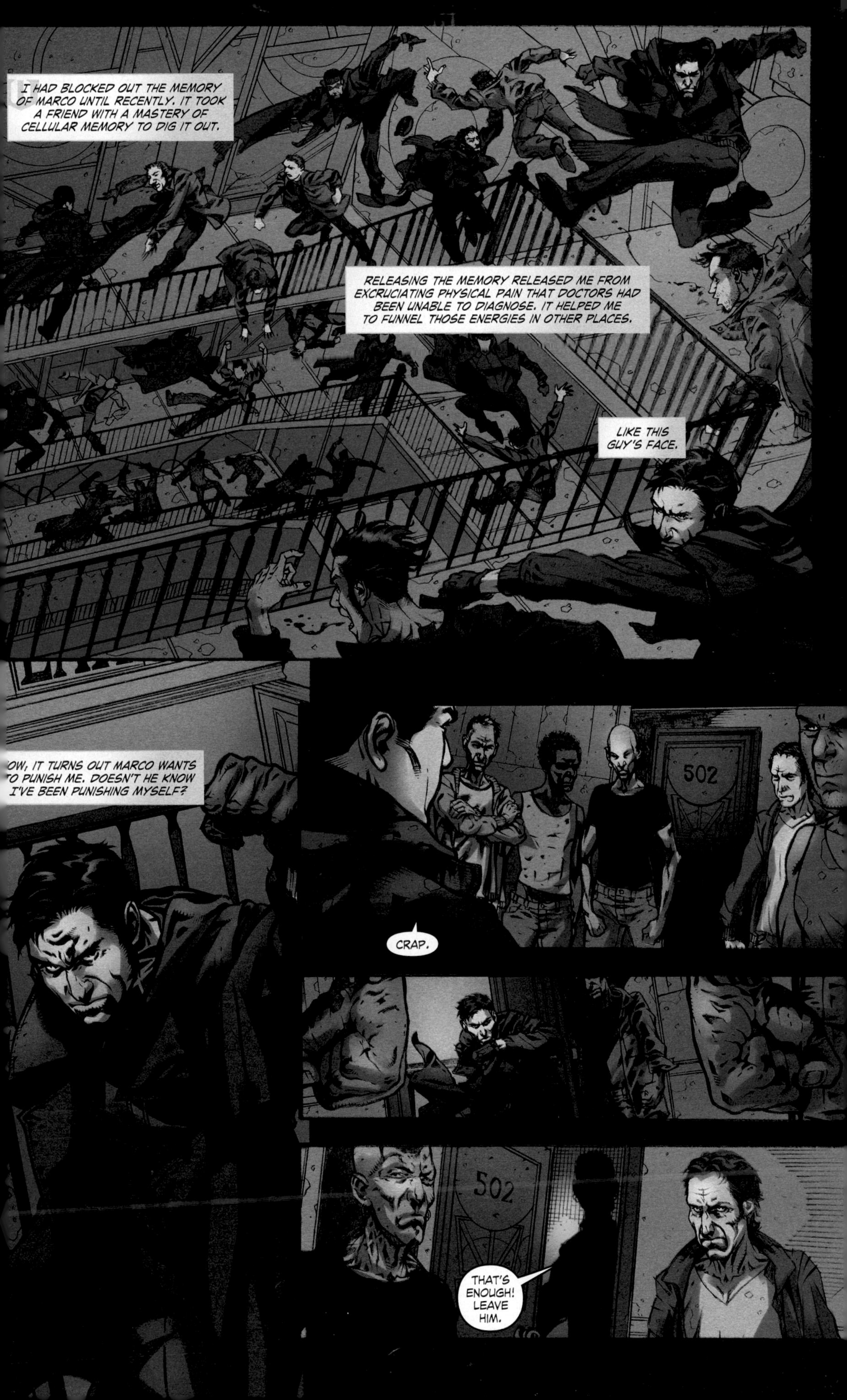
I HAD BLOCKED OUT THE MEMORY OF MARCO UNTIL RECENTLY. IT TOOK A FRIEND WITH A MASTERY OF CELLULAR MEMORY TO DIG IT OUT.
RELEASING THE MEMORY RELEASED ME FROM EXCRUCIATING PHYSICAL PAIN THAT DOCTORS HAD BEEN UNABLE TO DIAGNOSE. IT HELPED ME TO FUNNEL THOSE ENERGIES IN OTHER PLACES.
LIKE THIS GUY'S FACE.
OW, IT TURNS OUT MARCO WANTS TO PUNISH ME. DOESN'T HE KNOW I'VE BEEN PUNISHING MYSELF?
502
CRAP.
502
THAT'S ENOUGH! LEAVE HIM.

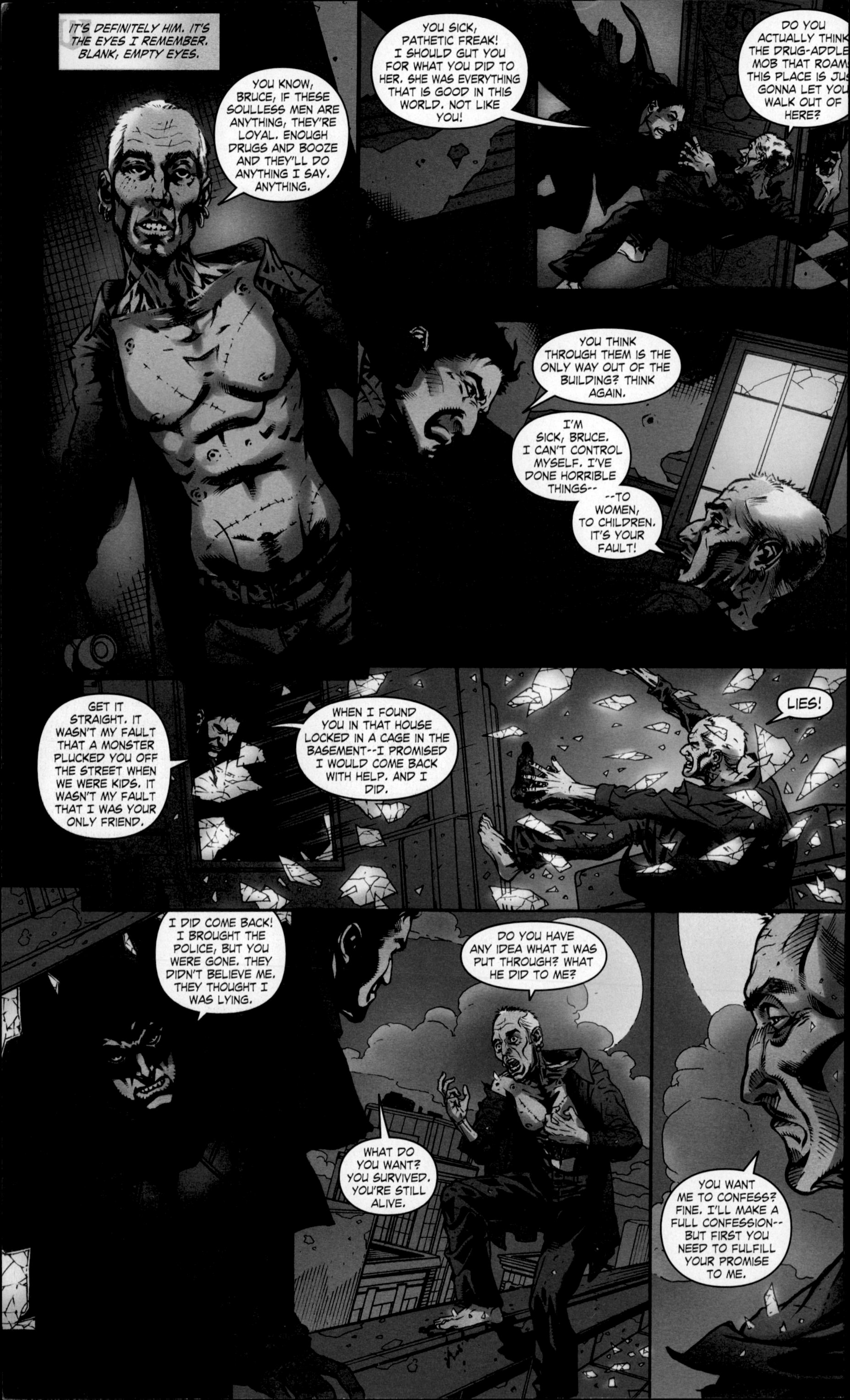
IT'S DEFINITELY HIM. IT'S THE EYES I REMEMBER. BLANK, EMPTY EYES.
YOU KNOW, BRUCE, IF THESE SOULLESS MEN ARE ANYTHING, THEY'RE LOYAL. ENOUGH DRUGS AND BOOZE AND THEY'LL DO ANYTHING I SAY. ANYTHING.
YOU SICK, PATHETIC FREAK! I SHOULD GUT YOU FOR WHAT YOU DID TO HER. SHE WAS EVERYTHING THAT IS GOOD IN THIS WORLD. NOT LIKE YOU!
DO YOU ACTUALLY THINK THE DRUG-ADDLE MOB THAT ROAM THIS PLACE IS JUS GONNA LET YOU WALK OUT OF HERE?
YOU THINK THROUGH THEM IS THE ONLY WAY OUT OF THE BUILDING? THINK AGAIN.
I'M SICK, BRUCE. I CAN'T CONTROL MYSELF. I'VE DONE HORRIBLE THINGS--
--TO WOMEN, TO CHILDREN. IT'S YOUR FAULT!
GET IT STRAIGHT. IT WASN'T MY FAULT THAT A MONSTER PLUCKED YOU OFF THE STREET WHEN WE WERE KIDS. IT WASN'T MY FAULT THAT I WAS YOUR ONLY FRIEND.
WHEN I FOUND YOU IN THAT HOUSE LOCKED IN A CAGE IN THE BASEMENT--I PROMISED I WOULD COME BACK WITH HELP. AND I DID.
LIES!
I DID COME BACK! I BROUGHT THE POLICE, BUT YOU WERE GONE. THEY DIDN'T BELIEVE ME. THEY THOUGHT I WAS LYING.
DO YOU HAVE ANY IDEA WHAT I WAS PUT THROUGH? WHAT HE DID TO ME?
WHAT DO YOU WANT? YOU SURVIVED. YOU'RE STILL ALIVE.
YOU WANT ME TO CONFESS? FINE. I'LL MAKE A FULL CONFESSION-- BUT FIRST YOU NEED TO FULFILL YOUR PROMISE TO ME.

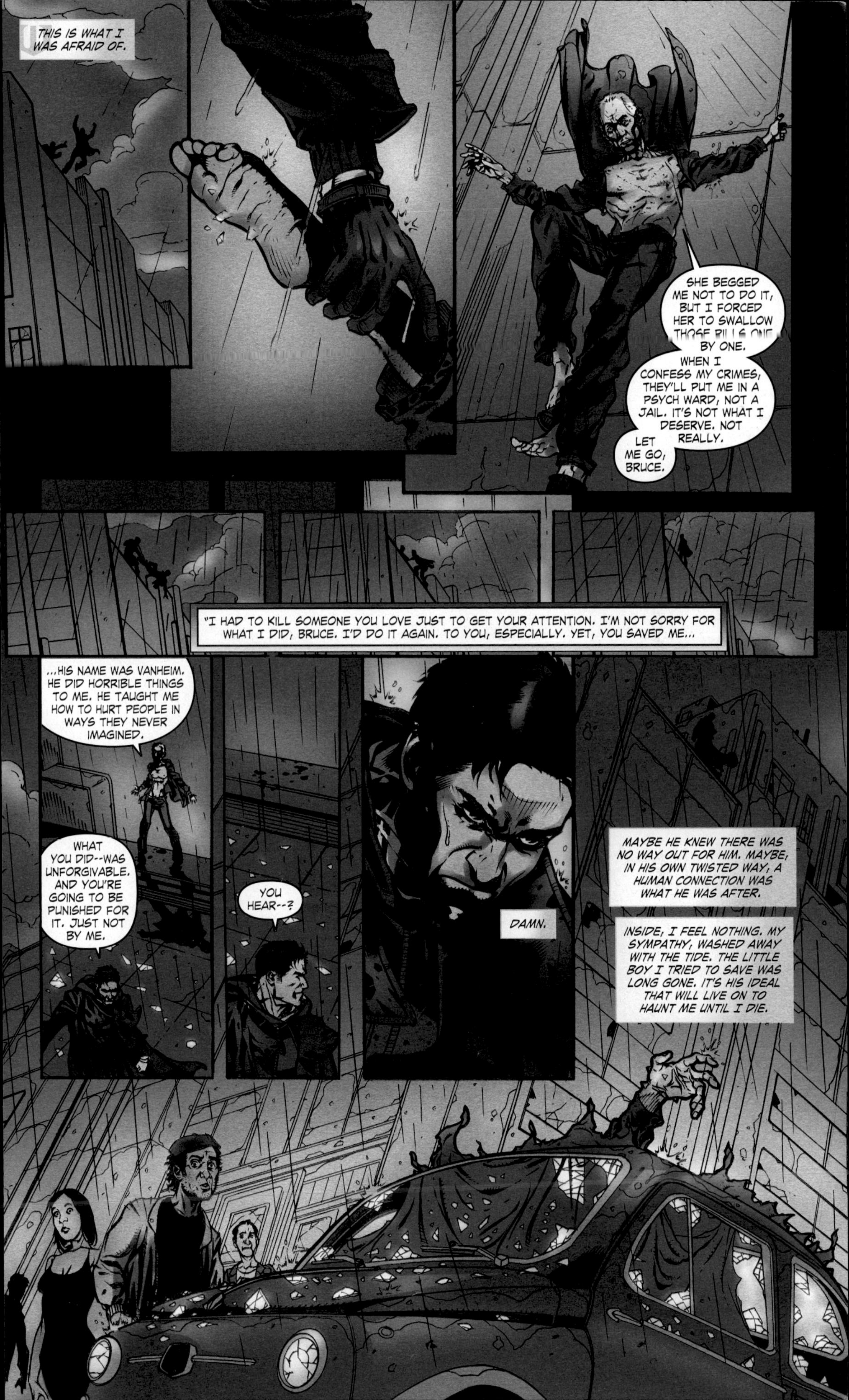
THIS IS WHAT I WAS AFRAID OF.
SHE BEGGED ME NOT TO DO IT, BUT I FORCED HER TO SWALLOW THOSE PILLS ONE BY ONE.
WHEN I CONFESS MY CRIMES, THEY'LL PUT ME IN A PSYCH WARD, NOT A JAIL. IT'S NOT WHAT I DESERVE. NOT REALLY.
LET ME GO, BRUCE.
"I HAD TO KILL SOMEONE YOU LOVE JUST TO GET YOUR ATTENTION. I'M NOT SORRY FOR WHAT I DID, BRUCE. I'D DO IT AGAIN. TO YOU, ESPECIALLY. YET, YOU SAVED ME...
...HIS NAME WAS VANHEIM. HE DID HORRIBLE THINGS TO ME. HE TAUGHT ME HOW TO HURT PEOPLE IN WAYS THEY NEVER IMAGINED.
WHAT YOU DID--WAS UNFORGIVABLE. AND YOU'RE GOING TO BE PUNISHED FOR IT. JUST NOT BY ME.
YOU HEAR--?
DAMN.
MAYBE HE KNEW THERE WAS NO WAY OUT FOR HIM. MAYBE, IN HIS OWN TWISTED WAY, A HUMAN CONNECTION WAS WHAT HE WAS AFTER.
INSIDE, I FEEL NOTHING. MY SYMPATHY, WASHED AWAY WITH THE TIDE. THE LITTLE BOY I TRIED TO SAVE WAS LONG GONE. IT'S HIS IDEAL THAT WILL LIVE ON TO HAUNT ME UNTIL I DIE.

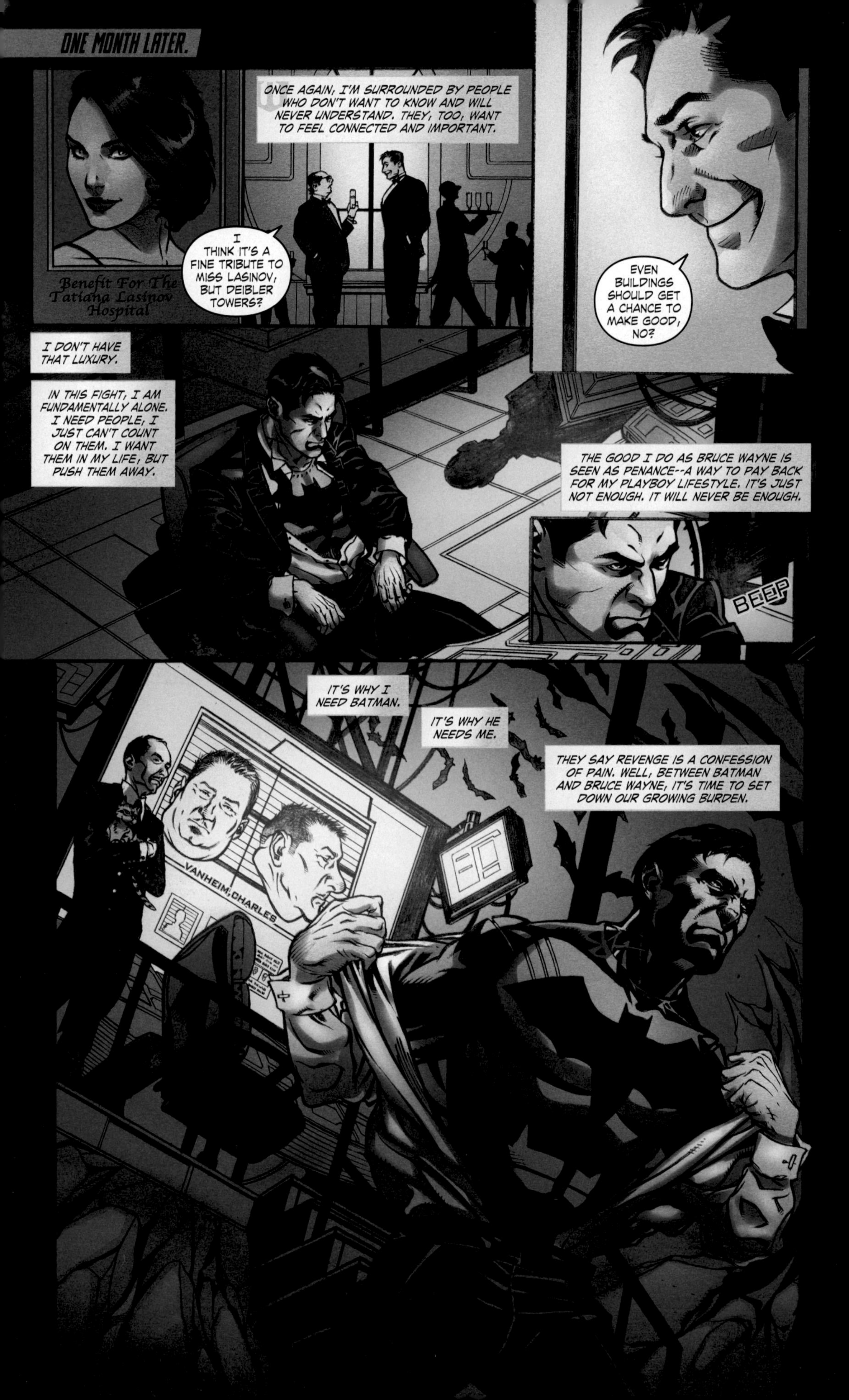
ONE MONTH LATER.
ONCE AGAIN, I'M SURROUNDED BY PEOPLE WHO DON'T WANT TO KNOW AND WILL NEVER UNDERSTAND. THEY, TOO, WANT TO FEEL CONNECTED AND IMPORTANT.
Benefit For The Tatiana Lasinov Hospital
I THINK IT'S A FINE TRIBUTE TO MISS LASINOV, BUT DEIBLER TOWERS?
EVEN BUILDINGS SHOULD GET A CHANCE TO MAKE GOOD, NO?
I DON'T HAVE THAT LUXURY.
IN THIS FIGHT, I AM FUNDAMENTALLY ALONE. I NEED PEOPLE, I JUST CAN'T COUNT ON THEM. I WANT THEM IN MY LIFE, BUT PUSH THEM AWAY.
THE GOOD I DO AS BRUCE WAYNE IS SEEN AS PENANCE--A WAY TO PAY BACK FOR MY PLAYBOY LIFESTYLE. IT'S JUST NOT ENOUGH. IT WILL NEVER BE ENOUGH.
BEEP
IT'S WHY I NEED BATMAN.
IT'S WHY HE NEEDS ME.
THEY SAY REVENGE IS A CONFESSION OF PAIN. WELL, BETWEEN BATMAN AND BRUCE WAYNE, IT'S TIME TO SET DOWN OUR GROWING BURDEN.
VANHEIM, CHARLES

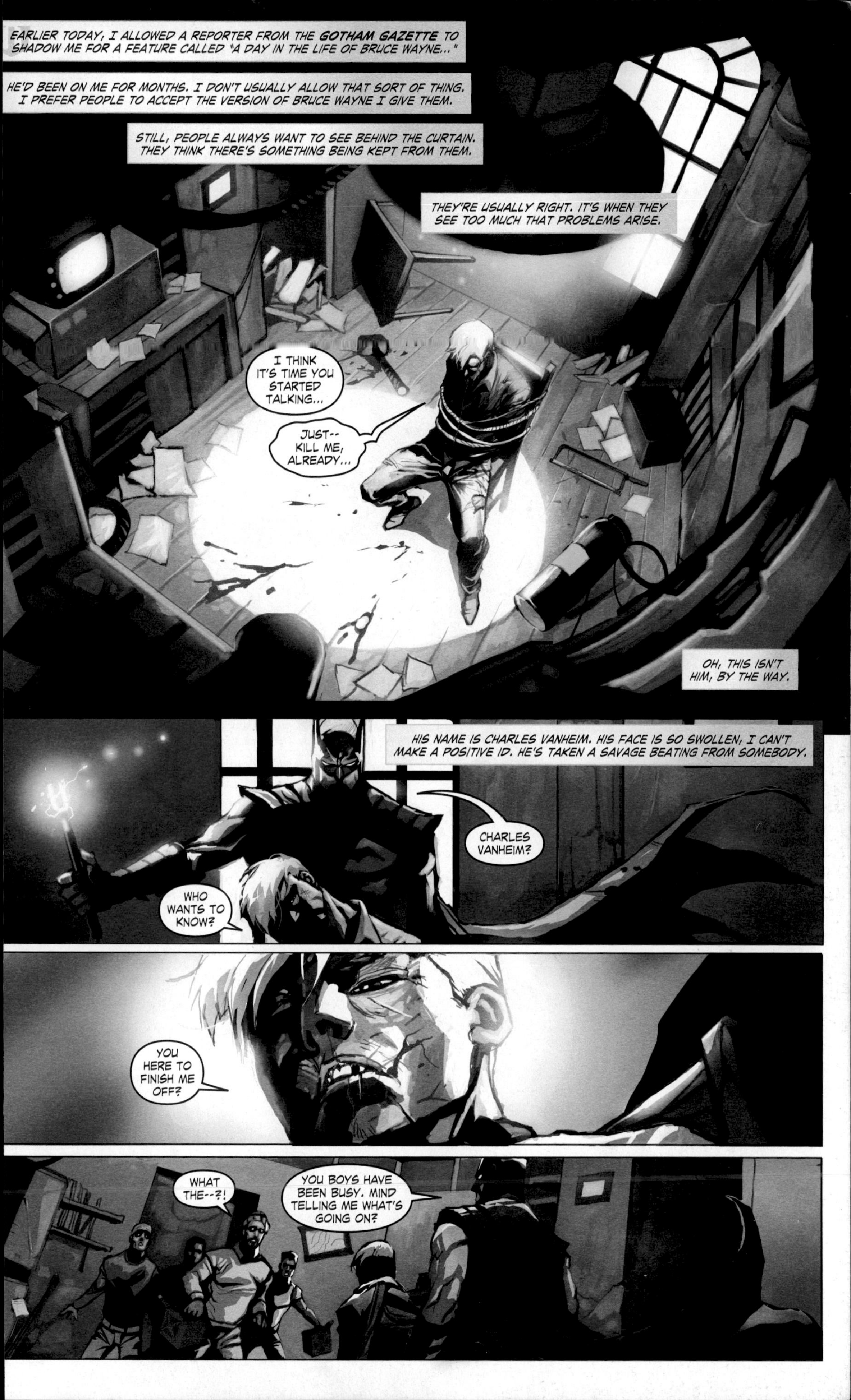
EARLIER TODAY, I ALLOWED A REPORTER FROM THE GOTHAM GAZETTE TO SHADOW ME FOR A FEATURE CALLED "A DAY IN THE LIFE OF BRUCE WAYNE..."
HE'D BEEN ON ME FOR MONTHS. I DON'T USUALLY ALLOW THAT SORT OF THING. I PREFER PEOPLE TO ACCEPT THE VERSION OF BRUCE WAYNE I GIVE THEM.
STILL, PEOPLE ALWAYS WANT TO SEE BEHIND THE CURTAIN. THEY THINK THERE'S SOMETHING BEING KEPT FROM THEM.
THEY'RE USUALLY RIGHT. IT'S WHEN THEY SEE TOO MUCH THAT PROBLEMS ARISE.
I THINK IT'S TIME YOU STARTED TALKING...
JUST-- KILL ME, ALREADY...
OH, THIS ISN'T HIM, BY THE WAY.
HIS NAME IS CHARLES VANHEIM. HIS FACE IS SO SWOLLEN, I CAN'T MAKE A POSITIVE ID. HE'S TAKEN A SAVAGE BEATING FROM SOMEBODY.
CHARLES VANHEIM?
WHO WANTS TO KNOW?
YOU HERE TO FINISH ME OFF?
WHAT THE--?!
YOU BOYS HAVE BEEN BUSY. MIND TELLING ME WHAT'S GOING ON?

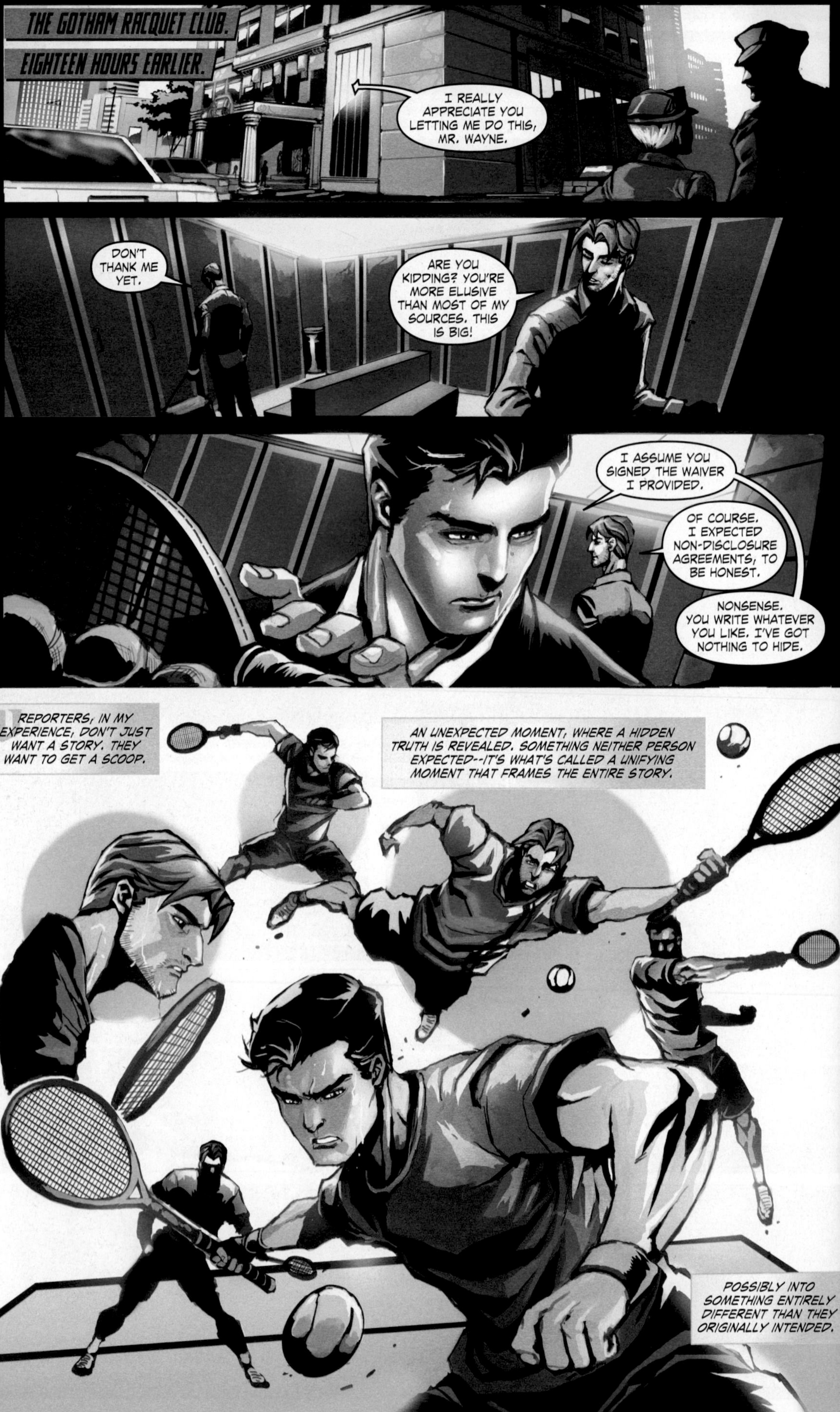
THE GOTHAM RACQUET CLUB.
EIGHTEEN HOURS EARLIER.
I REALLY APPRECIATE YOU LETTING ME DO THIS, MR. WAYNE.
DON'T THANK ME YET.
ARE YOU KIDDING? YOU'RE MORE ELUSIVE THAN MOST OF MY SOURCES. THIS IS BIG!
I ASSUME YOU SIGNED THE WAIVER I PROVIDED.
OF COURSE. I EXPECTED NON-DISCLOSURE AGREEMENTS, TO BE HONEST.
NONSENSE. YOU WRITE WHATEVER YOU LIKE. I'VE GOT NOTHING TO HIDE.
REPORTERS, IN MY EXPERIENCE, DON'T JUST WANT A STORY. THEY WANT TO GET A SCOOP.
AN UNEXPECTED MOMENT, WHERE A HIDDEN TRUTH IS REVEALED. SOMETHING NEITHER PERSON EXPECTED--IT'S WHAT'S CALLED A UNIFYING MOMENT THAT FRAMES THE ENTIRE STORY.
POSSIBLY INTO SOMETHING ENTIRELY DIFFERENT THAN THEY ORIGINALLY INTENDED.

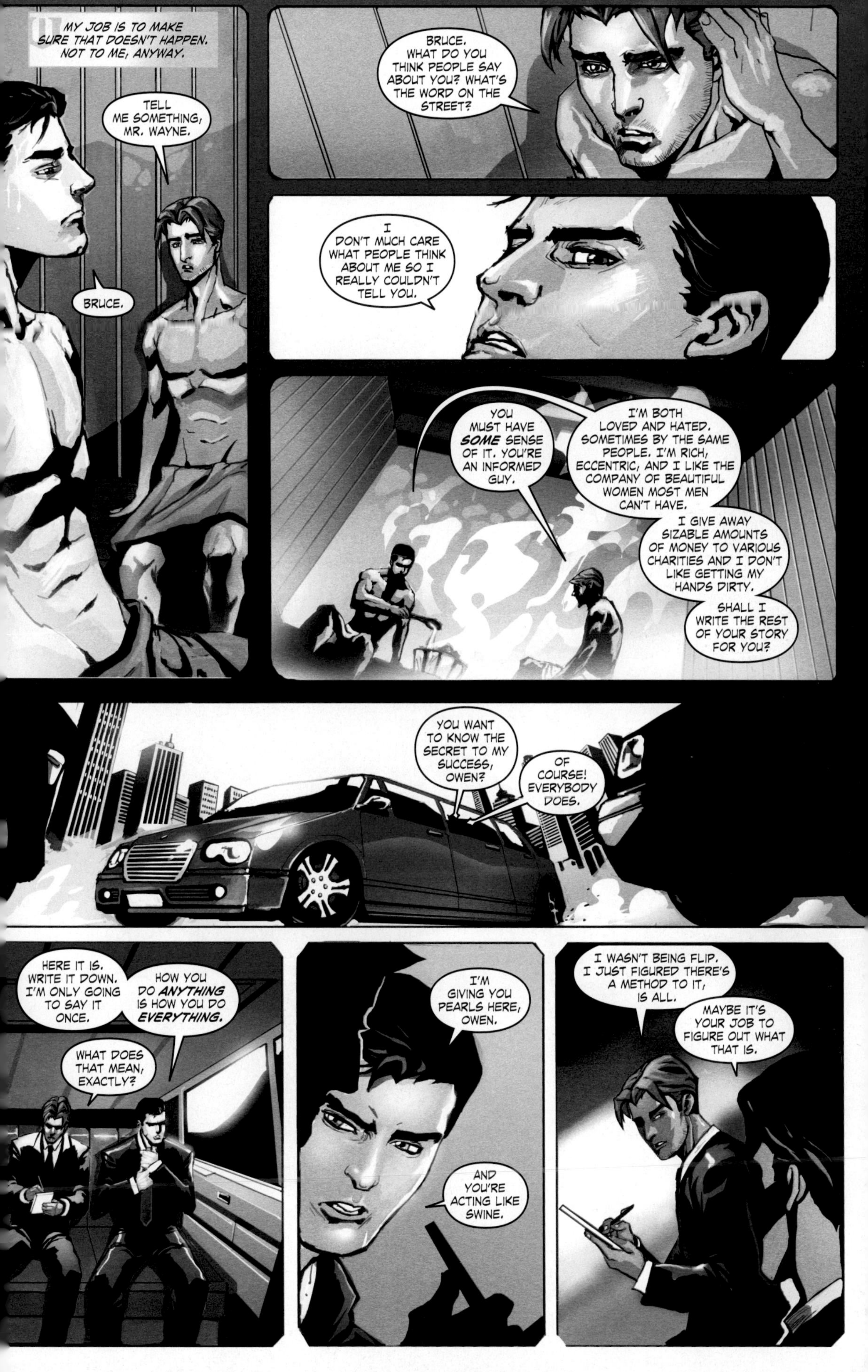
MY JOB IS TO MAKE SURE THAT DOESN'T HAPPEN. NOT TO ME, ANYWAY.
TELL ME SOMETHING, MR. WAYNE.
BRUCE.
BRUCE. WHAT DO YOU THINK PEOPLE SAY ABOUT YOU? WHAT'S THE WORD ON THE STREET?
I DON'T MUCH CARE WHAT PEOPLE THINK ABOUT ME SO I REALLY COULDN'T TELL YOU.
YOU MUST HAVE SOME SENSE OF IT. YOU'RE AN INFORMED GUY.
I'M BOTH LOVED AND HATED. SOMETIMES BY THE SAME PEOPLE. I'M RICH, ECCENTRIC, AND I LIKE THE COMPANY OF BEAUTIFUL WOMEN MOST MEN CAN'T HAVE.
I GIVE AWAY SIZABLE AMOUNTS OF MONEY TO VARIOUS CHARITIES AND I DON'T LIKE GETTING MY HANDS DIRTY.
SHALL I WRITE THE REST OF YOUR STORY FOR YOU?
YOU WANT TO KNOW THE SECRET TO MY SUCCESS, OWEN?
OF COURSE! EVERYBODY DOES.
HERE IT IS. WRITE IT DOWN. I'M ONLY GOING TO SAY IT ONCE.
HOW YOU DO ANYTHING IS HOW YOU DO EVERYTHING.
WHAT DOES THAT MEAN, EXACTLY?
I'M GIVING YOU PEARLS HERE, OWEN.
AND YOU'RE ACTING LIKE SWINE.
I WASN'T BEING FLIP. I JUST FIGURED THERE'S A METHOD TO IT, IS ALL.
MAYBE IT'S YOUR JOB TO FIGURE OUT WHAT THAT IS.

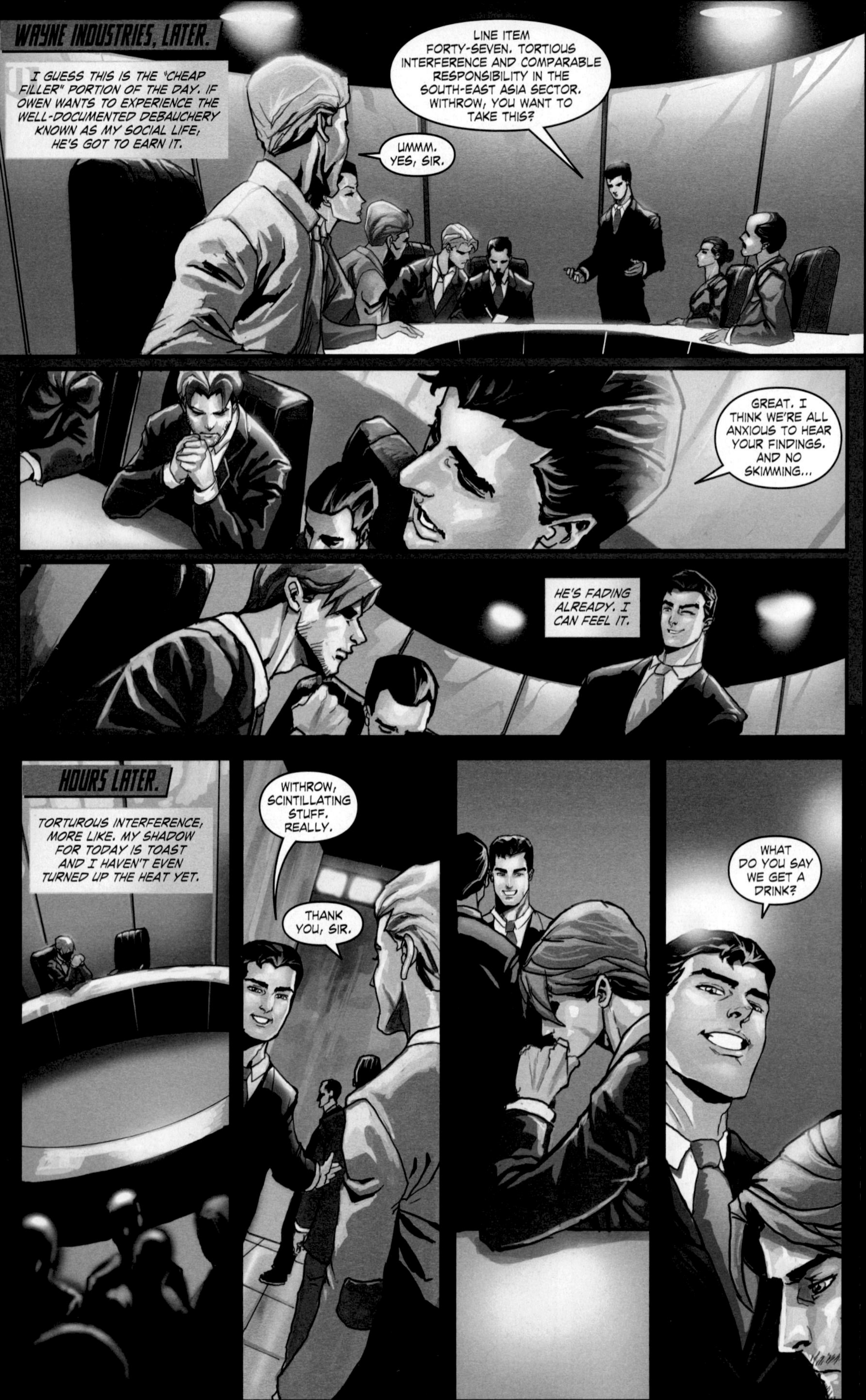
WAYNE INDUSTRIES, LATER.
I GUESS THIS IS THE "CHEAP FILLER" PORTION OF THE DAY. IF OWEN WANTS TO EXPERIENCE THE WELL-DOCUMENTED DEBAUCHERY KNOWN AS MY SOCIAL LIFE, HE'S GOT TO EARN IT.
LINE ITEM FORTY-SEVEN. TORTIOUS INTERFERENCE AND COMPARABLE RESPONSIBILITY IN THE SOUTH-EAST ASIA SECTOR. WITHROW, YOU WANT TO TAKE THIS?
UMMM. YES, SIR.
GREAT. I THINK WE'RE ALL ANXIOUS TO HEAR YOUR FINDINGS. AND NO SKIMMING...
HE'S FADING ALREADY. I CAN FEEL IT.
HOURS LATER.
TORTUROUS INTERFERENCE, MORE LIKE. MY SHADOW FOR TODAY IS TOAST AND I HAVEN'T EVEN TURNED UP THE HEAT YET.
WITHROW, SCINTILLATING STUFF. REALLY.
THANK YOU, SIR.
WHAT DO YOU SAY WE GET A DRINK?

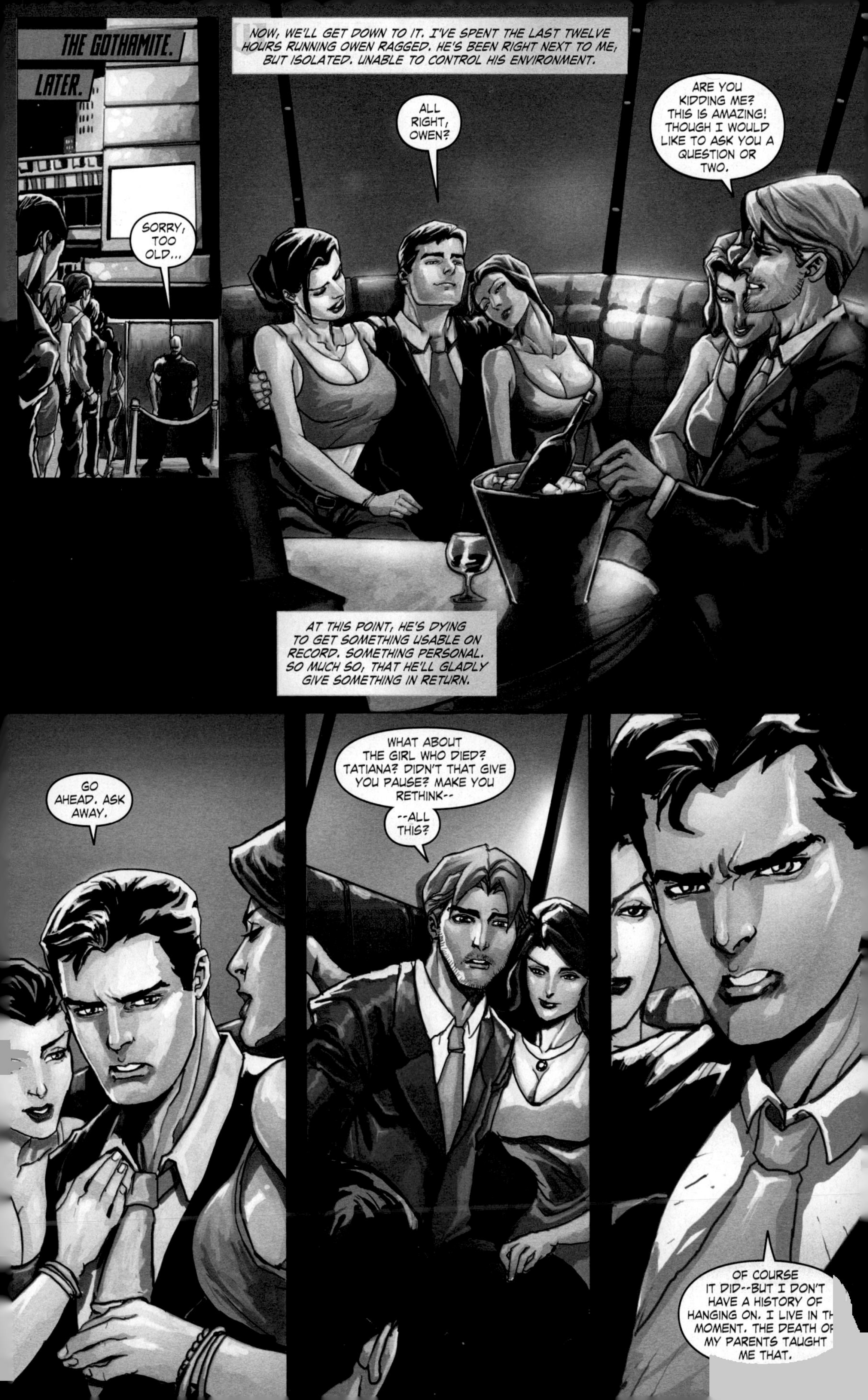
THE GOTHAMITE.
LATER.
SORRY, TOO OLD...
NOW, WE'LL GET DOWN TO IT. I'VE SPENT THE LAST TWELVE HOURS RUNNING OWEN RAGGED. HE'S BEEN RIGHT NEXT TO ME, BUT ISOLATED. UNABLE TO CONTROL HIS ENVIRONMENT.
ALL RIGHT, OWEN?
ARE YOU KIDDING ME? THIS IS AMAZING! THOUGH I WOULD LIKE TO ASK YOU A QUESTION OR TWO.
AT THIS POINT, HE'S DYING TO GET SOMETHING USABLE ON RECORD. SOMETHING PERSONAL. SO MUCH SO, THAT HE'LL GLADLY GIVE SOMETHING IN RETURN.
GO AHEAD. ASK AWAY.
WHAT ABOUT THE GIRL WHO DIED? TATIANA? DIDN'T THAT GIVE YOU PAUSE? MAKE YOU RETHINK--
--ALL THIS?
OF COURSE IT DID--BUT I DON'T HAVE A HISTORY OF HANGING ON. I LIVE IN TH MOMENT. THE DEATH OF MY PARENTS TAUGHT ME THAT.

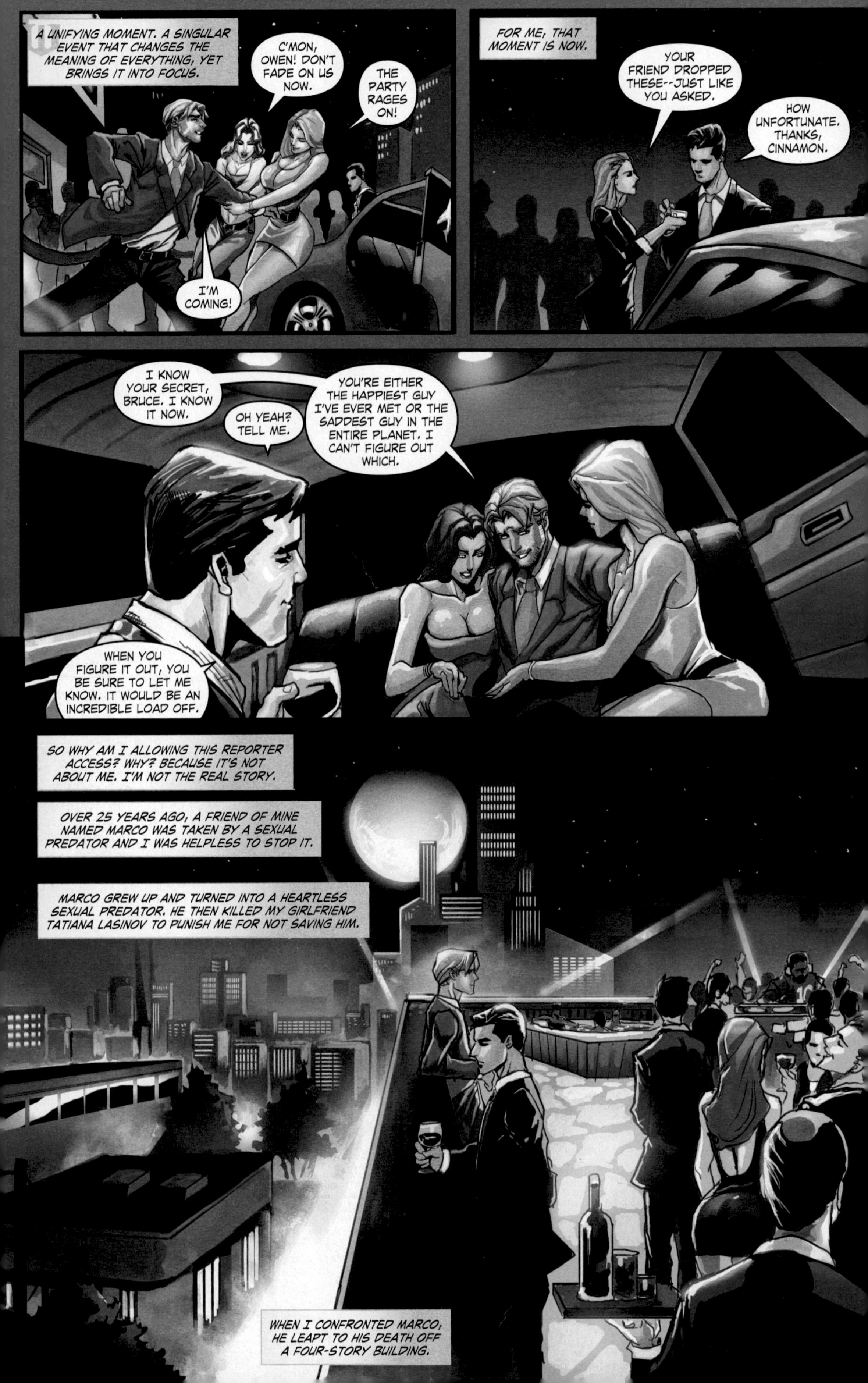
A UNIFYING MOMENT. A SINGULAR EVENT THAT CHANGES THE MEANING OF EVERYTHING, YET BRINGS IT INTO FOCUS.
C'MON, OWEN! DON'T FADE ON US NOW.
THE PARTY RAGES ON!
I'M COMING!
FOR ME, THAT MOMENT IS NOW.
YOUR FRIEND DROPPED THESE--JUST LIKE YOU ASKED.
HOW UNFORTUNATE. THANKS, CINNAMON.
I KNOW YOUR SECRET, BRUCE. I KNOW IT NOW.
OH YEAH? TELL ME.
YOU'RE EITHER THE HAPPIEST GUY I'VE EVER MET OR THE SADDEST GUY IN THE ENTIRE PLANET. I CAN'T FIGURE OUT WHICH.
WHEN YOU FIGURE IT OUT, YOU BE SURE TO LET ME KNOW. IT WOULD BE AN INCREDIBLE LOAD OFF.
SO WHY AM I ALLOWING THIS REPORTER ACCESS? WHY? BECAUSE IT'S NOT ABOUT ME. I'M NOT THE REAL STORY.
OVER 25 YEARS AGO, A FRIEND OF MINE NAMED MARCO WAS TAKEN BY A SEXUAL PREDATOR AND I WAS HELPLESS TO STOP IT.
MARCO GREW UP AND TURNED INTO A HEARTLESS SEXUAL PREDATOR. HE THEN KILLED MY GIRLFRIEND TATIANA LASINOV TO PUNISH ME FOR NOT SAVING HIM.
WHEN I CONFRONTED MARCO, HE LEAPT TO HIS DEATH OFF A FOUR-STORY BUILDING.

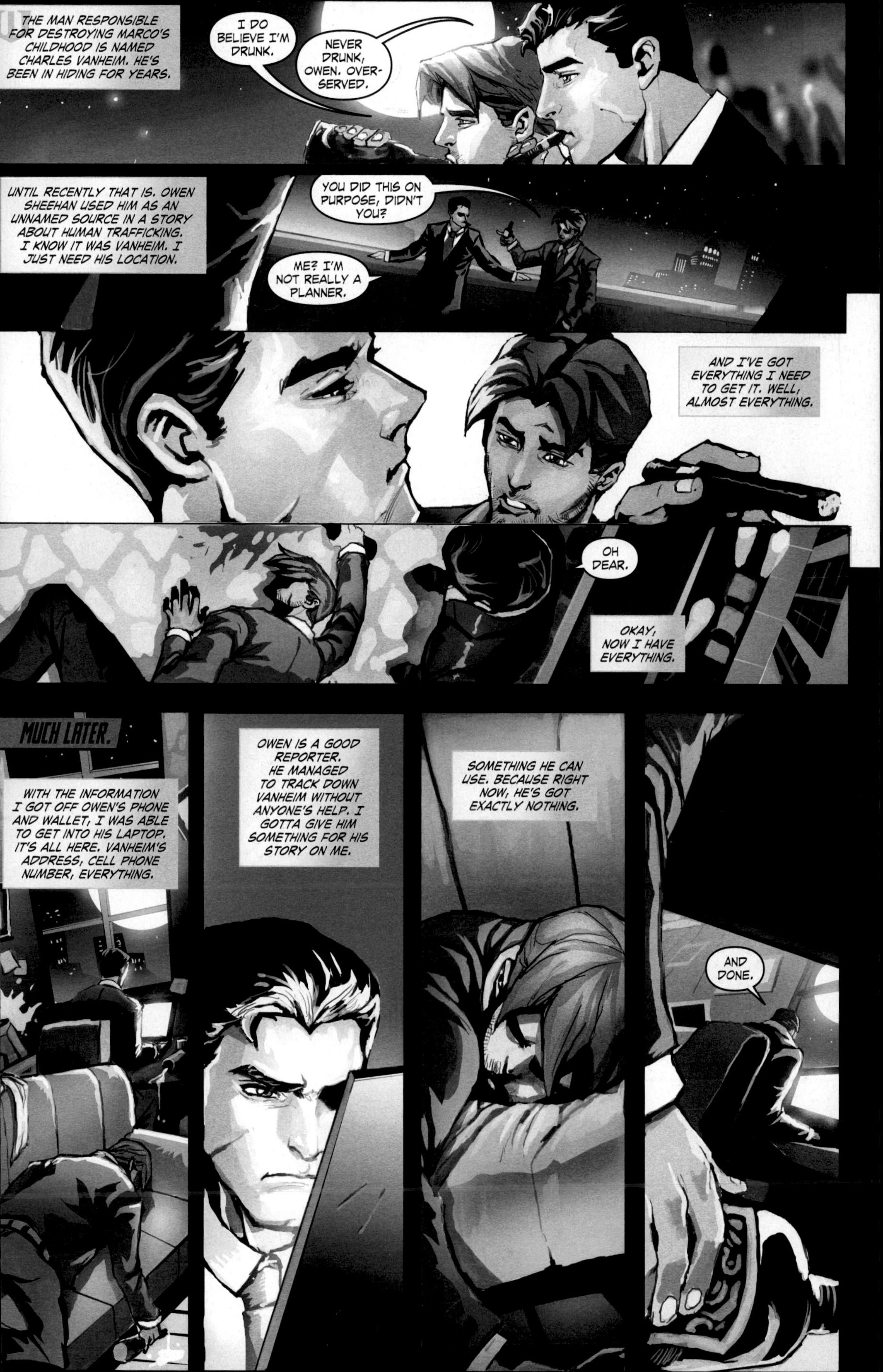
THE MAN RESPONSIBLE FOR DESTROYING MARCO'S CHILDHOOD IS NAMED CHARLES VANHEIM. HE'S BEEN IN HIDING FOR YEARS.
I DO BELIEVE I'M DRUNK.
NEVER DRUNK, OWEN. OVER-SERVED.
UNTIL RECENTLY THAT IS. OWEN SHEEHAN USED HIM AS AN UNNAMED SOURCE IN A STORY ABOUT HUMAN TRAFFICKING. I KNOW IT WAS VANHEIM. I JUST NEED HIS LOCATION.
YOU DID THIS ON PURPOSE, DIDN'T YOU?
ME? I'M NOT REALLY A PLANNER.
AND I'VE GOT EVERYTHING I NEED TO GET IT. WELL, ALMOST EVERYTHING.
OH DEAR.
OKAY, NOW I HAVE EVERYTHING.
MUCH LATER.
WITH THE INFORMATION I GOT OFF OWEN'S PHONE AND WALLET, I WAS ABLE TO GET INTO HIS LAPTOP. IT'S ALL HERE. VANHEIM'S ADDRESS, CELL PHONE NUMBER, EVERYTHING.
OWEN IS A GOOD REPORTER. HE MANAGED TO TRACK DOWN VANHEIM WITHOUT ANYONE'S HELP. I GOTTA GIVE HIM SOMETHING FOR HIS STORY ON ME.
SOMETHING HE CAN USE. BECAUSE RIGHT NOW, HE'S GOT EXACTLY NOTHING.
AND DONE.

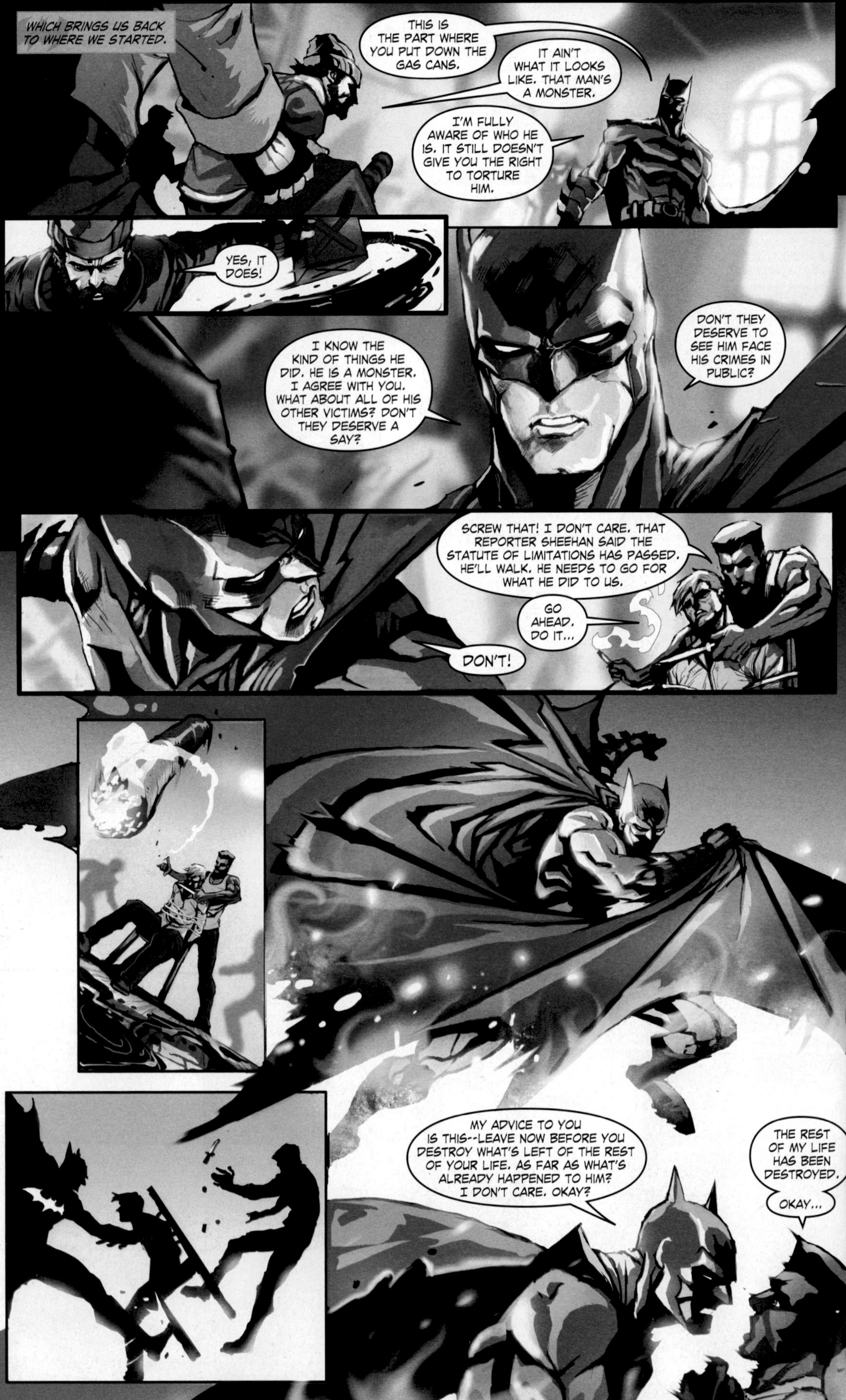
WHICH BRINGS US BACK TO WHERE WE STARTED.
THIS IS THE PART WHERE YOU PUT DOWN THE GAS CANS.
IT AIN'T WHAT IT LOOKS LIKE. THAT MAN'S A MONSTER.
I'M FULLY AWARE OF WHO HE IS. IT STILL DOESN'T GIVE YOU THE RIGHT TO TORTURE HIM.
YES, IT DOES!
I KNOW THE KIND OF THINGS HE DID. HE IS A MONSTER. I AGREE WITH YOU. WHAT ABOUT ALL OF HIS OTHER VICTIMS? DON'T THEY DESERVE A SAY?
DON'T THEY DESERVE TO SEE HIM FACE HIS CRIMES IN PUBLIC?
SCREW THAT! I DON'T CARE. THAT REPORTER SHEEHAN SAID THE STATUTE OF LIMITATIONS HAS PASSED. HE'LL WALK. HE NEEDS TO GO FOR WHAT HE DID TO US.
GO AHEAD. DO IT...
DON'T!
MY ADVICE TO YOU IS THIS--LEAVE NOW BEFORE YOU DESTROY WHAT'S LEFT OF THE REST OF YOUR LIFE. AS FAR AS WHAT'S ALREADY HAPPENED TO HIM? I DON'T CARE. OKAY?
THE REST OF MY LIFE HAS BEEN DESTROYED.
OKAY...

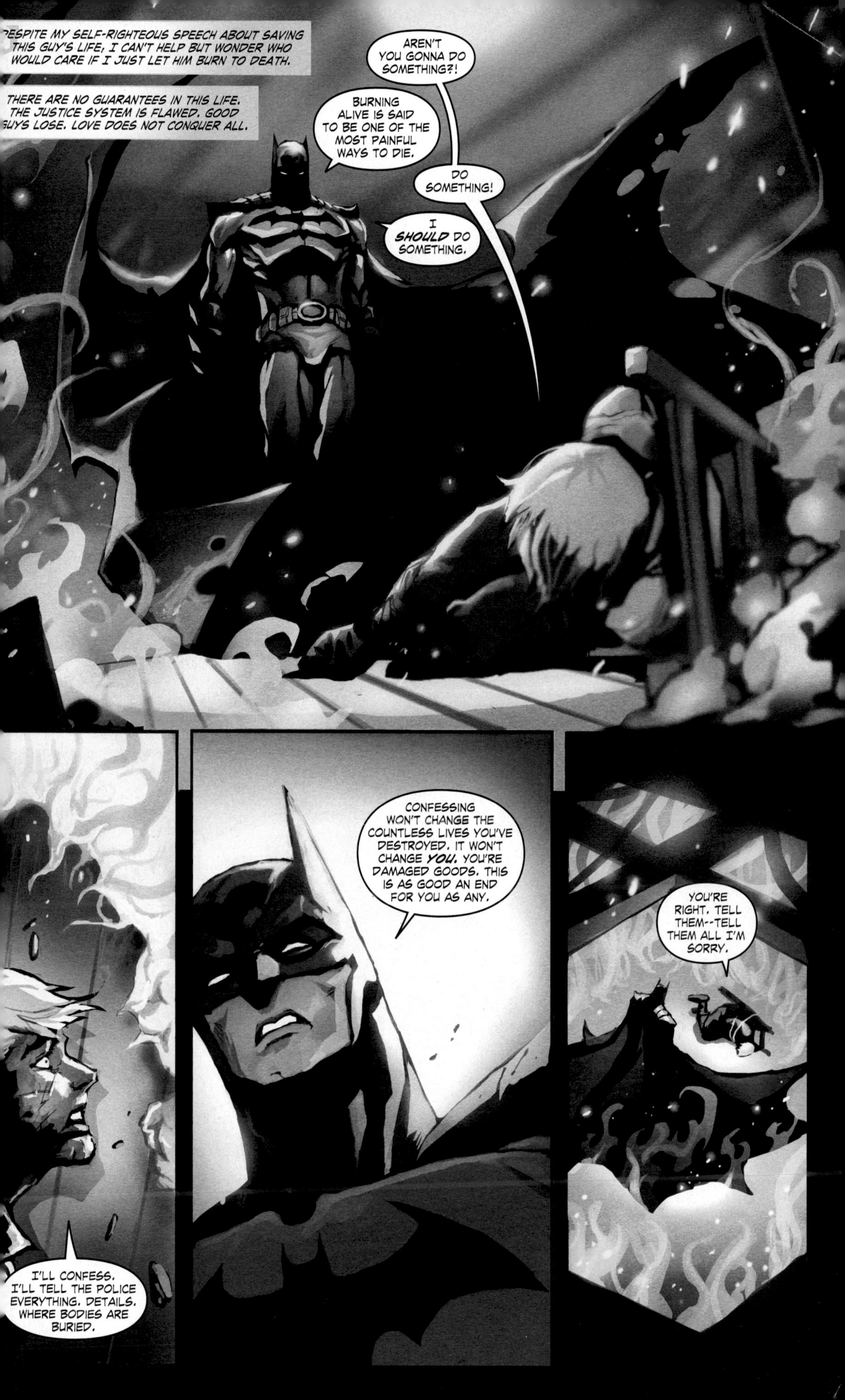
ESPITE MY SELF-RIGHTEOUS SPEECH ABOUT SAVING THIS GUY'S LIFE, I CAN'T HELP BUT WONDER WHO WOULD CARE IF I JUST LET HIM BURN TO DEATH.
THERE ARE NO GUARANTEES IN THIS LIFE. THE JUSTICE SYSTEM IS FLAWED. GOOD GUYS LOSE. LOVE DOES NOT CONQUER ALL.
AREN'T YOU GONNA DO SOMETHING?!
BURNING ALIVE IS SAID TO BE ONE OF THE MOST PAINFUL WAYS TO DIE.
DO SOMETHING!
I *SHOULD* DO SOMETHING.
I'LL CONFESS. I'LL TELL THE POLICE EVERYTHING. DETAILS. WHERE BODIES ARE BURIED.
CONFESSING WON'T CHANGE THE COUNTLESS LIVES YOU'VE DESTROYED. IT WON'T CHANGE *YOU*. YOU'RE DAMAGED GOODS. THIS IS AS GOOD AN END FOR YOU AS ANY.
YOU'RE RIGHT. TELL THEM--TELL THEM ALL I'M SORRY.

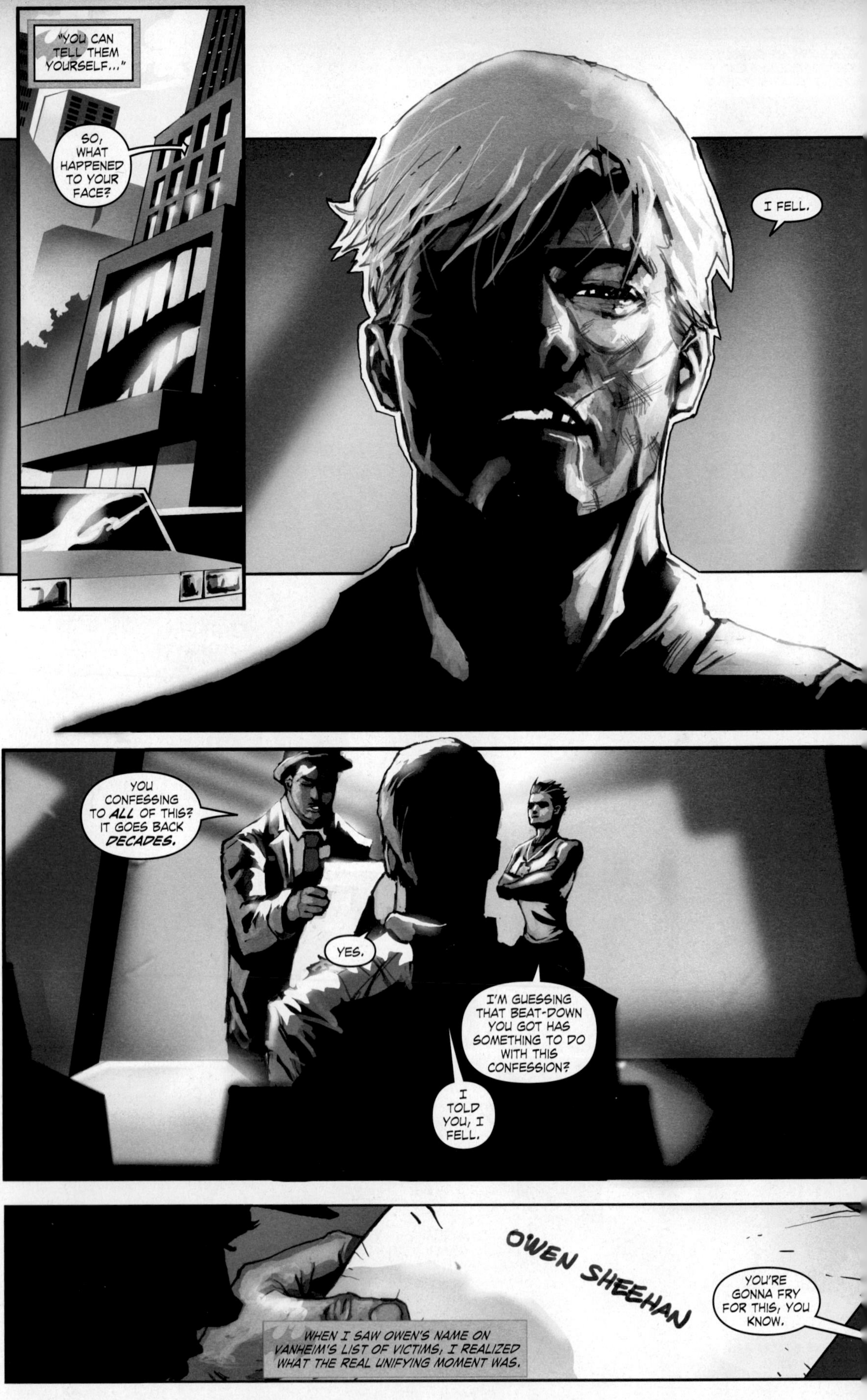
"YOU CAN TELL THEM YOURSELF..."
SO, WHAT HAPPENED TO YOUR FACE?
I FELL.
YOU CONFESSING TO ALL OF THIS? IT GOES BACK DECADES.
YES.
I'M GUESSING THAT BEAT-DOWN YOU GOT HAS SOMETHING TO DO WITH THIS CONFESSION?
I TOLD YOU, I FELL.
OWEN SHEEHAN
YOU'RE GONNA FRY FOR THIS, YOU KNOW.
WHEN I SAW OWEN'S NAME ON VANHEIM'S LIST OF VICTIMS, I REALIZED WHAT THE REAL UNIFYING MOMENT WAS.

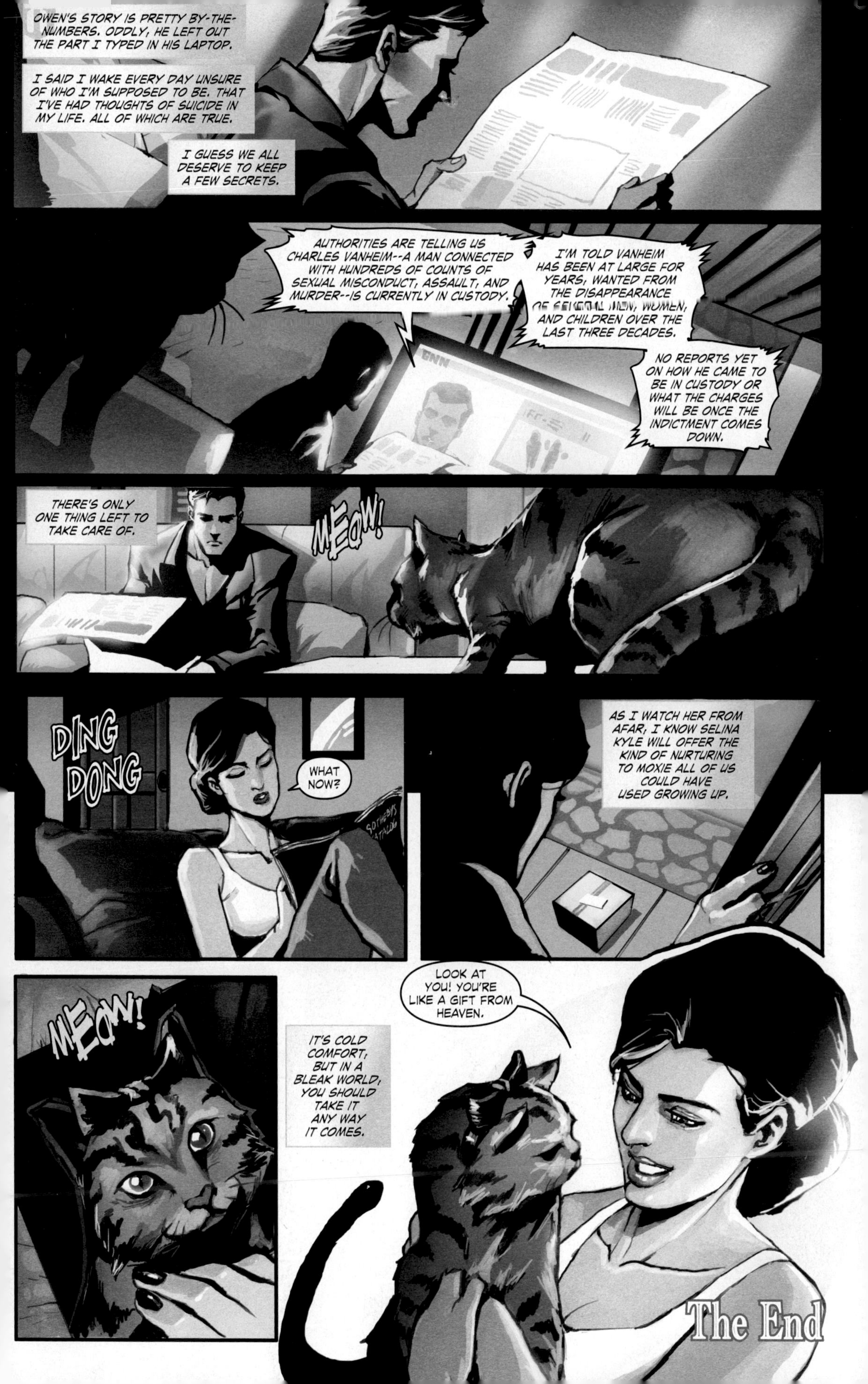
OWEN'S STORY IS PRETTY BY-THE-NUMBERS. ODDLY, HE LEFT OUT THE PART I TYPED IN HIS LAPTOP.
I SAID I WAKE EVERY DAY UNSURE OF WHO I'M SUPPOSED TO BE. THAT I'VE HAD THOUGHTS OF SUICIDE IN MY LIFE. ALL OF WHICH ARE TRUE.
I GUESS WE ALL DESERVE TO KEEP A FEW SECRETS.
AUTHORITIES ARE TELLING US CHARLES VANHEIM--A MAN CONNECTED WITH HUNDREDS OF COUNTS OF SEXUAL MISCONDUCT, ASSAULT, AND MURDER--IS CURRENTLY IN CUSTODY.
I'M TOLD VANHEIM HAS BEEN AT LARGE FOR YEARS, WANTED FROM THE DISAPPEARANCE OF SEVERAL MEN, WOMEN, AND CHILDREN OVER THE LAST THREE DECADES.
NO REPORTS YET ON HOW HE CAME TO BE IN CUSTODY OR WHAT THE CHARGES WILL BE ONCE THE INDICTMENT COMES DOWN.
GNN
THERE'S ONLY ONE THING LEFT TO TAKE CARE OF.
MEOW!
DING DONG
WHAT NOW?
SOTHEBYS CATALOG
AS I WATCH HER FROM AFAR, I KNOW SELINA KYLE WILL OFFER THE KIND OF NURTURING TO MOXIE ALL OF US COULD HAVE USED GROWING UP.
MEOW!
IT'S COLD COMFORT, BUT IN A BLEAK WORLD, YOU SHOULD TAKE IT ANY WAY IT COMES.
LOOK AT YOU! YOU'RE LIKE A GIFT FROM HEAVEN.
The End

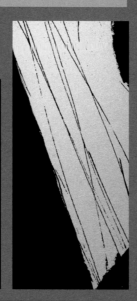

THE BEAUTIFUL UGLY

DEREK FRIDOLFS

KENNETH ELLIOTT JONES
Writers

JASON SHAWN ALEXANDER
Artist

SHERARD JACKSON
Colorist

DERON BENNETT
Letterer

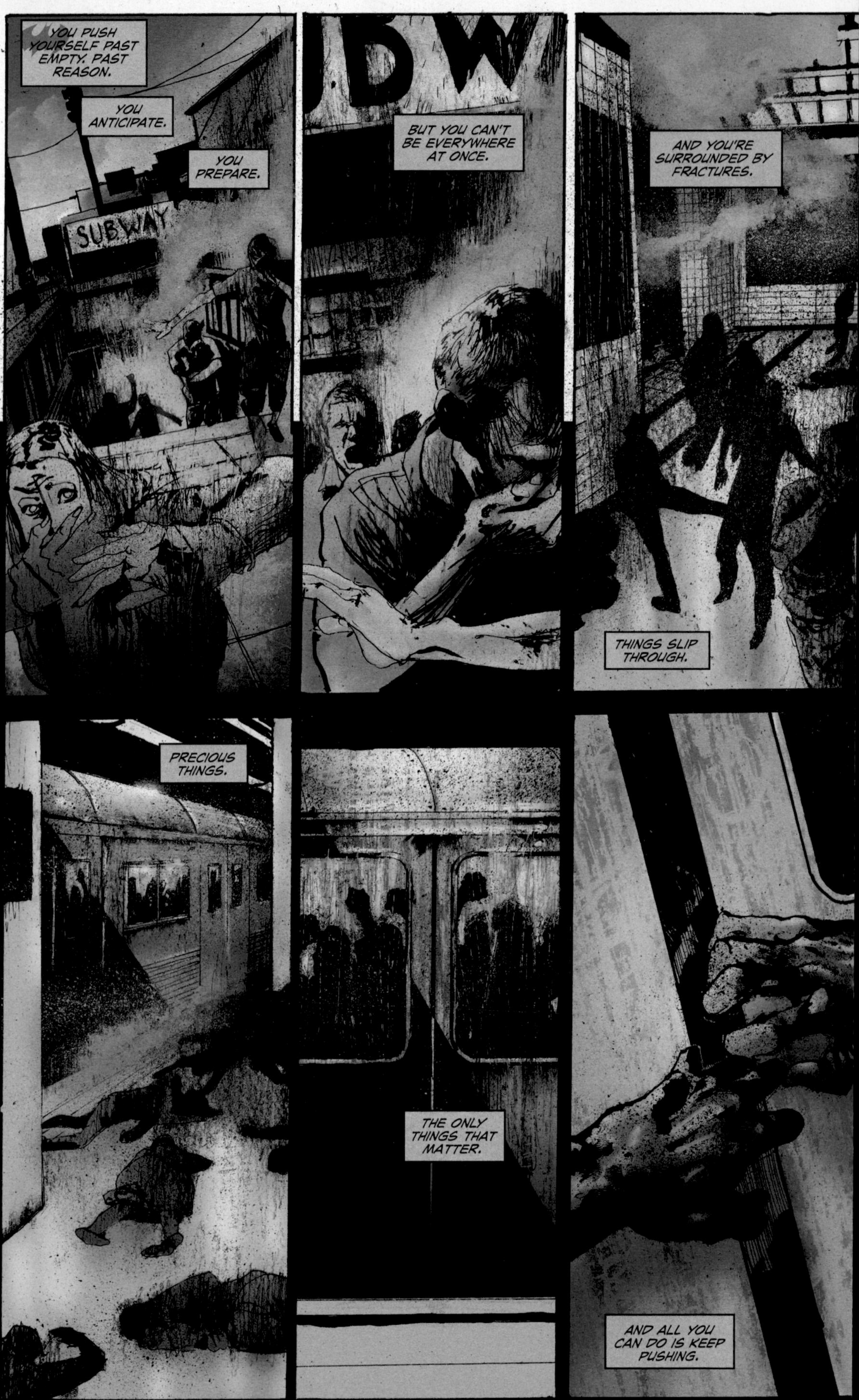
YOU PUSH YOURSELF PAST EMPTY. PAST REASON.
YOU ANTICIPATE.
YOU PREPARE.
SUBWAY
BUT YOU CAN'T BE EVERYWHERE AT ONCE.
AND YOU'RE SURROUNDED BY FRACTURES.
THINGS SLIP THROUGH.
PRECIOUS THINGS.
THE ONLY THINGS THAT MATTER.
AND ALL YOU CAN DO IS KEEP PUSHING.

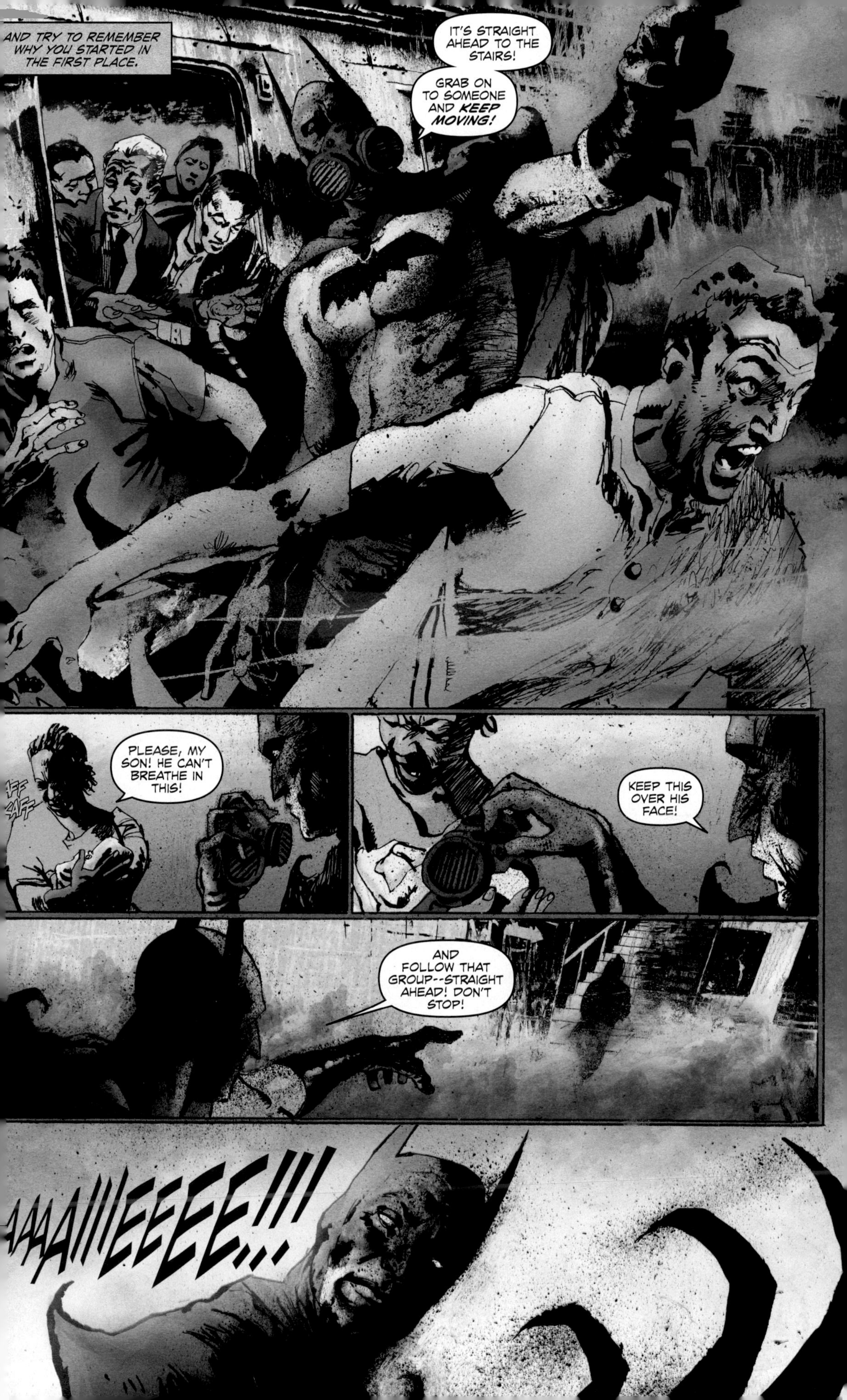

AND TRY TO REMEMBER WHY YOU STARTED IN THE FIRST PLACE.
IT'S STRAIGHT AHEAD TO THE STAIRS!
GRAB ON TO SOMEONE AND **KEEP MOVING!**
PLEASE, MY SON! HE CAN'T BREATHE IN THIS!
KEEP THIS OVER HIS FACE!
AND FOLLOW THAT GROUP--STRAIGHT AHEAD! DON'T STOP!
AAAAIIIEEEEE...!!!

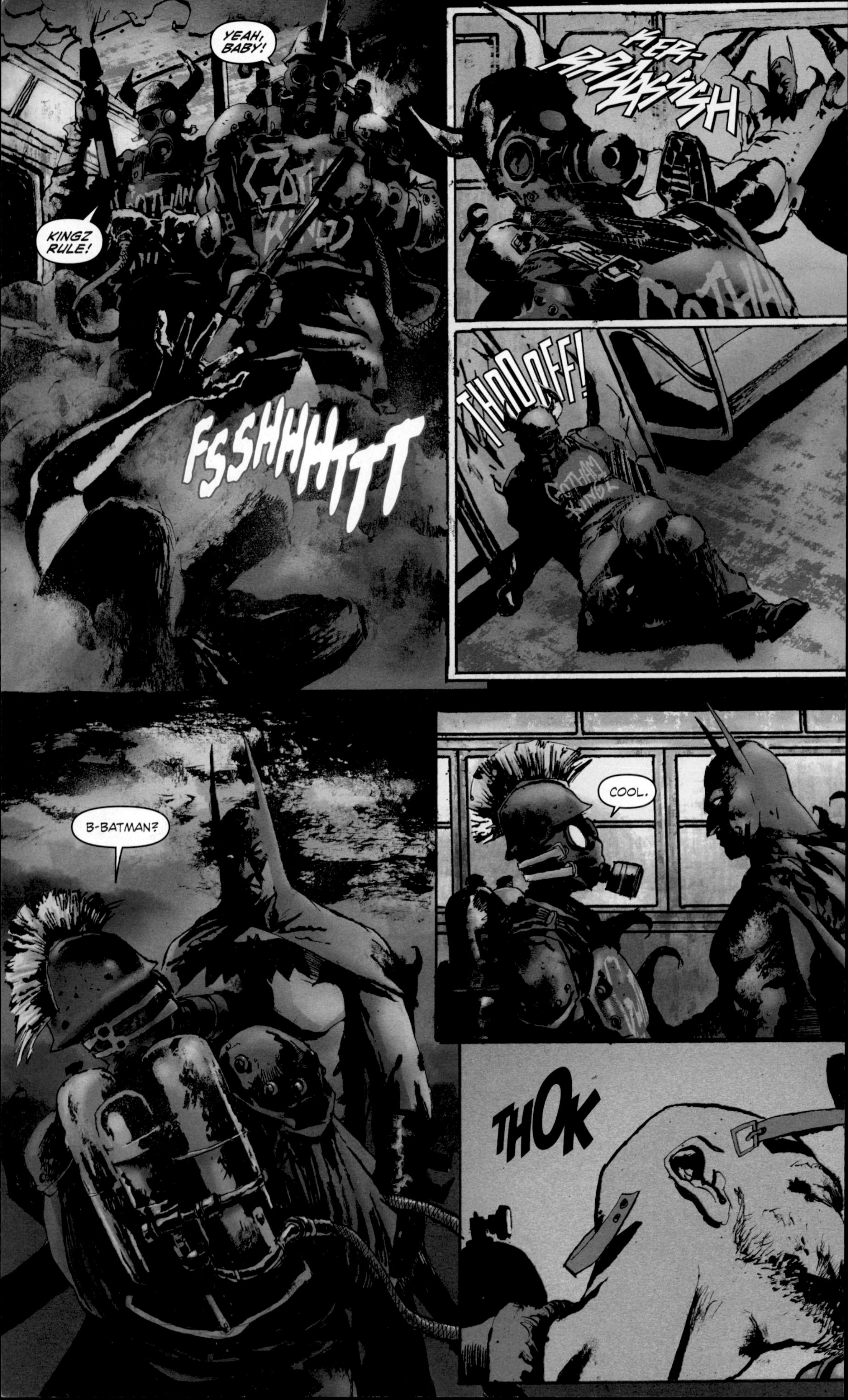
YEAH, BABY!
KINGZ RULE!
KER-BRAASSSH
FSSHHHTTT
THOOFF!
B-BATMAN?
COOL.
THOK

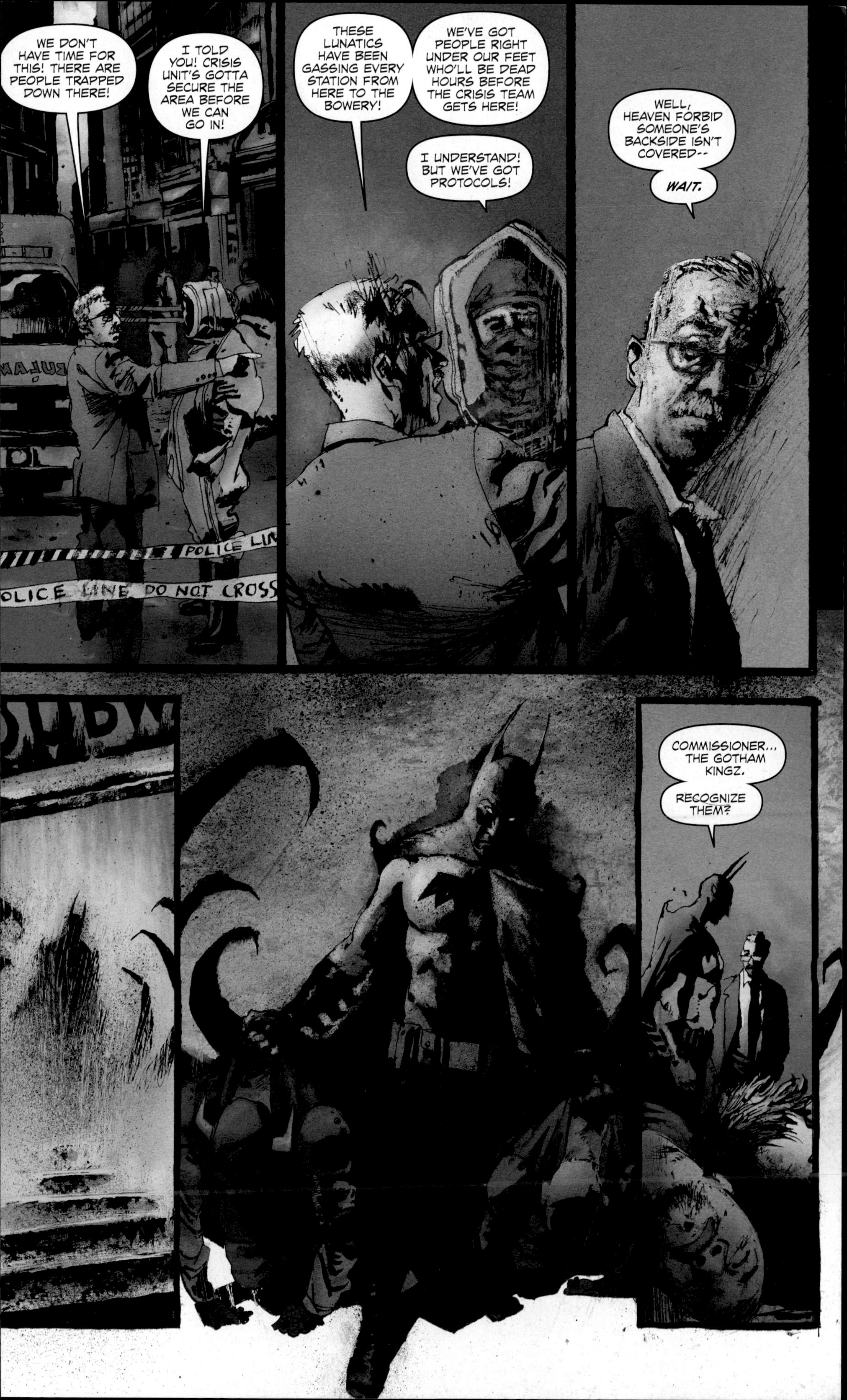
WE DON'T HAVE TIME FOR THIS! THERE ARE PEOPLE TRAPPED DOWN THERE!
I TOLD YOU! CRISIS UNIT'S GOTTA SECURE THE AREA BEFORE WE CAN GO IN!
POLICE LINE DO NOT CROSS
THESE LUNATICS HAVE BEEN GASSING EVERY STATION FROM HERE TO THE BOWERY!
WE'VE GOT PEOPLE RIGHT UNDER OUR FEET WHO'LL BE DEAD HOURS BEFORE THE CRISIS TEAM GETS HERE!
I UNDERSTAND! BUT WE'VE GOT PROTOCOLS!
WELL, HEAVEN FORBID SOMEONE'S BACKSIDE ISN'T COVERED--
WAIT.
COMMISSIONER... THE GOTHAM KINGZ.
RECOGNIZE THEM?

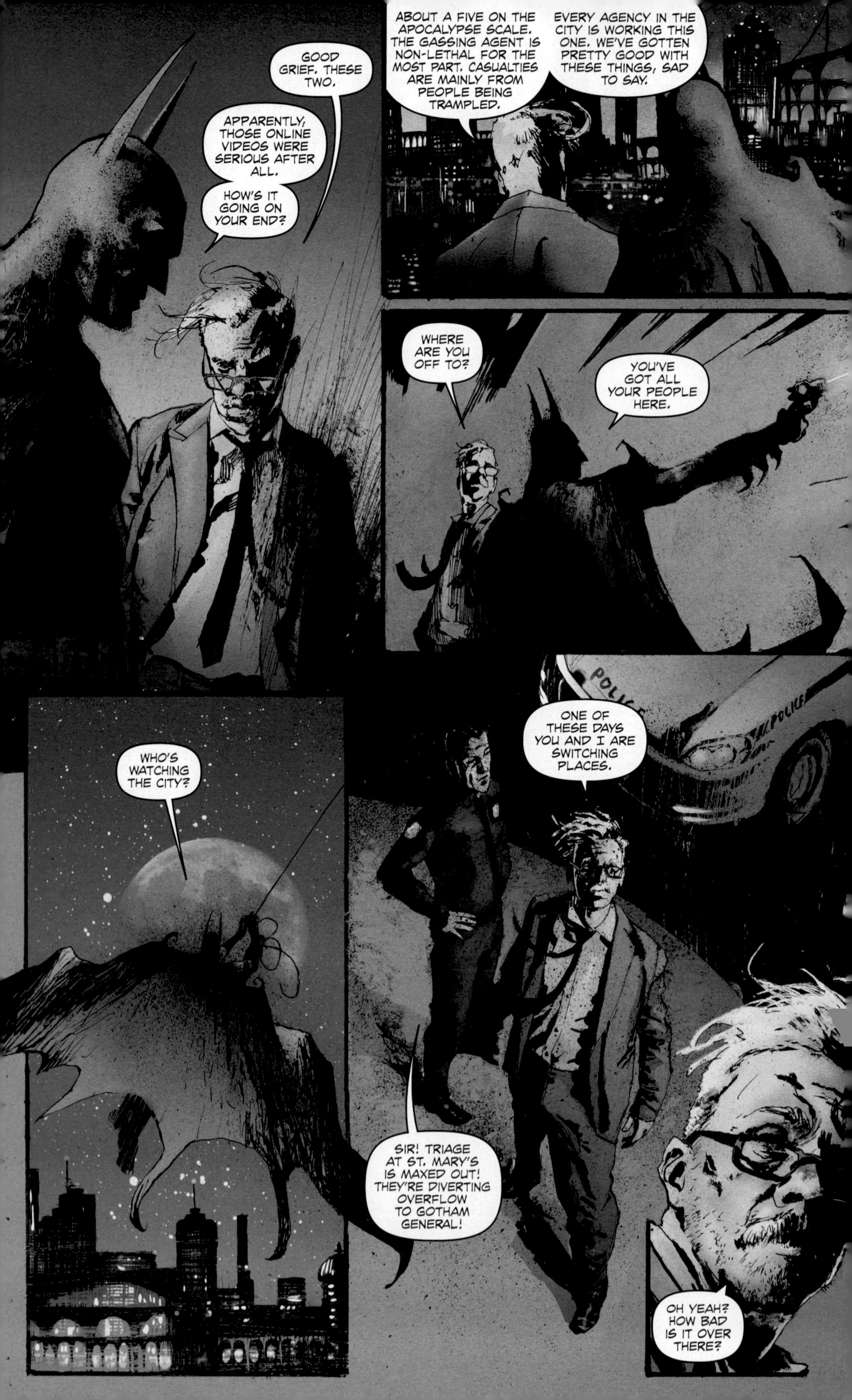
GOOD GRIEF. THESE TWO.
APPARENTLY, THOSE ONLINE VIDEOS WERE SERIOUS AFTER ALL.
HOW'S IT GOING ON YOUR END?
ABOUT A FIVE ON THE APOCALYPSE SCALE. THE GASSING AGENT IS NON-LETHAL FOR THE MOST PART. CASUALTIES ARE MAINLY FROM PEOPLE BEING TRAMPLED.
EVERY AGENCY IN THE CITY IS WORKING THIS ONE. WE'VE GOTTEN PRETTY GOOD WITH THESE THINGS, SAD TO SAY.
WHERE ARE YOU OFF TO?
YOU'VE GOT ALL YOUR PEOPLE HERE.
WHO'S WATCHING THE CITY?
POLICE
ONE OF THESE DAYS YOU AND I ARE SWITCHING PLACES.
SIR! TRIAGE AT ST. MARY'S IS MAXED OUT! THEY'RE DIVERTING OVERFLOW TO GOTHAM GENERAL!
OH YEAH? HOW BAD IS IT OVER THERE?

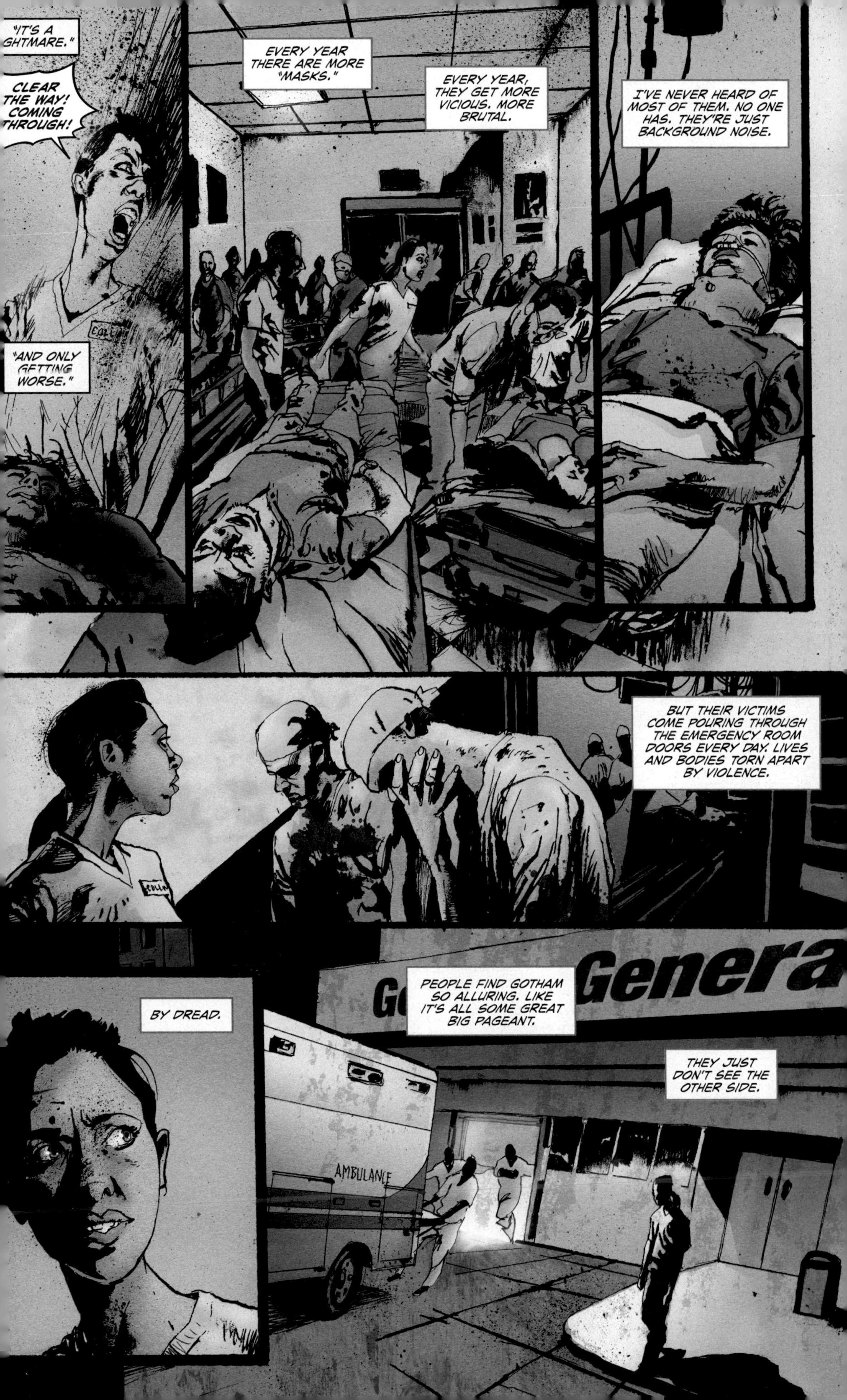
"IT'S A
GHTMARE."
CLEAR THE WAY! COMING THROUGH!
"AND ONLY GETTING WORSE."
EVERY YEAR THERE ARE MORE "MASKS."
EVERY YEAR, THEY GET MORE VICIOUS. MORE BRUTAL.
I'VE NEVER HEARD OF MOST OF THEM. NO ONE HAS. THEY'RE JUST BACKGROUND NOISE.
BUT THEIR VICTIMS COME POURING THROUGH THE EMERGENCY ROOM DOORS EVERY DAY. LIVES AND BODIES TORN APART BY VIOLENCE.
BY DREAD.
Genera
PEOPLE FIND GOTHAM SO ALLURING. LIKE IT'S ALL SOME GREAT BIG PAGEANT.
THEY JUST DON'T SEE THE OTHER SIDE.
AMBULANCE

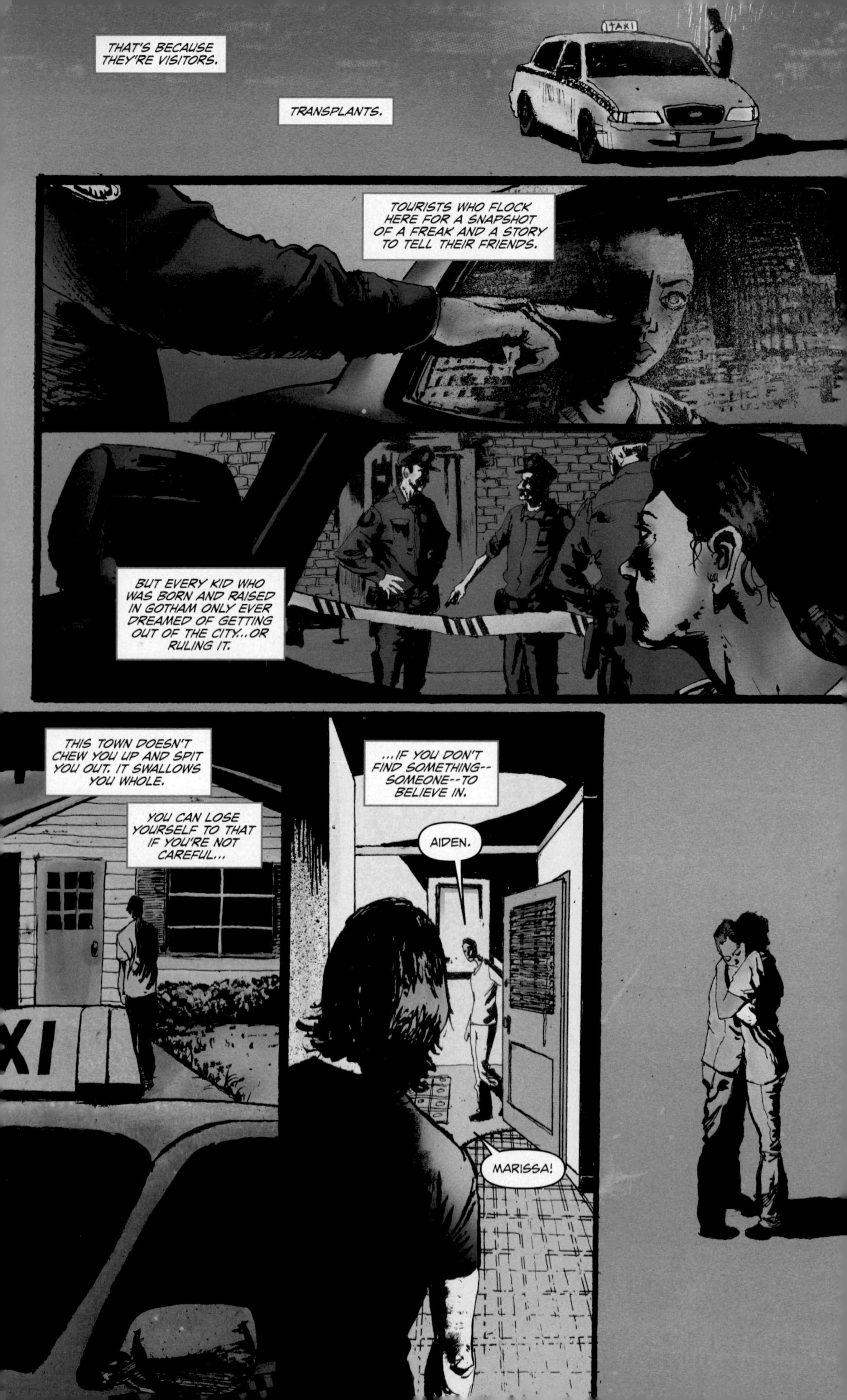
THAT'S BECAUSE THEY'RE VISITORS.
TRANSPLANTS.
TOURISTS WHO FLOCK HERE FOR A SNAPSHOT OF A FREAK AND A STORY TO TELL THEIR FRIENDS.
BUT EVERY KID WHO WAS BORN AND RAISED IN GOTHAM ONLY EVER DREAMED OF GETTING OUT OF THE CITY...OR RULING IT.
THIS TOWN DOESN'T CHEW YOU UP AND SPIT YOU OUT. IT SWALLOWS YOU WHOLE.
YOU CAN LOSE YOURSELF TO THAT IF YOU'RE NOT CAREFUL...
...IF YOU DON'T FIND SOMETHING--SOMEONE--TO BELIEVE IN.
AIDEN.
MARISSA!

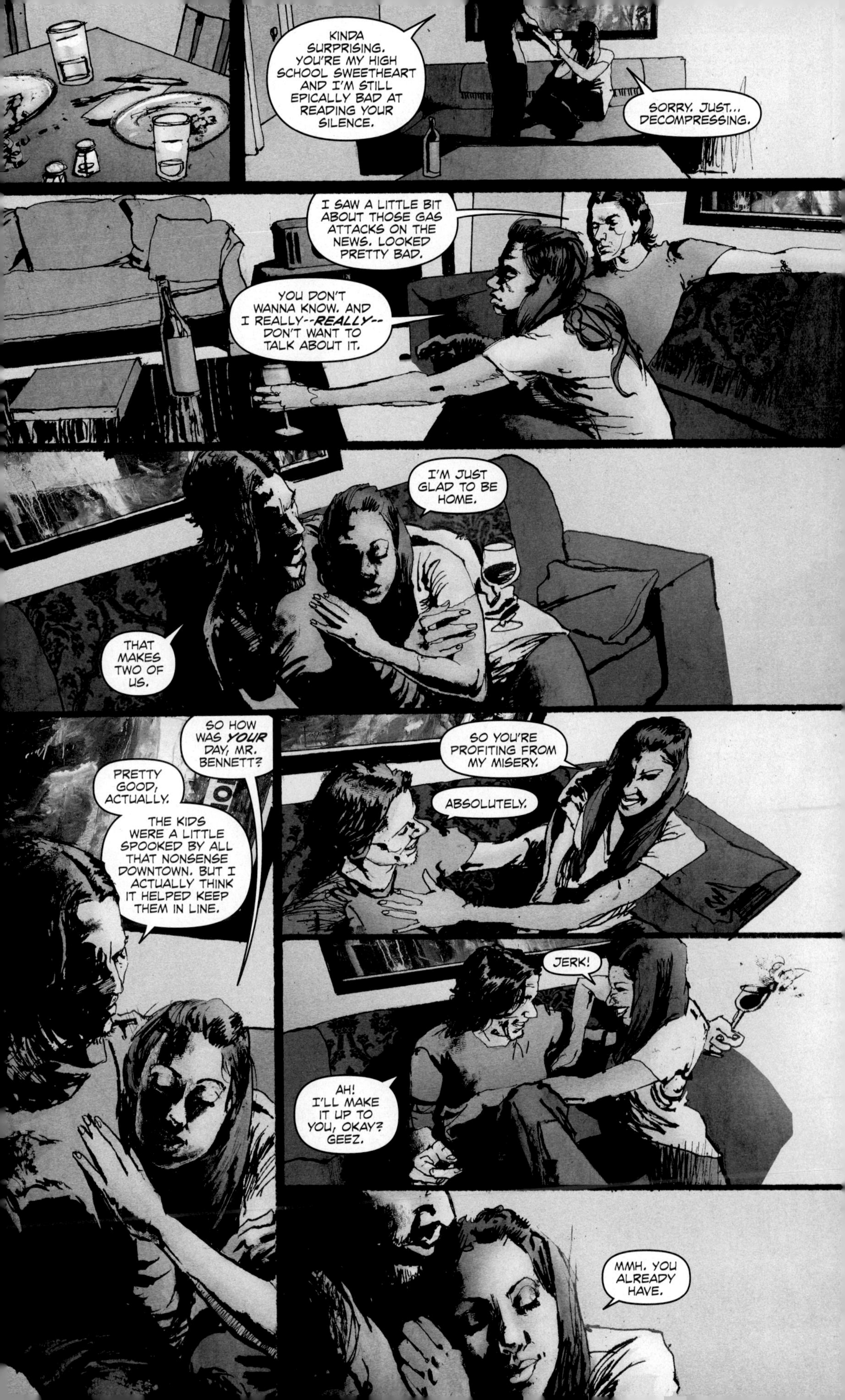

KINDA SURPRISING. YOU'RE MY HIGH SCHOOL SWEETHEART AND I'M STILL EPICALLY BAD AT READING YOUR SILENCE.
SORRY. JUST... DECOMPRESSING.
I SAW A LITTLE BIT ABOUT THOSE GAS ATTACKS ON THE NEWS. LOOKED PRETTY BAD.
YOU DON'T WANNA KNOW. AND I REALLY--*REALLY*--DON'T WANT TO TALK ABOUT IT.
I'M JUST GLAD TO BE HOME.
THAT MAKES TWO OF US.
SO HOW WAS *YOUR* DAY, MR. BENNETT?
PRETTY GOOD, ACTUALLY.
THE KIDS WERE A LITTLE SPOOKED BY ALL THAT NONSENSE DOWNTOWN. BUT I ACTUALLY THINK IT HELPED KEEP THEM IN LINE.
SO YOU'RE PROFITING FROM MY MISERY.
ABSOLUTELY.
JERK!
AH! I'LL MAKE IT UP TO YOU, OKAY? GEEZ.
MMH. YOU ALREADY HAVE.

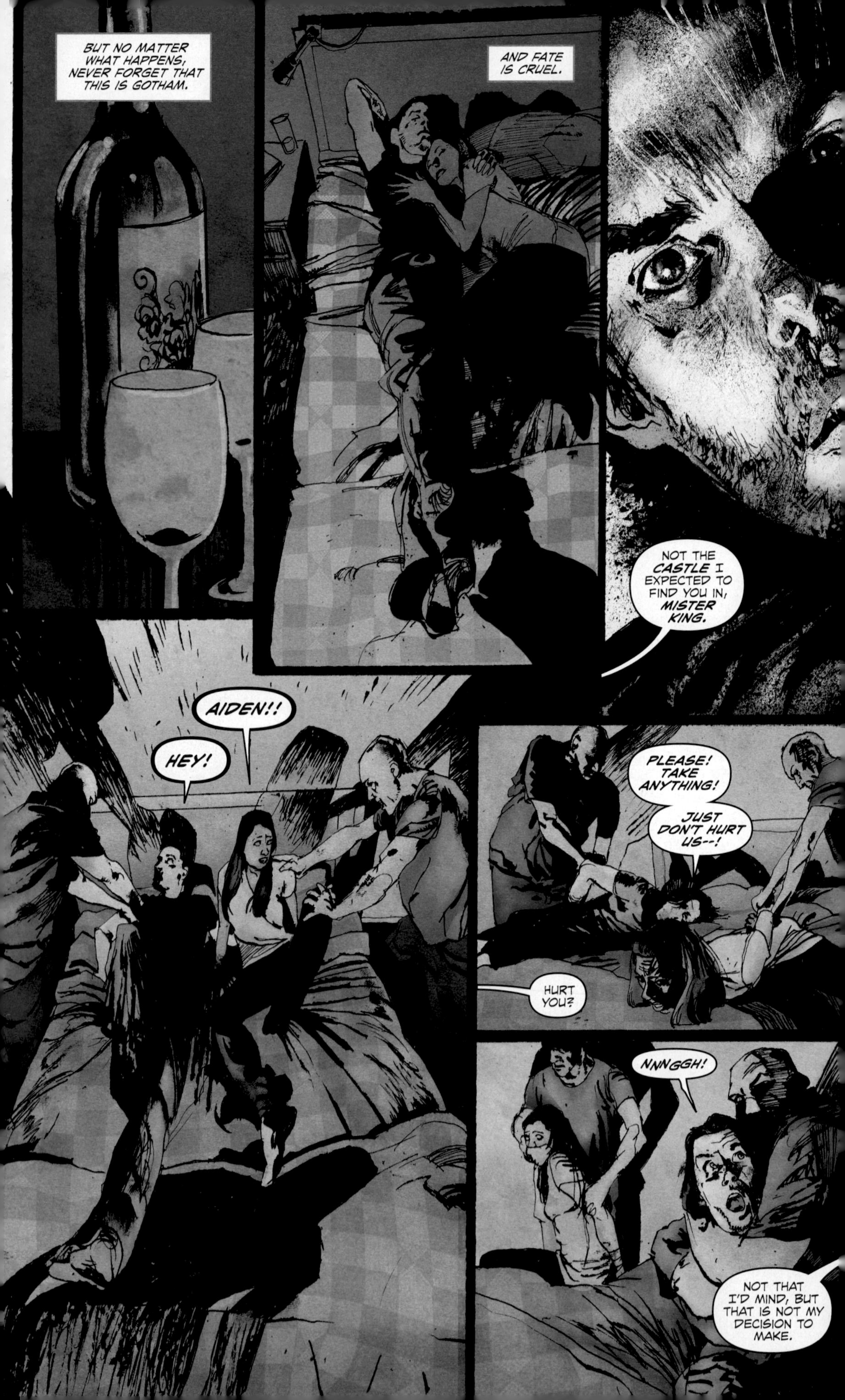
BUT NO MATTER WHAT HAPPENS, NEVER FORGET THAT THIS IS GOTHAM.
AND FATE IS CRUEL.
NOT THE CASTLE I EXPECTED TO FIND YOU IN, MISTER KING.
AIDEN!!
HEY!
PLEASE! TAKE ANYTHING!
JUST DON'T HURT US--!
HURT YOU?
NNNGGH!
NOT THAT I'D MIND, BUT THAT IS NOT MY DECISION TO MAKE.

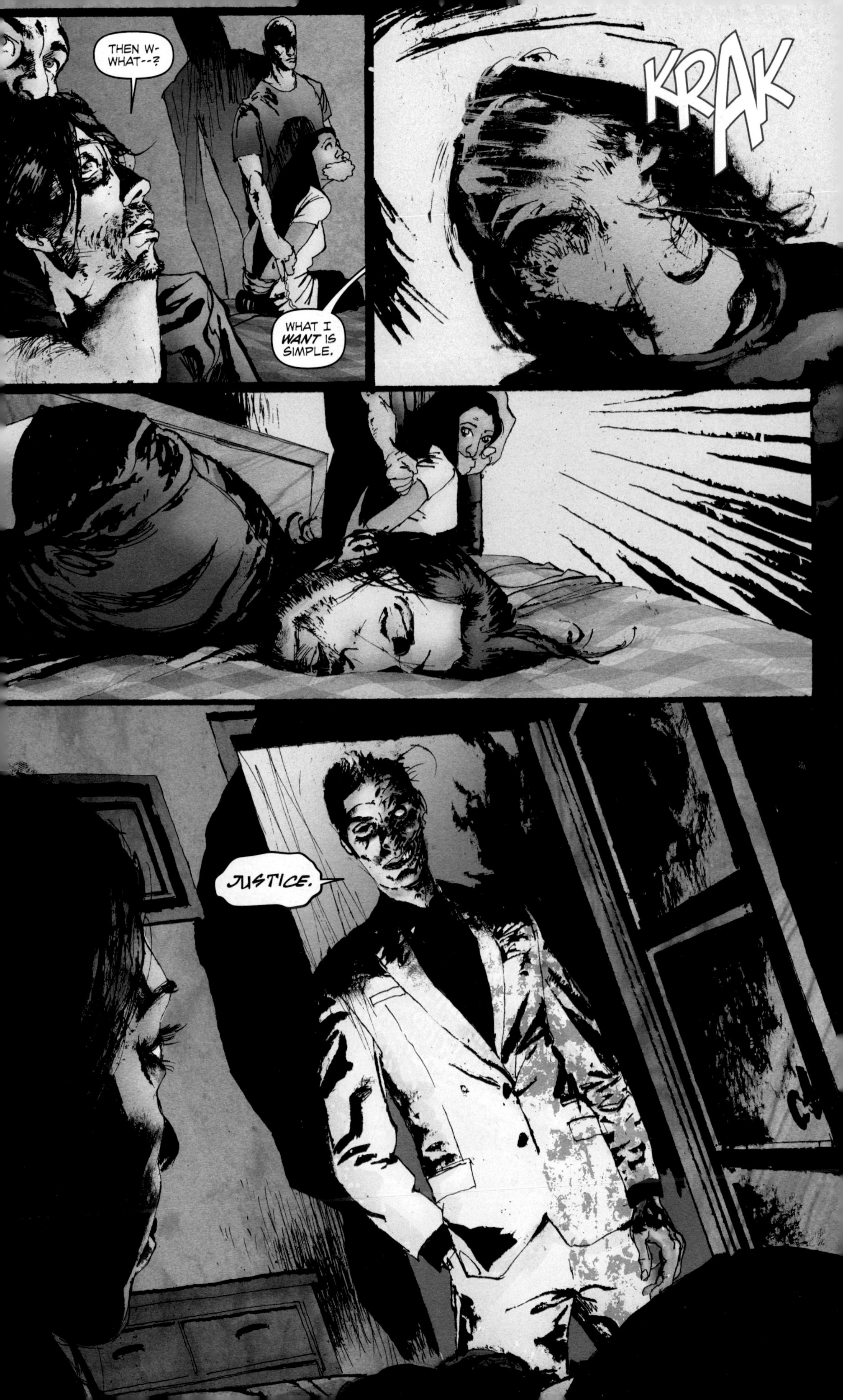
THEN W-WHAT--?
WHAT I WANT IS SIMPLE.
KRAK
JUSTICE.

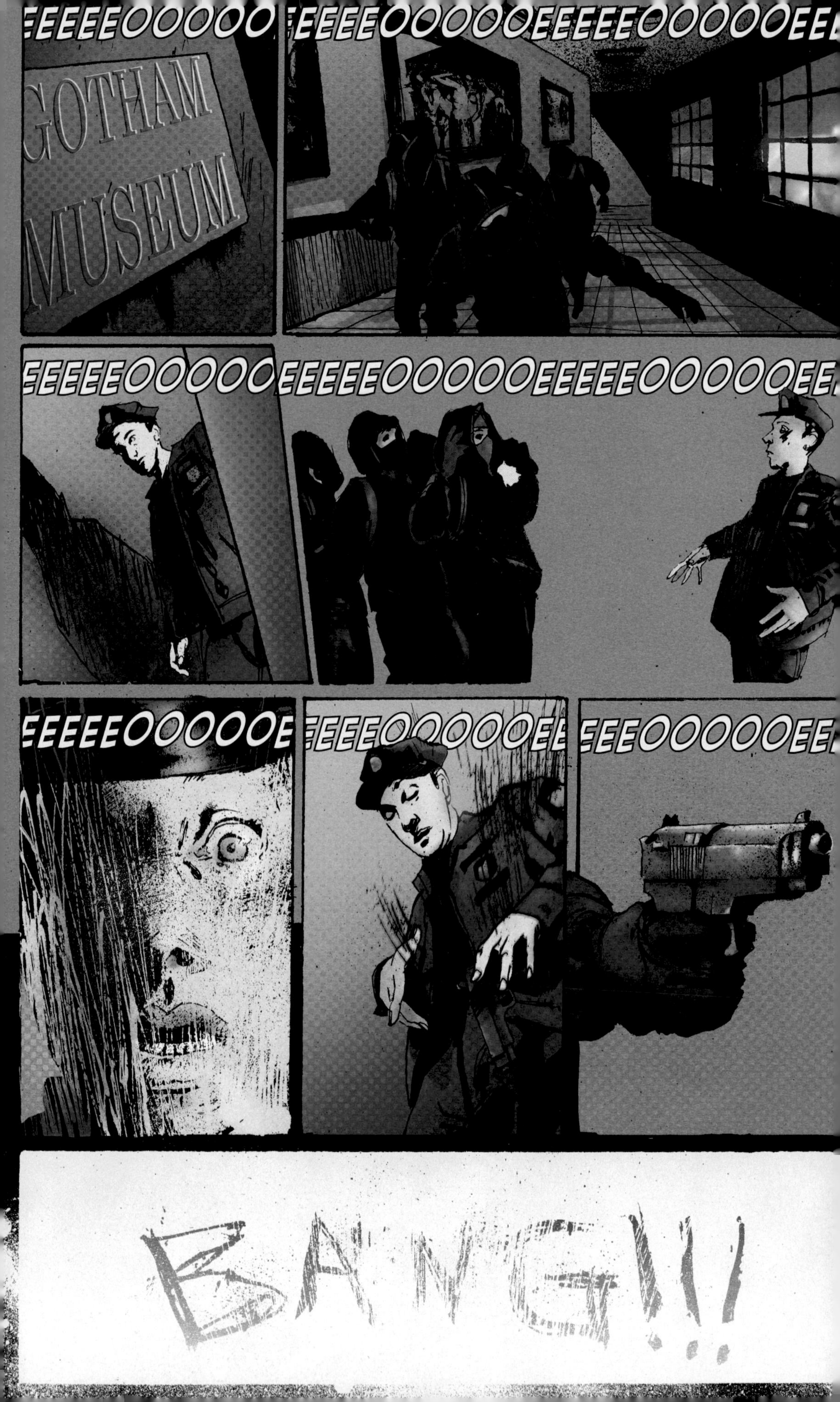

EEEEEOOOOO
EEEEEOOOOOEEEEEOOOOOEE
GOTHAM MUSEUM
EEEEEOOOOO
EEEEEOOOOOEEEEEOOOOOEE
EEEEEOOOOOE
EEEEOOOOOEE
EEEOOOOOEE
BANG!!

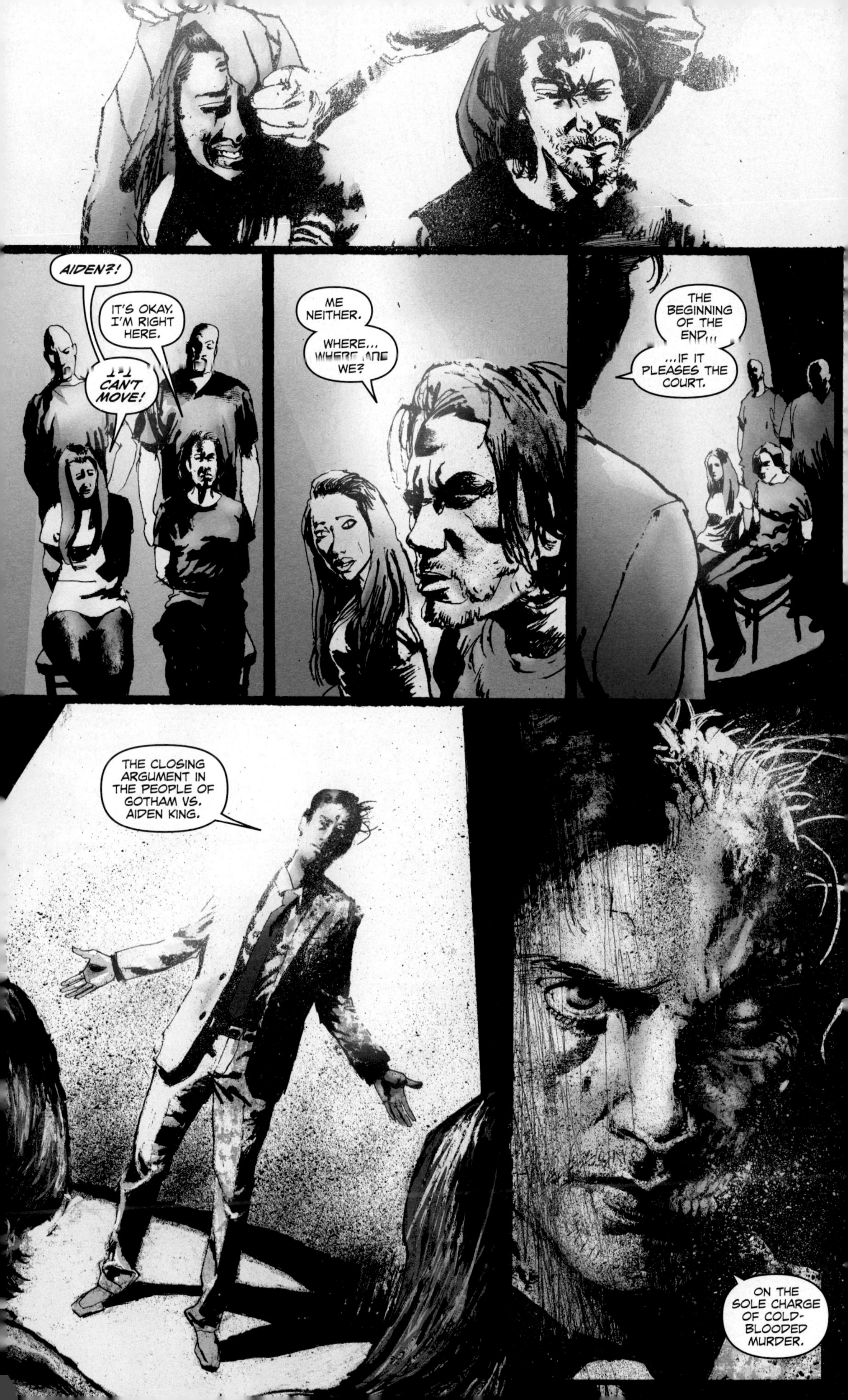
AIDEN?!
IT'S OKAY. I'M RIGHT HERE.
CAN'T MOVE!
ME NEITHER.
WHERE... WHERE ARE WE?
THE BEGINNING OF THE END...
...IF IT PLEASES THE COURT.
THE CLOSING ARGUMENT IN THE PEOPLE OF GOTHAM VS. AIDEN KING.
ON THE SOLE CHARGE OF COLD-BLOODED MURDER.

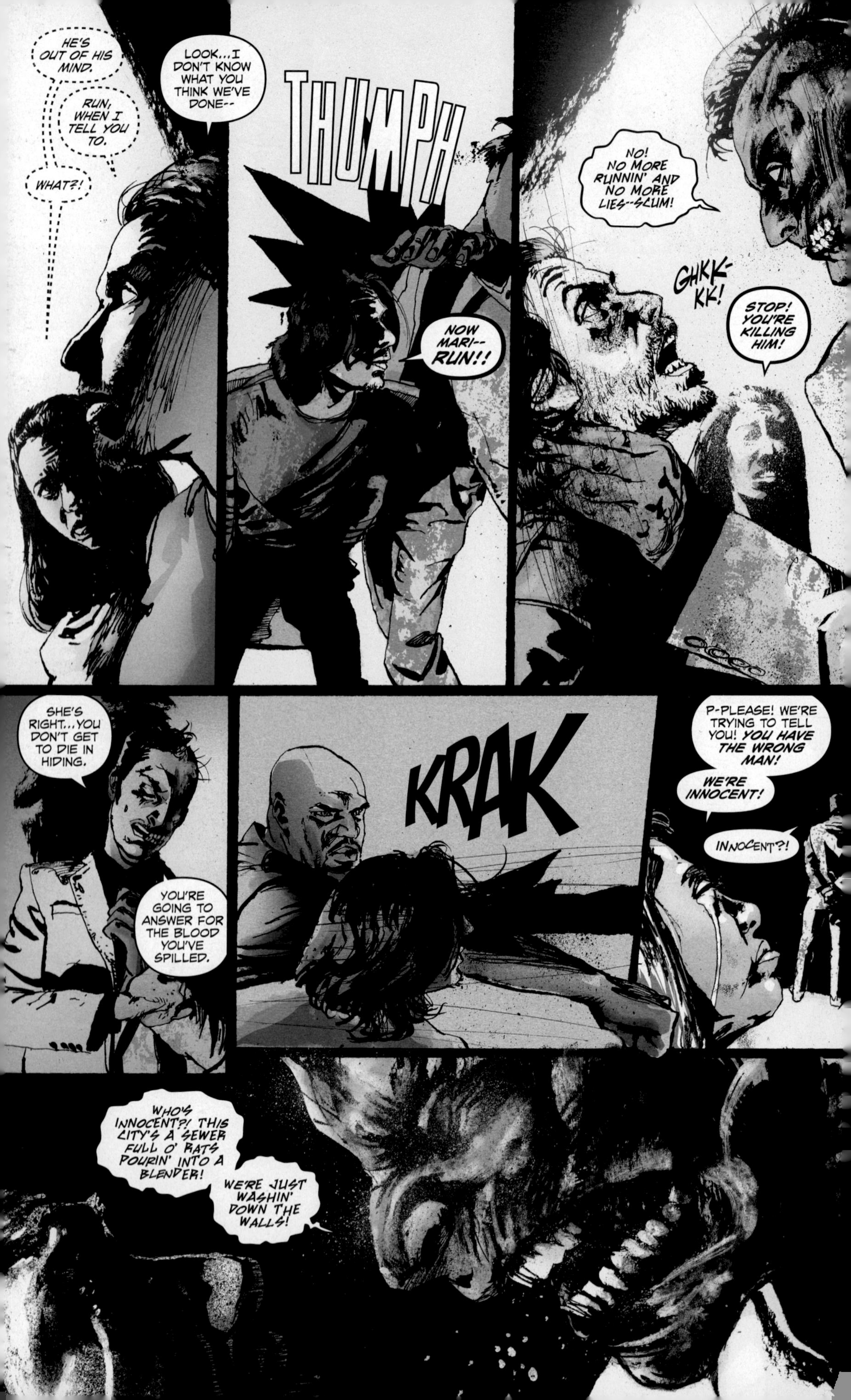
HE'S OUT OF HIS MIND.
RUN, WHEN I TELL YOU TO.
WHAT?!
LOOK...I DON'T KNOW WHAT YOU THINK WE'VE DONE--
THUMPH
NOW MARI-- RUN!!
NO! NO MORE RUNNIN' AND NO MORE LIES--SCUM!
GHKK-KK!
STOP! YOU'RE KILLING HIM!
SHE'S RIGHT...YOU DON'T GET TO DIE IN HIDING.
YOU'RE GOING TO ANSWER FOR THE BLOOD YOU'VE SPILLED.
KRAK
P-PLEASE! WE'RE TRYING TO TELL YOU! YOU HAVE THE WRONG MAN!
WE'RE INNOCENT!
INNOCENT?!
WHO'S INNOCENT?! THIS CITY'S A SEWER FULL O' RATS POURIN' INTO A BLENDER!
WE'RE JUST WASHIN' DOWN THE WALLS!

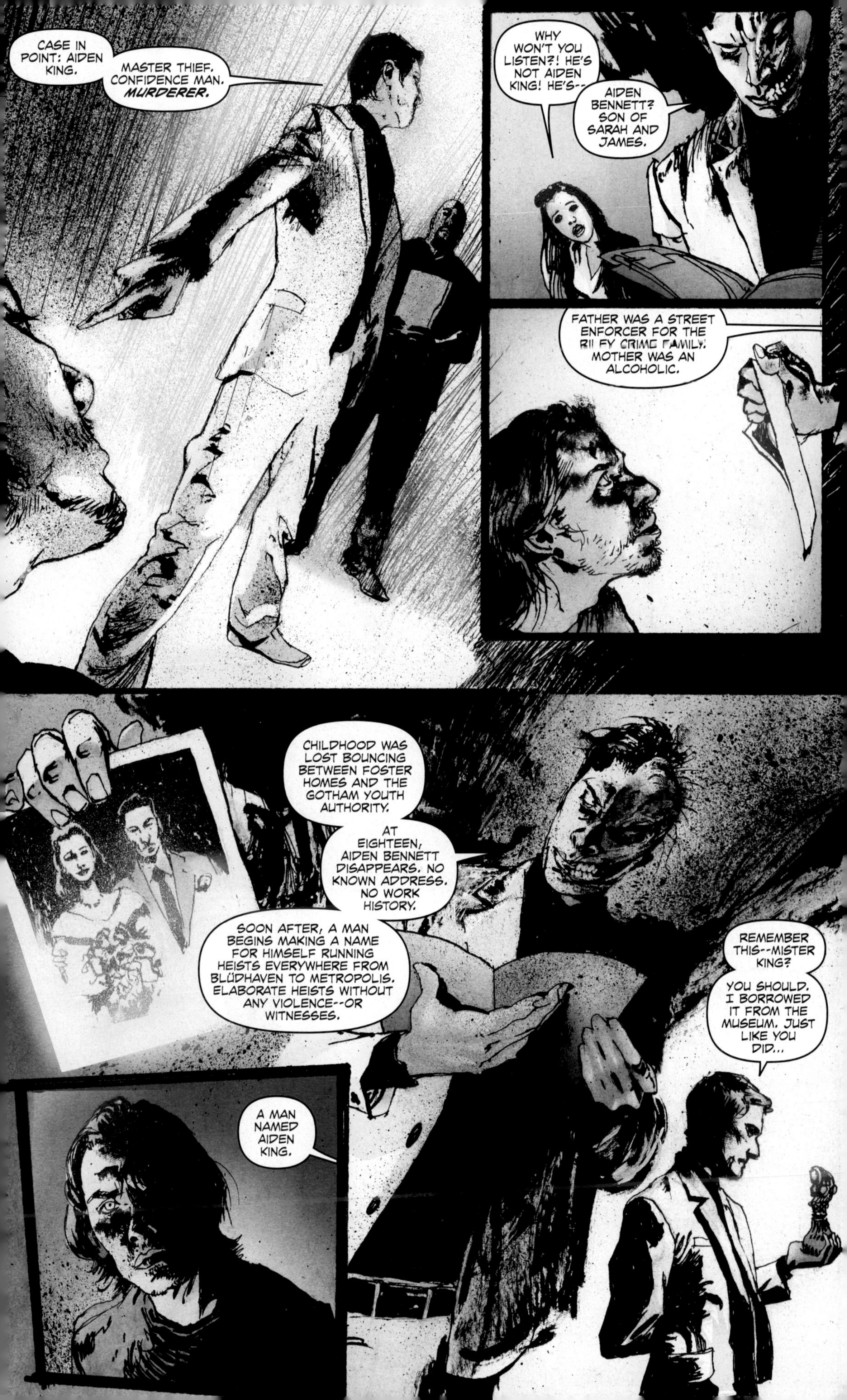
CASE IN POINT: AIDEN KING.
MASTER THIEF. CONFIDENCE MAN. ***MURDERER.***
WHY WON'T YOU LISTEN?! HE'S NOT AIDEN KING! HE'S--
AIDEN BENNETT? SON OF SARAH AND JAMES.
FATHER WAS A STREET ENFORCER FOR THE RILEY CRIME FAMILY. MOTHER WAS AN ALCOHOLIC.
CHILDHOOD WAS LOST BOUNCING BETWEEN FOSTER HOMES AND THE GOTHAM YOUTH AUTHORITY.
AT EIGHTEEN, AIDEN BENNETT DISAPPEARS. NO KNOWN ADDRESS. NO WORK HISTORY.
SOON AFTER, A MAN BEGINS MAKING A NAME FOR HIMSELF RUNNING HEISTS EVERYWHERE FROM BLÜDHAVEN TO METROPOLIS. ELABORATE HEISTS WITHOUT ANY VIOLENCE--OR WITNESSES.
A MAN NAMED AIDEN KING.
REMEMBER THIS--MISTER KING?
YOU SHOULD. I BORROWED IT FROM THE MUSEUM. JUST LIKE YOU DID...

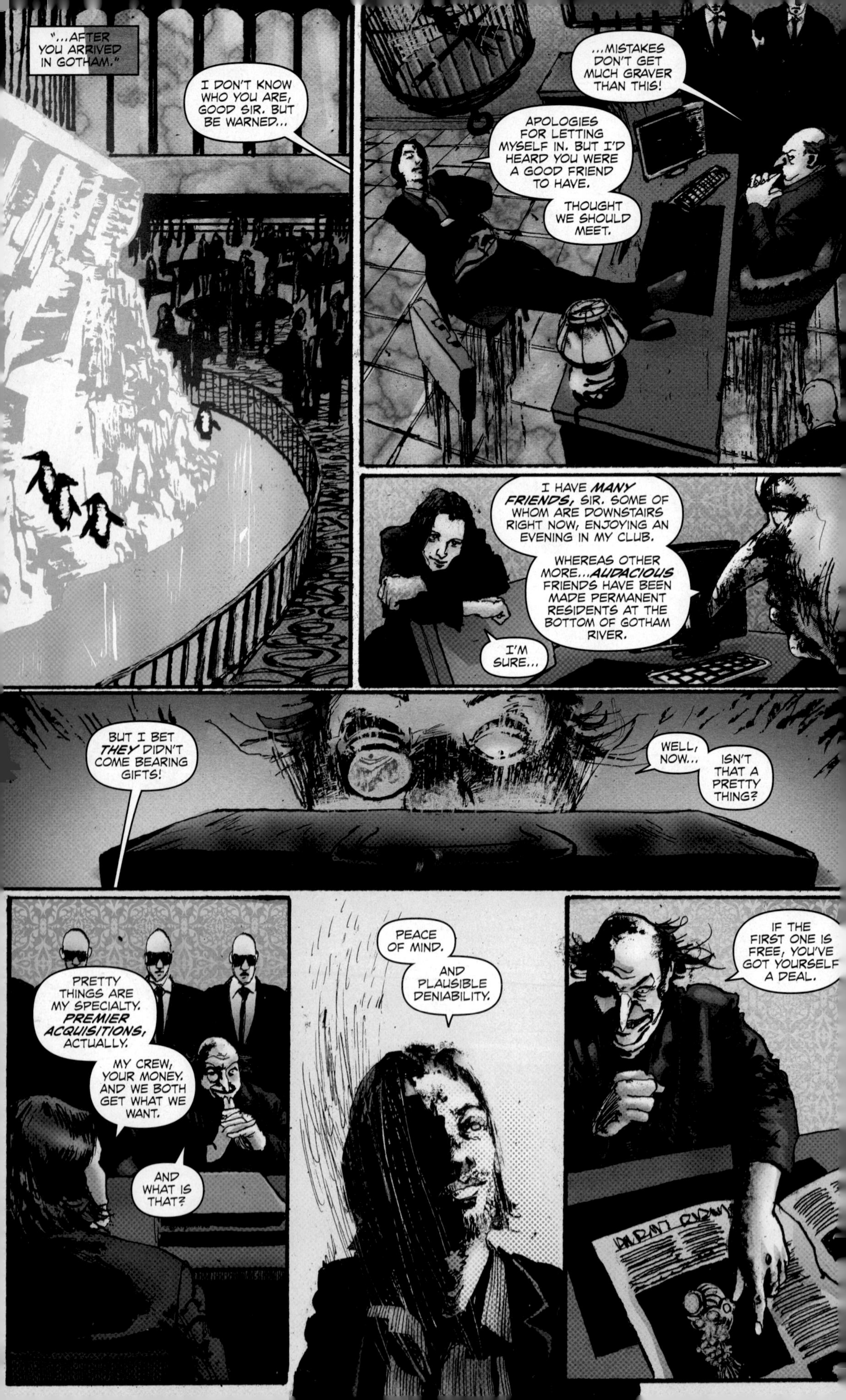
"...AFTER YOU ARRIVED IN GOTHAM."
I DON'T KNOW WHO YOU ARE, GOOD SIR. BUT BE WARNED...
APOLOGIES FOR LETTING MYSELF IN. BUT I'D HEARD YOU WERE A GOOD FRIEND TO HAVE.
THOUGHT WE SHOULD MEET.
...MISTAKES DON'T GET MUCH GRAVER THAN THIS!
I HAVE MANY FRIENDS, SIR. SOME OF WHOM ARE DOWNSTAIRS RIGHT NOW, ENJOYING AN EVENING IN MY CLUB.
WHEREAS OTHER MORE...AUDACIOUS FRIENDS HAVE BEEN MADE PERMANENT RESIDENTS AT THE BOTTOM OF GOTHAM RIVER.
I'M SURE...
BUT I BET THEY DIDN'T COME BEARING GIFTS!
WELL, NOW...
ISN'T THAT A PRETTY THING?
PRETTY THINGS ARE MY SPECIALTY. PREMIER ACQUISITIONS, ACTUALLY.
MY CREW, YOUR MONEY. AND WE BOTH GET WHAT WE WANT.
AND WHAT IS THAT?
PEACE OF MIND.
AND PLAUSIBLE DENIABILITY.
IF THE FIRST ONE IS FREE, YOU'VE GOT YOURSELF A DEAL.

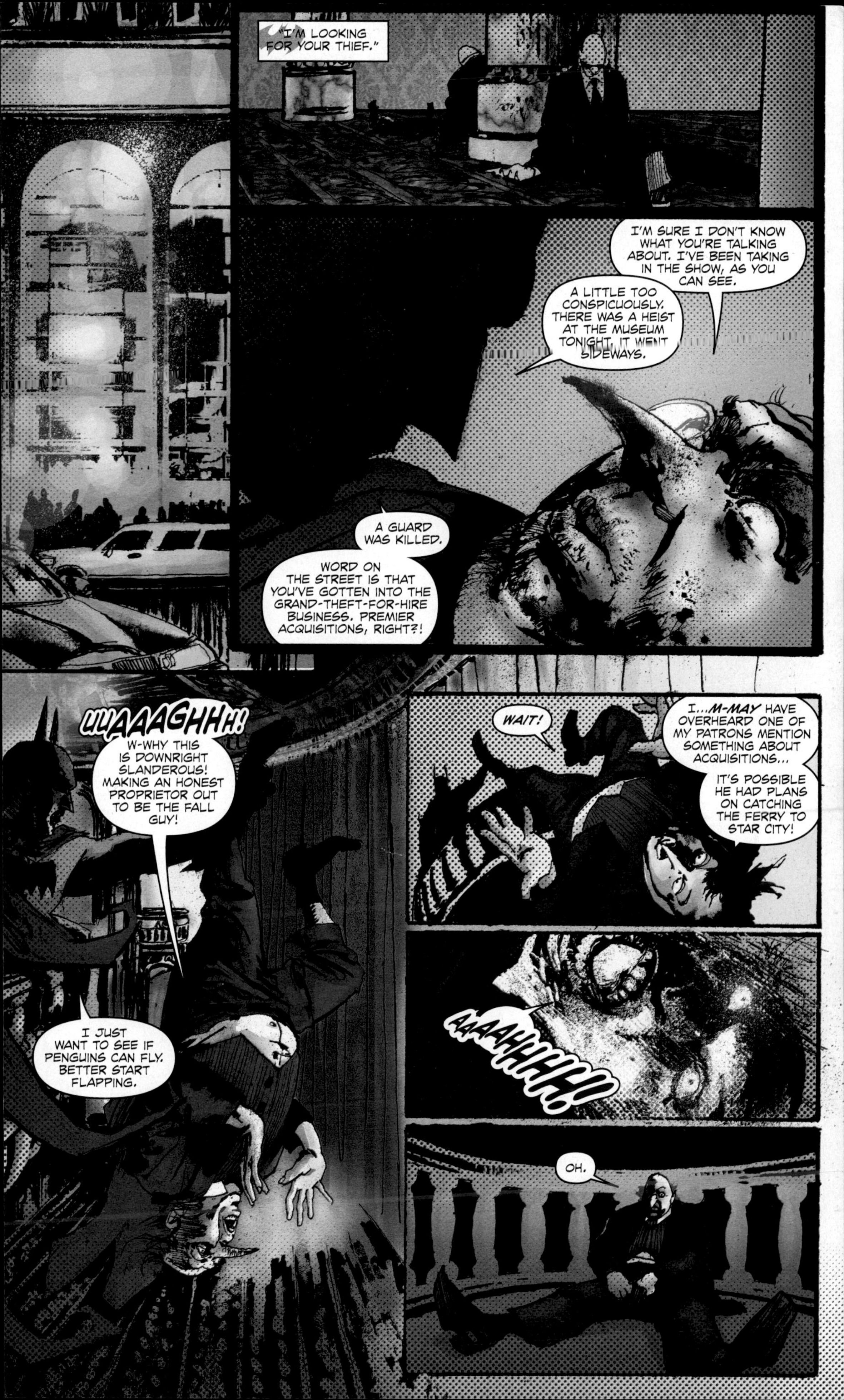
"I'M LOOKING FOR YOUR THIEF."
I'M SURE I DON'T KNOW WHAT YOU'RE TALKING ABOUT. I'VE BEEN TAKING IN THE SHOW, AS YOU CAN SEE.
A LITTLE TOO CONSPICUOUSLY. THERE WAS A HEIST AT THE MUSEUM TONIGHT. IT WENT SIDEWAYS.
A GUARD WAS KILLED.
WORD ON THE STREET IS THAT YOU'VE GOTTEN INTO THE GRAND-THEFT-FOR-HIRE BUSINESS. PREMIER ACQUISITIONS, RIGHT?!
UUAAAGHHH!
W-WHY THIS IS DOWNRIGHT SLANDEROUS! MAKING AN HONEST PROPRIETOR OUT TO BE THE FALL GUY!
I JUST WANT TO SEE IF PENGUINS CAN FLY. BETTER START FLAPPING.
WAIT!
I...M-MAY HAVE OVERHEARD ONE OF MY PATRONS MENTION SOMETHING ABOUT ACQUISITIONS...
IT'S POSSIBLE HE HAD PLANS ON CATCHING THE FERRY TO STAR CITY!
AAAAHHHH!
OH.

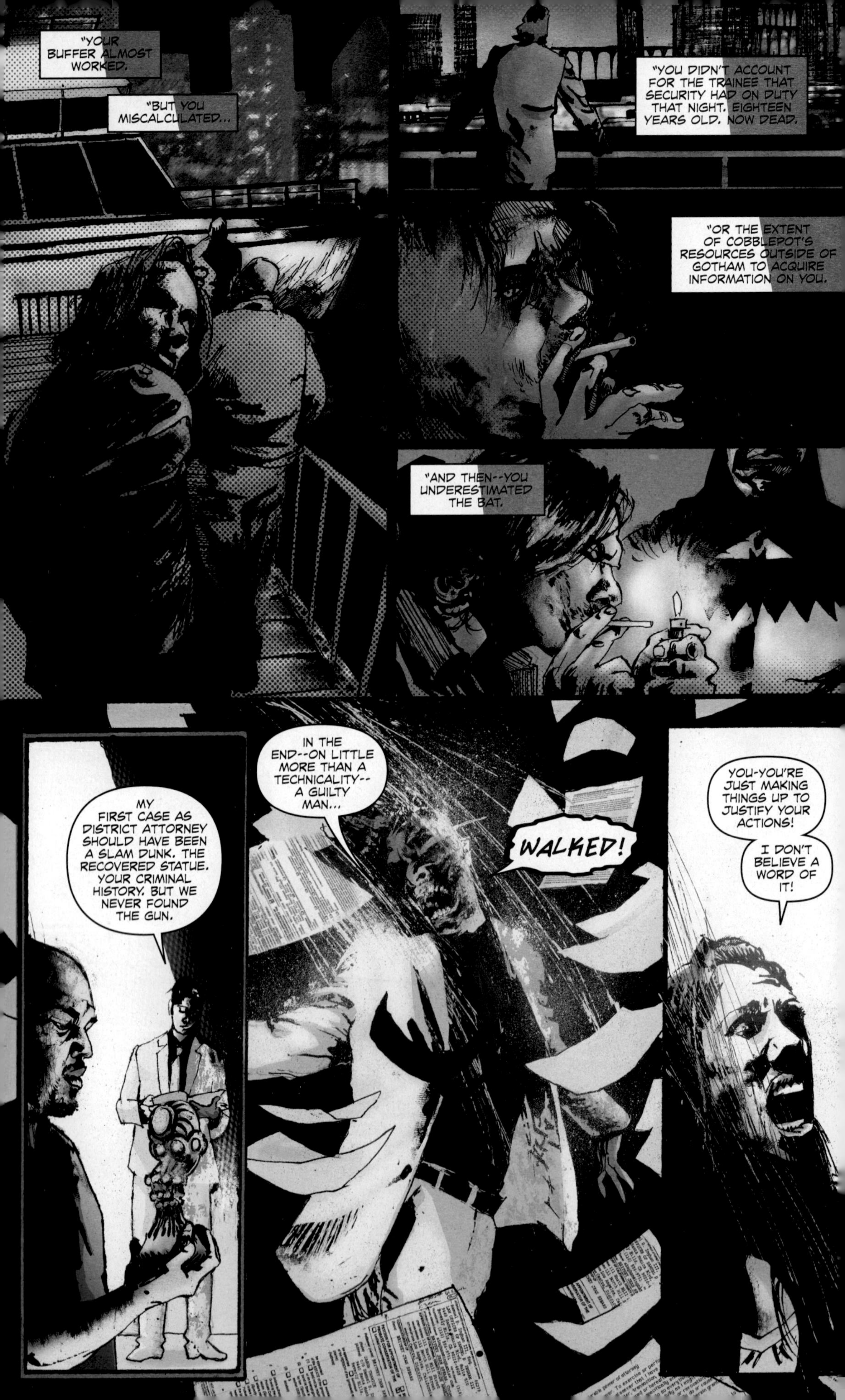
"YOUR BUFFER ALMOST WORKED.
"BUT YOU MISCALCULATED...
"YOU DIDN'T ACCOUNT FOR THE TRAINEE THAT SECURITY HAD ON DUTY THAT NIGHT. EIGHTEEN YEARS OLD. NOW DEAD.
"OR THE EXTENT OF COBBLEPOT'S RESOURCES OUTSIDE OF GOTHAM TO ACQUIRE INFORMATION ON YOU.
"AND THEN--YOU UNDERESTIMATED THE BAT.
MY FIRST CASE AS DISTRICT ATTORNEY SHOULD HAVE BEEN A SLAM DUNK. THE RECOVERED STATUE. YOUR CRIMINAL HISTORY. BUT WE NEVER FOUND THE GUN.
IN THE END--ON LITTLE MORE THAN A TECHNICALITY--A GUILTY MAN...
WALKED!
YOU-YOU'RE JUST MAKING THINGS UP TO JUSTIFY YOUR ACTIONS!
I DON'T BELIEVE A WORD OF IT!

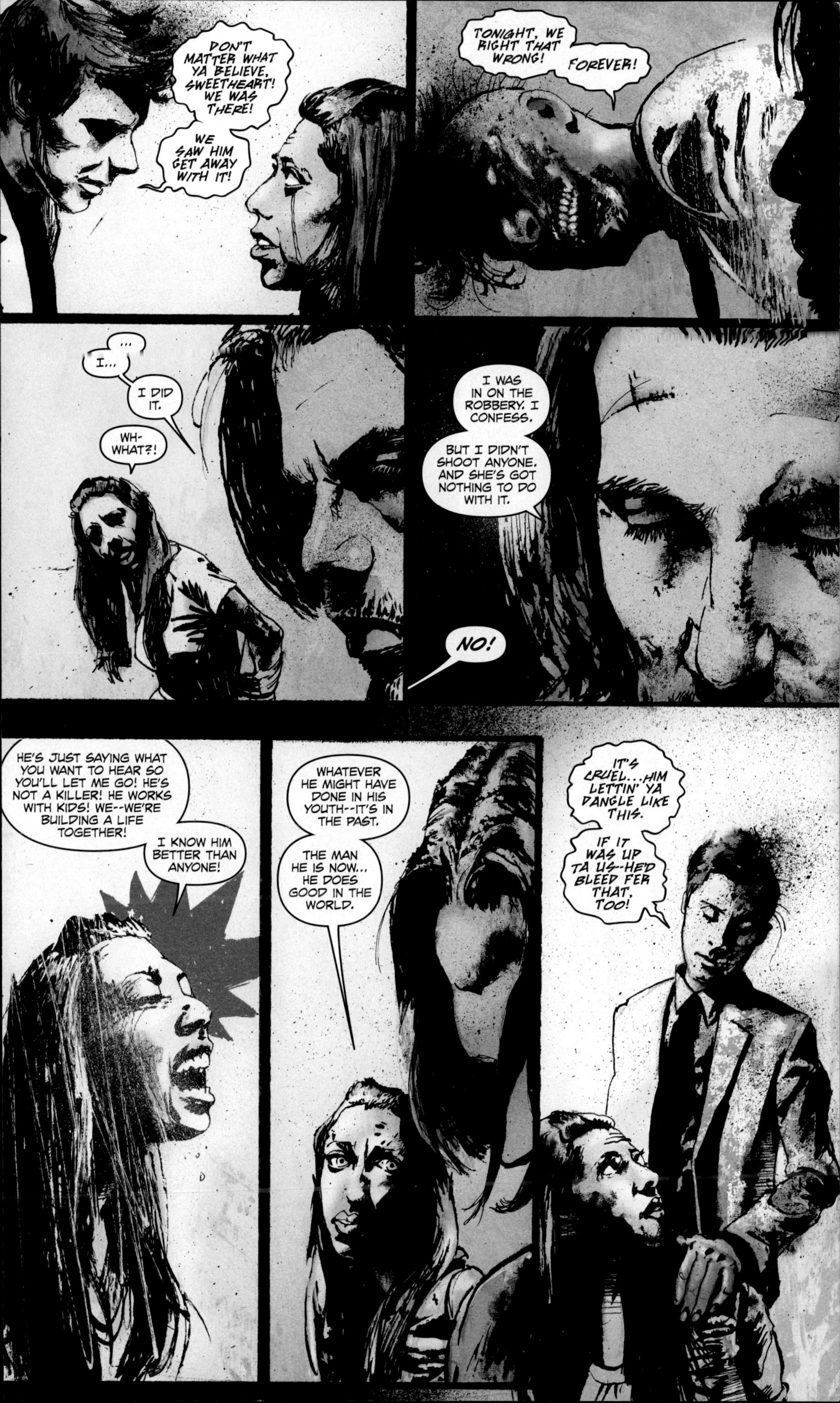
DON'T MATTER WHAT YA BELIEVE, SWEETHEART! WE WAS THERE!
WE SAW HIM GET AWAY WITH IT!
TONIGHT, WE RIGHT THAT WRONG!
FOREVER!
...
I...
I DID IT.
WH-WHAT?!
I WAS IN ON THE ROBBERY. I CONFESS.
BUT I DIDN'T SHOOT ANYONE. AND SHE'S GOT NOTHING TO DO WITH IT.
NO!
HE'S JUST SAYING WHAT YOU WANT TO HEAR SO YOU'LL LET ME GO! HE'S NOT A KILLER! HE WORKS WITH KIDS! WE--WE'RE BUILDING A LIFE TOGETHER!
I KNOW HIM BETTER THAN ANYONE!
WHATEVER HE MIGHT HAVE DONE IN HIS YOUTH--IT'S IN THE PAST.
THE MAN HE IS NOW... HE DOES GOOD IN THE WORLD.
IT'S CRUEL...HIM LETTIN' YA DANGLE LIKE THIS.
IF IT WAS UP TA US--HE'D BLEED FER THAT, TOO!

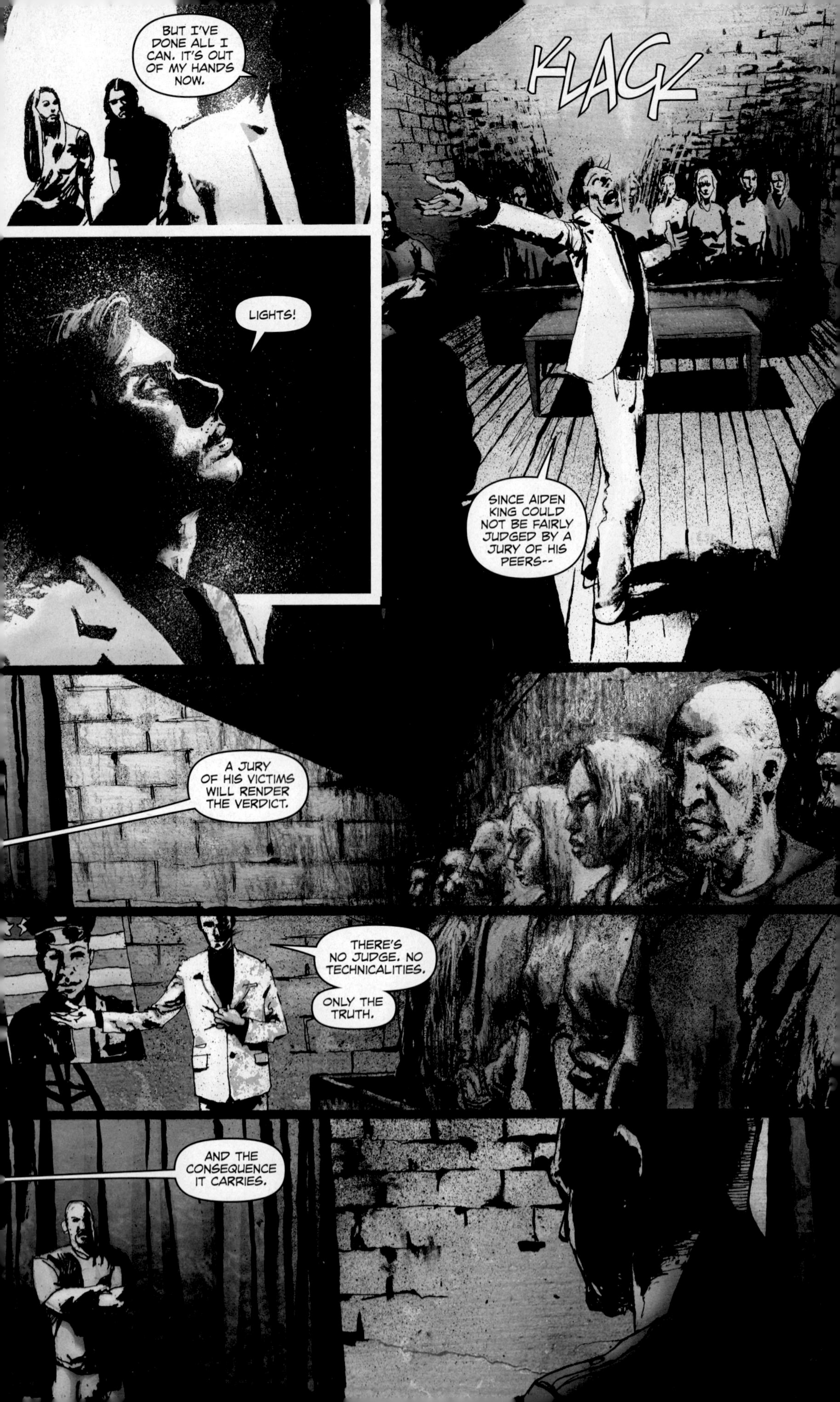
BUT I'VE DONE ALL I CAN. IT'S OUT OF MY HANDS NOW.
LIGHTS!
KLACK
SINCE AIDEN KING COULD NOT BE FAIRLY JUDGED BY A JURY OF HIS PEERS--
A JURY OF HIS VICTIMS WILL RENDER THE VERDICT.
THERE'S NO JUDGE. NO TECHNICALITIES.
ONLY THE TRUTH.
AND THE CONSEQUENCE IT CARRIES.

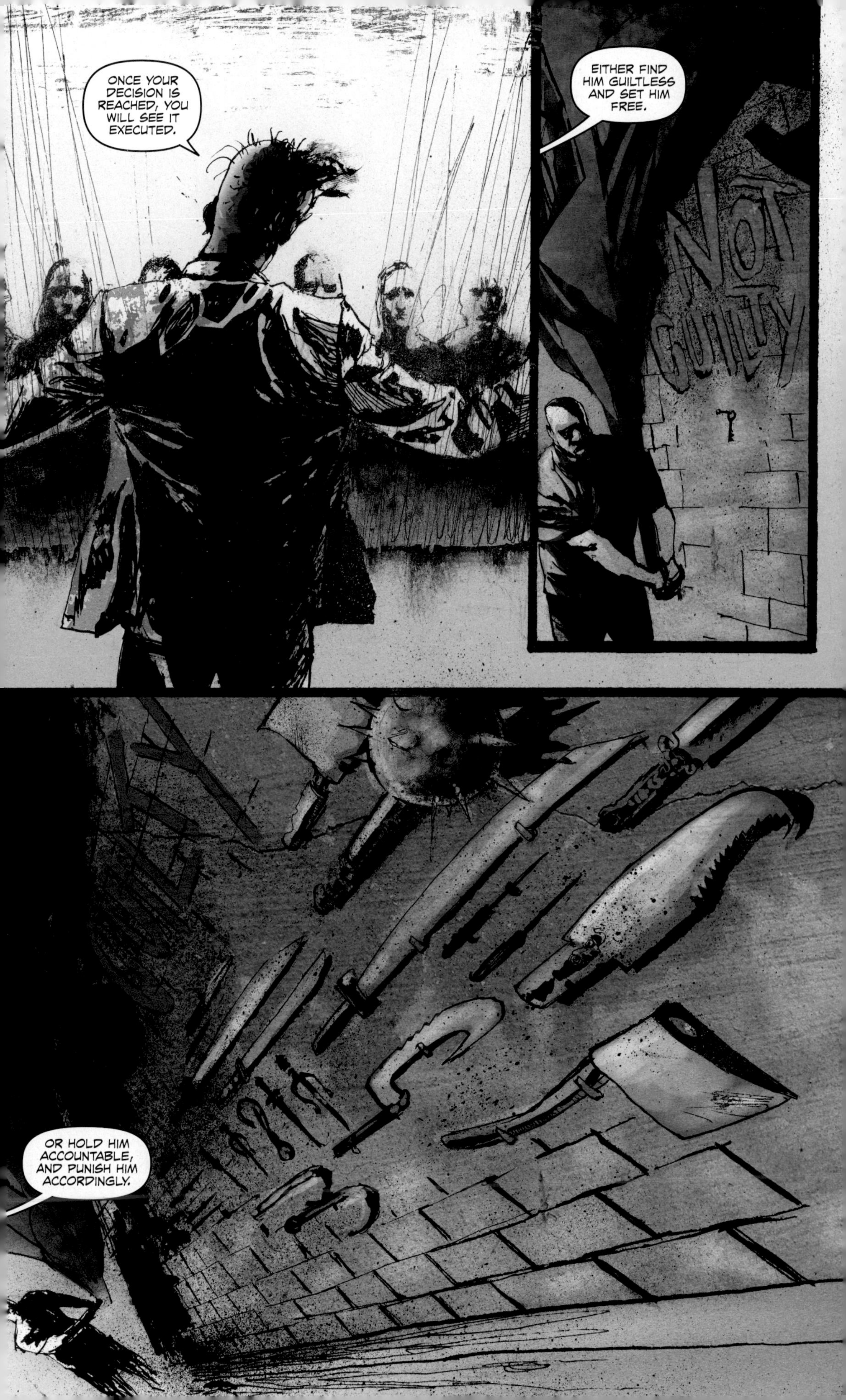
ONCE YOUR DECISION IS REACHED, YOU WILL SEE IT EXECUTED.
EITHER FIND HIM GUILTLESS AND SET HIM FREE.
NOT GUILTY
OR HOLD HIM ACCOUNTABLE, AND PUNISH HIM ACCORDINGLY.

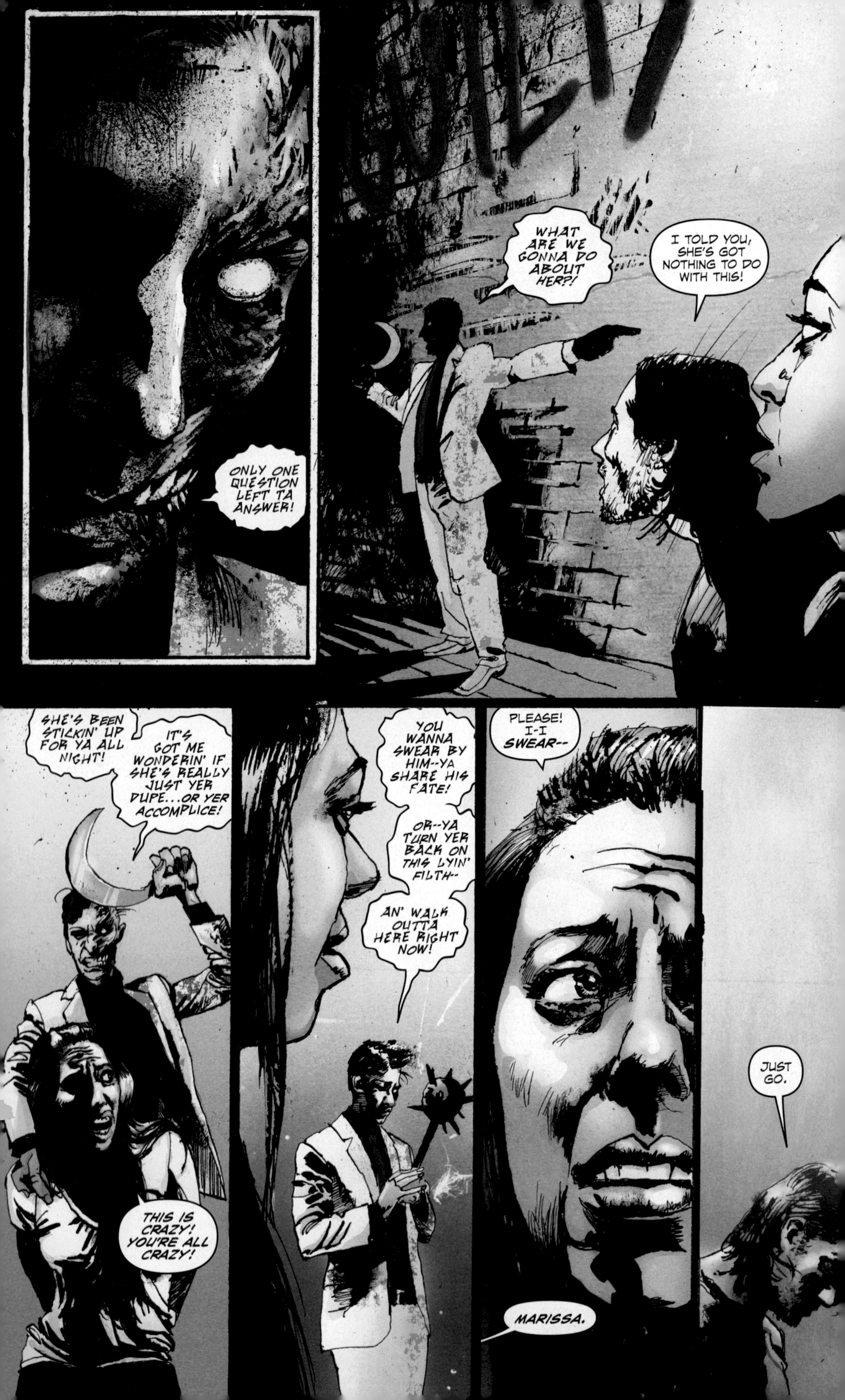
ONLY ONE QUESTION LEFT TA ANSWER!
WHAT ARE WE GONNA DO ABOUT HER?!
I TOLD YOU, SHE'S GOT NOTHING TO DO WITH THIS!
SHE'S BEEN STICKIN' UP FOR YA ALL NIGHT!
IT'S GOT ME WONDERIN' IF SHE'S REALLY JUST YER DUPE...OR YER ACCOMPLICE!
THIS IS CRAZY! YOU'RE ALL CRAZY!
YOU WANNA SWEAR BY HIM--YA SHARE HIS FATE!
OR--YA TURN YER BACK ON THIS LYIN' FILTH--
AN' WALK OUTTA HERE RIGHT NOW!
PLEASE! I-I SWEAR--
MARISSA.
JUST GO.

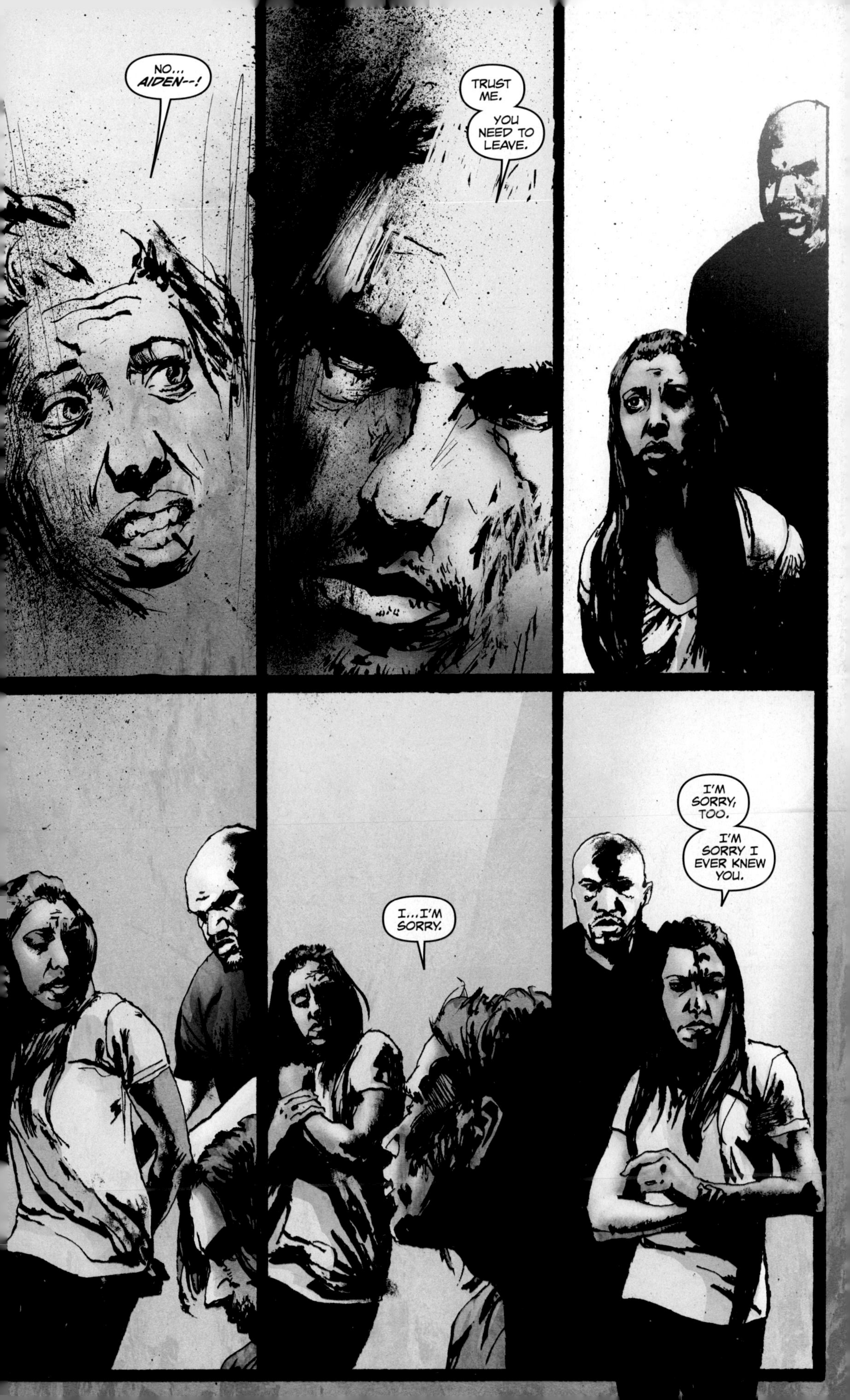
NO... AIDEN--!
TRUST ME.
YOU NEED TO LEAVE.
I...I'M SORRY.
I'M SORRY, TOO.
I'M SORRY I EVER KNEW YOU.

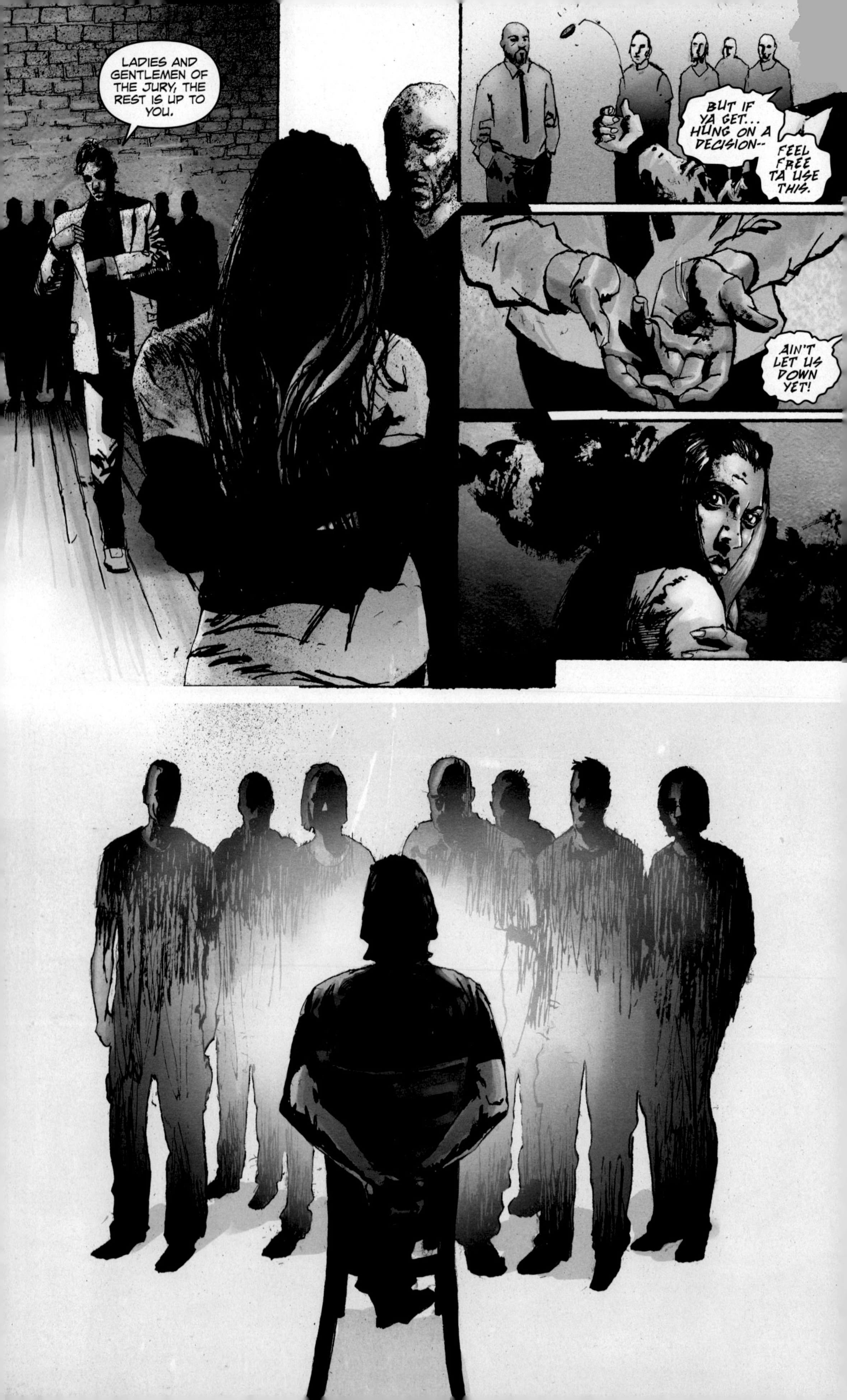
LADIES AND GENTLEMEN OF THE JURY, THE REST IS UP TO YOU.
BUT IF YA GET... HUNG ON A DECISION--
FEEL FREE TA USE THIS.
AIN'T LET US DOWN YET!

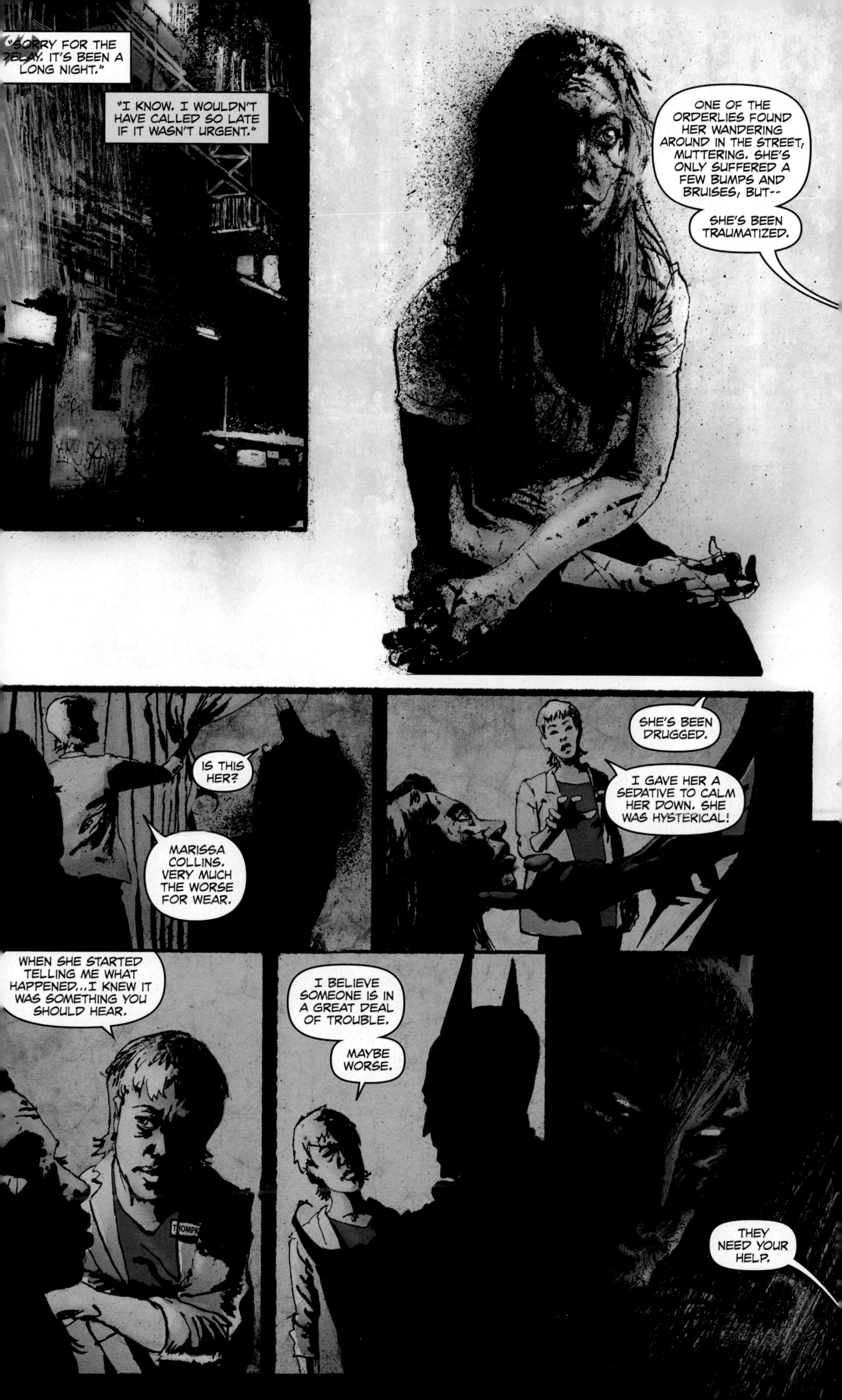
"SORRY FOR THE DELAY. IT'S BEEN A LONG NIGHT."
"I KNOW. I WOULDN'T HAVE CALLED SO LATE IF IT WASN'T URGENT."
ONE OF THE ORDERLIES FOUND HER WANDERING AROUND IN THE STREET, MUTTERING. SHE'S ONLY SUFFERED A FEW BUMPS AND BRUISES, BUT--
SHE'S BEEN TRAUMATIZED.
IS THIS HER?
MARISSA COLLINS. VERY MUCH THE WORSE FOR WEAR.
SHE'S BEEN DRUGGED.
I GAVE HER A SEDATIVE TO CALM HER DOWN. SHE WAS HYSTERICAL!
WHEN SHE STARTED TELLING ME WHAT HAPPENED...I KNEW IT WAS SOMETHING YOU SHOULD HEAR.
THOMPK
I BELIEVE SOMEONE IS IN A GREAT DEAL OF TROUBLE.
MAYBE WORSE.
THEY NEED YOUR HELP.

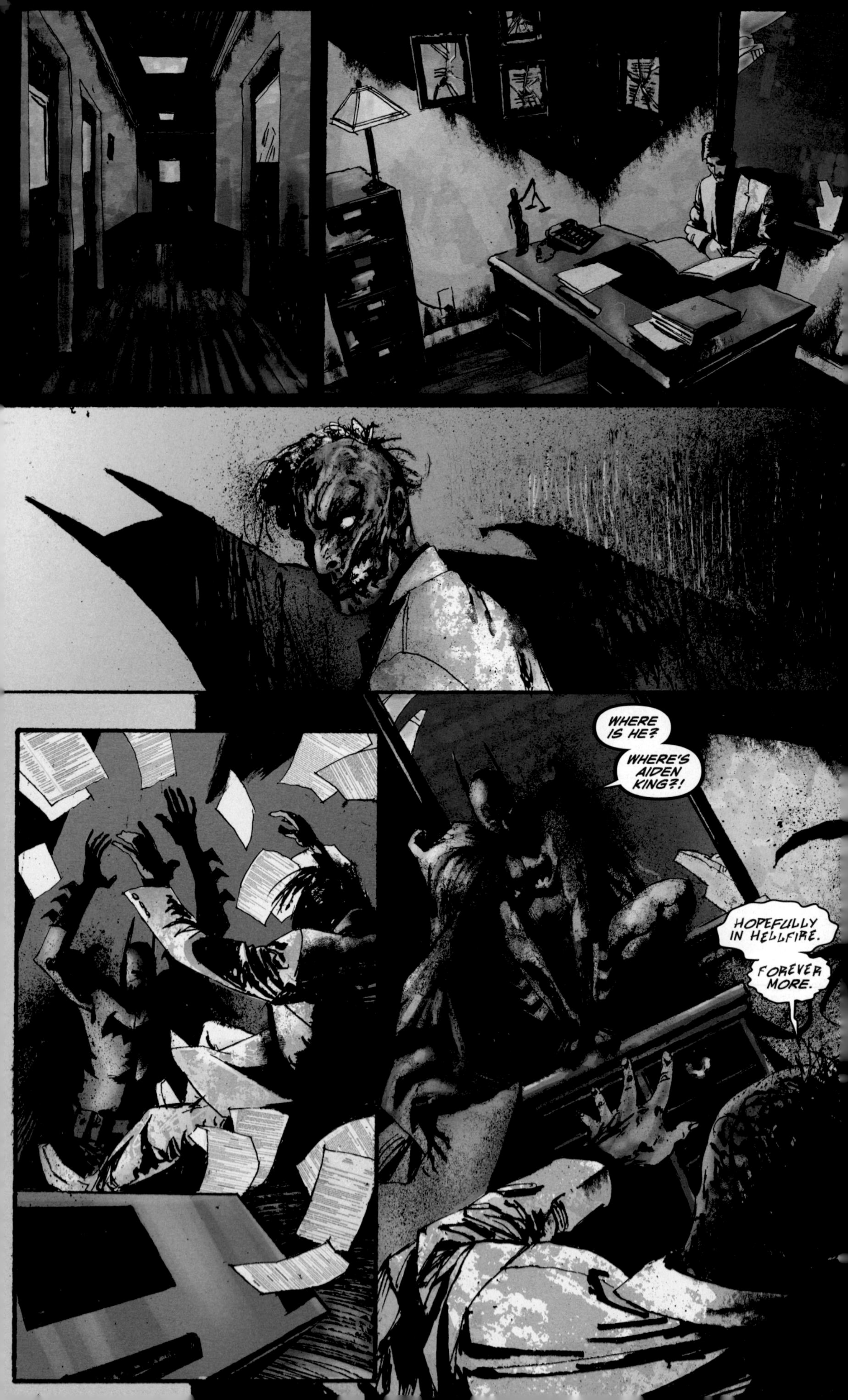
WHERE IS HE?
WHERE'S AIDEN KING?!
HOPEFULLY IN HELLFIRE.
FOREVER MORE.

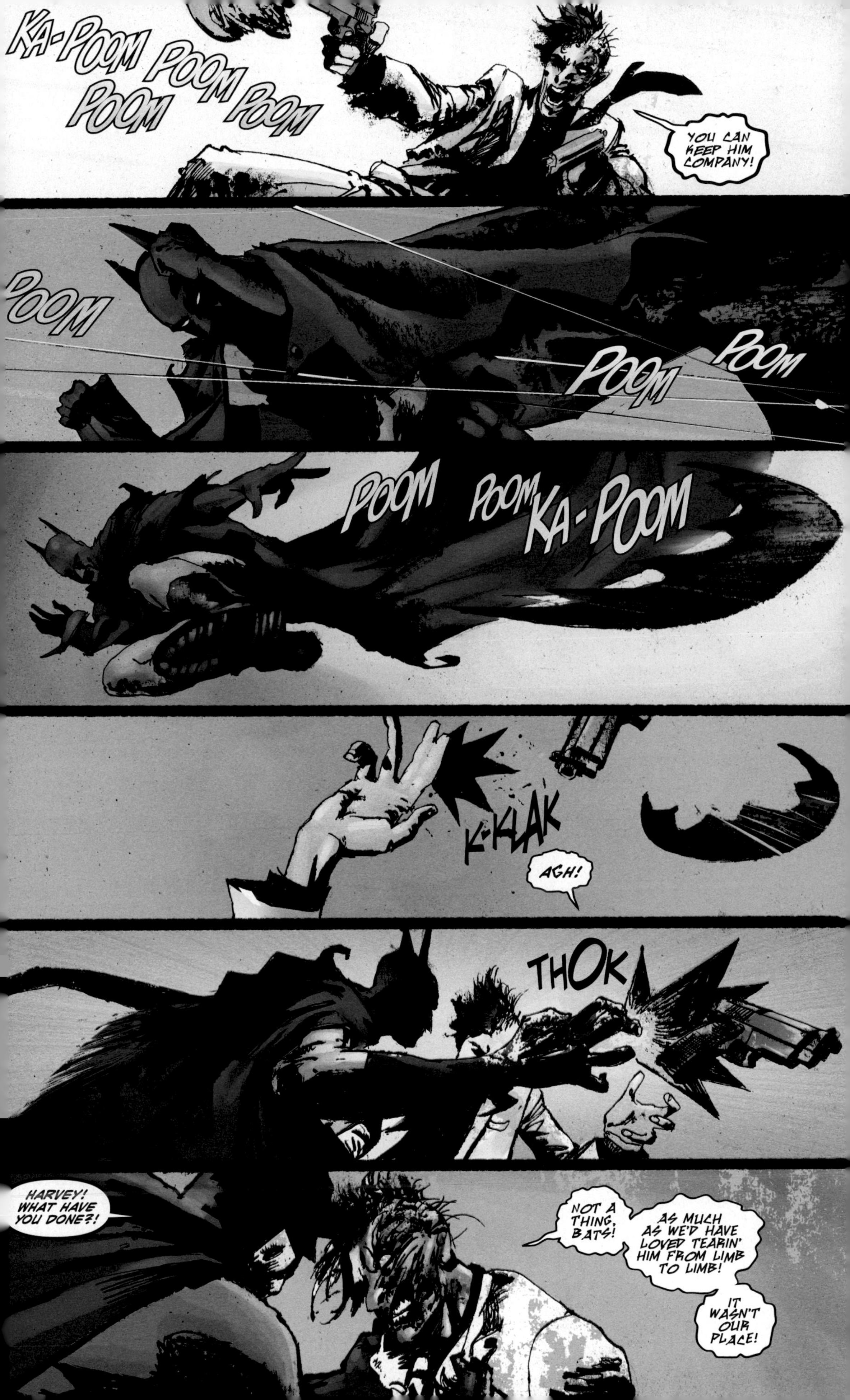
KA-POOM POOM POOM POOM
YOU CAN KEEP HIM COMPANY!
POOM
POOM POOM
POOM POOM KA-POOM
K-KLAK
AGH!
THOK
HARVEY! WHAT HAVE YOU DONE?!
NOT A THING, BATS!
AS MUCH AS WE'D HAVE LOVED TEARIN' HIM FROM LIMB TO LIMB!
IT WASN'T OUR PLACE!

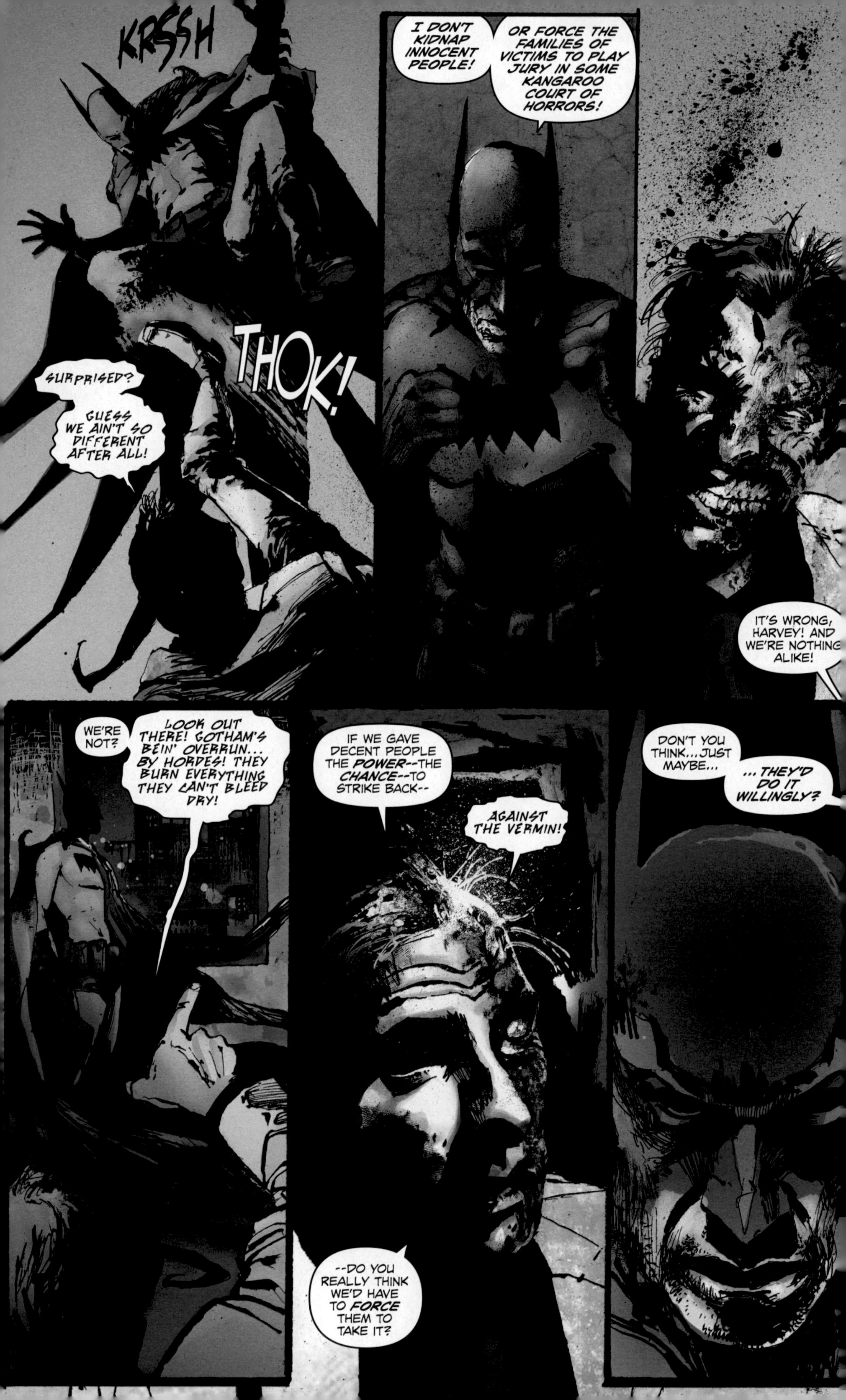
KRSSH
THOK!
SURPRISED?
GUESS WE AIN'T SO DIFFERENT AFTER ALL!
I DON'T KIDNAP INNOCENT PEOPLE!
OR FORCE THE FAMILIES OF VICTIMS TO PLAY JURY IN SOME KANGAROO COURT OF HORRORS!
IT'S WRONG, HARVEY! AND WE'RE NOTHING ALIKE!
WE'RE NOT?
LOOK OUT THERE! GOTHAM'S BEIN' OVERRUN... BY HORDES! THEY BURN EVERYTHING THEY CAN'T BLEED DRY!
IF WE GAVE DECENT PEOPLE THE POWER--THE CHANCE--TO STRIKE BACK--
AGAINST THE VERMIN!
--DO YOU REALLY THINK WE'D HAVE TO FORCE THEM TO TAKE IT?
DON'T YOU THINK...JUST MAYBE...
...THEY'D DO IT WILLINGLY?

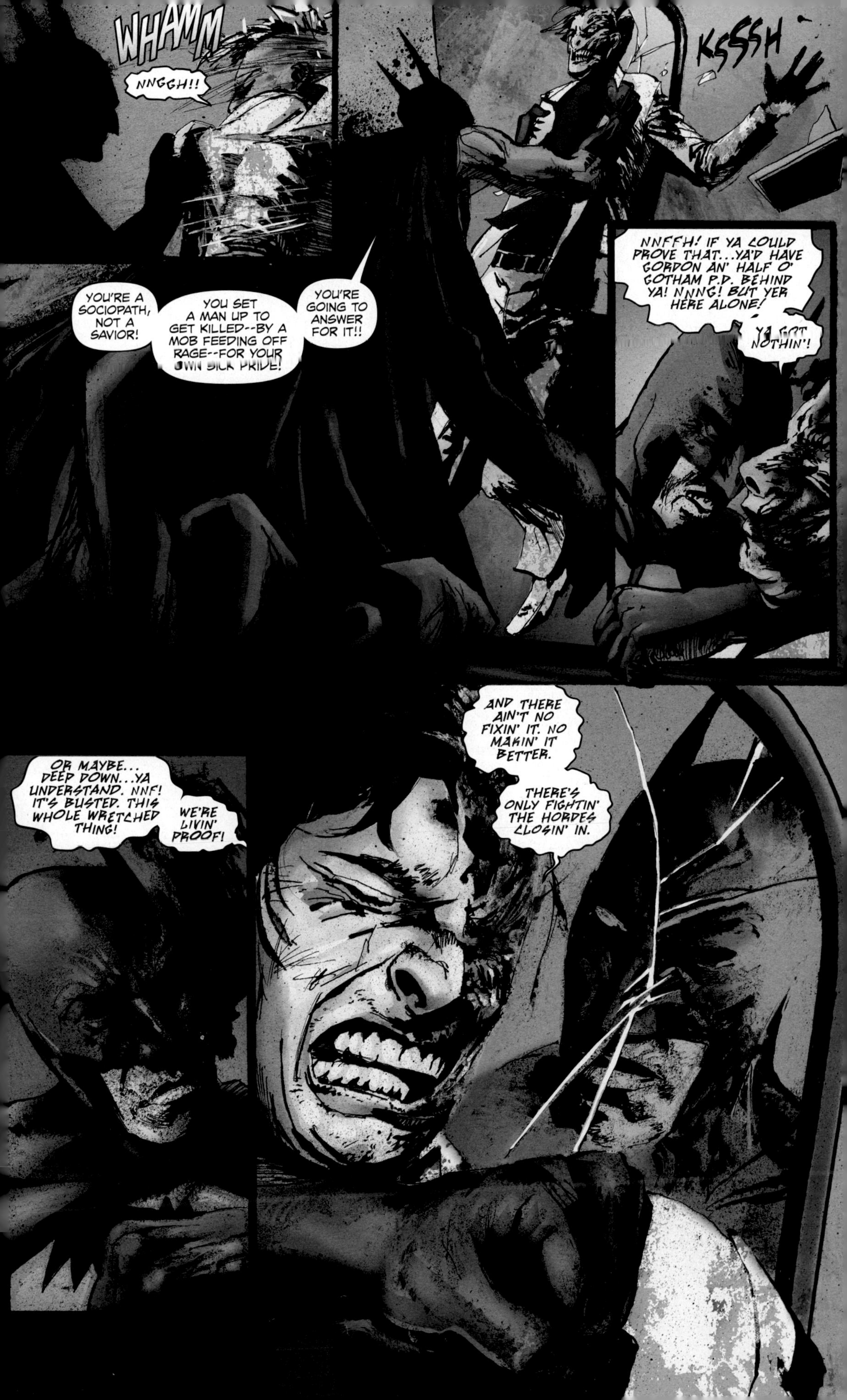
WHAMM
NNGGH!!
KSSSH
YOU'RE A SOCIOPATH, NOT A SAVIOR!
YOU SET A MAN UP TO GET KILLED--BY A MOB FEEDING OFF RAGE--FOR YOUR OWN SICK PRIDE!
YOU'RE GOING TO ANSWER FOR IT!!
NNFFH! IF YA COULD PROVE THAT...YA'D HAVE GORDON AN' HALF O' GOTHAM P.D. BEHIND YA! NNNG! BUT YER HERE ALONE!
YA GOT NOTHIN'!
OR MAYBE... DEEP DOWN...YA UNDERSTAND. NNF! IT'S BUSTED. THIS WHOLE WRETCHED THING!
WE'RE LIVIN' PROOF!
AND THERE AIN'T NO FIXIN' IT. NO MAKIN' IT BETTER.
THERE'S ONLY FIGHTIN' THE HORDES CLOSIN' IN.

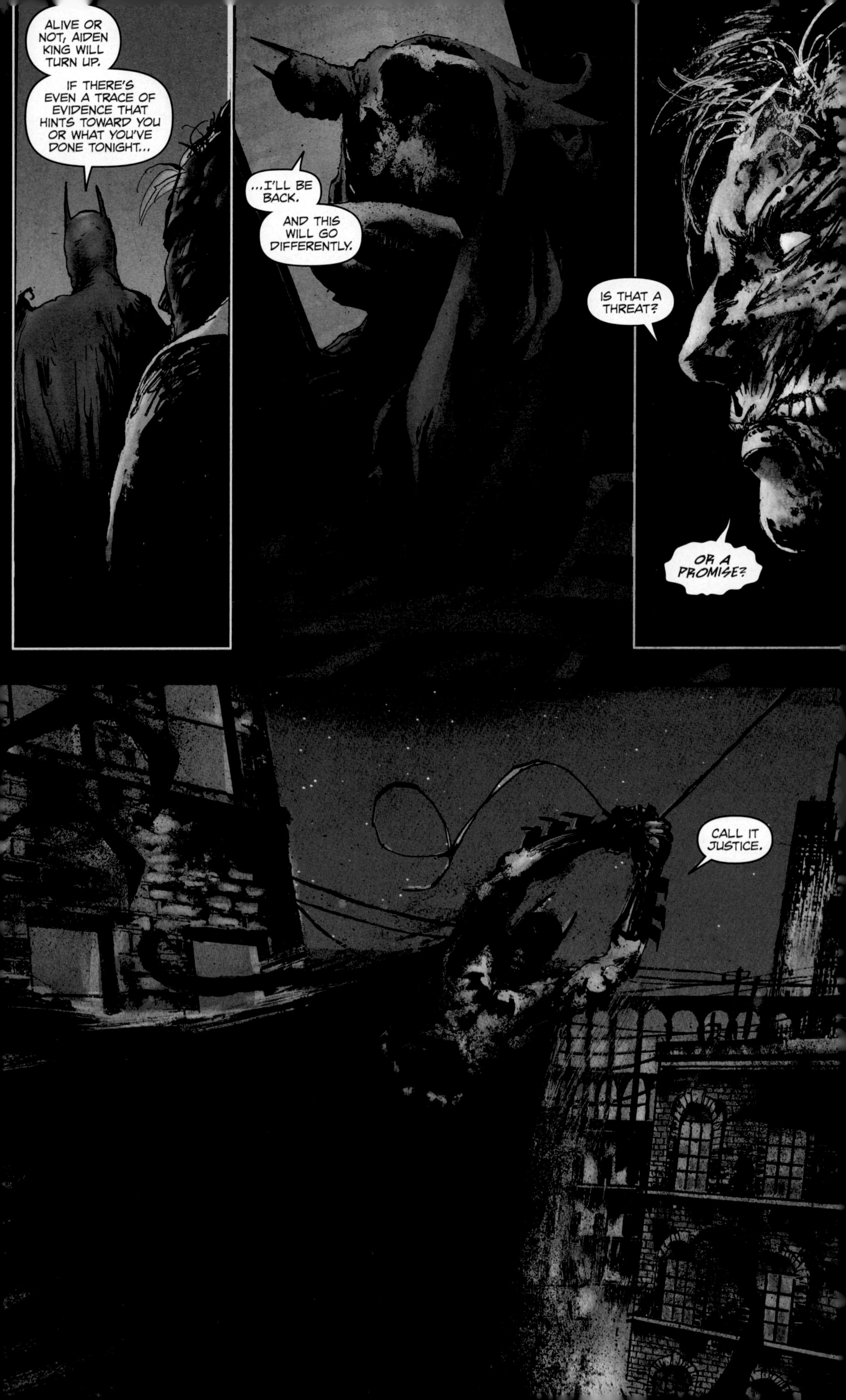
ALIVE OR NOT, AIDEN KING WILL TURN UP.
IF THERE'S EVEN A TRACE OF EVIDENCE THAT HINTS TOWARD YOU OR WHAT YOU'VE DONE TONIGHT...
...I'LL BE BACK.
AND THIS WILL GO DIFFERENTLY.
IS THAT A THREAT?
OR A PROMISE?
CALL IT JUSTICE.

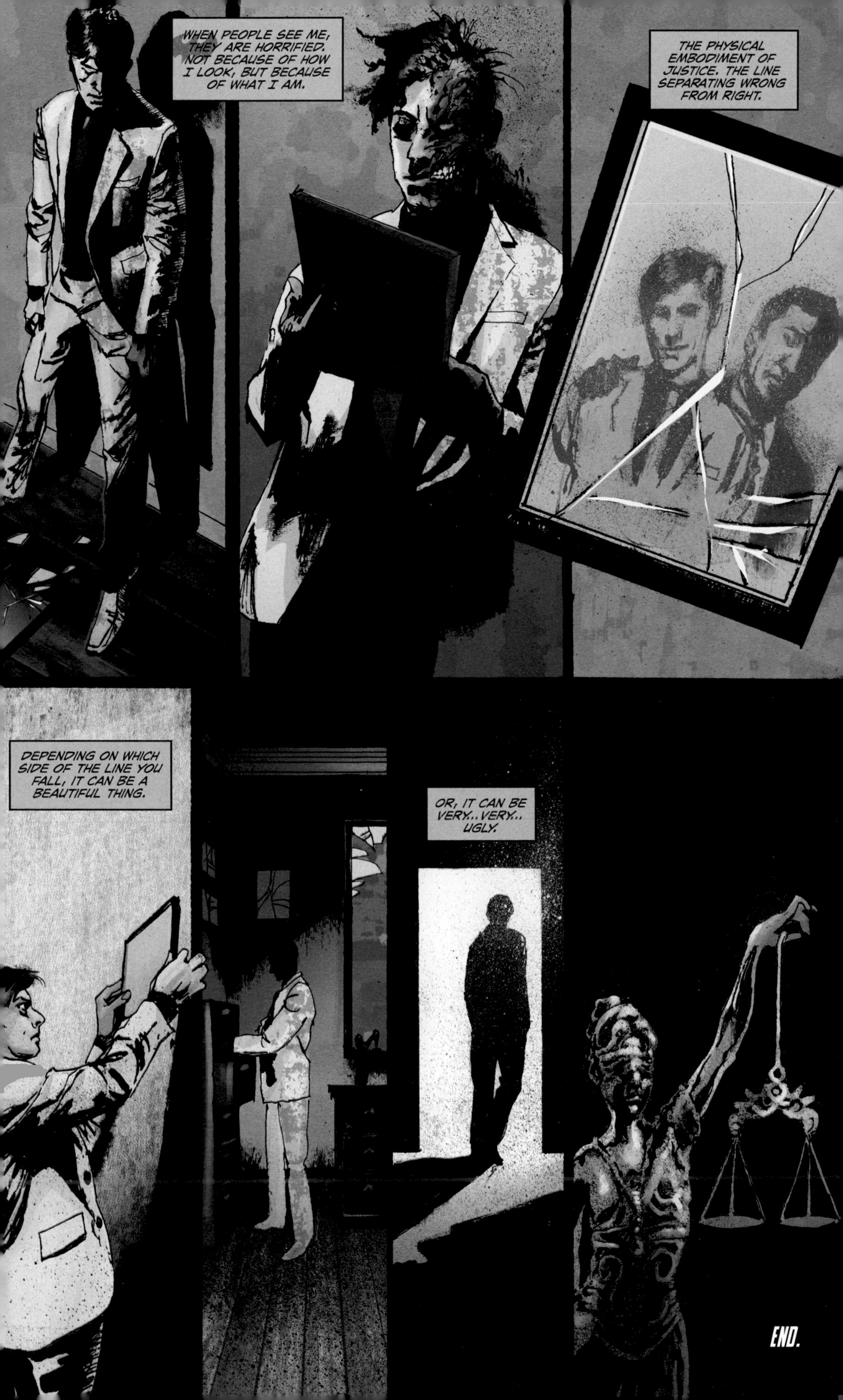
WHEN PEOPLE SEE ME, THEY ARE HORRIFIED. NOT BECAUSE OF HOW I LOOK, BUT BECAUSE OF WHAT I AM.
THE PHYSICAL EMBODIMENT OF JUSTICE. THE LINE SEPARATING WRONG FROM RIGHT.
DEPENDING ON WHICH SIDE OF THE LINE YOU FALL, IT CAN BE A BEAUTIFUL THING.
OR, IT CAN BE VERY...VERY... UGLY.
END.

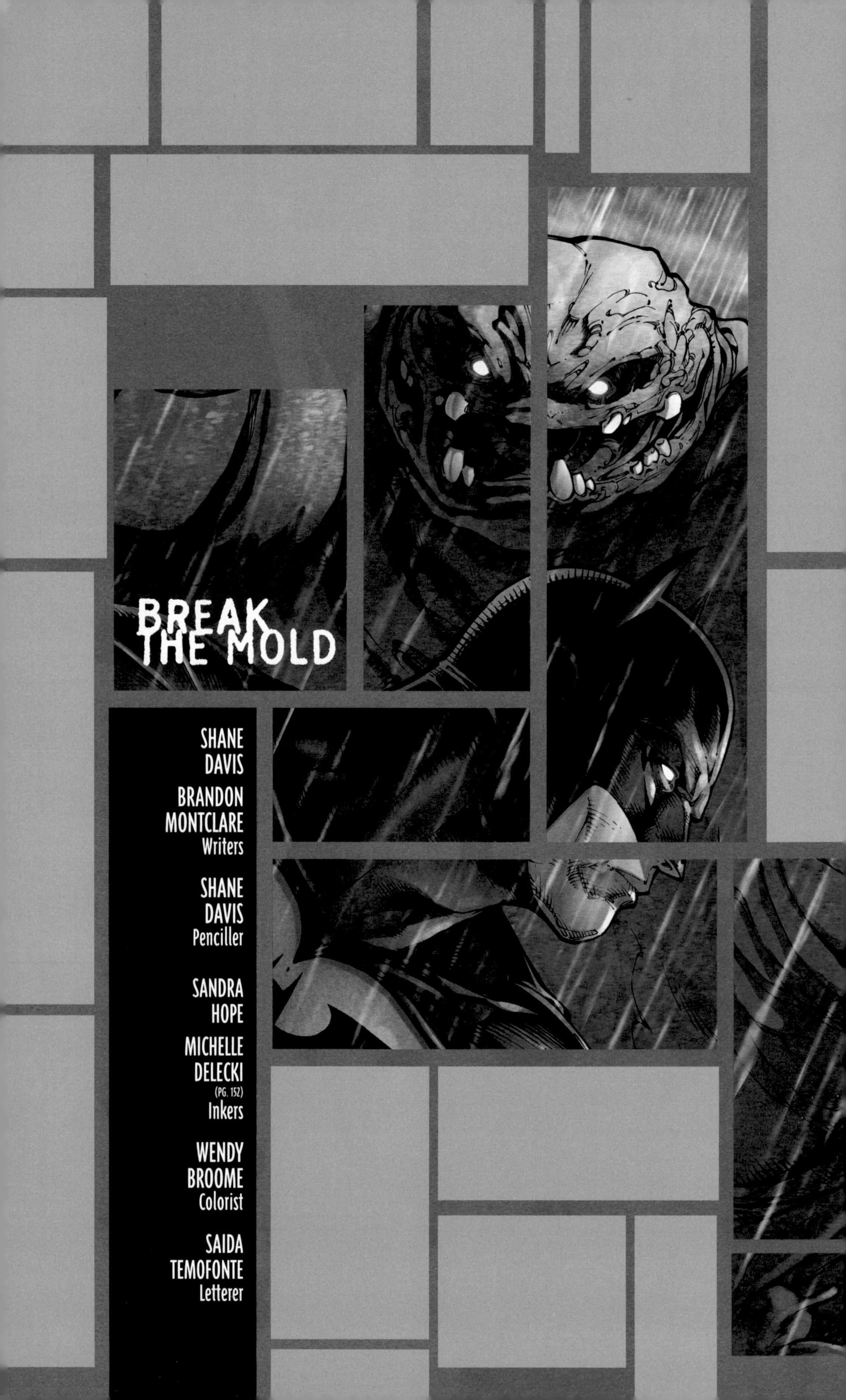

BREAK THE MOLD

SHANE DAVIS
BRANDON MONTCLARE
Writers

SHANE DAVIS
Penciller

SANDRA HOPE
MICHELLE DELECKI (PG. 152)
Inkers

WENDY BROOME
Colorist

SAIDA TEMOFONTE
Letterer

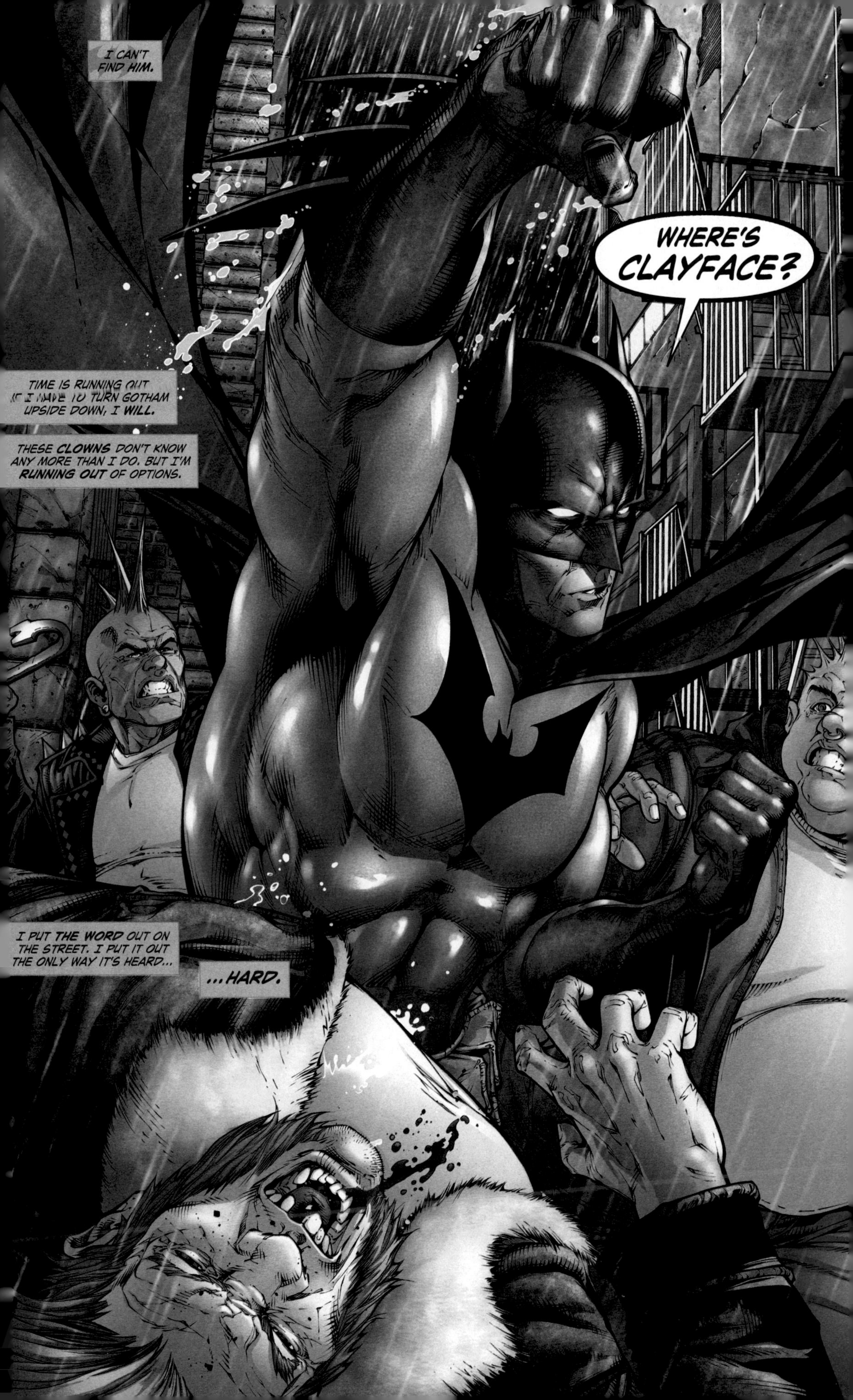
I CAN'T FIND HIM.
WHERE'S CLAYFACE?
TIME IS RUNNING OUT. IF I HAVE TO TURN GOTHAM UPSIDE DOWN, I WILL.
THESE CLOWNS DON'T KNOW ANY MORE THAN I DO. BUT I'M RUNNING OUT OF OPTIONS.
I PUT THE WORD OUT ON THE STREET. I PUT IT OUT THE ONLY WAY IT'S HEARD...
...HARD.

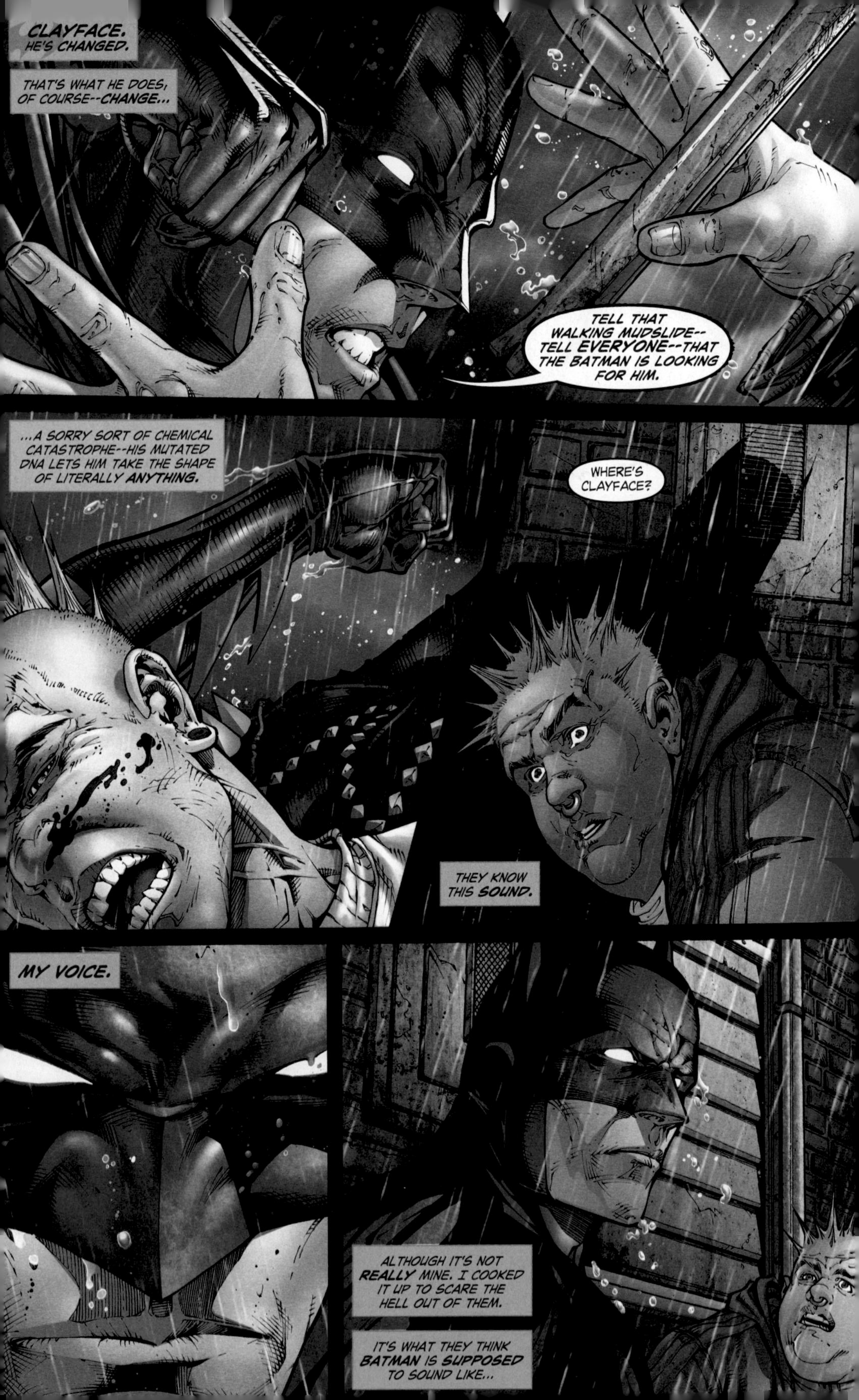
CLAYFACE. HE'S CHANGED.
THAT'S WHAT HE DOES, OF COURSE--CHANGE...
TELL THAT WALKING MUDSLIDE--TELL EVERYONE--THAT THE BATMAN IS LOOKING FOR HIM.
...A SORRY SORT OF CHEMICAL CATASTROPHE--HIS MUTATED DNA LETS HIM TAKE THE SHAPE OF LITERALLY ANYTHING.
WHERE'S CLAYFACE?
THEY KNOW THIS SOUND.
MY VOICE.
ALTHOUGH IT'S NOT REALLY MINE. I COOKED IT UP TO SCARE THE HELL OUT OF THEM.
IT'S WHAT THEY THINK BATMAN IS SUPPOSED TO SOUND LIKE...

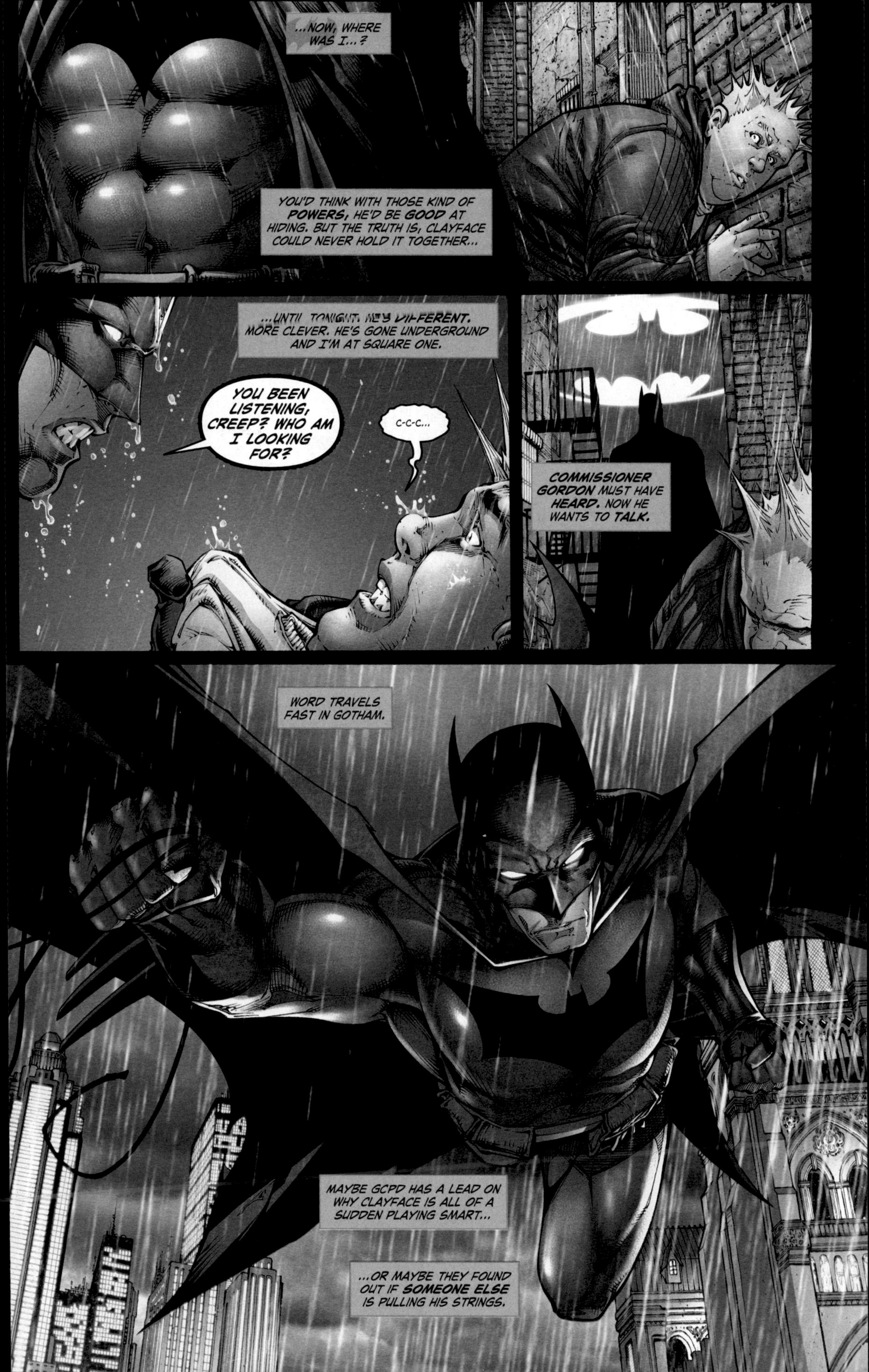
...NOW, WHERE WAS I...?
YOU'D THINK WITH THOSE KIND OF **POWERS,** HE'D BE **GOOD** AT HIDING. BUT THE TRUTH IS, CLAYFACE COULD NEVER HOLD IT TOGETHER...
...UNTIL TONIGHT. HE'S DIFFERENT. MORE CLEVER. HE'S GONE UNDERGROUND AND I'M AT SQUARE ONE.
YOU BEEN LISTENING, CREEP? WHO AM I LOOKING FOR?
C-C-C...
COMMISSIONER GORDON MUST HAVE **HEARD.** NOW HE WANTS TO **TALK.**
WORD TRAVELS FAST IN GOTHAM.
MAYBE GCPD HAS A LEAD ON WHY CLAYFACE IS ALL OF A SUDDEN PLAYING SMART...
...OR MAYBE THEY FOUND OUT IF **SOMEONE ELSE** IS PULLING HIS STRINGS.

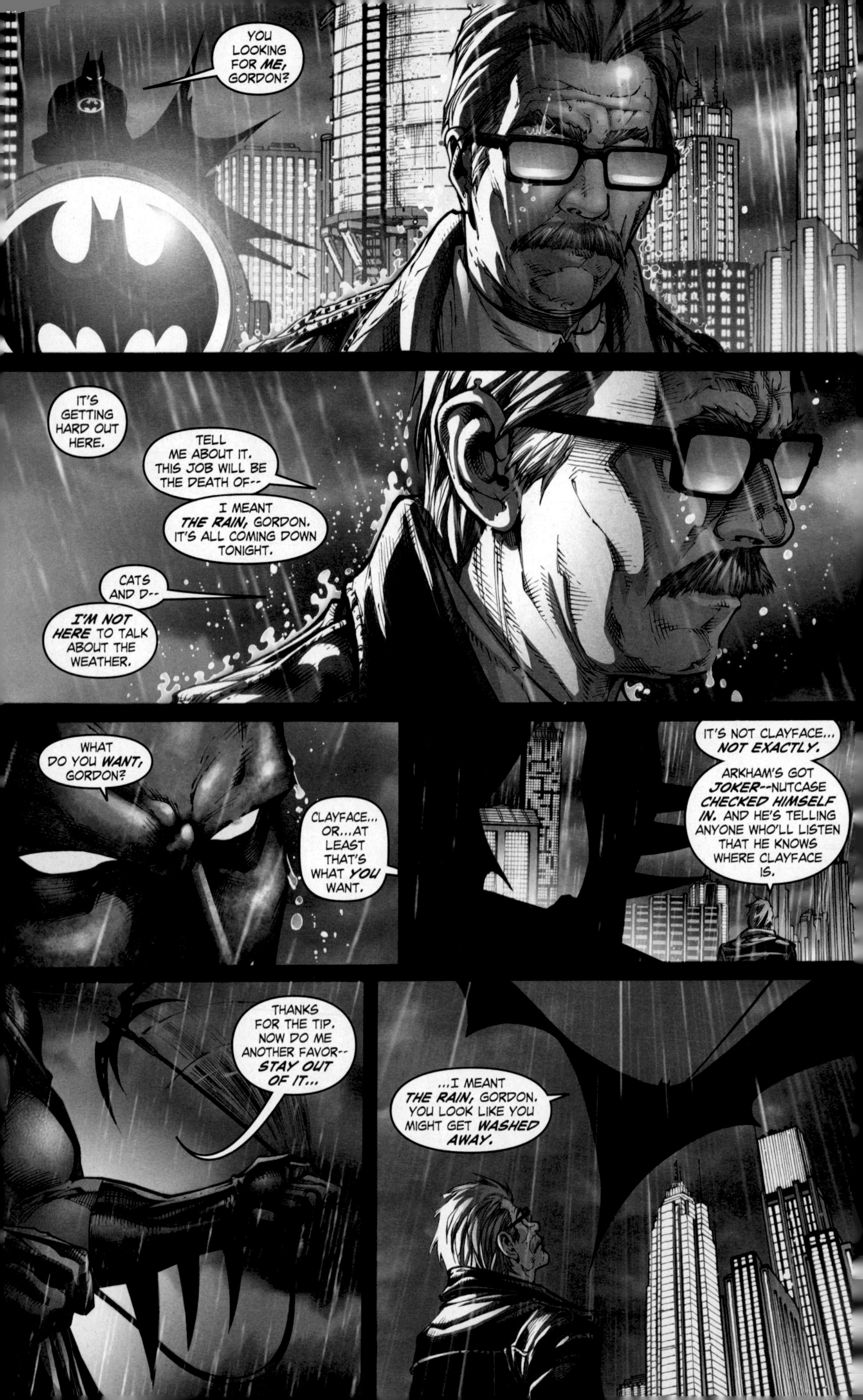
YOU LOOKING FOR ME, GORDON?
IT'S GETTING HARD OUT HERE.
TELL ME ABOUT IT. THIS JOB WILL BE THE DEATH OF--
I MEANT THE RAIN, GORDON. IT'S ALL COMING DOWN TONIGHT.
CATS AND D--
I'M NOT HERE TO TALK ABOUT THE WEATHER.
WHAT DO YOU WANT, GORDON?
CLAYFACE... OR...AT LEAST THAT'S WHAT YOU WANT.
IT'S NOT CLAYFACE... NOT EXACTLY.
ARKHAM'S GOT JOKER--NUTCASE CHECKED HIMSELF IN. AND HE'S TELLING ANYONE WHO'LL LISTEN THAT HE KNOWS WHERE CLAYFACE IS.
THANKS FOR THE TIP. NOW DO ME ANOTHER FAVOR-- STAY OUT OF IT...
...I MEANT THE RAIN, GORDON. YOU LOOK LIKE YOU MIGHT GET WASHED AWAY.

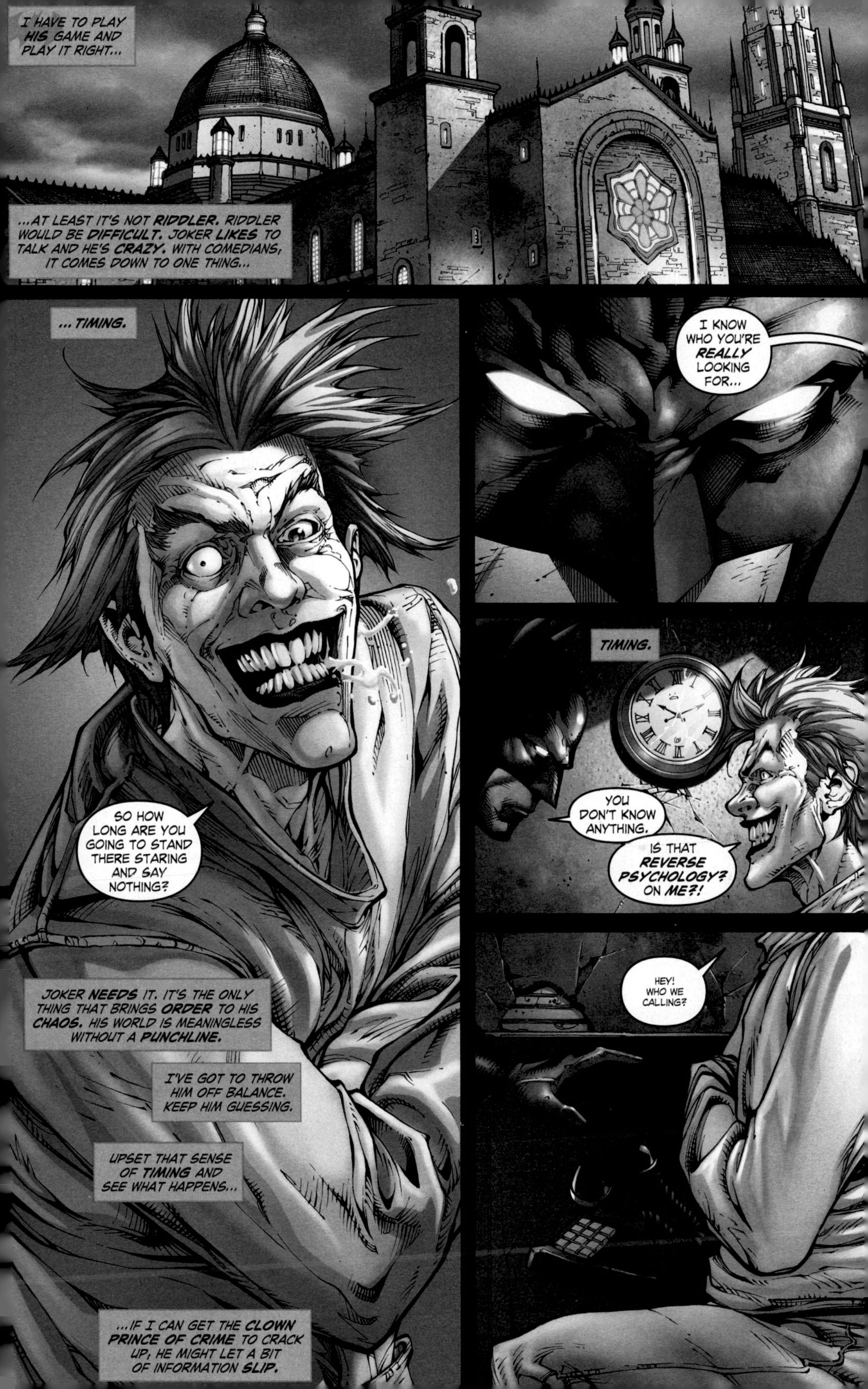
I HAVE TO PLAY HIS GAME AND PLAY IT RIGHT...
...AT LEAST IT'S NOT RIDDLER. RIDDLER WOULD BE DIFFICULT. JOKER LIKES TO TALK AND HE'S CRAZY. WITH COMEDIANS, IT COMES DOWN TO ONE THING...
...TIMING.
SO HOW LONG ARE YOU GOING TO STAND THERE STARING AND SAY NOTHING?
JOKER NEEDS IT. IT'S THE ONLY THING THAT BRINGS ORDER TO HIS CHAOS. HIS WORLD IS MEANINGLESS WITHOUT A PUNCHLINE.
I'VE GOT TO THROW HIM OFF BALANCE. KEEP HIM GUESSING.
UPSET THAT SENSE OF TIMING AND SEE WHAT HAPPENS...
...IF I CAN GET THE CLOWN PRINCE OF CRIME TO CRACK UP, HE MIGHT LET A BIT OF INFORMATION SLIP.
I KNOW WHO YOU'RE REALLY LOOKING FOR...
TIMING.
YOU DON'T KNOW ANYTHING.
IS THAT REVERSE PSYCHOLOGY? ON ME?!
HEY! WHO WE CALLING?

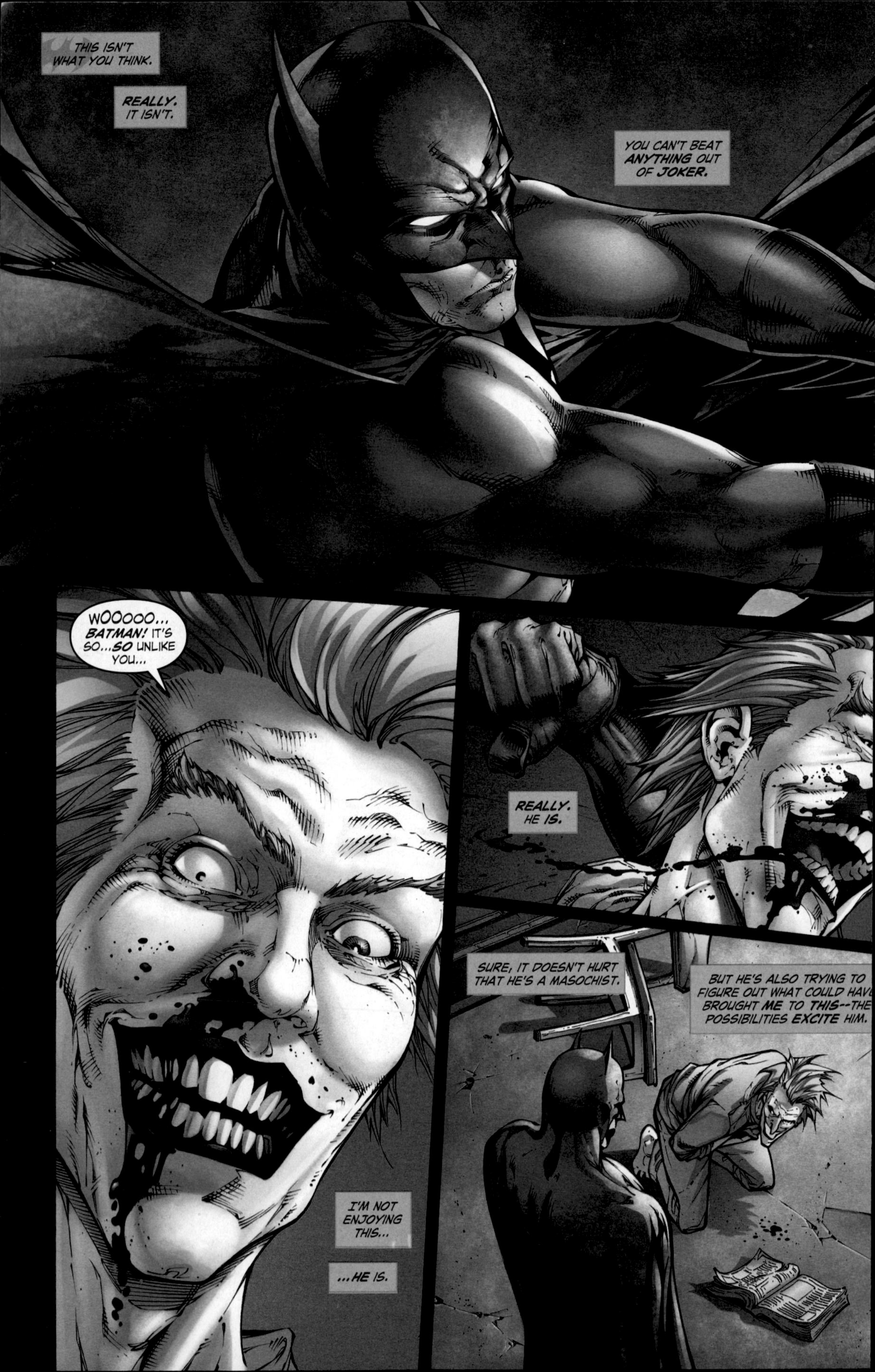
THIS ISN'T WHAT YOU THINK.
REALLY. IT ISN'T.
YOU CAN'T BEAT ANYTHING OUT OF JOKER.
WOOOOO... BATMAN! IT'S SO...SO UNLIKE YOU...
I'M NOT ENJOYING THIS...
...HE IS.
REALLY. HE IS.
SURE, IT DOESN'T HURT THAT HE'S A MASOCHIST.
BUT HE'S ALSO TRYING TO FIGURE OUT WHAT COULD HAVE BROUGHT ME TO THIS--THE POSSIBILITIES EXCITE HIM.

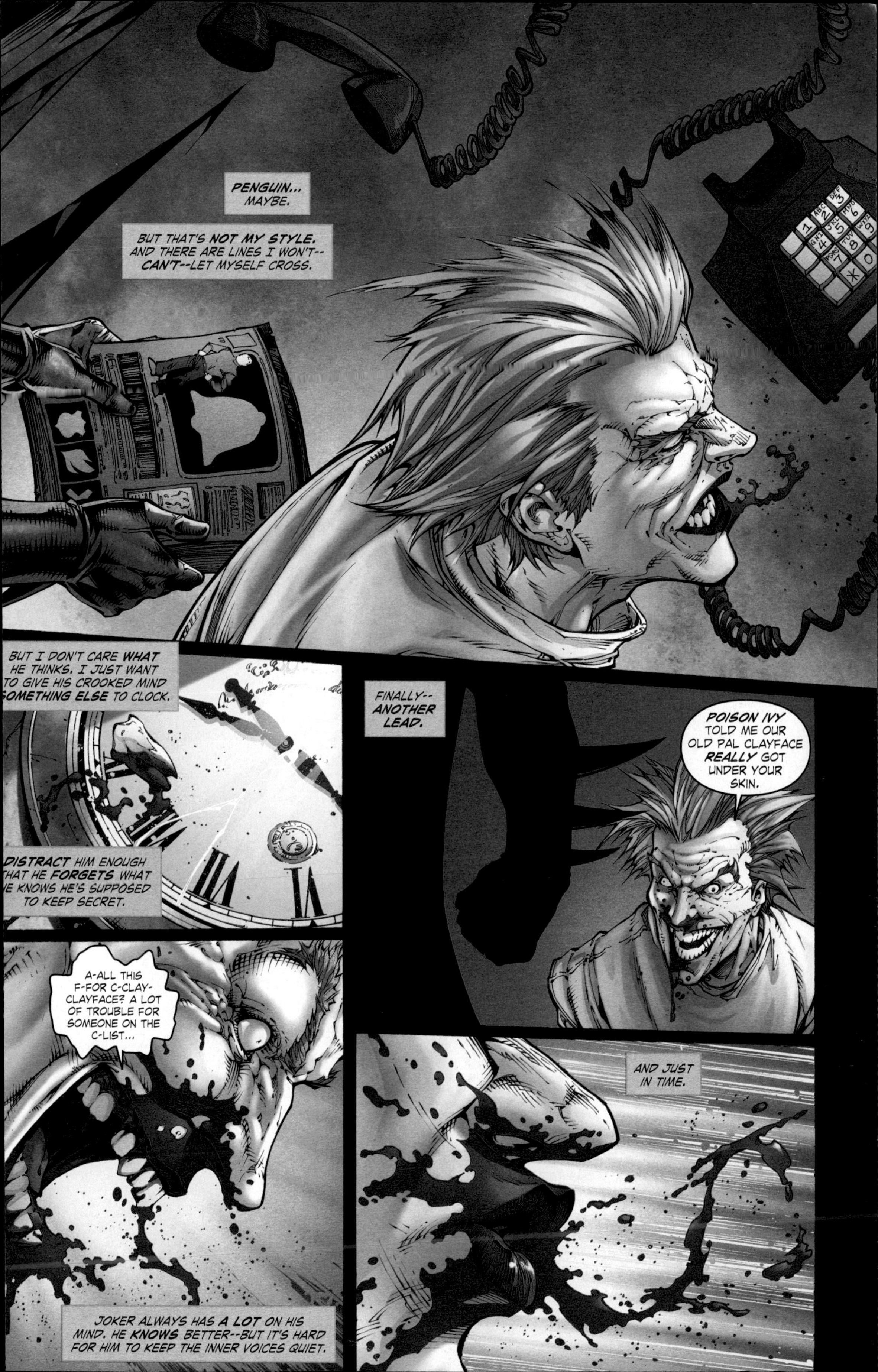
PENGUIN... MAYBE.
BUT THAT'S NOT MY STYLE. AND THERE ARE LINES I WON'T--CAN'T--LET MYSELF CROSS.
BUT I DON'T CARE WHAT HE THINKS. I JUST WANT TO GIVE HIS CROOKED MIND SOMETHING ELSE TO CLOCK.
DISTRACT HIM ENOUGH THAT HE FORGETS WHAT HE KNOWS HE'S SUPPOSED TO KEEP SECRET.
FINALLY--ANOTHER LEAD.
POISON IVY TOLD ME OUR OLD PAL CLAYFACE REALLY GOT UNDER YOUR SKIN.
A-ALL THIS F-FOR C-CLAY-CLAYFACE? A LOT OF TROUBLE FOR SOMEONE ON THE C-LIST...
AND JUST IN TIME.
JOKER ALWAYS HAS A LOT ON HIS MIND. HE KNOWS BETTER--BUT IT'S HARD FOR HIM TO KEEP THE INNER VOICES QUIET.

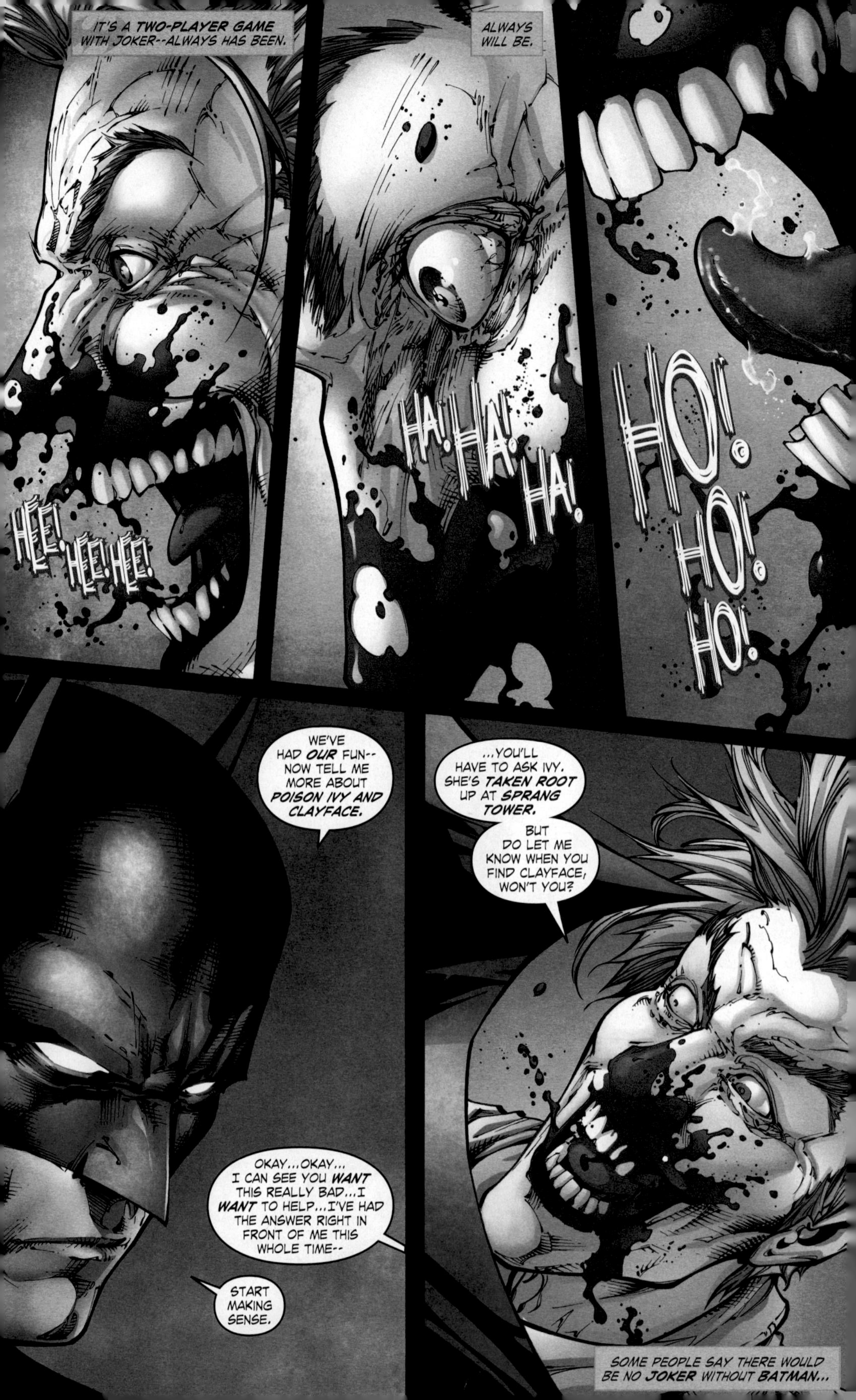

IT'S A TWO-PLAYER GAME WITH JOKER--ALWAYS HAS BEEN.
HEE! HEE! HEE!
ALWAYS WILL BE.
HA! HA! HA!
HO! HO! HO! HO!
WE'VE HAD OUR FUN--NOW TELL ME MORE ABOUT POISON IVY AND CLAYFACE.
OKAY...OKAY... I CAN SEE YOU WANT THIS REALLY BAD...I WANT TO HELP...I'VE HAD THE ANSWER RIGHT IN FRONT OF ME THIS WHOLE TIME--
START MAKING SENSE.
...YOU'LL HAVE TO ASK IVY. SHE'S TAKEN ROOT UP AT SPRANG TOWER.
BUT DO LET ME KNOW WHEN YOU FIND CLAYFACE, WON'T YOU?
SOME PEOPLE SAY THERE WOULD BE NO JOKER WITHOUT BATMAN...

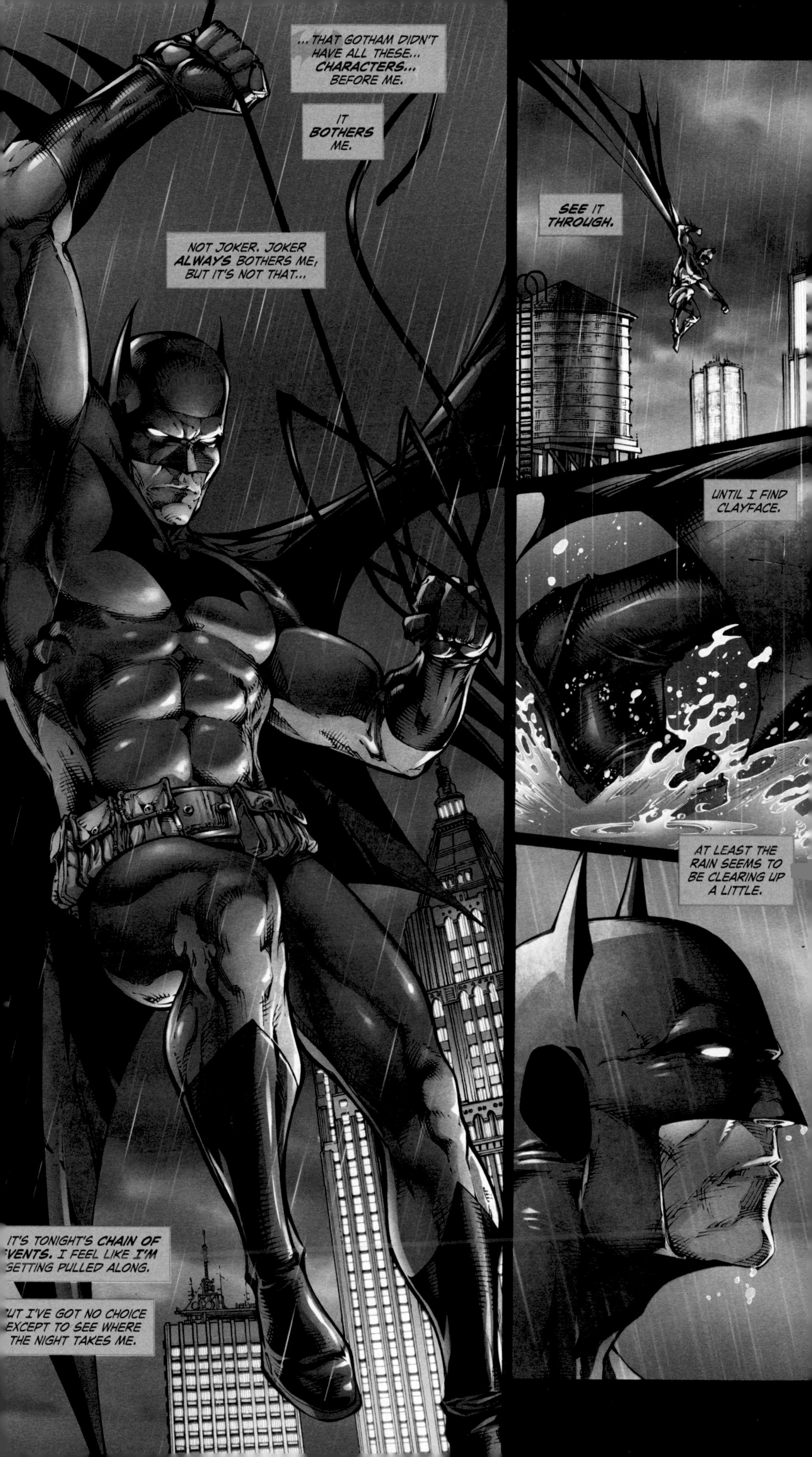
...THAT GOTHAM DIDN'T HAVE ALL THESE... **CHARACTERS...** BEFORE ME.
IT **BOTHERS** ME.
NOT JOKER. JOKER **ALWAYS** BOTHERS ME, BUT IT'S NOT THAT...
IT'S TONIGHT'S **CHAIN OF EVENTS.** I FEEL LIKE **I'M** GETTING PULLED ALONG.
UT I'VE GOT NO CHOICE EXCEPT TO SEE WHERE THE NIGHT TAKES ME.
SEE IT **THROUGH.**
UNTIL I FIND CLAYFACE.
AT LEAST THE RAIN SEEMS TO BE CLEARING UP A LITTLE.

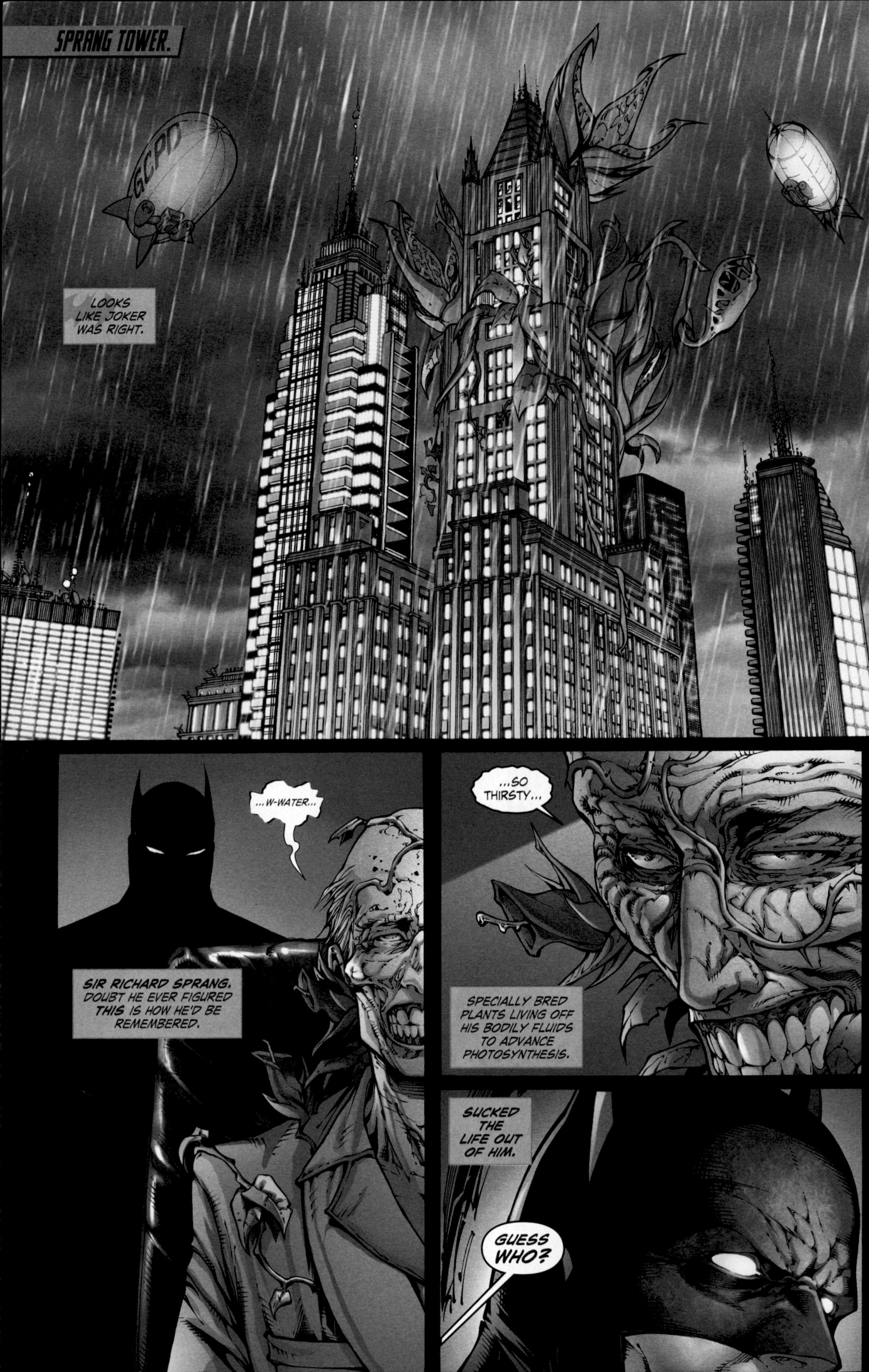
SPRANG TOWER.
GCPD
LOOKS LIKE JOKER WAS RIGHT.
...W-WATER...
SIR RICHARD SPRANG. DOUBT HE EVER FIGURED THIS IS HOW HE'D BE REMEMBERED.
...SO THIRSTY...
SPECIALLY BRED PLANTS LIVING OFF HIS BODILY FLUIDS TO ADVANCE PHOTOSYNTHESIS.
SUCKED THE LIFE OUT OF HIM.
GUESS WHO?

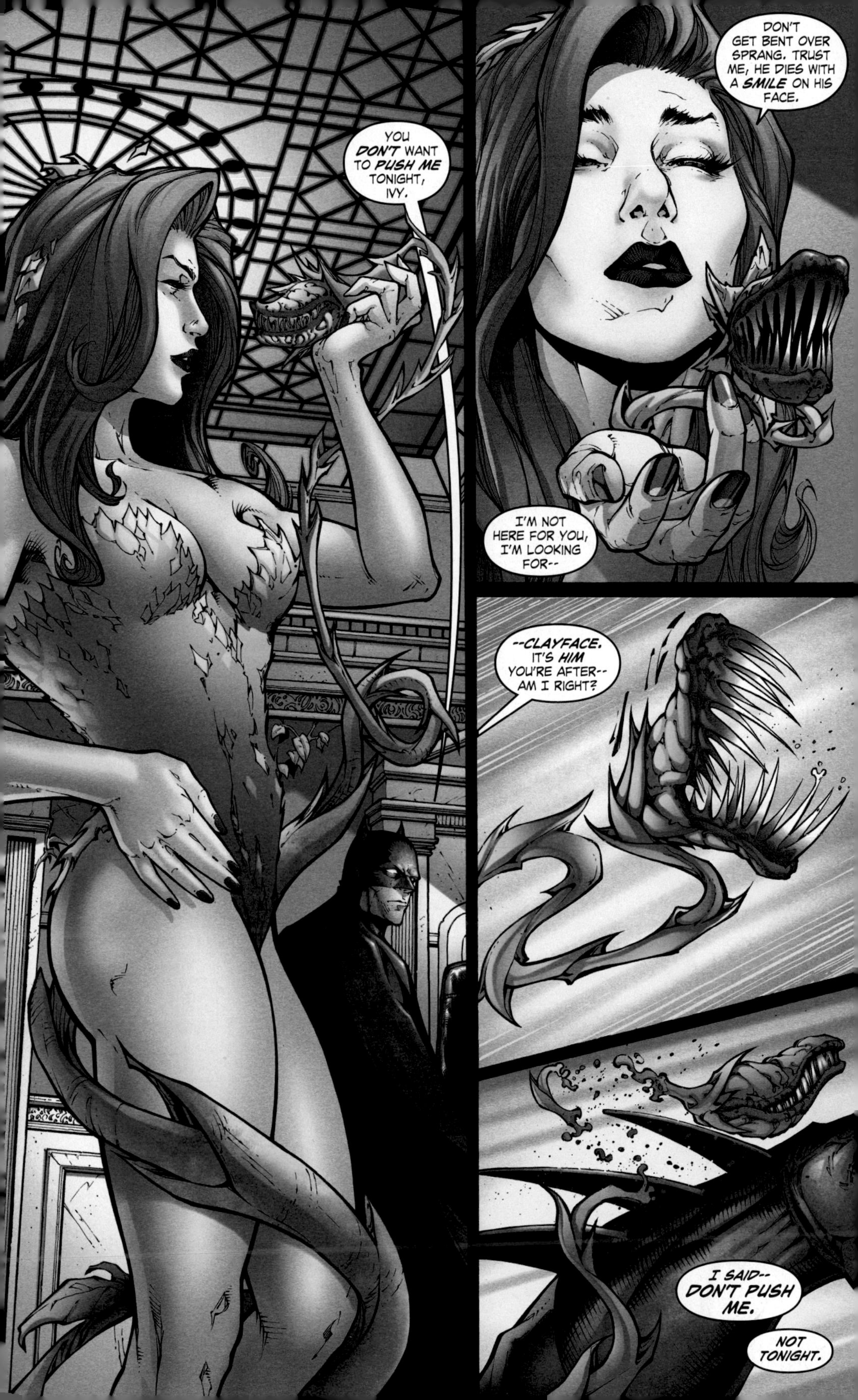
YOU DON'T WANT TO PUSH ME TONIGHT, IVY.
DON'T GET BENT OVER SPRANG. TRUST ME, HE DIES WITH A SMILE ON HIS FACE.
I'M NOT HERE FOR YOU, I'M LOOKING FOR--
--CLAYFACE. IT'S HIM YOU'RE AFTER--AM I RIGHT?
I SAID--DON'T PUSH ME.
NOT TONIGHT.

OVERGROWN VENUS FLYTRAPS I CAN *DEAL* WITH.

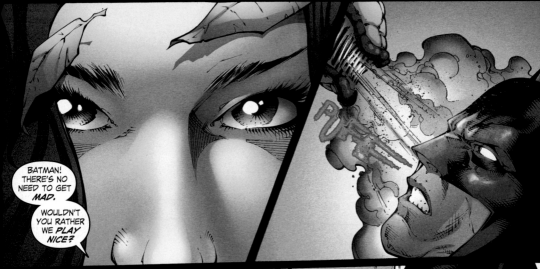

BATMAN! THERE'S NO NEED TO GET *MAD*.

WOULDN'T YOU RATHER WE *PLAY NICE?*

THERE! ISN'T THAT *BETTER?*

NOW LET'S SEE IF I CAN PUT A *SMILE* ON YOUR *FACE.*

THESE SPORES PARALYZE ALL MOTOR FUNCTION...

...BUT *POISON IVY'S* BIOENGINEERED FLORA ISN'T THE *WORST* PART...

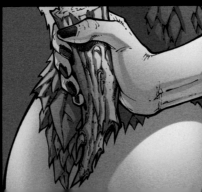

...*WORST* IS WHEN SHE GIVES YOU THAT ITCH YOU CAN'T *EVER* SCRATCH.

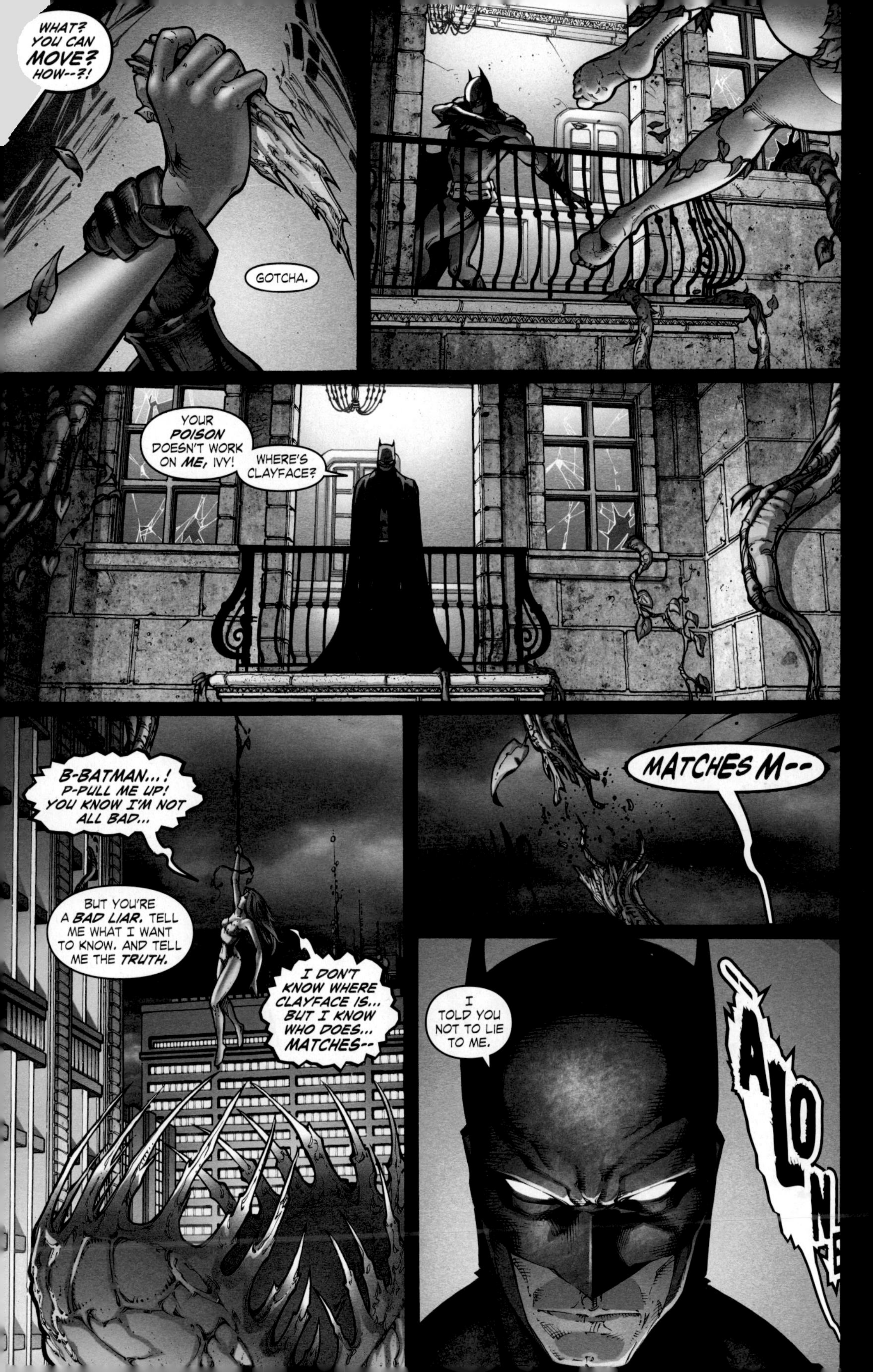
WHAT? YOU CAN MOVE? HOW--?!
GOTCHA.
YOUR POISON DOESN'T WORK ON ME, IVY!
WHERE'S CLAYFACE?
B-BATMAN...! P-PULL ME UP! YOU KNOW I'M NOT ALL BAD...
BUT YOU'RE A BAD LIAR. TELL ME WHAT I WANT TO KNOW. AND TELL ME THE TRUTH.
I DON'T KNOW WHERE CLAYFACE IS... BUT I KNOW WHO DOES... MATCHES--
MATCHES M--
I TOLD YOU NOT TO LIE TO ME.
ALONE

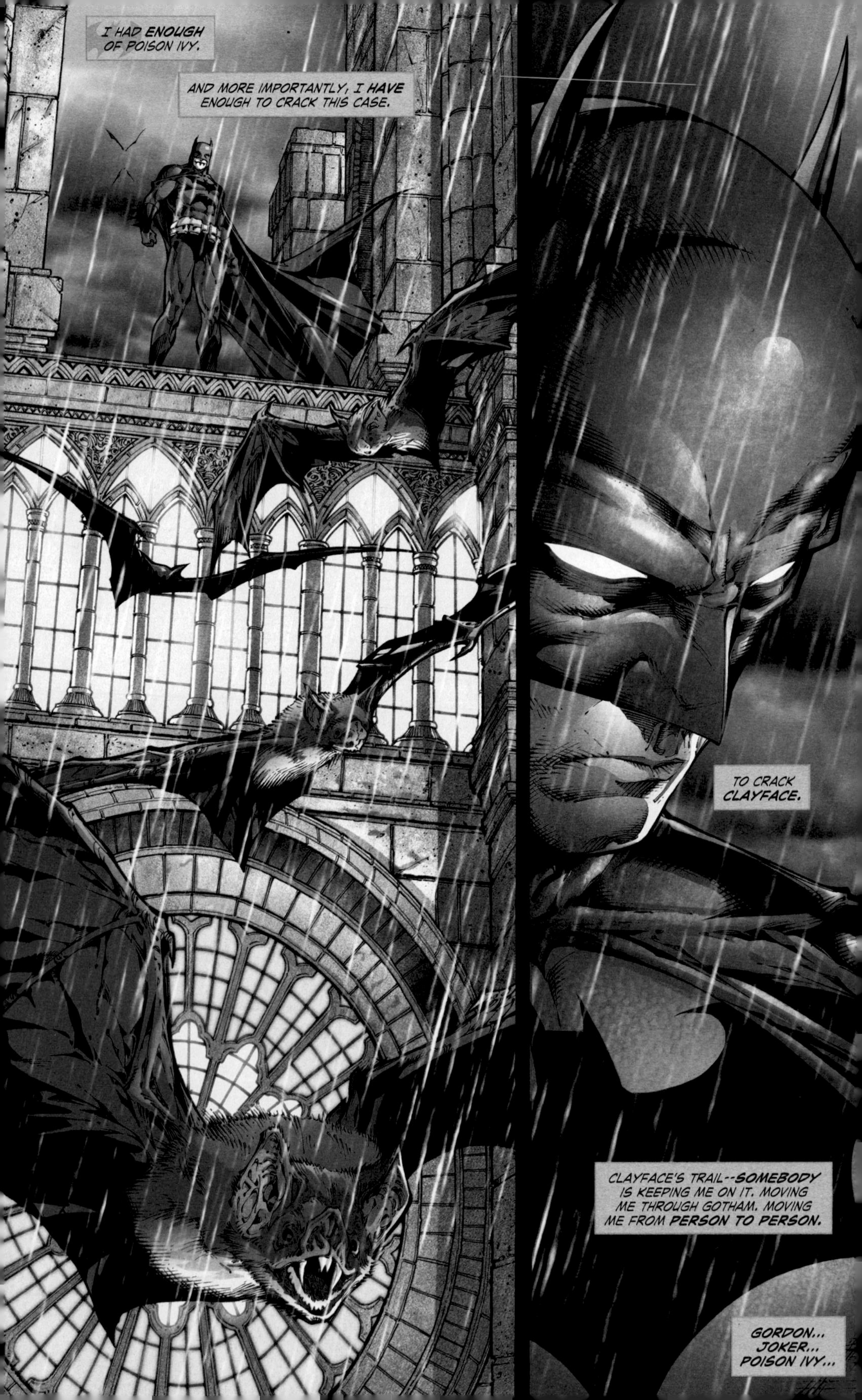
I HAD ENOUGH OF POISON IVY.
AND MORE IMPORTANTLY, I HAVE ENOUGH TO CRACK THIS CASE.
TO CRACK CLAYFACE.
CLAYFACE'S TRAIL--SOMEBODY IS KEEPING ME ON IT. MOVING ME THROUGH GOTHAM. MOVING ME FROM PERSON TO PERSON.
GORDON... JOKER... POISON IVY...

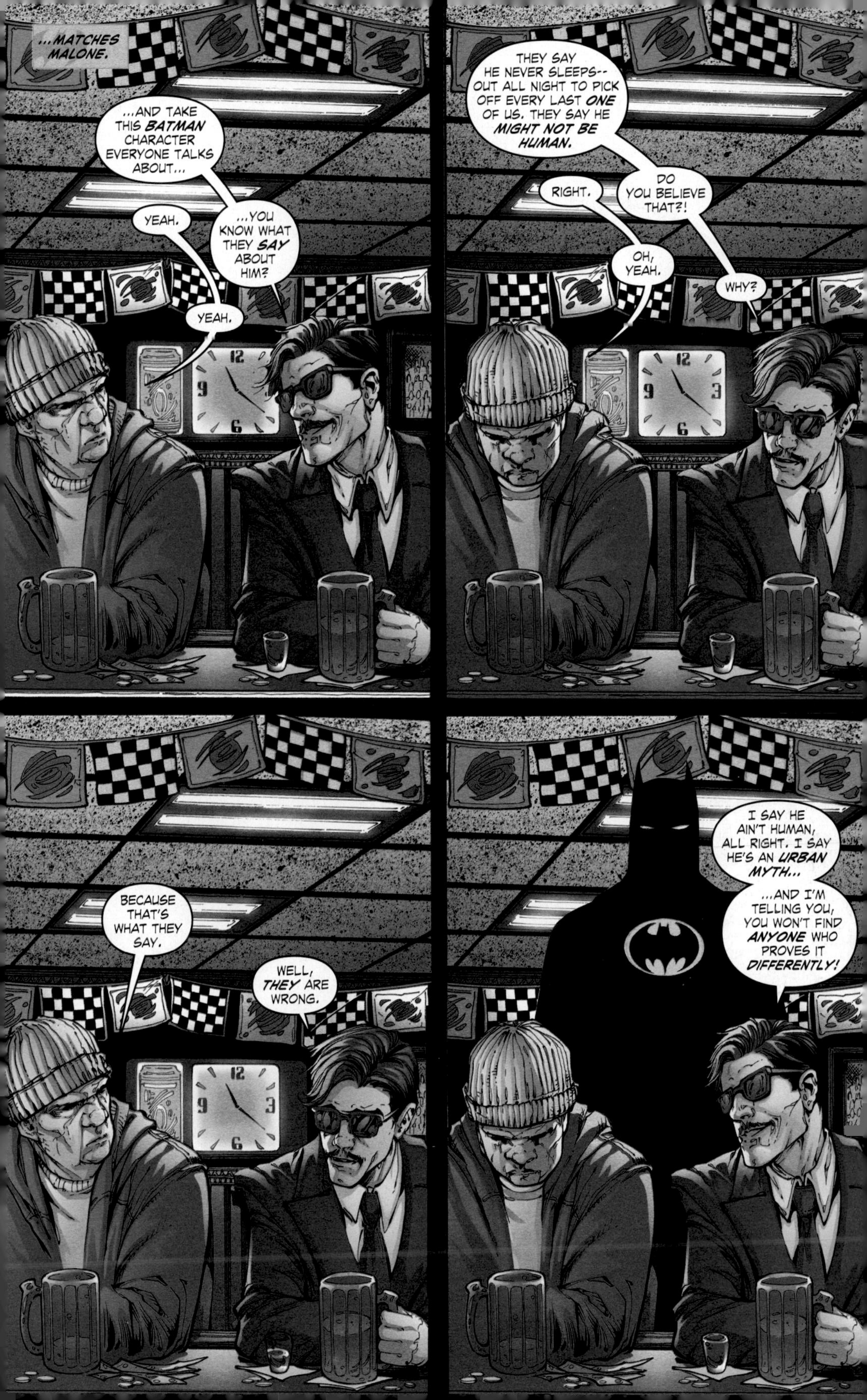
...MATCHES MALONE.
...AND TAKE THIS BATMAN CHARACTER EVERYONE TALKS ABOUT...
YEAH.
...YOU KNOW WHAT THEY SAY ABOUT HIM?
YEAH.
THEY SAY HE NEVER SLEEPS-- OUT ALL NIGHT TO PICK OFF EVERY LAST ONE OF US. THEY SAY HE MIGHT NOT BE HUMAN.
RIGHT.
DO YOU BELIEVE THAT?!
OH, YEAH.
WHY?
BECAUSE THAT'S WHAT THEY SAY.
WELL, THEY ARE WRONG.
I SAY HE AIN'T HUMAN, ALL RIGHT. I SAY HE'S AN URBAN MYTH...
...AND I'M TELLING YOU, YOU WON'T FIND ANYONE WHO PROVES IT DIFFERENTLY!

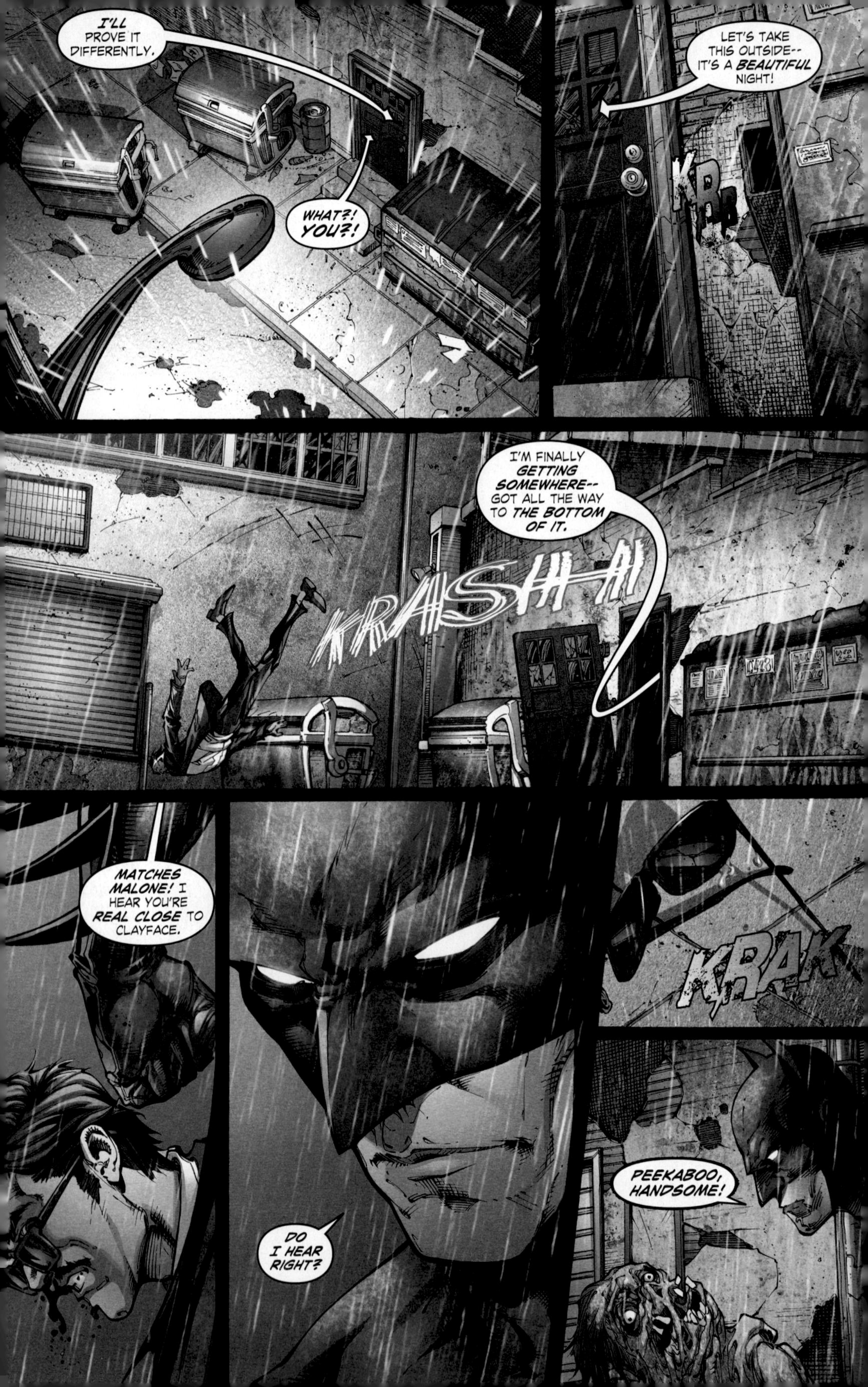
I'LL PROVE IT DIFFERENTLY.
WHAT?! YOU?!
LET'S TAKE THIS OUTSIDE-- IT'S A BEAUTIFUL NIGHT!
KRR
I'M FINALLY GETTING SOMEWHERE-- GOT ALL THE WAY TO THE BOTTOM OF IT.
KRASHH
MATCHES MALONE! I HEAR YOU'RE REAL CLOSE TO CLAYFACE.
DO I HEAR RIGHT?
KRAK
PEEKABOO, HANDSOME!

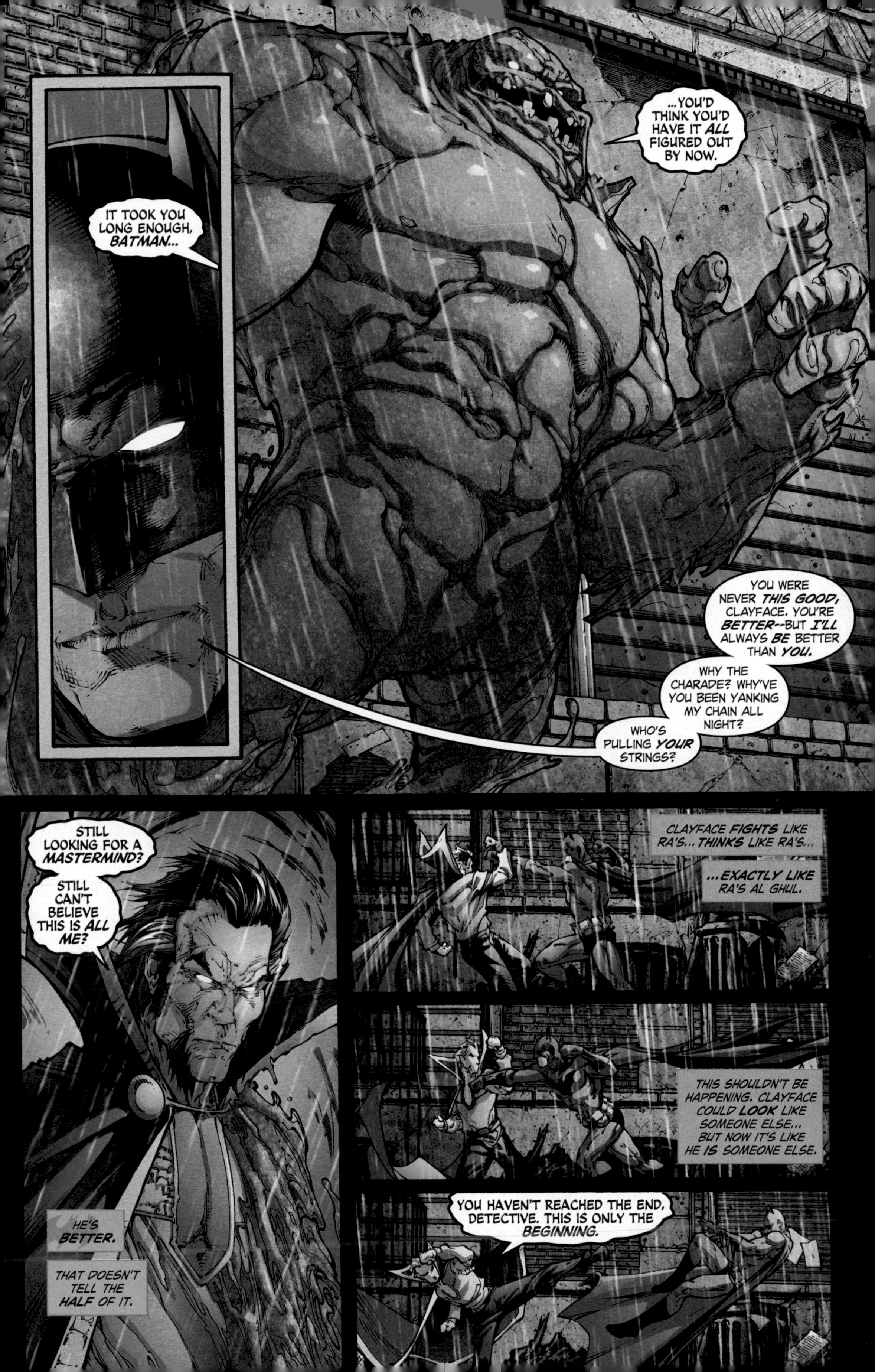
IT TOOK YOU LONG ENOUGH, BATMAN...
...YOU'D THINK YOU'D HAVE IT ALL FIGURED OUT BY NOW.
YOU WERE NEVER THIS GOOD, CLAYFACE. YOU'RE BETTER--BUT I'LL ALWAYS BE BETTER THAN YOU.
WHY THE CHARADE? WHY'VE YOU BEEN YANKING MY CHAIN ALL NIGHT?
WHO'S PULLING YOUR STRINGS?
STILL LOOKING FOR A MASTERMIND?
STILL CAN'T BELIEVE THIS IS ALL ME?
HE'S BETTER.
THAT DOESN'T TELL THE HALF OF IT.
CLAYFACE FIGHTS LIKE RA'S...THINKS LIKE RA'S...
...EXACTLY LIKE RA'S AL GHUL.
THIS SHOULDN'T BE HAPPENING. CLAYFACE COULD LOOK LIKE SOMEONE ELSE... BUT NOW IT'S LIKE HE IS SOMEONE ELSE.
YOU HAVEN'T REACHED THE END, DETECTIVE. THIS IS ONLY THE BEGINNING.

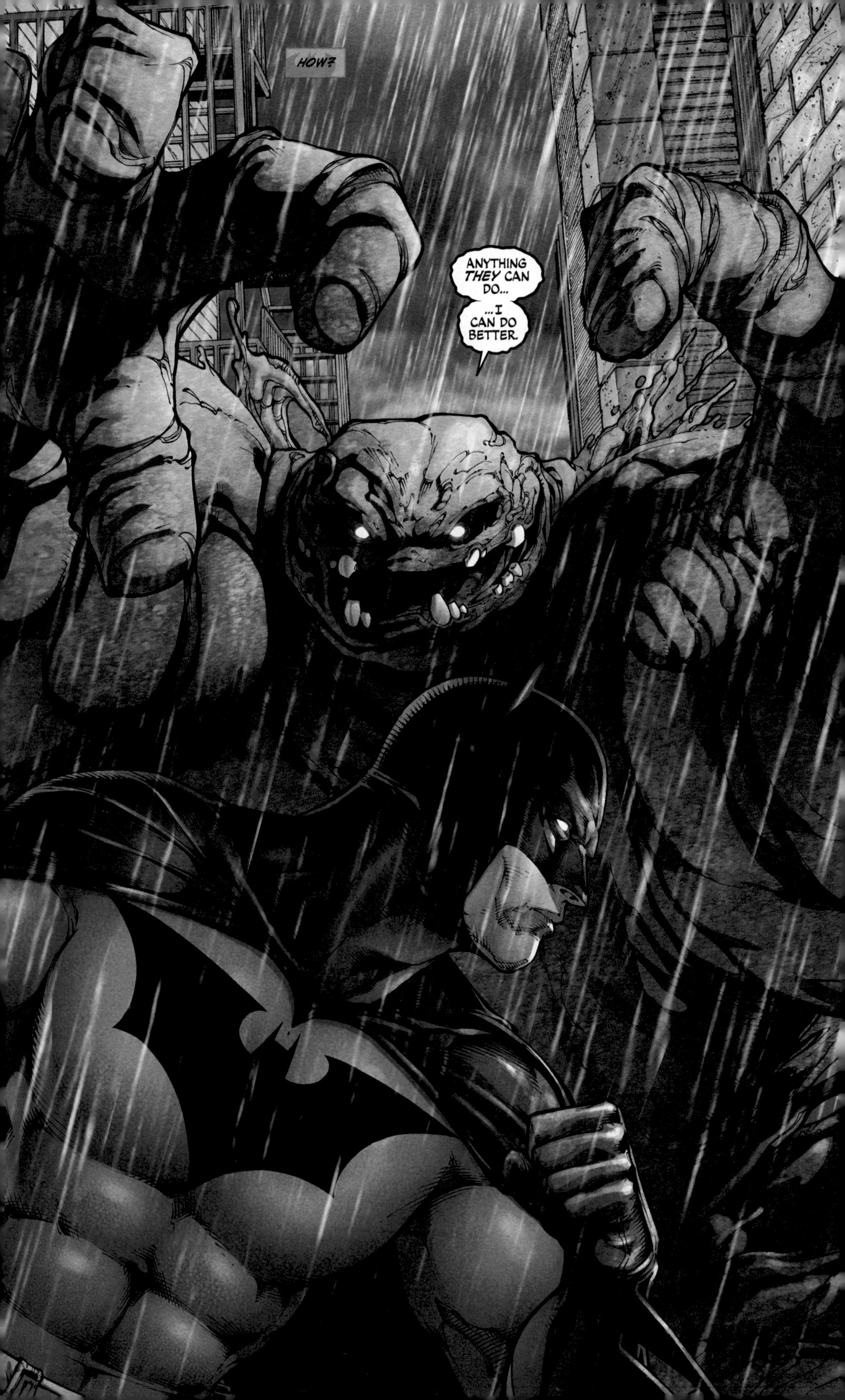
HOW?
ANYTHING THEY CAN DO...
...I CAN DO BETTER.

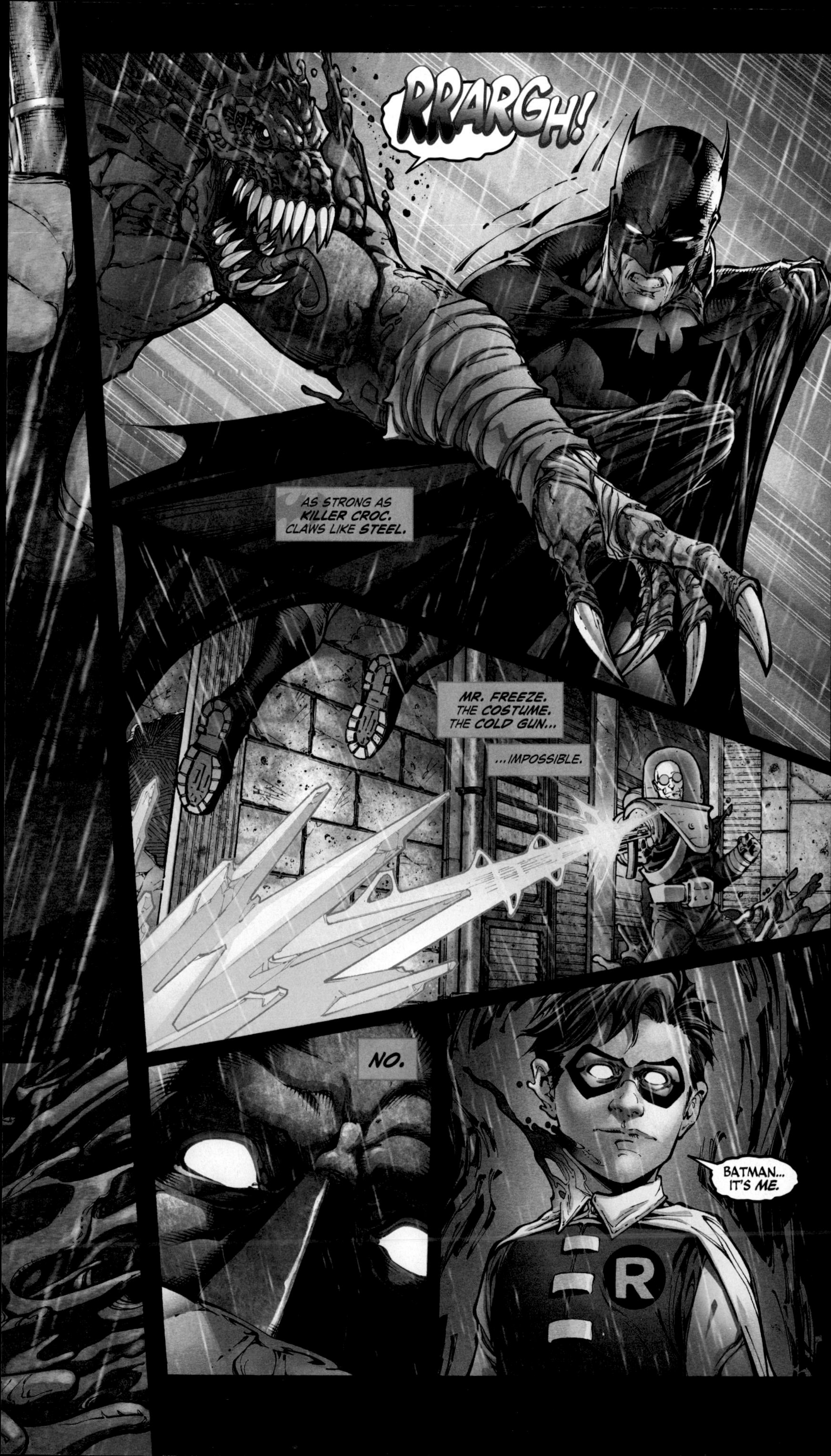
RRARGH!
AS STRONG AS KILLER CROC. CLAWS LIKE STEEL.
MR. FREEZE. THE COSTUME. THE COLD GUN...
...IMPOSSIBLE.
NO.
BATMAN... IT'S ME.

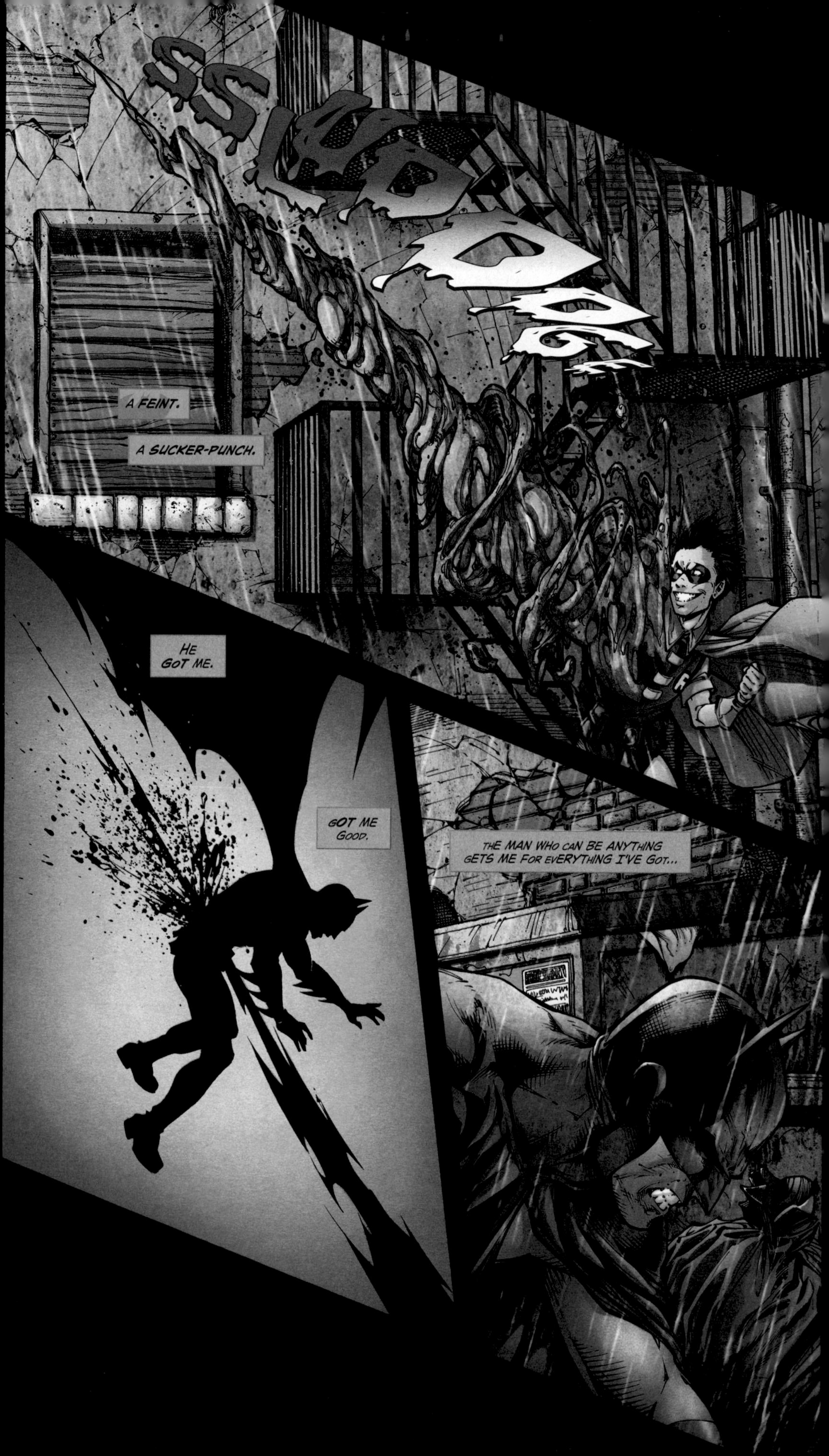
SSLUD
A FEINT.
A SUCKER-PUNCH.
HE GOT ME.
GOT ME GOOD.
THE MAN WHO CAN BE ANYTHING GETS ME FOR EVERYTHING I'VE GOT...

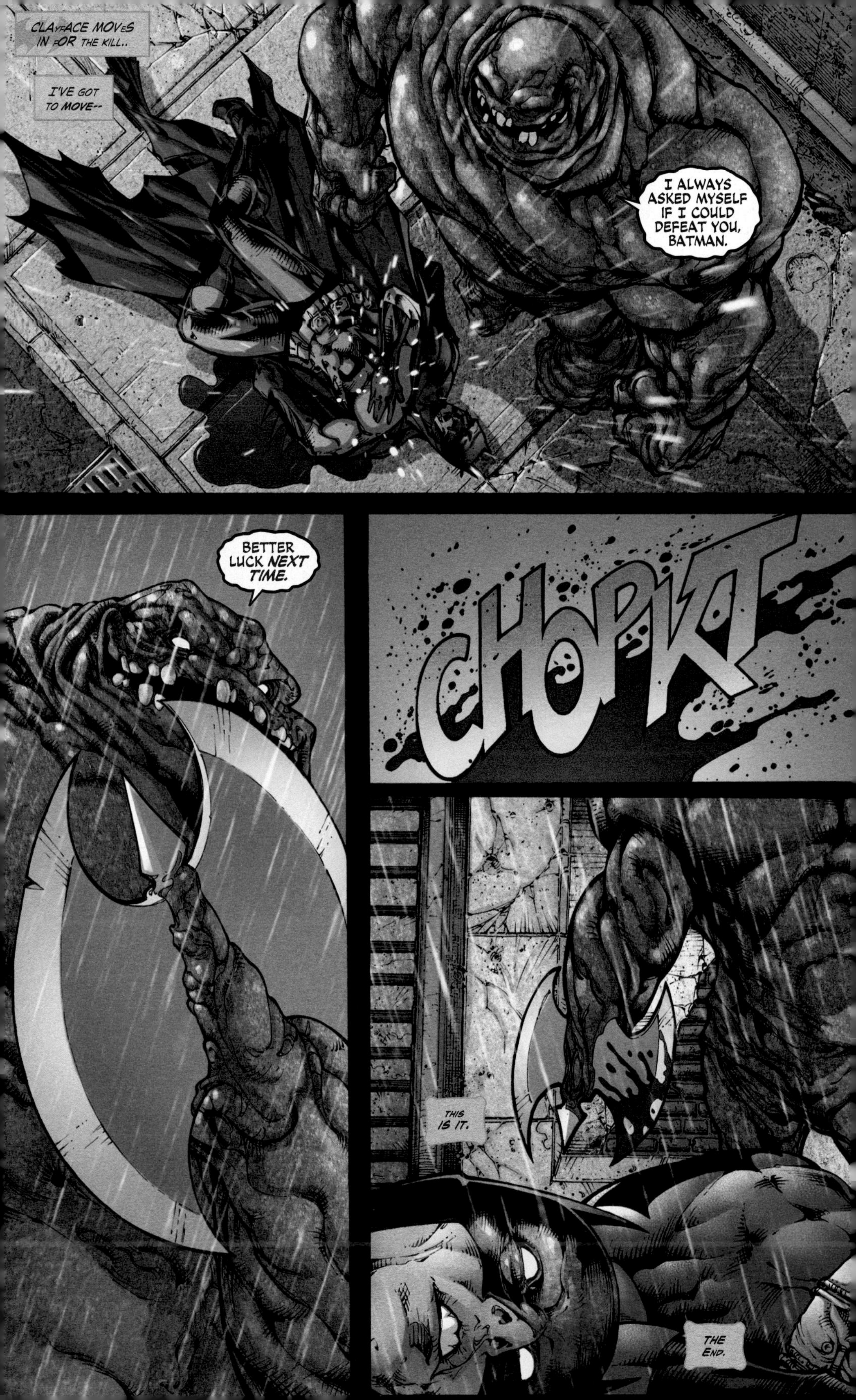
CLAYFACE MOVES IN FOR THE KILL..
I'VE GOT TO MOVE--
I ALWAYS ASKED MYSELF IF I COULD DEFEAT YOU, BATMAN.
BETTER LUCK NEXT TIME.
CHOPKT
THIS IS IT.
THE END.

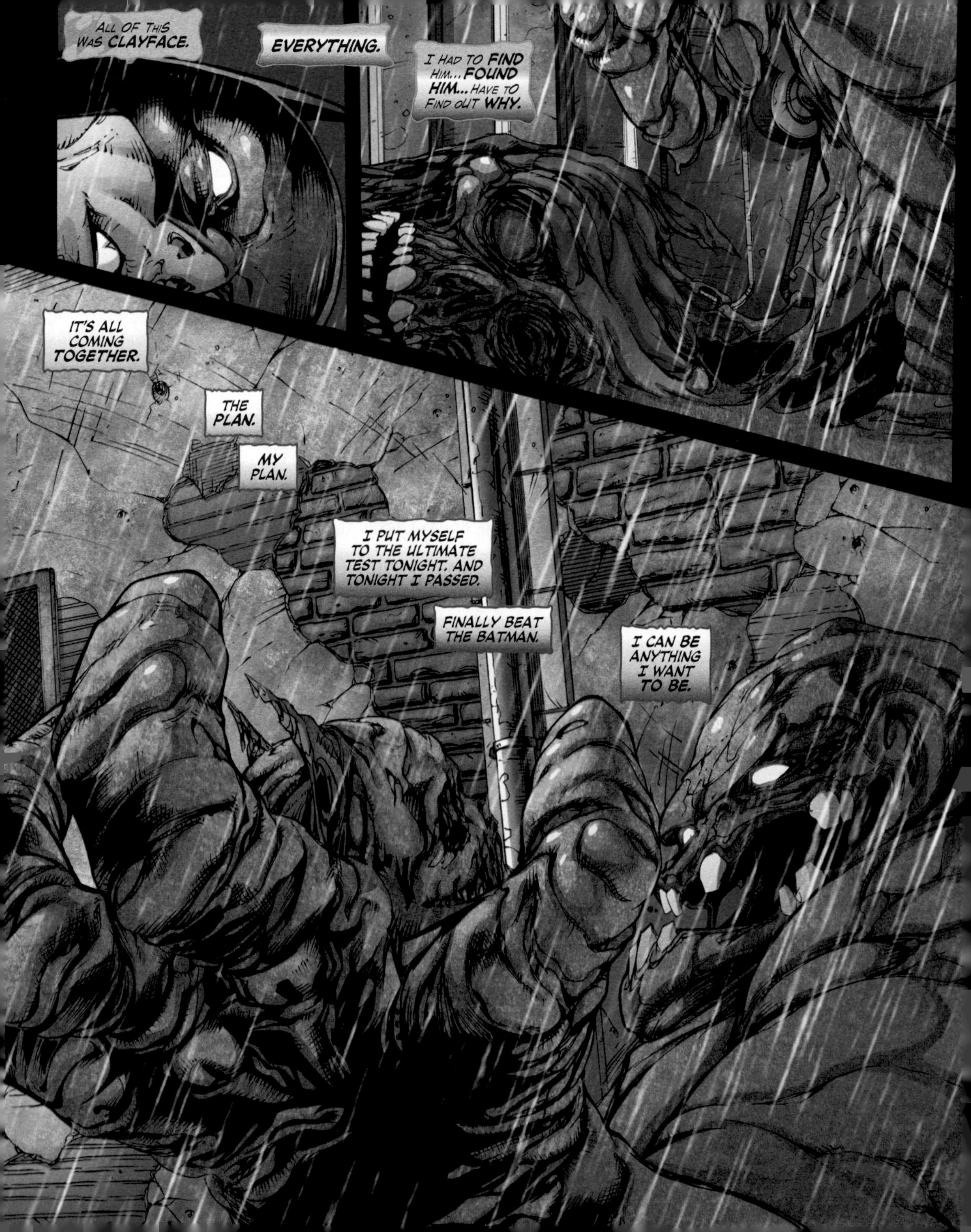
ALL OF THIS WAS CLAYFACE.
EVERYTHING.
I HAD TO FIND HIM... FOUND HIM... HAVE TO FIND OUT WHY.
IT'S ALL COMING TOGETHER.
THE PLAN.
MY PLAN.
I PUT MYSELF TO THE ULTIMATE TEST TONIGHT. AND TONIGHT I PASSED.
FINALLY BEAT THE BATMAN.
I CAN BE ANYTHING I WANT TO BE.

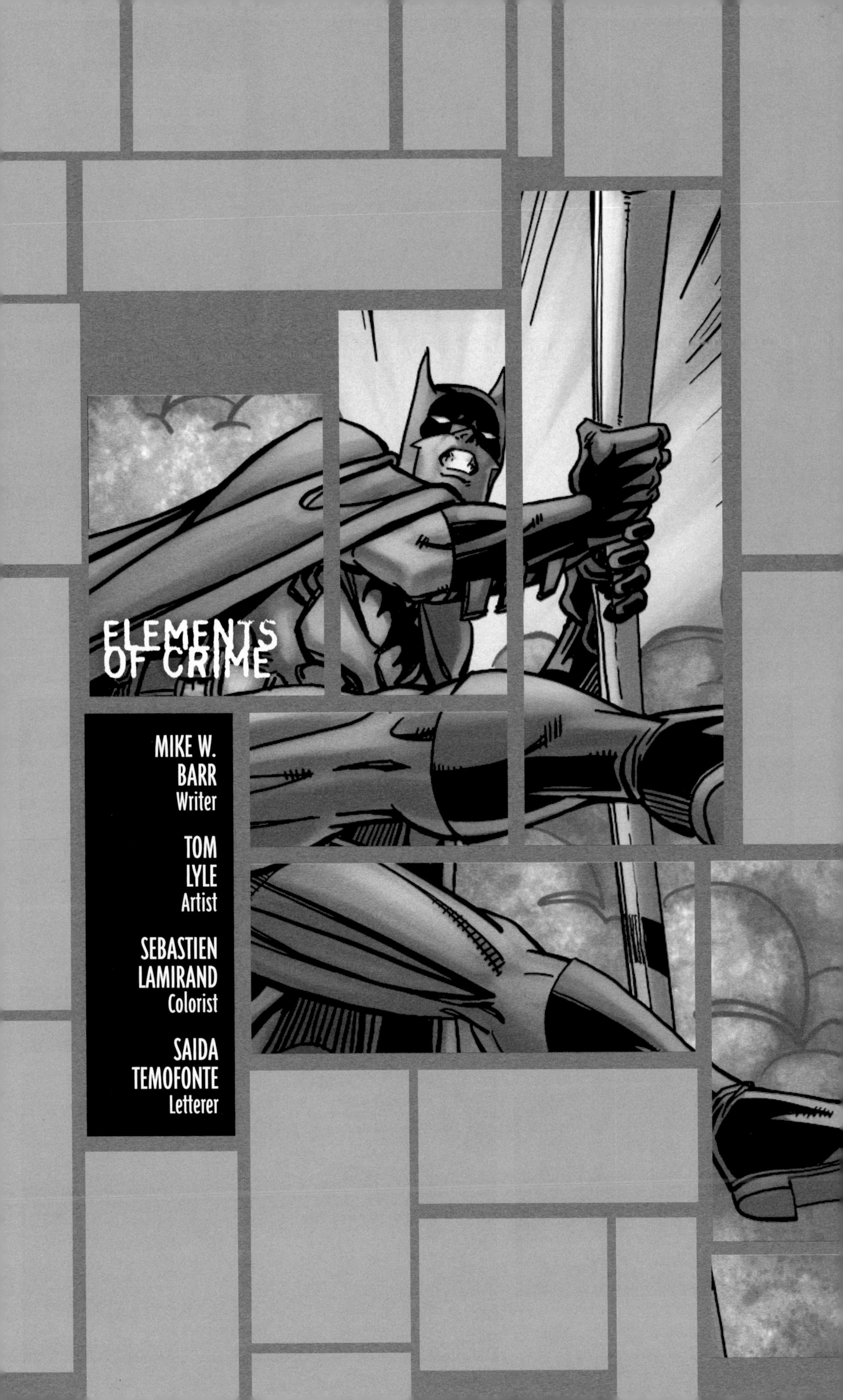
ELEMENTS OF CRIME
MIKE W. BARR Writer
TOM LYLE Artist
SEBASTIEN LAMIRAND Colorist
SAIDA TEMOFONTE Letterer

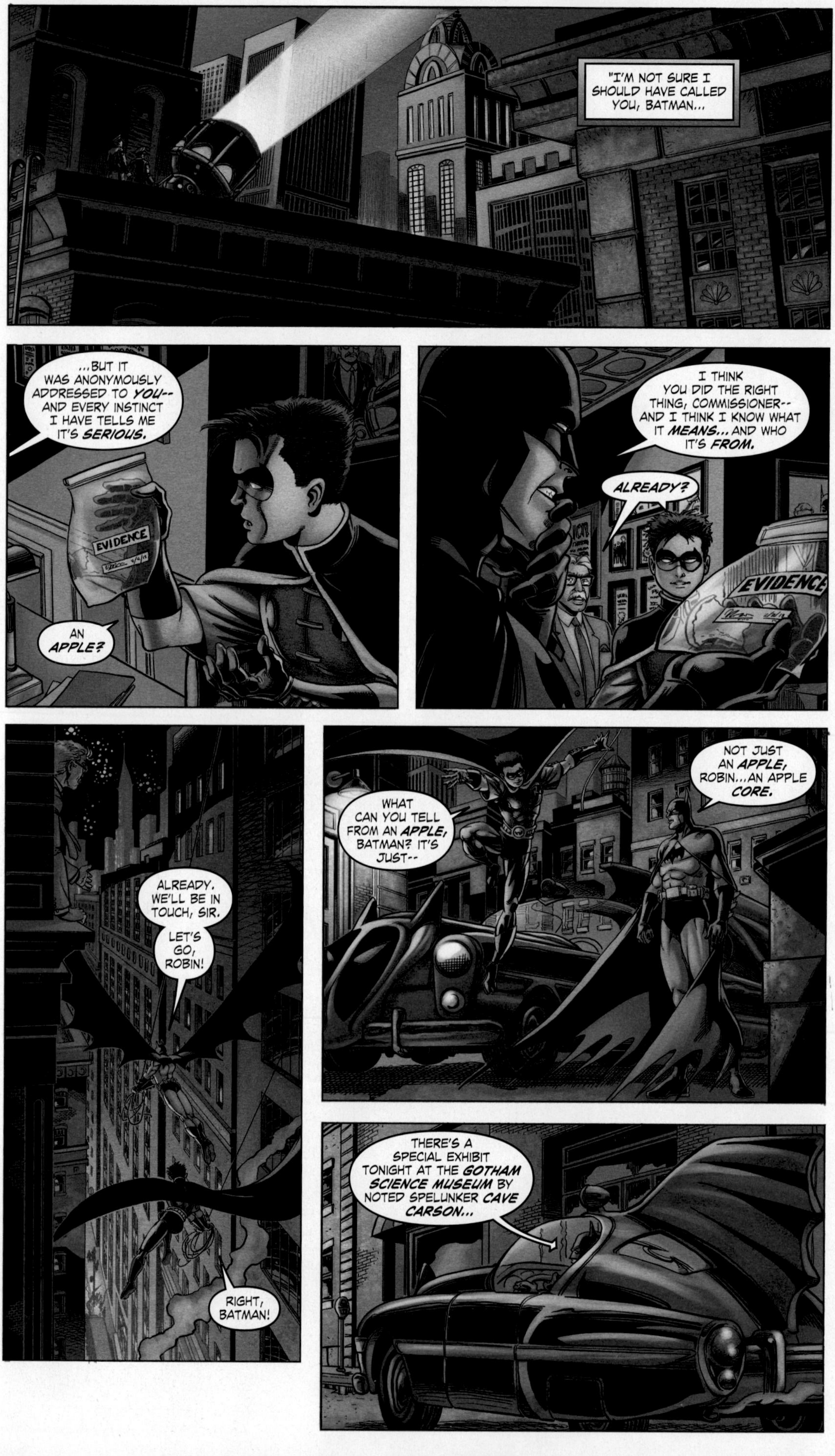
"I'M NOT SURE I SHOULD HAVE CALLED YOU, BATMAN...
...BUT IT WAS ANONYMOUSLY ADDRESSED TO YOU--AND EVERY INSTINCT I HAVE TELLS ME IT'S SERIOUS.
EVIDENCE
AN APPLE?
I THINK YOU DID THE RIGHT THING, COMMISSIONER--AND I THINK I KNOW WHAT IT MEANS... AND WHO IT'S FROM.
ALREADY?
EVIDENCE
ALREADY. WE'LL BE IN TOUCH, SIR.
LET'S GO, ROBIN!
RIGHT, BATMAN!
WHAT CAN YOU TELL FROM AN APPLE, BATMAN? IT'S JUST--
NOT JUST AN APPLE, ROBIN...AN APPLE CORE.
THERE'S A SPECIAL EXHIBIT TONIGHT AT THE GOTHAM SCIENCE MUSEUM BY NOTED SPELUNKER CAVE CARSON...

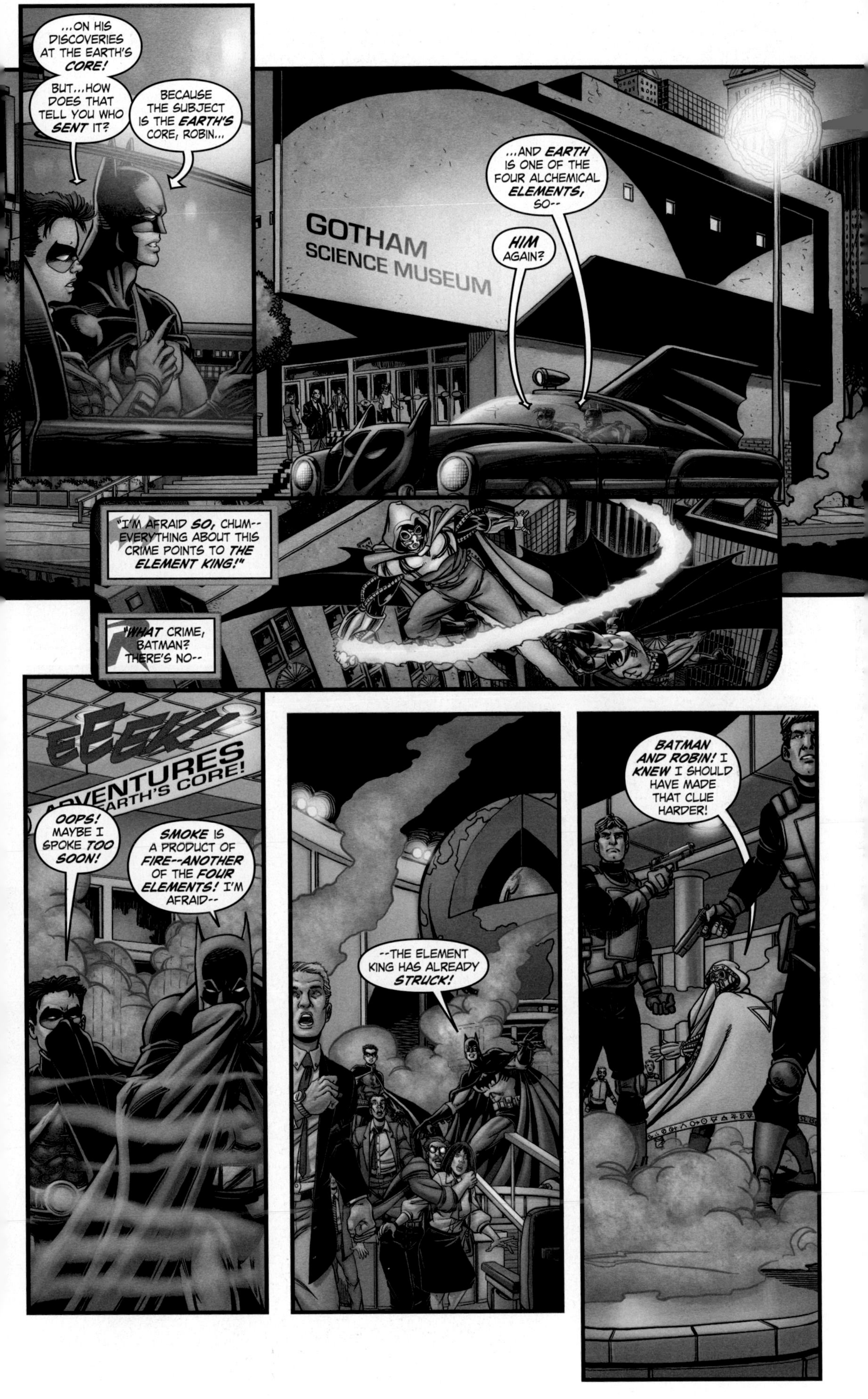
...ON HIS DISCOVERIES AT THE EARTH'S CORE!
BUT...HOW DOES THAT TELL YOU WHO SENT IT?
BECAUSE THE SUBJECT IS THE EARTH'S CORE, ROBIN...
GOTHAM SCIENCE MUSEUM
...AND EARTH IS ONE OF THE FOUR ALCHEMICAL ELEMENTS, SO--
HIM AGAIN?
"I'M AFRAID SO, CHUM-- EVERYTHING ABOUT THIS CRIME POINTS TO THE ELEMENT KING!"
"WHAT CRIME, BATMAN? THERE'S NO--
EEEK!
ADVENTURES EARTH'S CORE!
OOPS! MAYBE I SPOKE TOO SOON!
SMOKE IS A PRODUCT OF FIRE--ANOTHER OF THE FOUR ELEMENTS! I'M AFRAID--
--THE ELEMENT KING HAS ALREADY STRUCK!
BATMAN AND ROBIN! I KNEW I SHOULD HAVE MADE THAT CLUE HARDER!

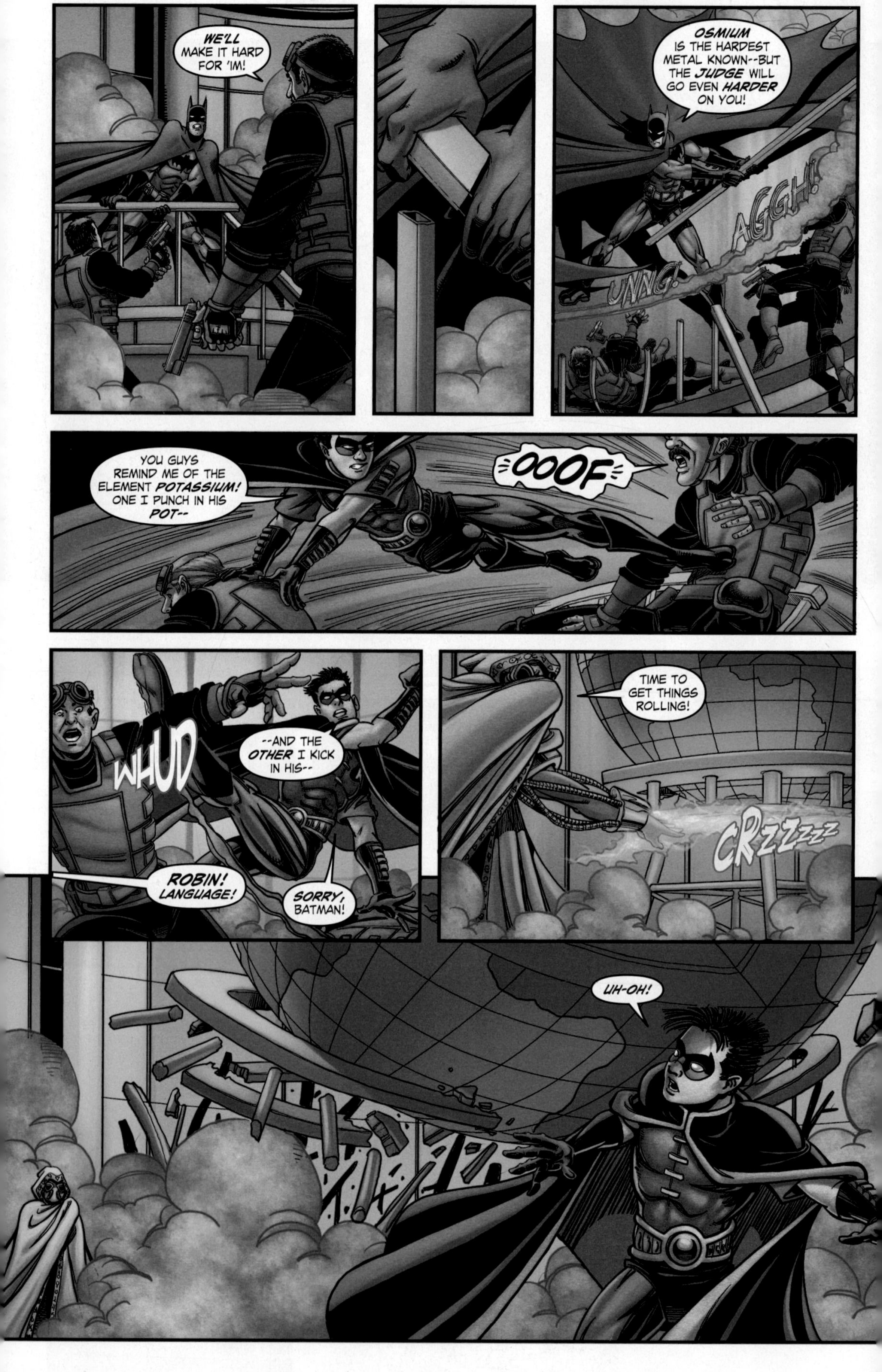
WE'LL MAKE IT HARD FOR 'IM!
OSMIUM IS THE HARDEST METAL KNOWN--BUT THE JUDGE WILL GO EVEN HARDER ON YOU!
AGGH!
UNNG!
YOU GUYS REMIND ME OF THE ELEMENT POTASSIUM! ONE I PUNCH IN HIS POT--
OOOF
WHUD
--AND THE OTHER I KICK IN HIS--
ROBIN! LANGUAGE!
SORRY, BATMAN!
TIME TO GET THINGS ROLLING!
CRZZZZZZ
UH-OH!

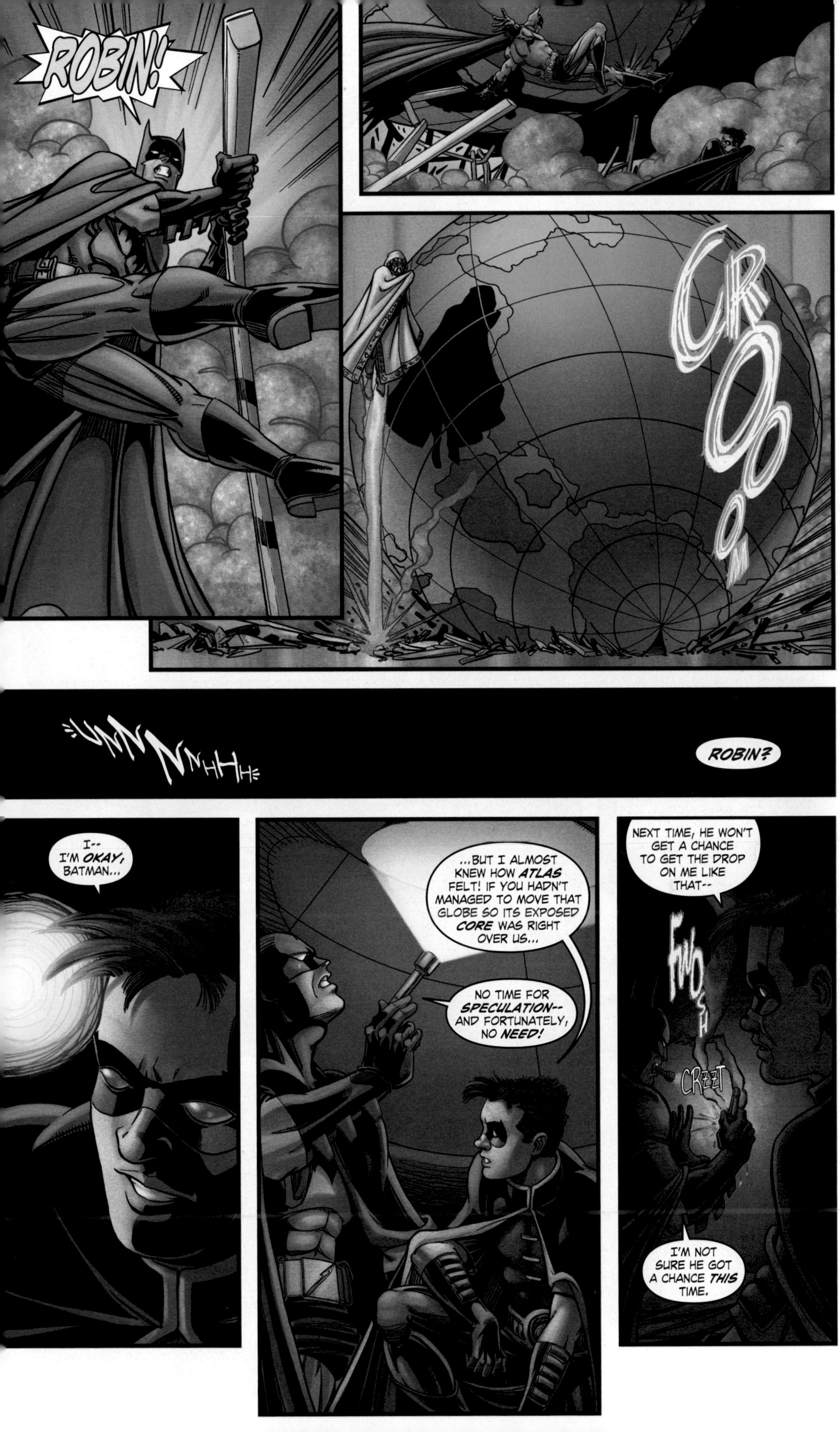
ROBIN!
CRROOOOM
UNNNNHHH
ROBIN?
I-- I'M OKAY, BATMAN...
...BUT I ALMOST KNEW HOW ATLAS FELT! IF YOU HADN'T MANAGED TO MOVE THAT GLOBE SO ITS EXPOSED CORE WAS RIGHT OVER US...
NO TIME FOR SPECULATION-- AND FORTUNATELY, NO NEED!
NEXT TIME, HE WON'T GET A CHANCE TO GET THE DROP ON ME LIKE THAT--
FWOOSH
CRZZT
I'M NOT SURE HE GOT A CHANCE THIS TIME.

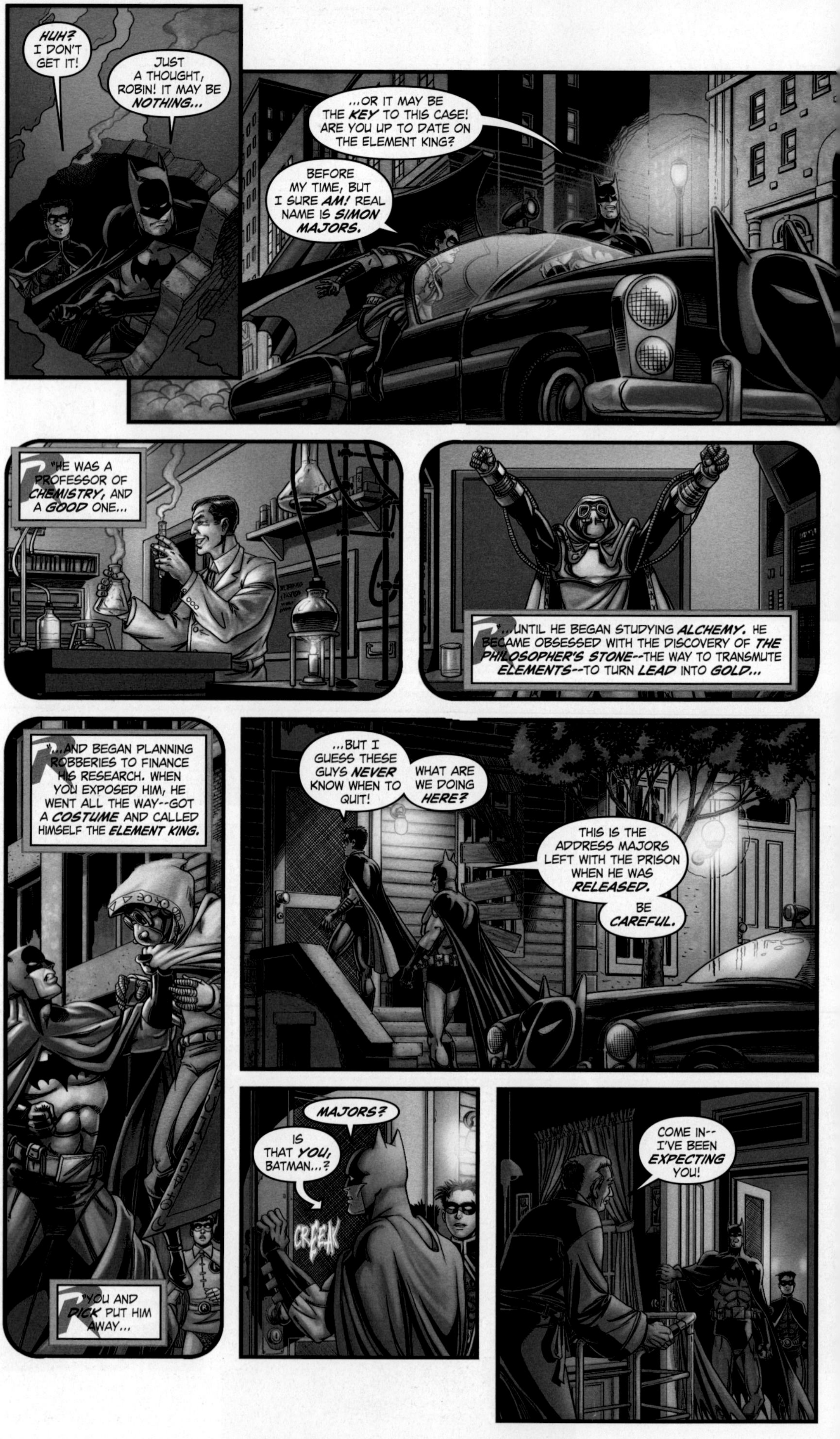
HUH? I DON'T GET IT!
JUST A THOUGHT, ROBIN! IT MAY BE NOTHING...
...OR IT MAY BE THE KEY TO THIS CASE! ARE YOU UP TO DATE ON THE ELEMENT KING?
BEFORE MY TIME, BUT I SURE AM! REAL NAME IS SIMON MAJORS.
"HE WAS A PROFESSOR OF CHEMISTRY, AND A GOOD ONE...
"...UNTIL HE BEGAN STUDYING ALCHEMY. HE BECAME OBSESSED WITH THE DISCOVERY OF THE PHILOSOPHER'S STONE--THE WAY TO TRANSMUTE ELEMENTS--TO TURN LEAD INTO GOLD...
"...AND BEGAN PLANNING ROBBERIES TO FINANCE HIS RESEARCH. WHEN YOU EXPOSED HIM, HE WENT ALL THE WAY--GOT A COSTUME AND CALLED HIMSELF THE ELEMENT KING.
"YOU AND DICK PUT HIM AWAY...
...BUT I GUESS THESE GUYS NEVER KNOW WHEN TO QUIT!
WHAT ARE WE DOING HERE?
THIS IS THE ADDRESS MAJORS LEFT WITH THE PRISON WHEN HE WAS RELEASED.
BE CAREFUL.
MAJORS?
CREEAK
IS THAT YOU, BATMAN...?
COME IN-- I'VE BEEN EXPECTING YOU!

PRISON LIFE WASN'T *GOOD* TO YOU, SIMON.

KEEP YOUR *HANDS* WHERE I CAN *SEE* THEM.

OF *COURSE*, BATMAN--BUT IT WAS THE *CHEMICALS* I USED IN MY RESEARCH THAT DID THIS TO ME... KNOWLEDGE IS A *JEALOUS* MISTRESS.

I *KNOW*. DO YOU HAVE AN *ALIBI* FOR TONIGHT, MAJORS?

I DON'T *NEED* ONE, BATMAN! I'M AWARE OF THE *ROBBERY* AT THE SCIENCE HALL, YES--IT WAS ON THE *NEWS*--BUT I DIDN'T COMMIT IT.

THEN WHO *DID*?

IT'S *YOUR* JOB TO PROVE THAT...BUT I CAN *HELP*. I THINK THE CULPRIT IS ONE OF THE PEOPLE I CORRESPONDED WITH IN PRISON...

...A YOUNG SCIENTIST WHO WAS VERY INQUISITIVE ABOUT MY ATTEMPTS TO CREATE A PHILOSOPHER'S STONE--*DR. SANDRA AURUM*. THAT'S HER ADDRESS.

I HOPE THIS IS THE *TRUTH*--FOR *YOUR* SAKE.

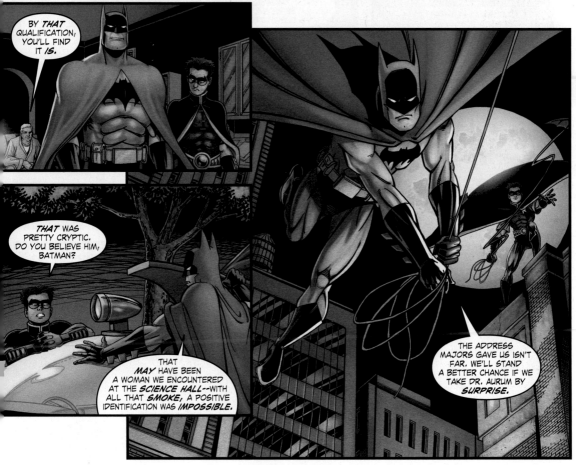

BY *THAT* QUALIFICATION, YOU'LL FIND IT *IS*.

THAT WAS PRETTY CRYPTIC. DO YOU BELIEVE HIM, BATMAN?

THAT *MAY* HAVE BEEN A WOMAN WE ENCOUNTERED AT THE *SCIENCE HALL*--WITH ALL THAT *SMOKE*, A POSITIVE IDENTIFICATION WAS *IMPOSSIBLE*.

THE ADDRESS MAJORS GAVE US ISN'T FAR. WE'LL STAND A BETTER CHANCE IF WE TAKE DR. AURUM BY *SURPRISE*.

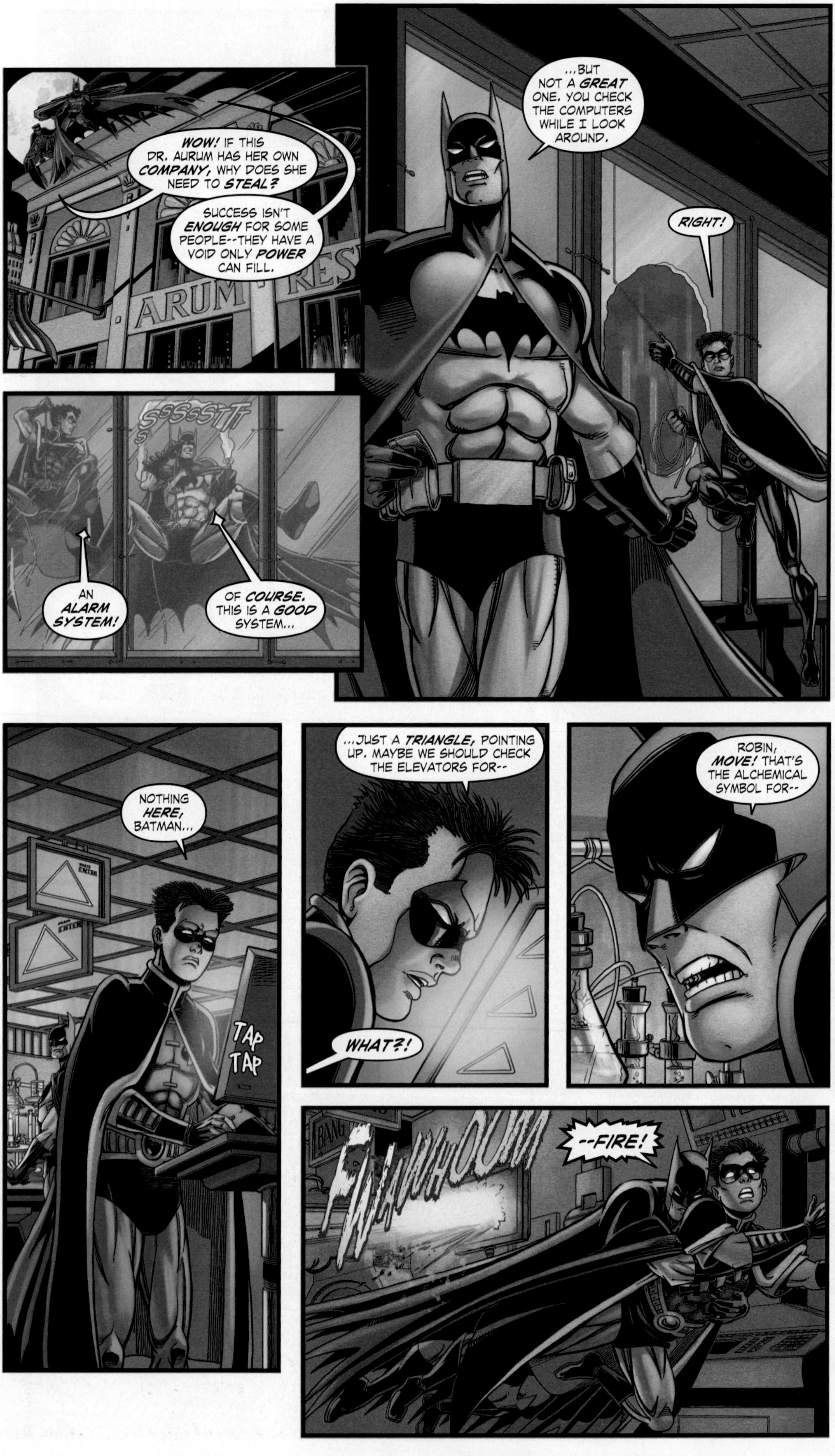
WOW! IF THIS DR. AURUM HAS HER OWN COMPANY, WHY DOES SHE NEED TO STEAL?
SUCCESS ISN'T ENOUGH FOR SOME PEOPLE--THEY HAVE A VOID ONLY POWER CAN FILL.
ARUM
SSSSSTT
AN ALARM SYSTEM!
OF COURSE. THIS IS A GOOD SYSTEM...
...BUT NOT A GREAT ONE. YOU CHECK THE COMPUTERS WHILE I LOOK AROUND.
RIGHT!
NOTHING HERE, BATMAN...
TAP TAP
...JUST A TRIANGLE, POINTING UP. MAYBE WE SHOULD CHECK THE ELEVATORS FOR--
WHAT?!
ROBIN, MOVE! THAT'S THE ALCHEMICAL SYMBOL FOR--
--FIRE!

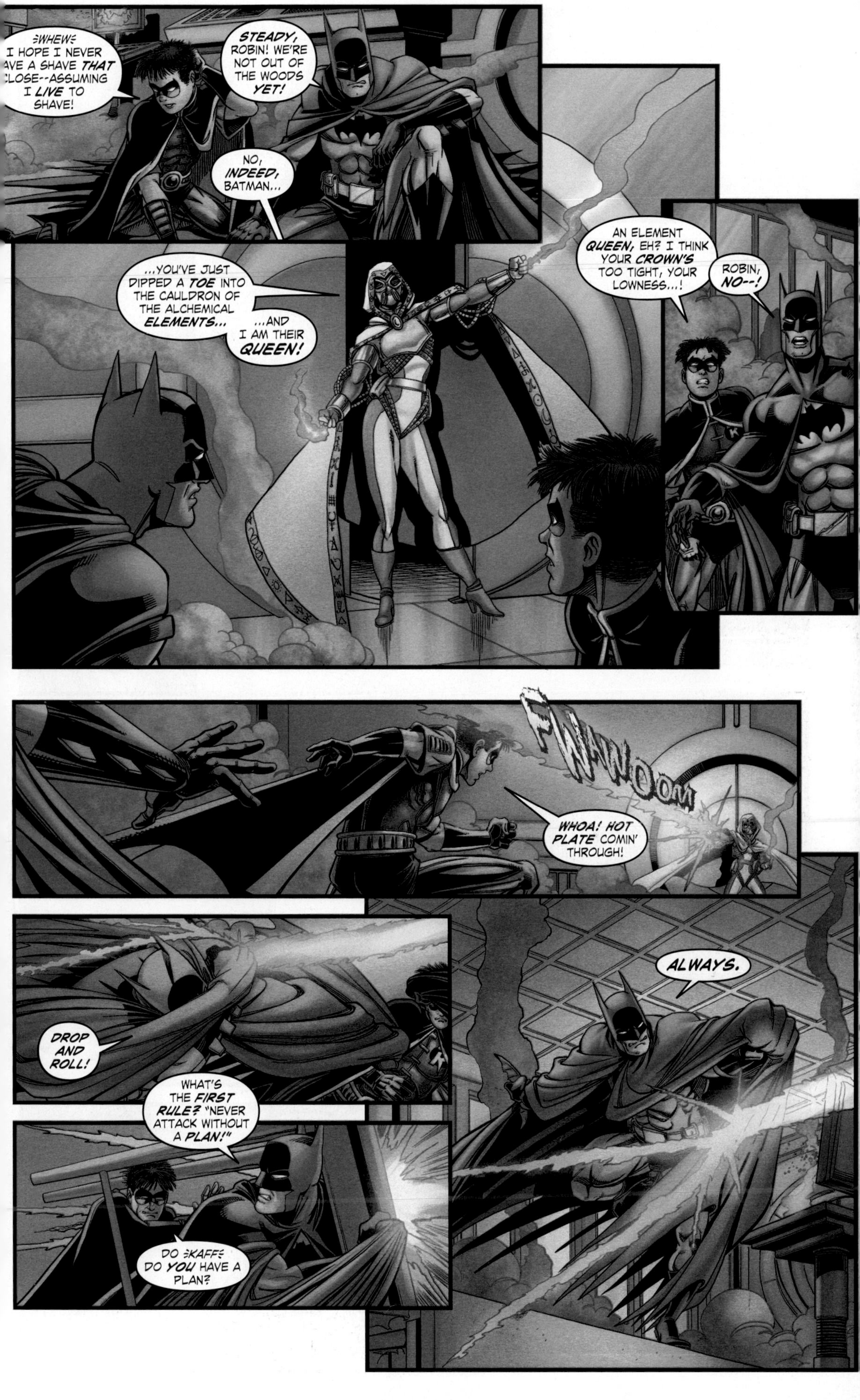

=WHEW= I HOPE I NEVER HAVE A SHAVE THAT CLOSE--ASSUMING I LIVE TO SHAVE!
STEADY, ROBIN! WE'RE NOT OUT OF THE WOODS YET!
NO, INDEED, BATMAN...
...YOU'VE JUST DIPPED A TOE INTO THE CAULDRON OF THE ALCHEMICAL ELEMENTS...
...AND I AM THEIR QUEEN!
AN ELEMENT QUEEN, EH? I THINK YOUR CROWN'S TOO TIGHT, YOUR LOWNESS...!
ROBIN, NO--!
FWAWOOM
WHOA! HOT PLATE COMIN' THROUGH!
DROP AND ROLL!
WHAT'S THE FIRST RULE? "NEVER ATTACK WITHOUT A PLAN!"
DO =KAFF= DO YOU HAVE A PLAN?
ALWAYS.

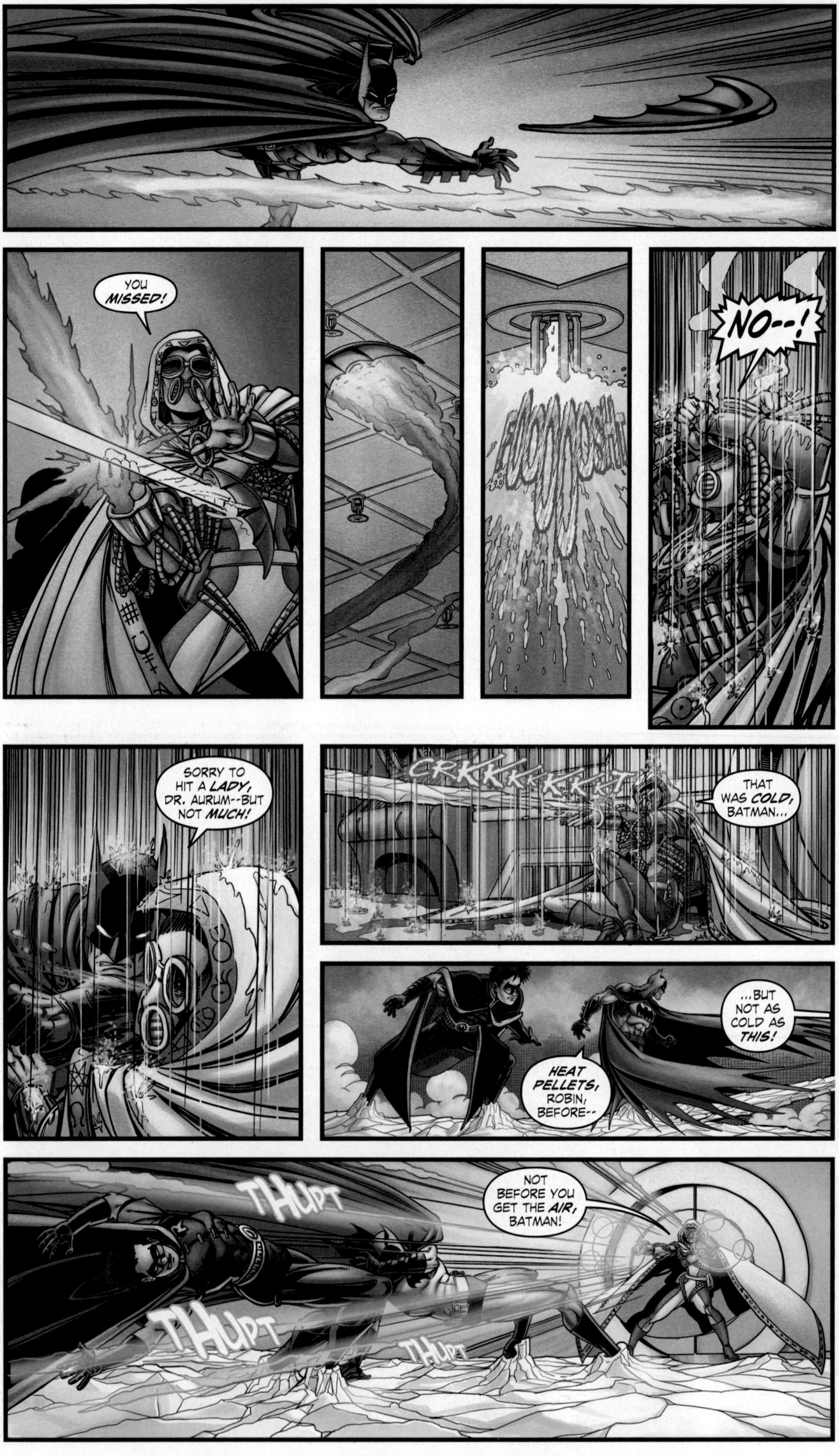

YOU MISSED!
NO--!
SORRY TO HIT A LADY, DR. AURUM--BUT NOT MUCH!
CRKKKKKKKT
THAT WAS COLD, BATMAN...
HEAT PELLETS, ROBIN, BEFORE--
...BUT NOT AS COLD AS THIS!
THUPT
NOT BEFORE YOU GET THE AIR, BATMAN!
THUPT
THUPT

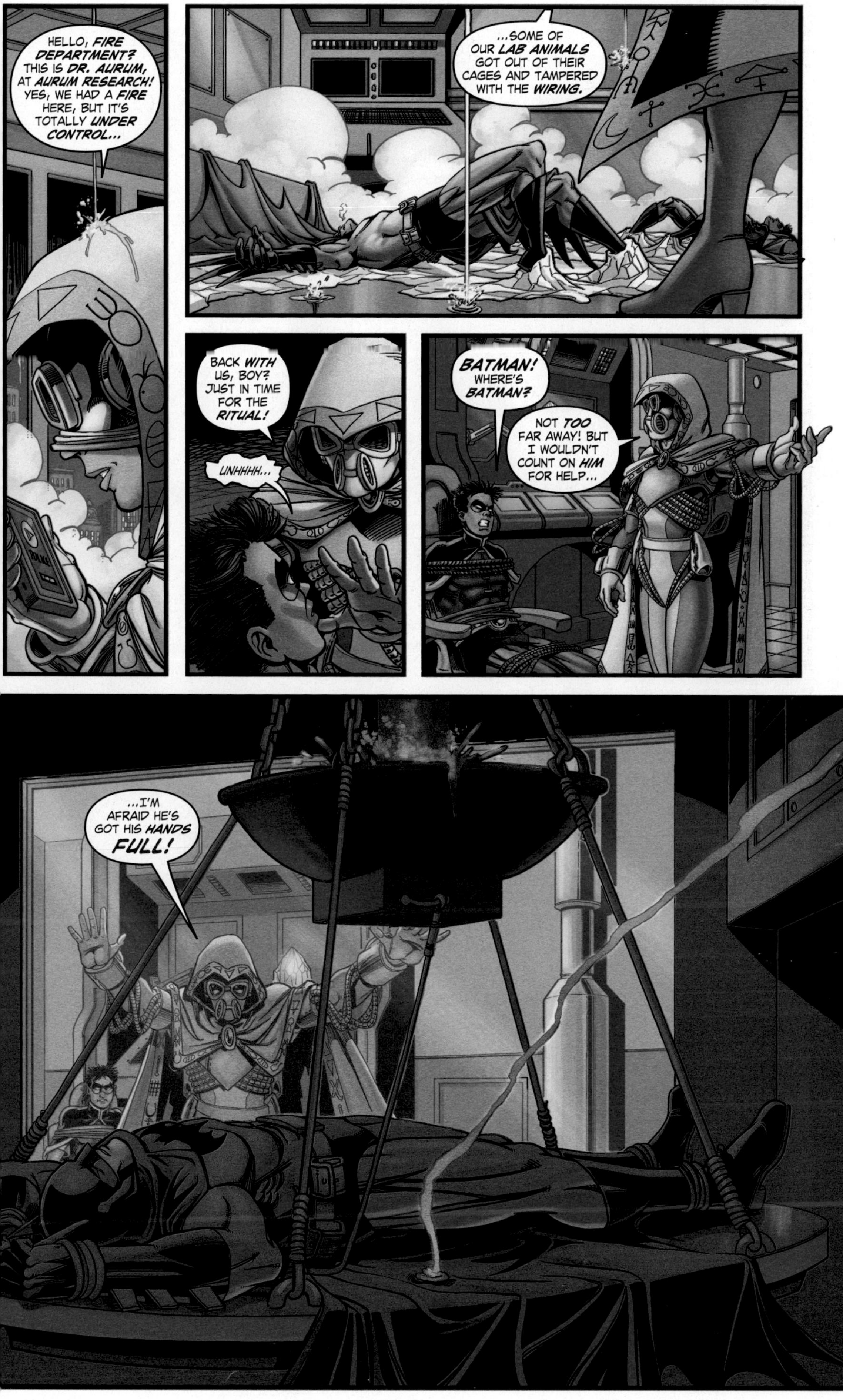
HELLO, FIRE DEPARTMENT? THIS IS DR. AURUM, AT AURUM RESEARCH! YES, WE HAD A FIRE HERE, BUT IT'S TOTALLY UNDER CONTROL...
...SOME OF OUR LAB ANIMALS GOT OUT OF THEIR CAGES AND TAMPERED WITH THE WIRING.
BACK WITH US, BOY? JUST IN TIME FOR THE RITUAL!
UNHHHH...
BATMAN! WHERE'S BATMAN?
NOT TOO FAR AWAY! BUT I WOULDN'T COUNT ON HIM FOR HELP...
...I'M AFRAID HE'S GOT HIS HANDS FULL!

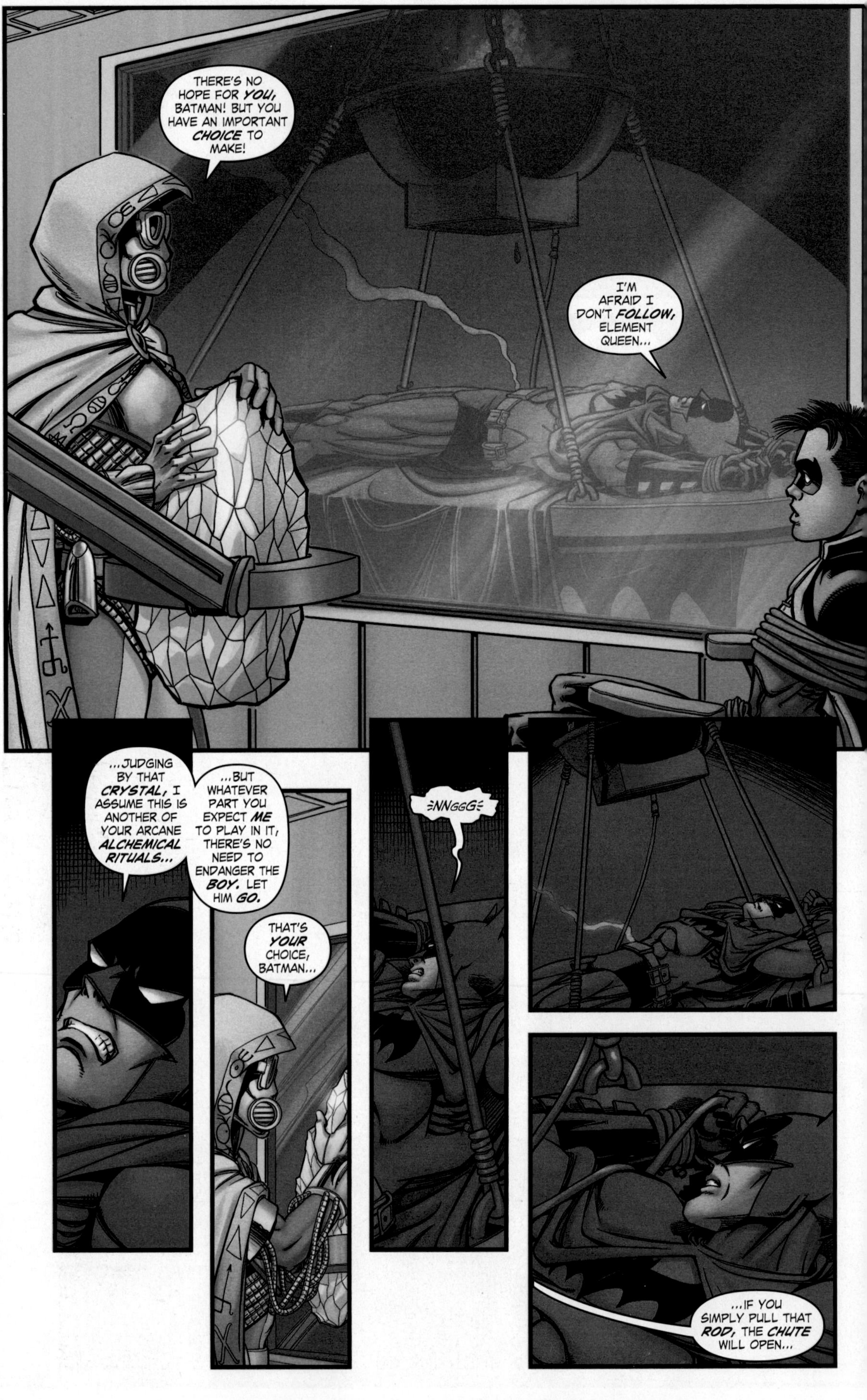
THERE'S NO HOPE FOR YOU, BATMAN! BUT YOU HAVE AN IMPORTANT CHOICE TO MAKE!
I'M AFRAID I DON'T FOLLOW, ELEMENT QUEEN...
...JUDGING BY THAT CRYSTAL, I ASSUME THIS IS ANOTHER OF YOUR ARCANE ALCHEMICAL RITUALS...
...BUT WHATEVER PART YOU EXPECT ME TO PLAY IN IT, THERE'S NO NEED TO ENDANGER THE BOY. LET HIM GO.
THAT'S YOUR CHOICE, BATMAN...
NNGGG
...IF YOU SIMPLY PULL THAT ROD, THE CHUTE WILL OPEN...

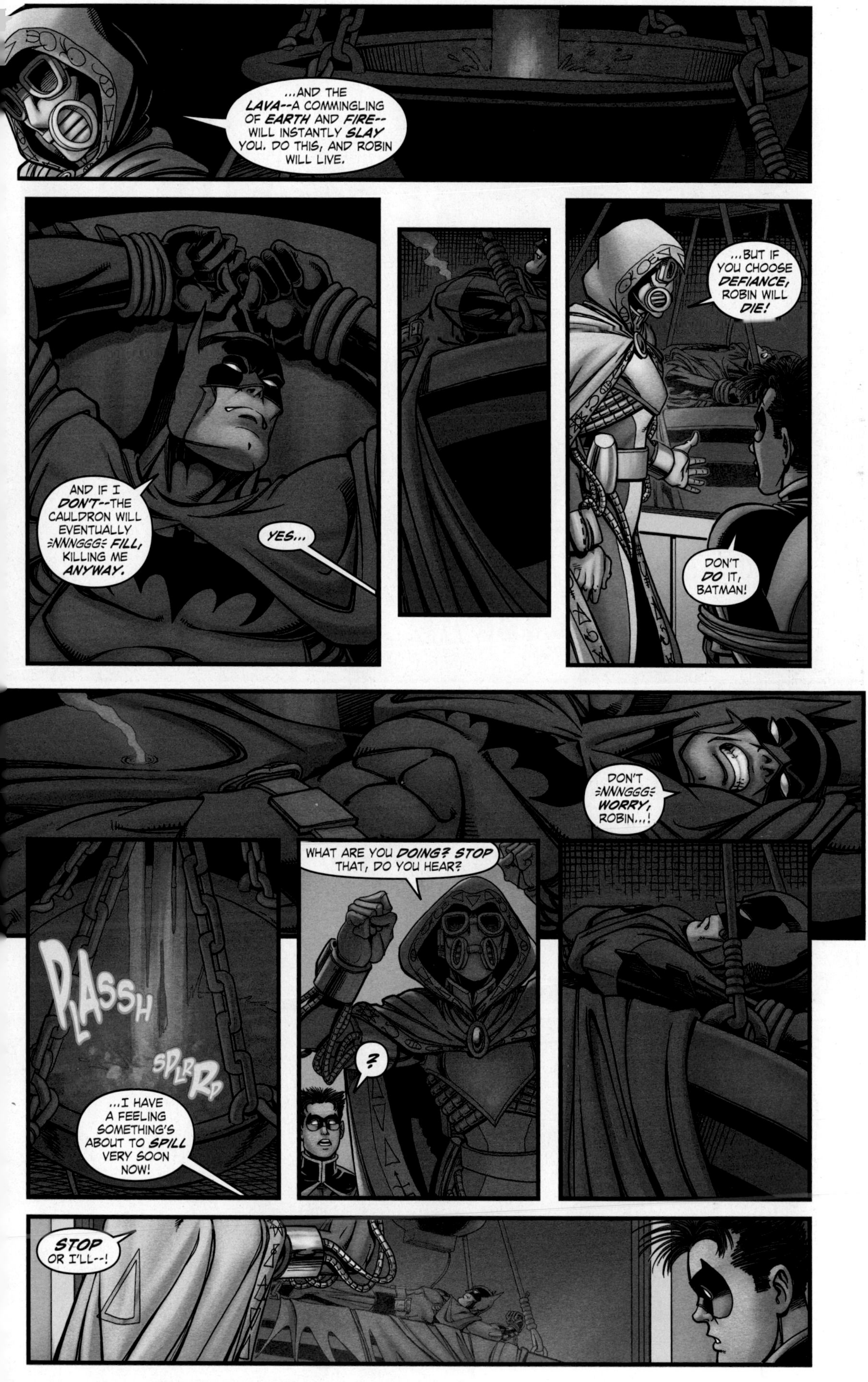
...AND THE LAVA--A COMMINGLING OF EARTH AND FIRE--WILL INSTANTLY SLAY YOU. DO THIS, AND ROBIN WILL LIVE.
AND IF I DON'T--THE CAULDRON WILL EVENTUALLY NNNGGG FILL, KILLING ME ANYWAY.
YES...
...BUT IF YOU CHOOSE DEFIANCE, ROBIN WILL DIE!
DON'T DO IT, BATMAN!
DON'T NNNGGG WORRY, ROBIN...!
PLASSH
SPLRRD
...I HAVE A FEELING SOMETHING'S ABOUT TO SPILL VERY SOON NOW!
WHAT ARE YOU DOING? STOP THAT, DO YOU HEAR?
?
STOP OR I'LL--!

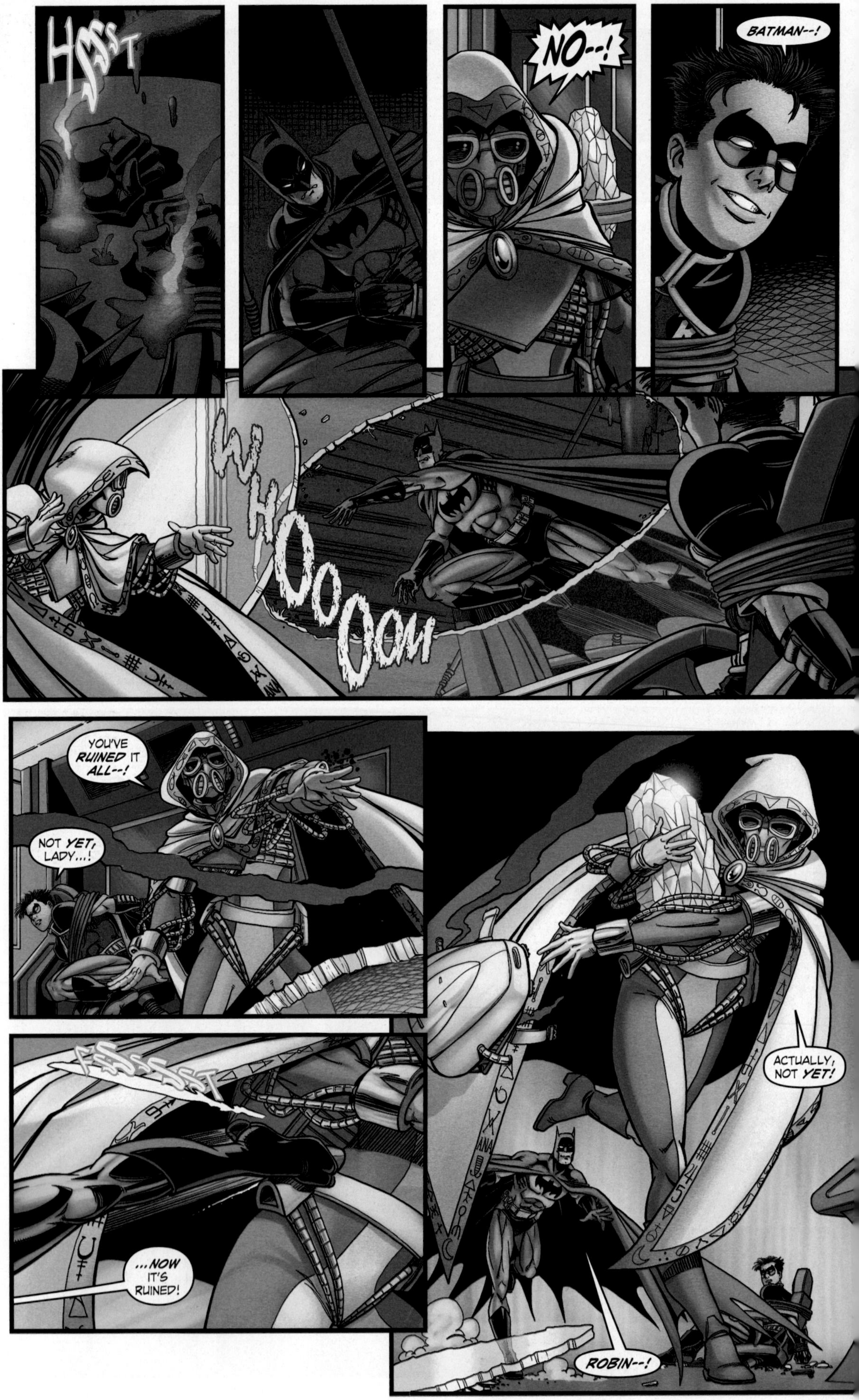
HSSST
NO--!
BATMAN--!
WHOOOOOM
YOU'VE RUINED IT ALL--!
NOT YET, LADY...!
ACTUALLY, NOT YET!
FSSSST
...NOW IT'S RUINED!
ROBIN--!

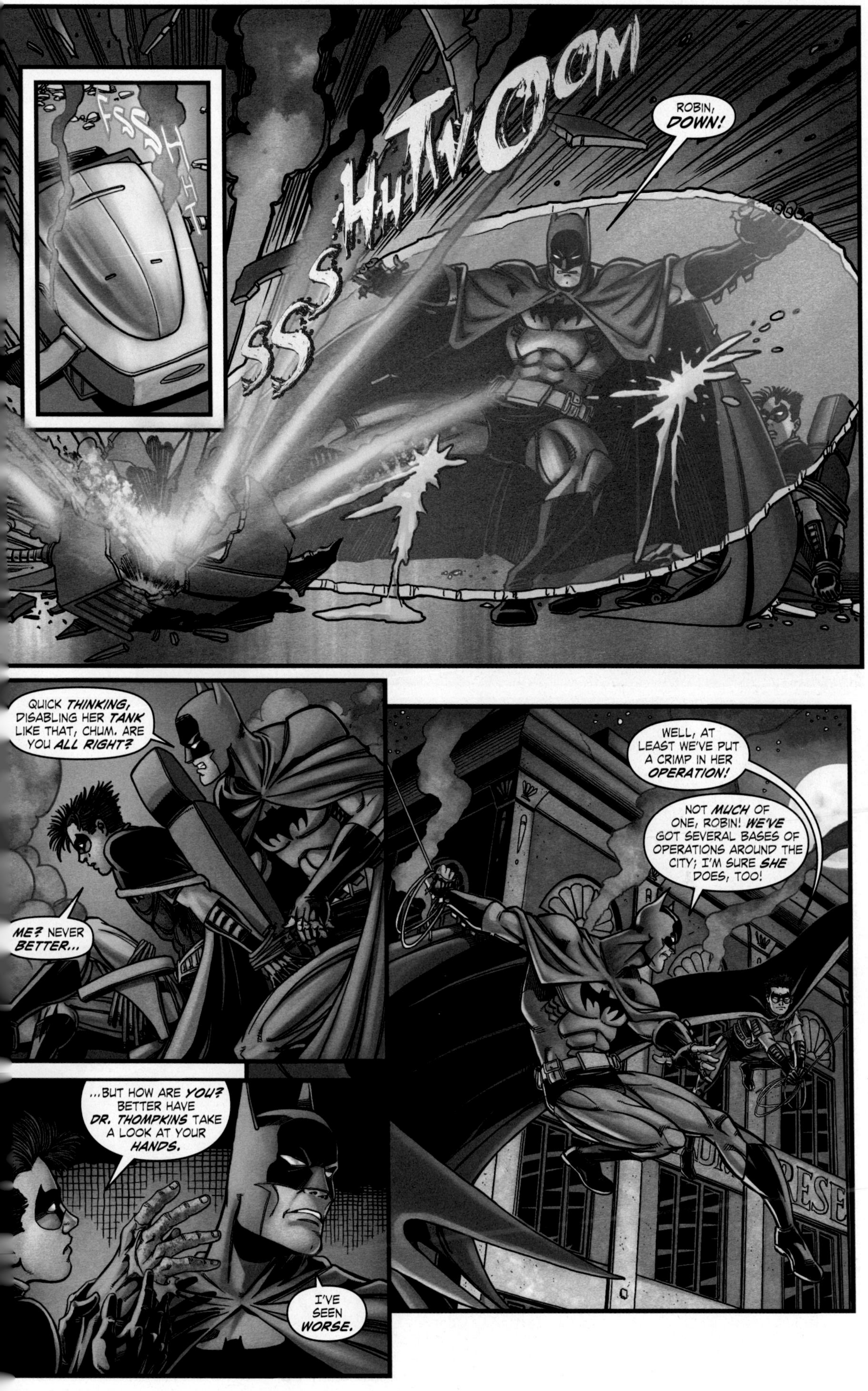
FSSHHH
SSSHHTVOOOM
ROBIN, DOWN!
QUICK THINKING, DISABLING HER TANK LIKE THAT, CHUM. ARE YOU ALL RIGHT?
ME? NEVER BETTER...
...BUT HOW ARE YOU? BETTER HAVE DR. THOMPKINS TAKE A LOOK AT YOUR HANDS.
I'VE SEEN WORSE.
WELL, AT LEAST WE'VE PUT A CRIMP IN HER OPERATION!
NOT MUCH OF ONE, ROBIN! WE'VE GOT SEVERAL BASES OF OPERATIONS AROUND THE CITY; I'M SURE SHE DOES, TOO!

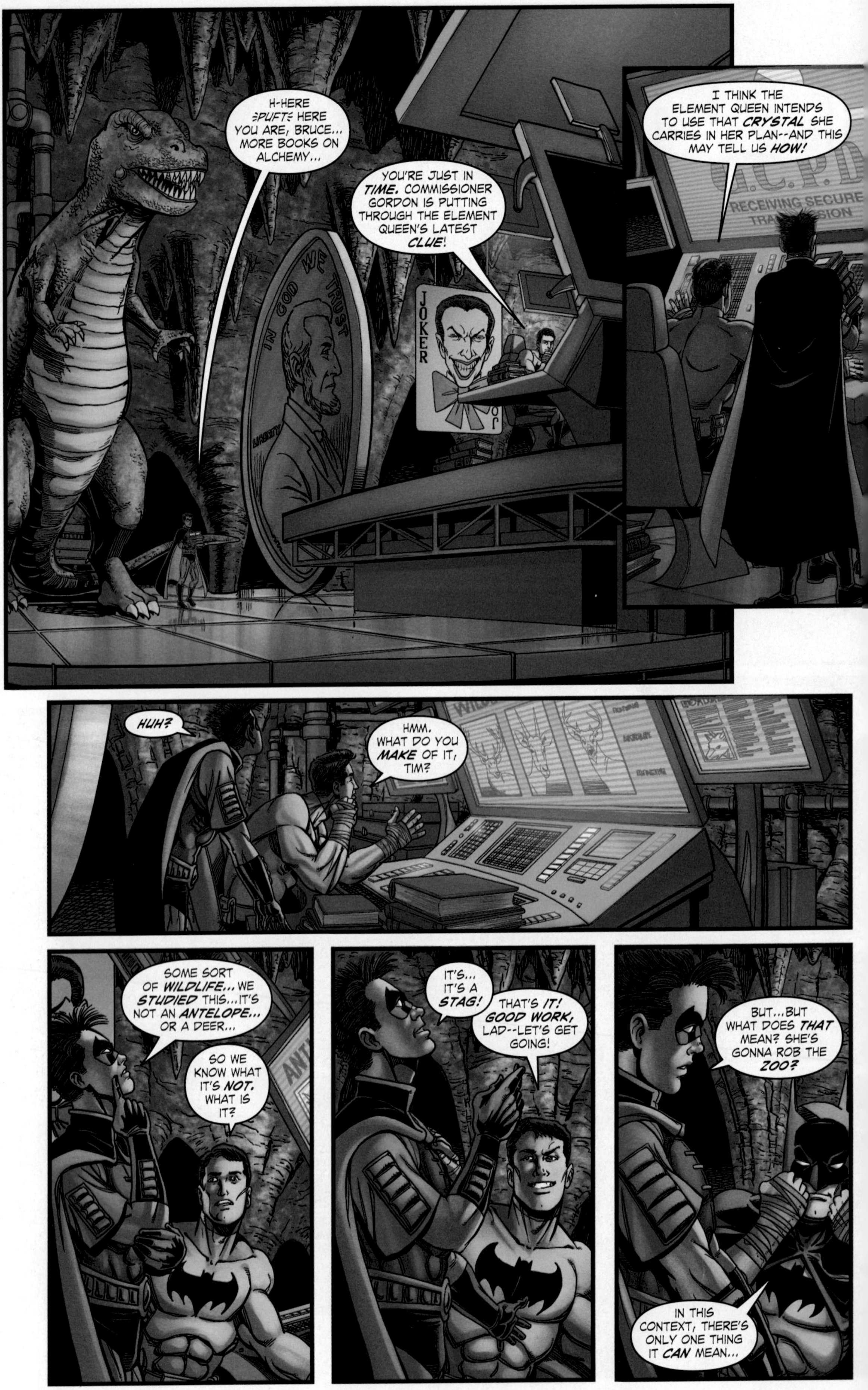
H-HERE *PUFT* HERE YOU ARE, BRUCE... MORE BOOKS ON ALCHEMY...
YOU'RE JUST IN TIME. COMMISSIONER GORDON IS PUTTING THROUGH THE ELEMENT QUEEN'S LATEST CLUE!
IN GOD WE TRUST
LIBERTY
JOKER
I THINK THE ELEMENT QUEEN INTENDS TO USE THAT CRYSTAL SHE CARRIES IN HER PLAN--AND THIS MAY TELL US HOW!
RECEIVING SECURE
HUH?
HMM. WHAT DO YOU MAKE OF IT, TIM?
SOME SORT OF WILDLIFE... WE STUDIED THIS...IT'S NOT AN ANTELOPE... OR A DEER...
SO WE KNOW WHAT IT'S NOT. WHAT IS IT?
IT'S... IT'S A STAG!
THAT'S IT! GOOD WORK, LAD--LET'S GET GOING!
BUT...BUT WHAT DOES THAT MEAN? SHE'S GONNA ROB THE ZOO?
IN THIS CONTEXT, THERE'S ONLY ONE THING IT CAN MEAN...

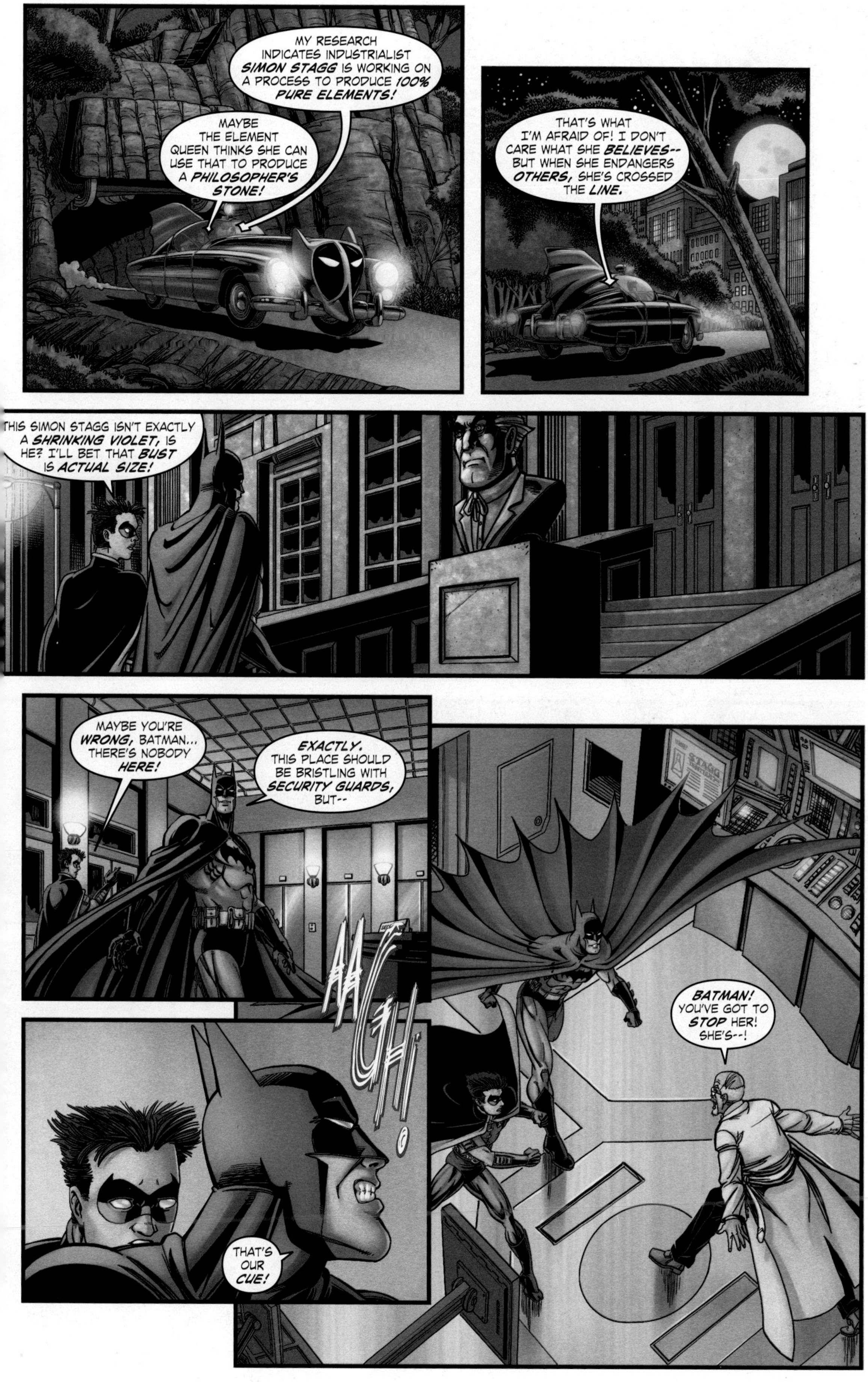
MY RESEARCH INDICATES INDUSTRIALIST SIMON STAGG IS WORKING ON A PROCESS TO PRODUCE 100% PURE ELEMENTS!
MAYBE THE ELEMENT QUEEN THINKS SHE CAN USE THAT TO PRODUCE A PHILOSOPHER'S STONE!
THAT'S WHAT I'M AFRAID OF! I DON'T CARE WHAT SHE BELIEVES-- BUT WHEN SHE ENDANGERS OTHERS, SHE'S CROSSED THE LINE.
THIS SIMON STAGG ISN'T EXACTLY A SHRINKING VIOLET, IS HE? I'LL BET THAT BUST IS ACTUAL SIZE!
MAYBE YOU'RE WRONG, BATMAN... THERE'S NOBODY HERE!
EXACTLY. THIS PLACE SHOULD BE BRISTLING WITH SECURITY GUARDS, BUT--
AAGH!
THAT'S OUR CUE!
STAGG
BATMAN! YOU'VE GOT TO STOP HER! SHE'S--!

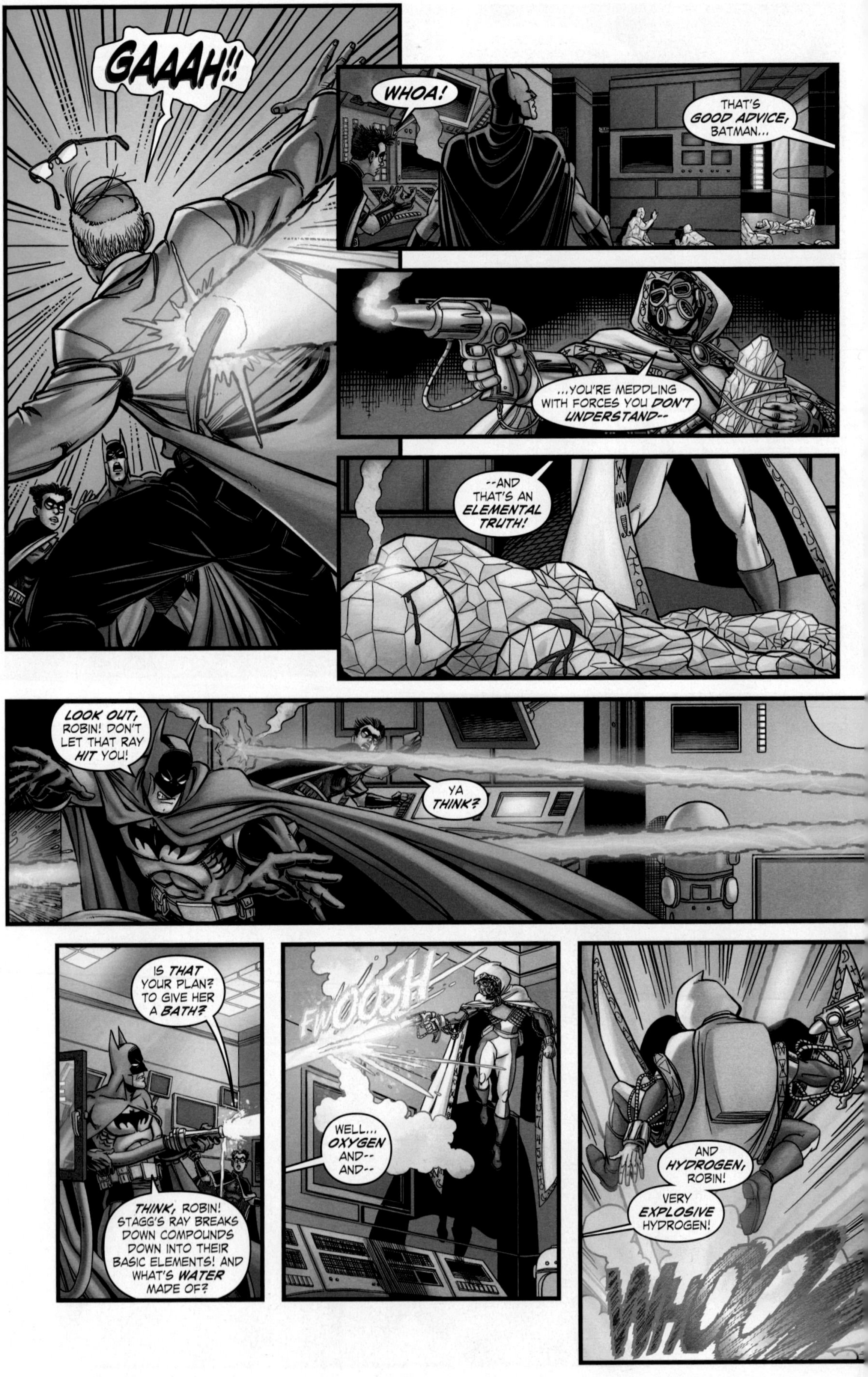
GAAAH!!
WHOA!
THAT'S GOOD ADVICE, BATMAN...
...YOU'RE MEDDLING WITH FORCES YOU DON'T UNDERSTAND--
--AND THAT'S AN ELEMENTAL TRUTH!
LOOK OUT, ROBIN! DON'T LET THAT RAY HIT YOU!
YA THINK?
IS THAT YOUR PLAN? TO GIVE HER A BATH?
THINK, ROBIN! STAGG'S RAY BREAKS DOWN COMPOUNDS DOWN INTO THEIR BASIC ELEMENTS! AND WHAT'S WATER MADE OF?
FWOOSH
WELL... OXYGEN AND-- AND--
AND HYDROGEN, ROBIN!
VERY EXPLOSIVE HYDROGEN!

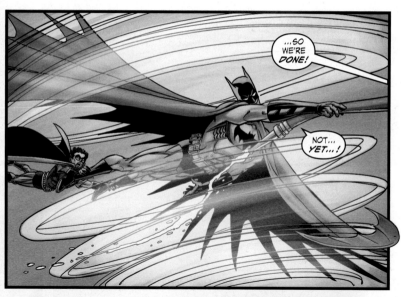

YOU DON'T *UNDERSTAND!* YOU KEEP *INTERFERING!* IF YOU DON'T LEAVE ME *ALONE,* IT WILL GO *BADLY* FOR YOU!

BUT I GOT WHAT I *CAME* FOR...

...SO WE'RE *DONE!*

NOT... *YET...!*

WHOOOOOSH

AFRAID *SO!*

COMMISSIONER, SEND *PARAMEDICS* TO THE *STAGG ENTERPRISES* BUILDING. I'M AFRAID IT'S TOO *LATE,* BUT--

THESE POOR *PEOPLE...*

...THEY'VE BEEN... BEEN...

SEPARATED TO THEIR BASIC CHEMICAL *COMPONENTS--* JUST WATER AND A FEW POUNDS OF *CHEMICALS.* THAT'S ALL THEY'RE *WORTH* TO THE ELEMENT QUEEN...

...BUT SHE'S *CROSSED* THAT LINE. SHE'S COMMITTED *MURDER...* AND SHE'S GOING TO *PAY.*

COME *ON,* ROBIN. WE CAN'T DO ANY GOOD *HERE...*

...BUT I *KNOW* WHERE WE *CAN!*

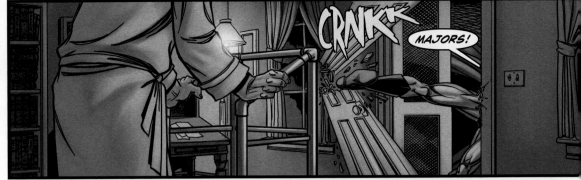

CRNKK

MAJORS!

WHERE *IS* SHE? WHERE'S THE *ELEMENT QUEEN?*

I... I *TOLD* YOU, I HAVE *NOTHING* TO DO WITH--!

DON'T TRY TO *LIE,* MAJORS--NOT TO *ME!* IT FINALLY OCCURRED TO ME...

...YOU ABSENTLY DREW THE ALCHEMICAL SYMBOLS FOR *MALE* AND *FEMALE, ALLIED,* ON THAT PAPER ROBIN FOUND! YOU AND AURUM *ARE* PARTNERS...!

WHERE

IS

SHE?

OKAY, BATMAN SAYS *SOMETHING'S* GOING TO BREAK, AND *SOON!* GOTTA STAY *FOCUSED,* AND--

--*THERE* SHE IS! BOY, WILL *SHE* BE SURPRISED!

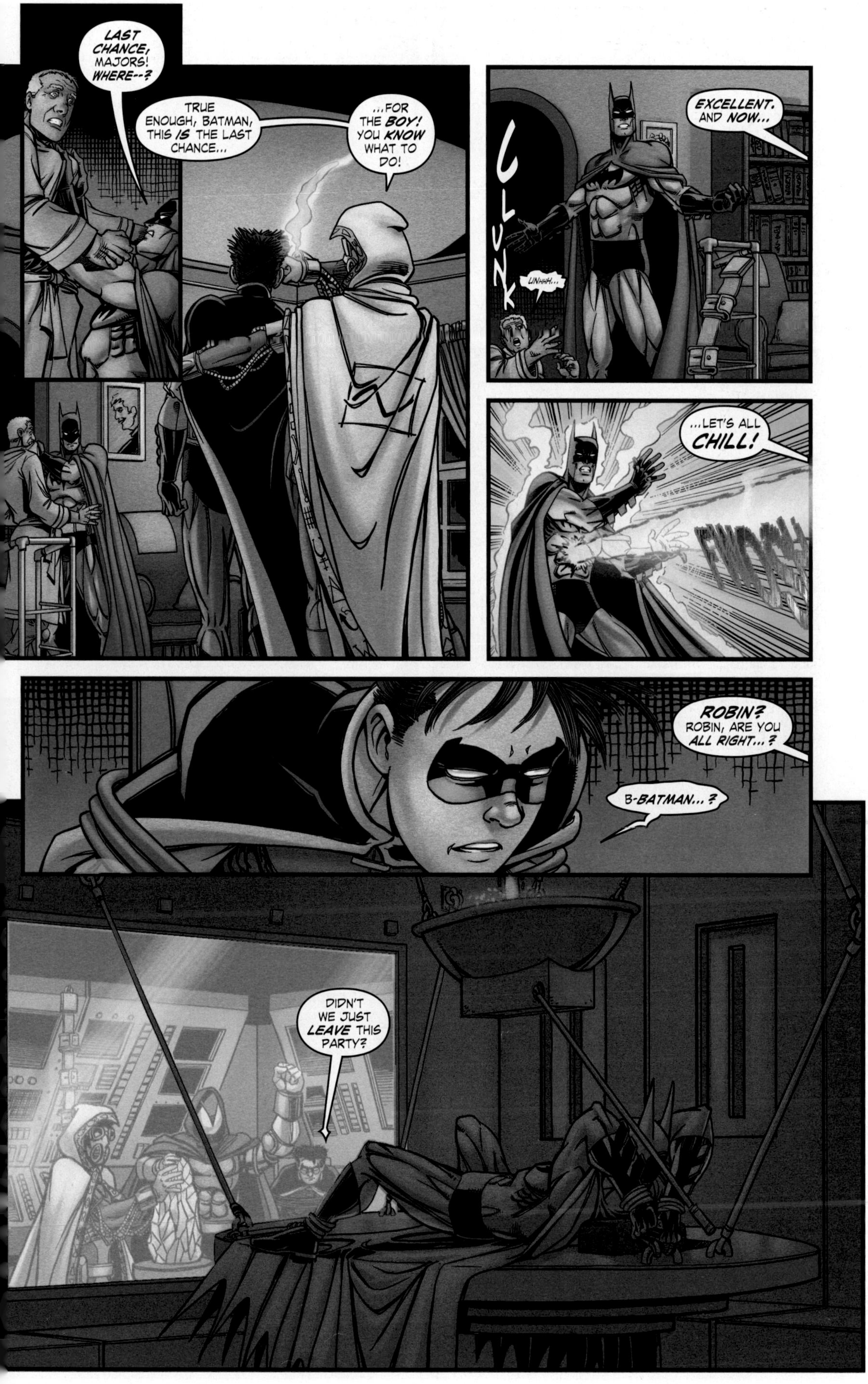
LAST CHANCE, MAJORS! WHERE--?
TRUE ENOUGH, BATMAN, THIS IS THE LAST CHANCE...
...FOR THE BOY! YOU KNOW WHAT TO DO!
EXCELLENT. AND NOW...
CLUNK
UNHHH...
...LET'S ALL CHILL!
ROBIN? ROBIN, ARE YOU ALL RIGHT...?
B-BATMAN...?
DIDN'T WE JUST LEAVE THIS PARTY?

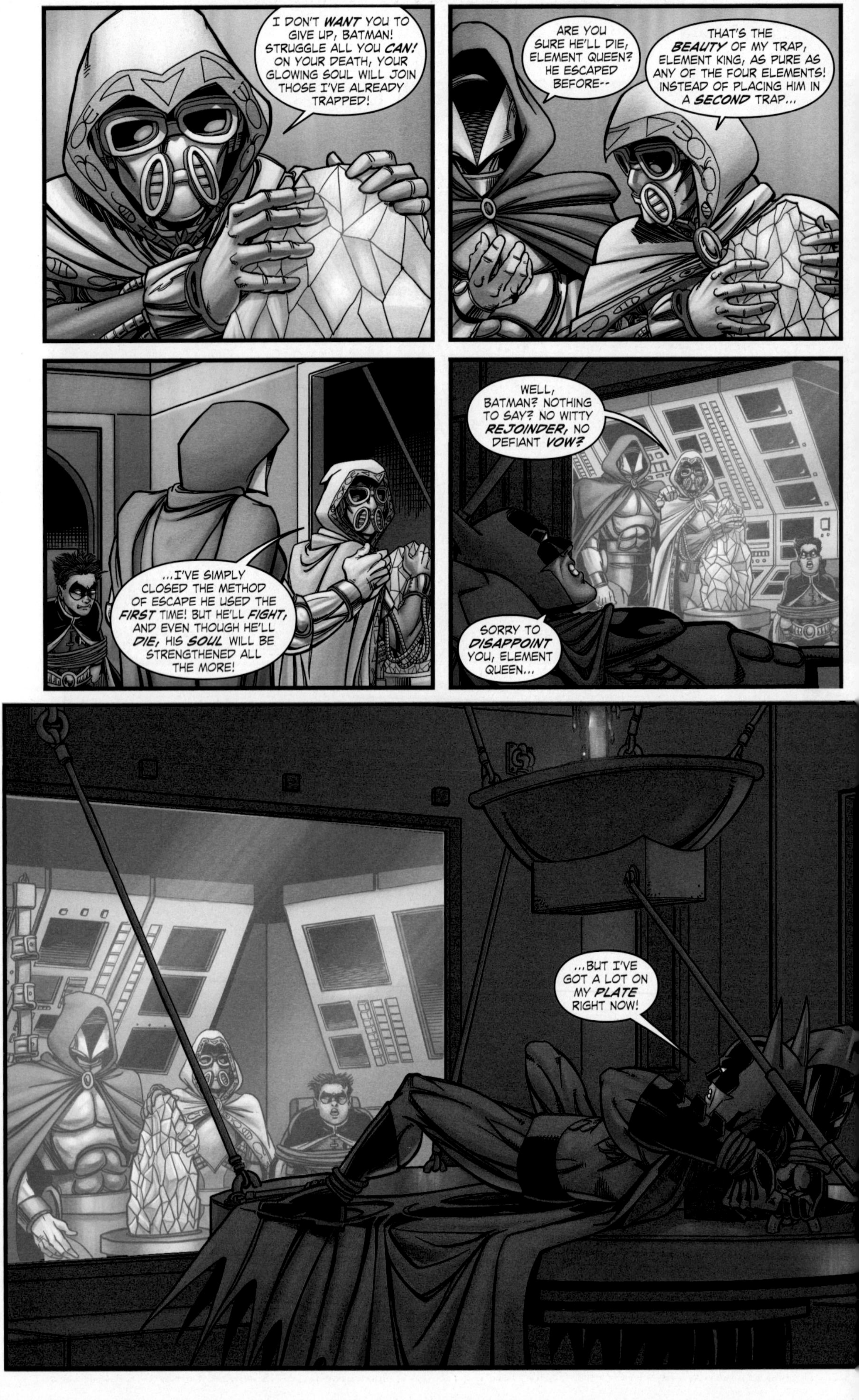
I DON'T WANT YOU TO GIVE UP, BATMAN! STRUGGLE ALL YOU CAN! ON YOUR DEATH, YOUR GLOWING SOUL WILL JOIN THOSE I'VE ALREADY TRAPPED!
ARE YOU SURE HE'LL DIE, ELEMENT QUEEN? HE ESCAPED BEFORE--
THAT'S THE BEAUTY OF MY TRAP, ELEMENT KING, AS PURE AS ANY OF THE FOUR ELEMENTS! INSTEAD OF PLACING HIM IN A SECOND TRAP...
...I'VE SIMPLY CLOSED THE METHOD OF ESCAPE HE USED THE FIRST TIME! BUT HE'LL FIGHT, AND EVEN THOUGH HE'LL DIE, HIS SOUL WILL BE STRENGTHENED ALL THE MORE!
WELL, BATMAN? NOTHING TO SAY? NO WITTY REJOINDER, NO DEFIANT VOW?
SORRY TO DISAPPOINT YOU, ELEMENT QUEEN...
...BUT I'VE GOT A LOT ON MY PLATE RIGHT NOW!

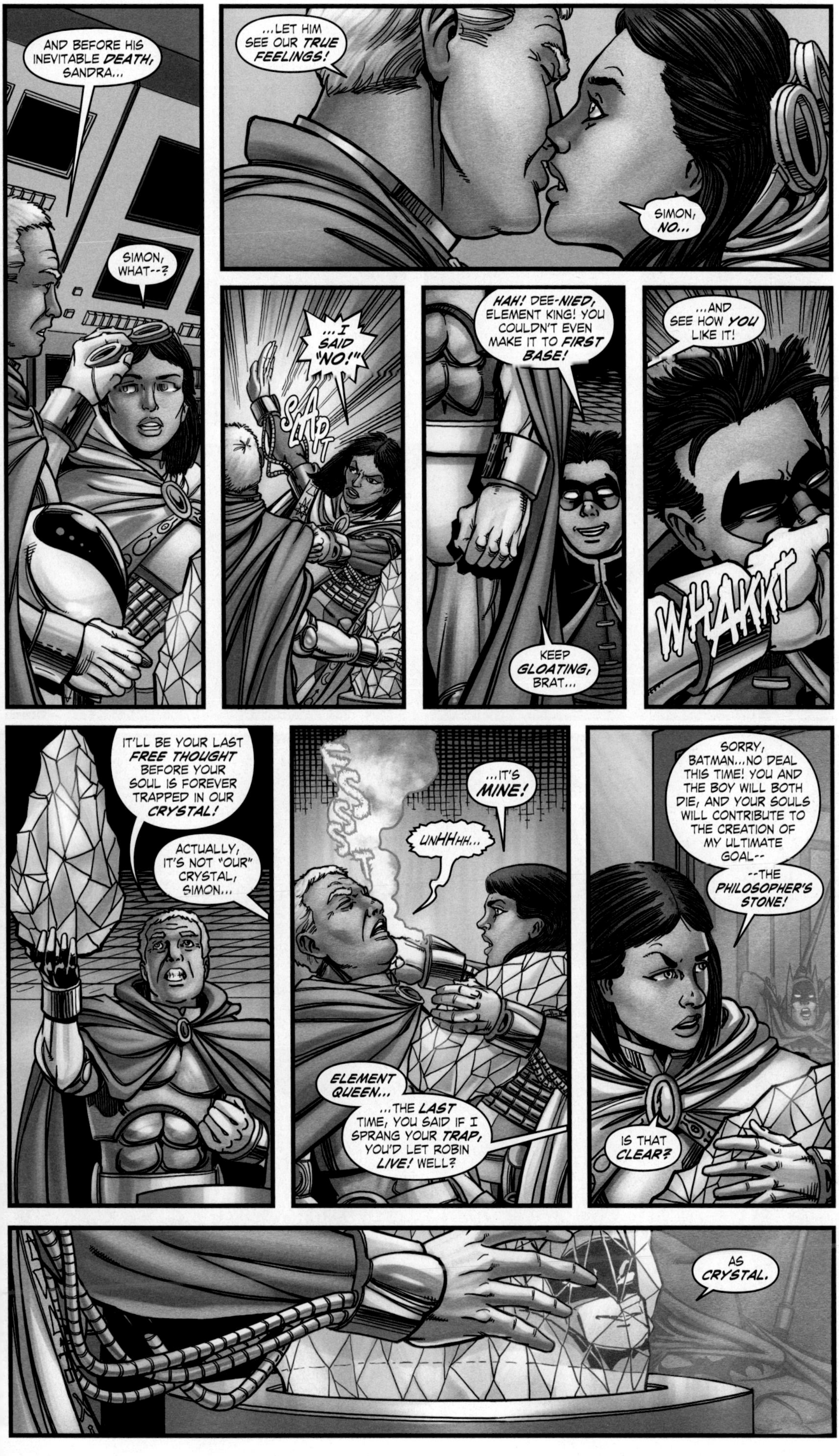
AND BEFORE HIS INEVITABLE DEATH, SANDRA...
SIMON, WHAT--?
...LET HIM SEE OUR TRUE FEELINGS!
SIMON, NO...
...I SAID "NO!"
SLAP
HAH! DEE-NIED, ELEMENT KING! YOU COULDN'T EVEN MAKE IT TO FIRST BASE!
KEEP GLOATING, BRAT...
...AND SEE HOW YOU LIKE IT!
WHAKK
IT'LL BE YOUR LAST FREE THOUGHT BEFORE YOUR SOUL IS FOREVER TRAPPED IN OUR CRYSTAL!
ACTUALLY, IT'S NOT "OUR" CRYSTAL, SIMON...
...IT'S MINE!
UNHHHH...
ELEMENT QUEEN...
...THE LAST TIME, YOU SAID IF I SPRANG YOUR TRAP, YOU'D LET ROBIN LIVE! WELL?
SORRY, BATMAN...NO DEAL THIS TIME! YOU AND THE BOY WILL BOTH DIE, AND YOUR SOULS WILL CONTRIBUTE TO THE CREATION OF MY ULTIMATE GOAL--
--THE PHILOSOPHER'S STONE!
IS THAT CLEAR?
AS CRYSTAL.

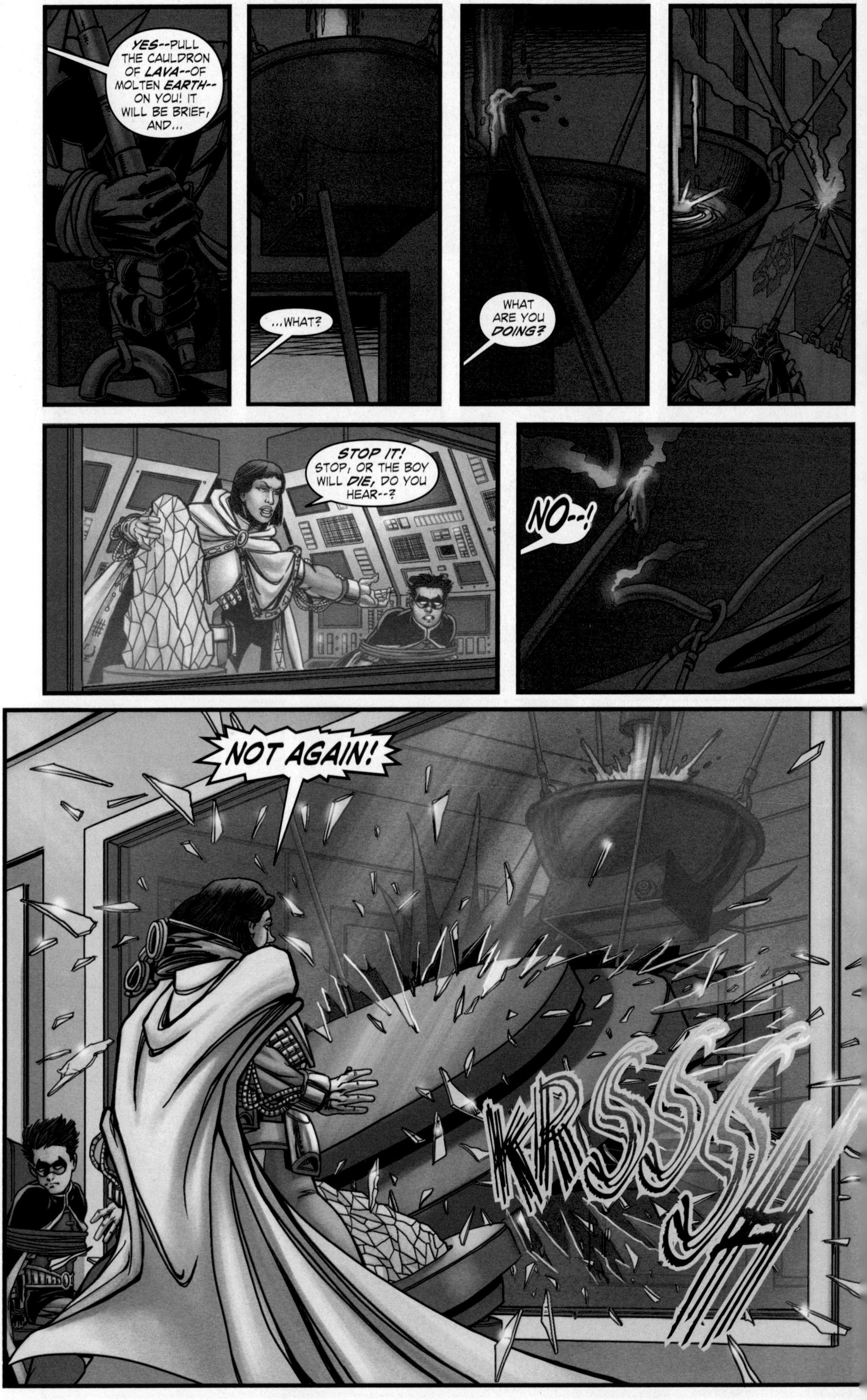
YES--PULL THE CAULDRON OF LAVA--OF MOLTEN EARTH--ON YOU! IT WILL BE BRIEF, AND...
...WHAT?
WHAT ARE YOU DOING?
STOP IT! STOP, OR THE BOY WILL DIE, DO YOU HEAR--?
NO--!
NOT AGAIN!
KRSSSH

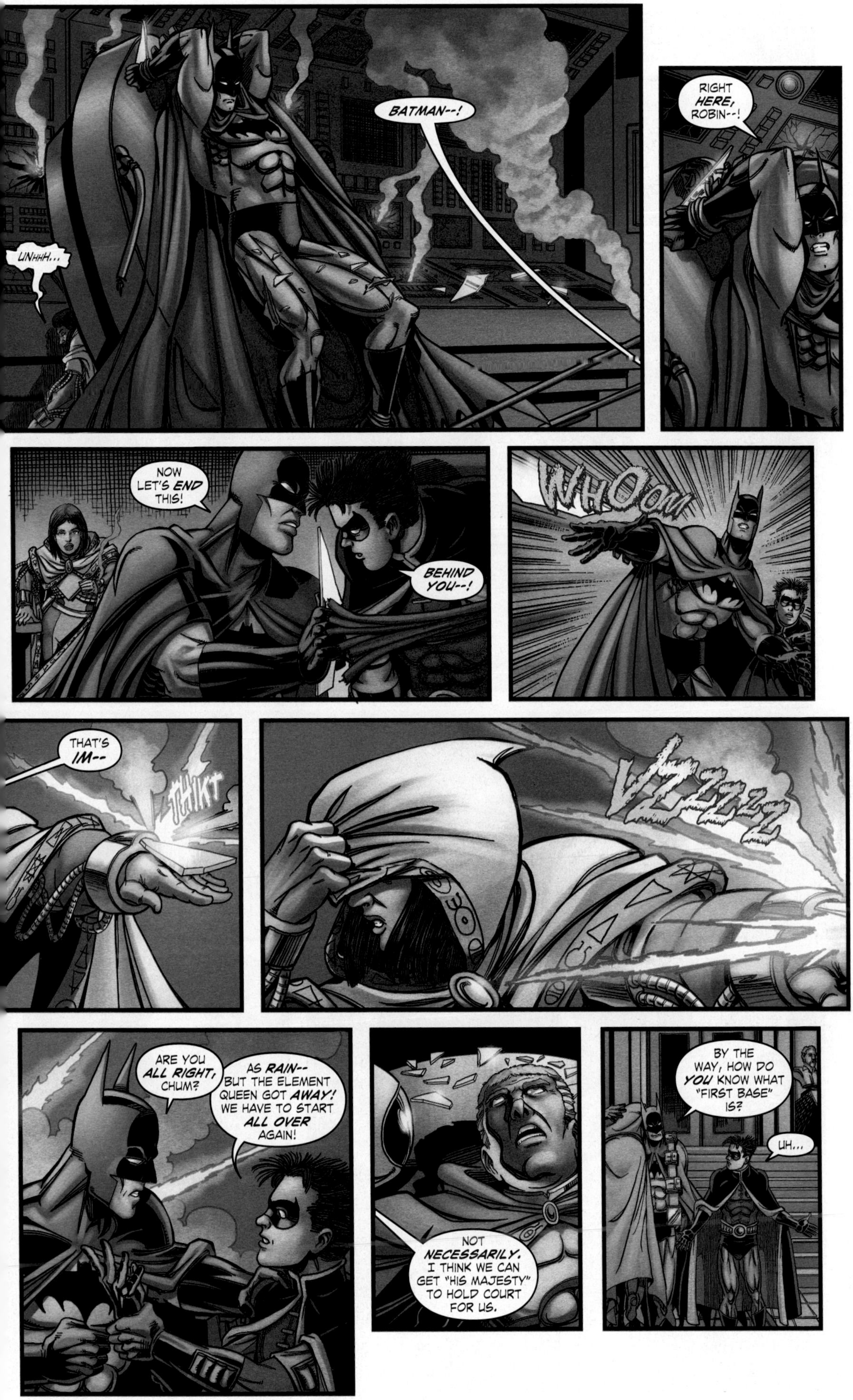
BATMAN--!
UNHHH...
RIGHT HERE, ROBIN--!
NOW LET'S END THIS!
BEHIND YOU--!
WHOOM
THAT'S IM--
THIKT
VZZZZZ
ARE YOU ALL RIGHT, CHUM?
AS RAIN-- BUT THE ELEMENT QUEEN GOT AWAY! WE HAVE TO START ALL OVER AGAIN!
NOT NECESSARILY. I THINK WE CAN GET "HIS MAJESTY" TO HOLD COURT FOR US.
BY THE WAY, HOW DO YOU KNOW WHAT "FIRST BASE" IS?
UH...

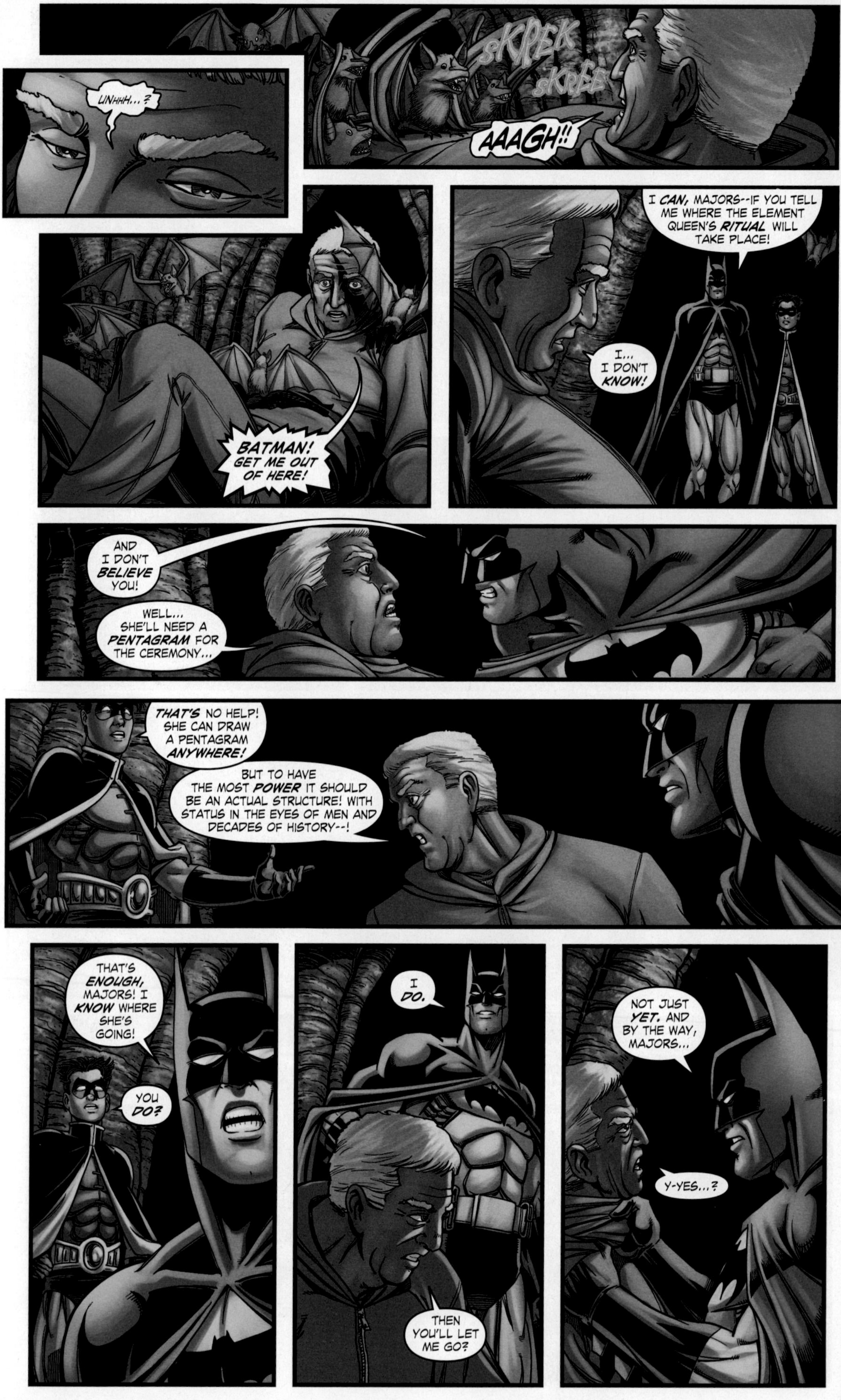
UNHHH...?
SKREEK
SKREE
AAAGH!!
BATMAN! GET ME OUT OF HERE!
I CAN, MAJORS--IF YOU TELL ME WHERE THE ELEMENT QUEEN'S RITUAL WILL TAKE PLACE!
I... I DON'T KNOW!
AND I DON'T BELIEVE YOU!
WELL... SHE'LL NEED A PENTAGRAM FOR THE CEREMONY...
THAT'S NO HELP! SHE CAN DRAW A PENTAGRAM ANYWHERE!
BUT TO HAVE THE MOST POWER IT SHOULD BE AN ACTUAL STRUCTURE! WITH STATUS IN THE EYES OF MEN AND DECADES OF HISTORY--!
THAT'S ENOUGH, MAJORS! I KNOW WHERE SHE'S GOING!
YOU DO?
I DO.
THEN YOU'LL LET ME GO?
NOT JUST YET. AND BY THE WAY, MAJORS...
Y-YES...?

WHAKT

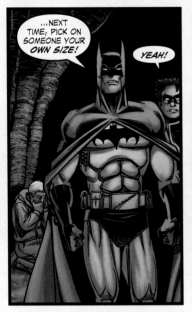

...NEXT TIME, PICK ON SOMEONE YOUR *OWN SIZE!*

YEAH!

SO WHAT'S THE *AGENDA?*

THINK, ROBIN! AN ACTUAL PENTAGRAM, FAMOUS AND WITH ITS OWN RICH *HISTORY...!*

OH, *WOW!* YOU DON'T *MEAN--?*

OUR DESTINATION ISN'T A PENTAGRAM, ROBIN...

"...IT'S THE PENTAGON!"

GOOD *EVENING,* MA'AM!

SOLDIER.

MAN, DON'T YOU *LOVE* A WOMAN IN *UNIFORM?*

THINK OF *DUTY* AND THE *FLAG,* MY FRIEND!

DOES THAT HELP?

NOT MUCH.

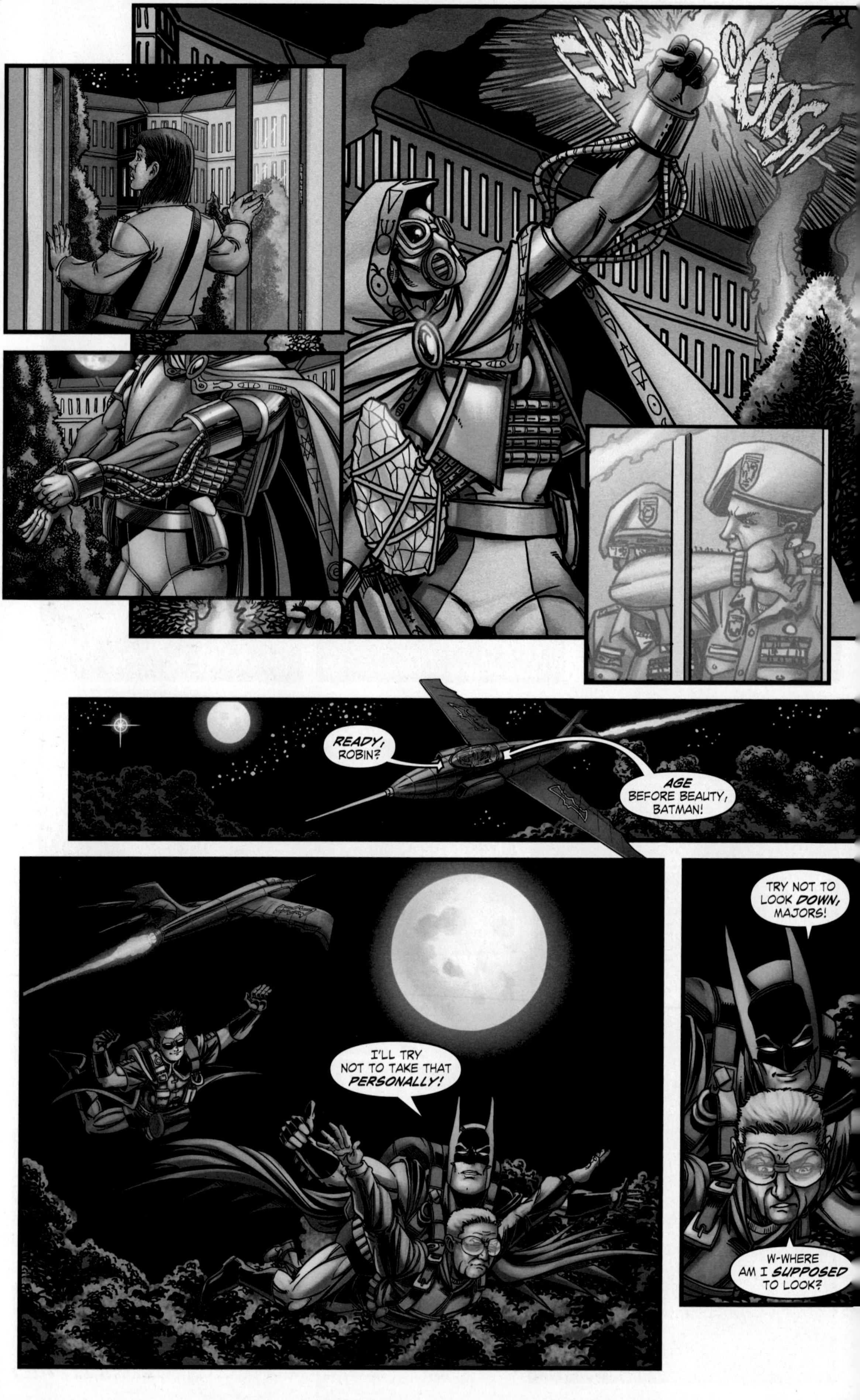
ZWOOOSH
READY, ROBIN?
AGE BEFORE BEAUTY, BATMAN!
I'LL TRY NOT TO TAKE THAT PERSONALLY!
TRY NOT TO LOOK DOWN, MAJORS!
W-WHERE AM I SUPPOSED TO LOOK?

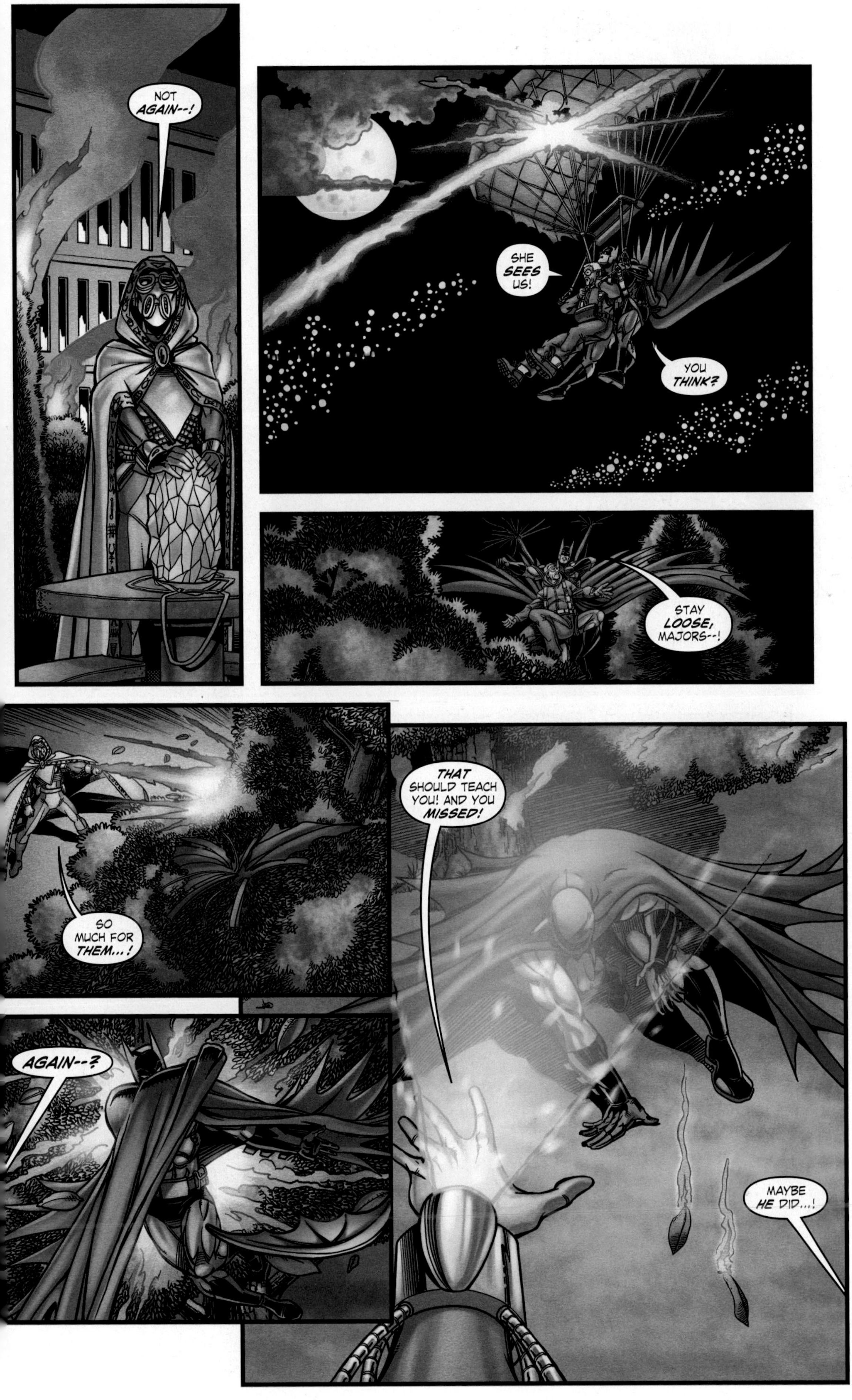
NOT AGAIN--!
SHE SEES US!
YOU THINK?
STAY LOOSE, MAJORS--!
SO MUCH FOR THEM...!
THAT SHOULD TEACH YOU! AND YOU MISSED!
AGAIN--?
MAYBE HE DID...!

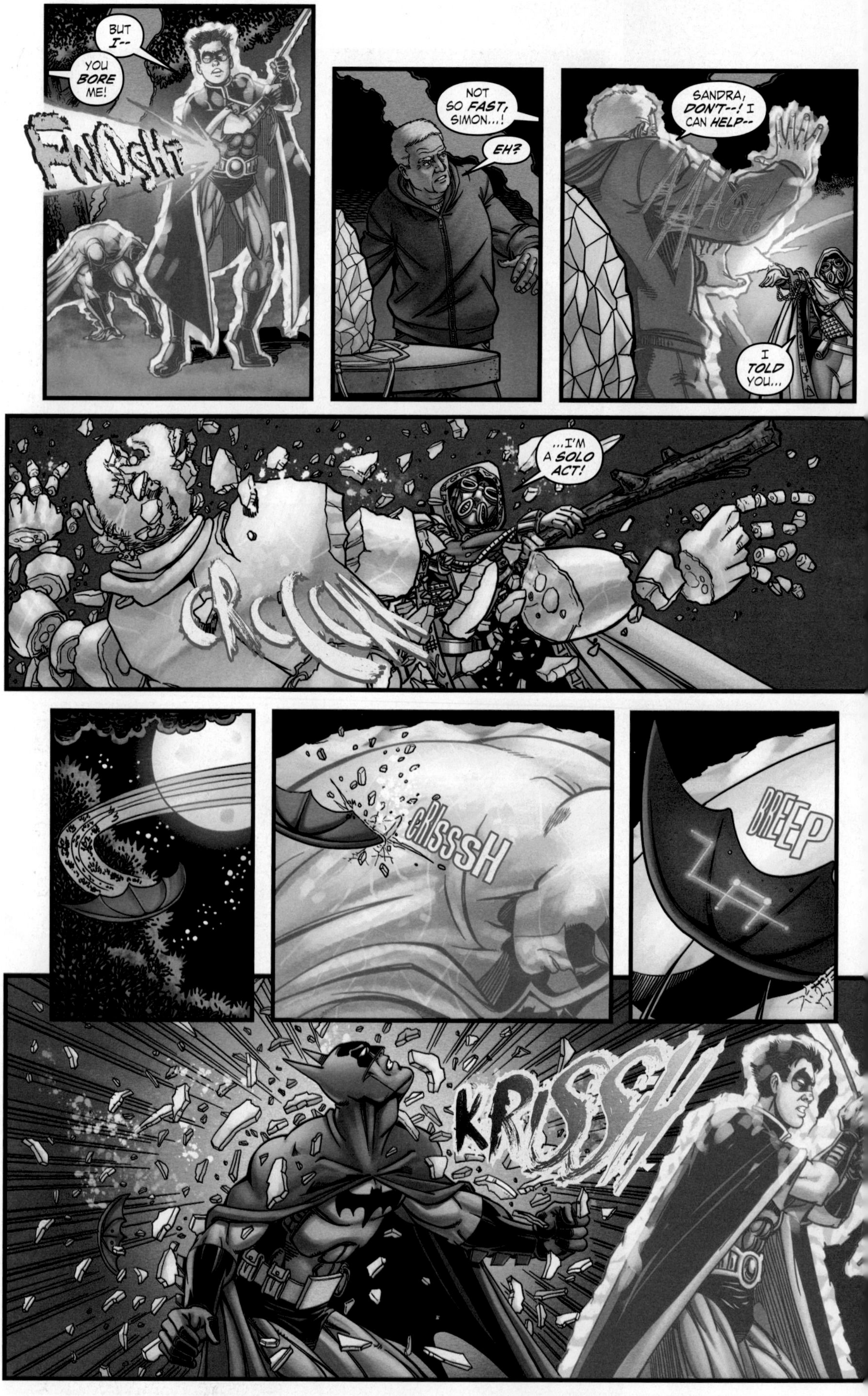
BUT I--
YOU BORE ME!
FWOSHT
NOT SO FAST, SIMON...!
EH?
SANDRA, DON'T--! I CAN HELP--
AAAGH!
I TOLD YOU...
...I'M A SOLO ACT!
CRCCK
CRISSSH
BREEP
KRISSH

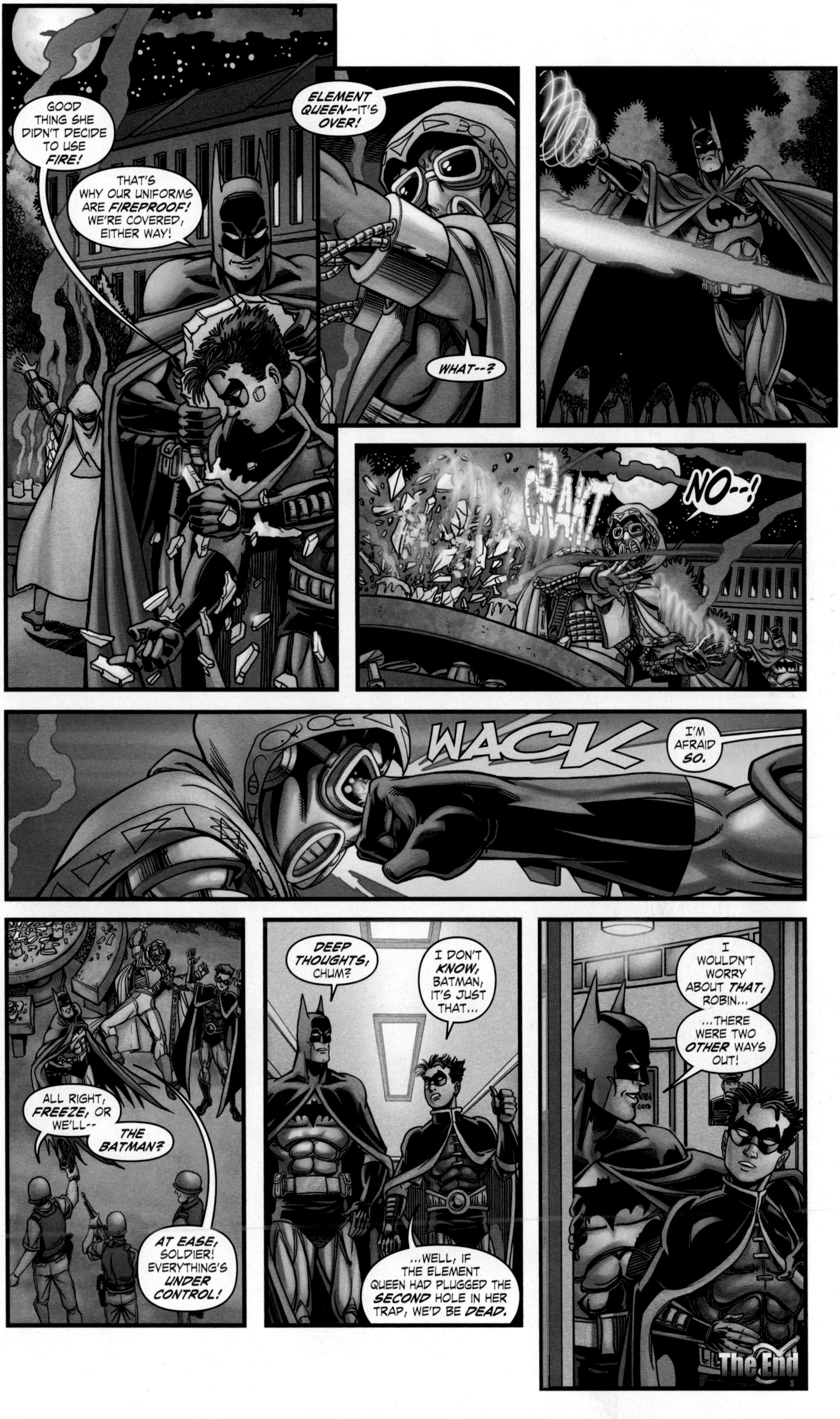
GOOD THING SHE DIDN'T DECIDE TO USE FIRE!
THAT'S WHY OUR UNIFORMS ARE FIREPROOF! WE'RE COVERED, EITHER WAY!
ELEMENT QUEEN--IT'S OVER!
WHAT--?
CRAKT
NO--!
WACK
I'M AFRAID SO.
ALL RIGHT, FREEZE, OR WE'LL--
THE BATMAN?
AT EASE, SOLDIER! EVERYTHING'S UNDER CONTROL!
DEEP THOUGHTS, CHUM?
I DON'T KNOW, BATMAN, IT'S JUST THAT...
...WELL, IF THE ELEMENT QUEEN HAD PLUGGED THE SECOND HOLE IN HER TRAP, WE'D BE DEAD.
I WOULDN'T WORRY ABOUT THAT, ROBIN...
...THERE WERE TWO OTHER WAYS OUT!
The End

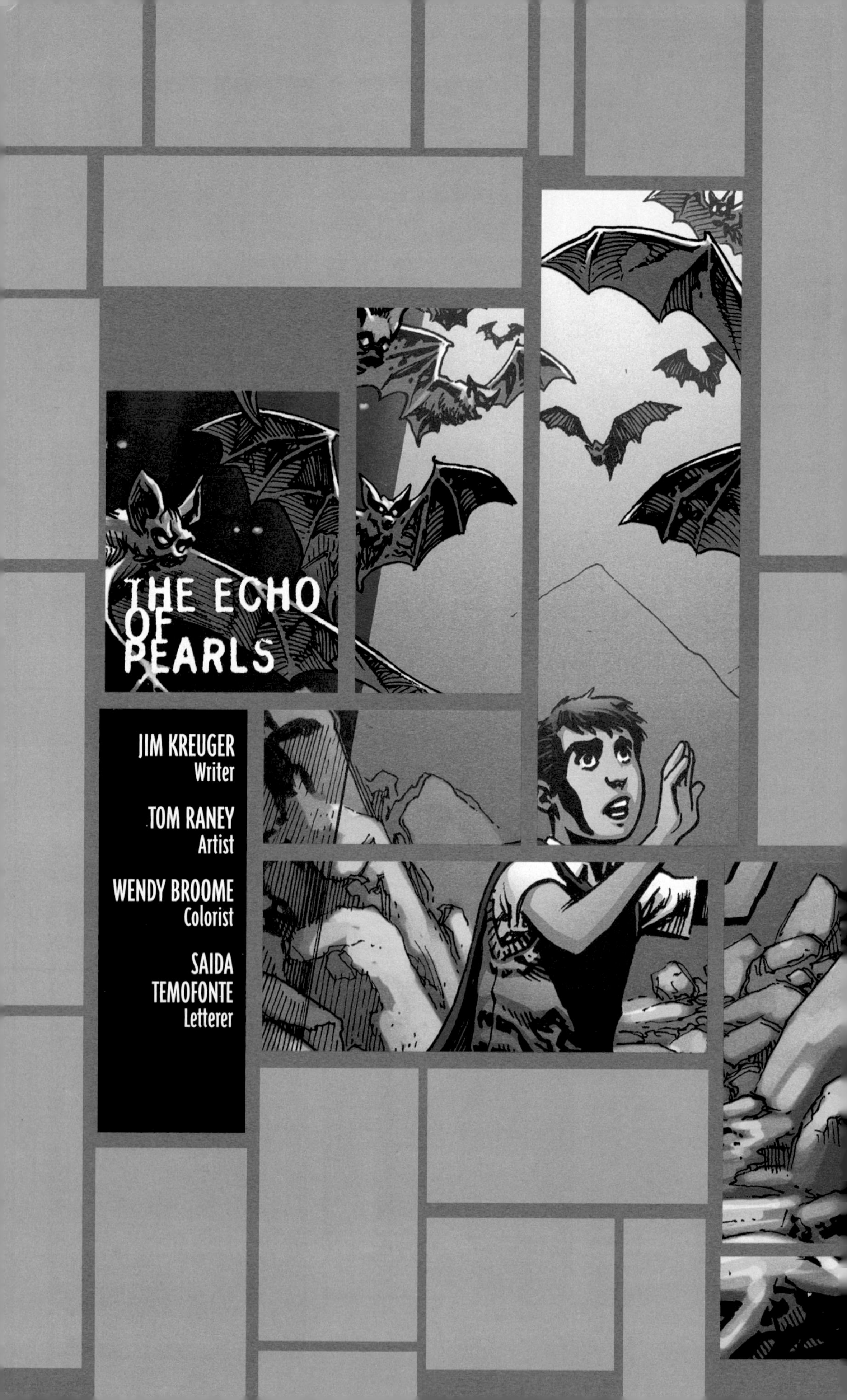
THE ECHO OF PEARLS
JIM KREUGER
Writer
TOM RANEY
Artist
WENDY BROOME
Colorist
SAIDA TEMOFONTE
Letterer

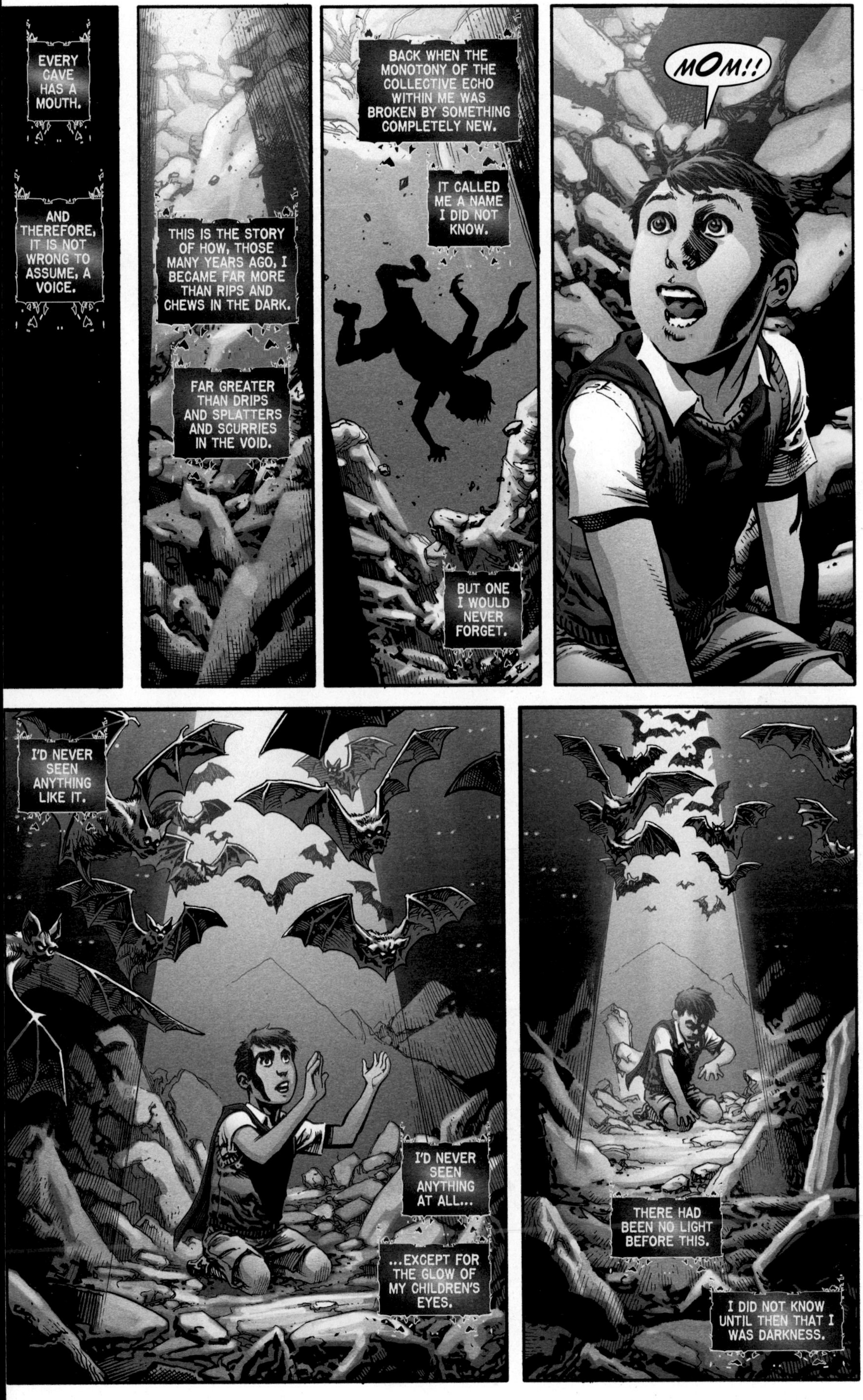
EVERY CAVE HAS A MOUTH.
AND THEREFORE, IT IS NOT WRONG TO ASSUME, A VOICE.
THIS IS THE STORY OF HOW, THOSE MANY YEARS AGO, I BECAME FAR MORE THAN RIPS AND CHEWS IN THE DARK.
FAR GREATER THAN DRIPS AND SPLATTERS AND SCURRIES IN THE VOID.
BACK WHEN THE MONOTONY OF THE COLLECTIVE ECHO WITHIN ME WAS BROKEN BY SOMETHING COMPLETELY NEW.
IT CALLED ME A NAME I DID NOT KNOW.
BUT ONE I WOULD NEVER FORGET.
MOM!!
I'D NEVER SEEN ANYTHING LIKE IT.
I'D NEVER SEEN ANYTHING AT ALL...
...EXCEPT FOR THE GLOW OF MY CHILDREN'S EYES.
THERE HAD BEEN NO LIGHT BEFORE THIS.
I DID NOT KNOW UNTIL THEN THAT I WAS DARKNESS.

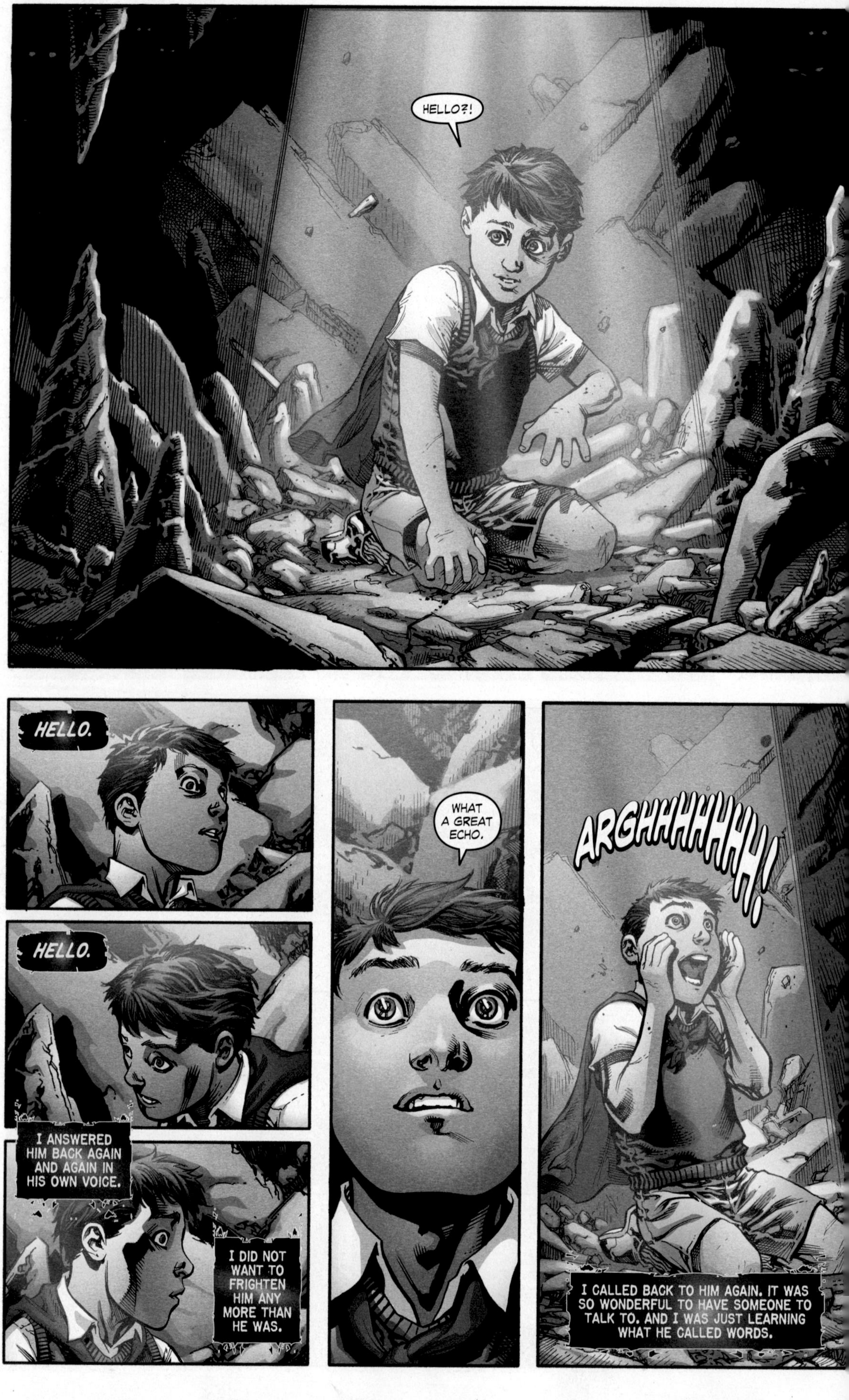
HELLO?!
HELLO.
HELLO.
I ANSWERED HIM BACK AGAIN AND AGAIN IN HIS OWN VOICE.
I DID NOT WANT TO FRIGHTEN HIM ANY MORE THAN HE WAS.
WHAT A GREAT ECHO.
ARGHHHHHHH!
I CALLED BACK TO HIM AGAIN. IT WAS SO WONDERFUL TO HAVE SOMEONE TO TALK TO. AND I WAS JUST LEARNING WHAT HE CALLED WORDS.

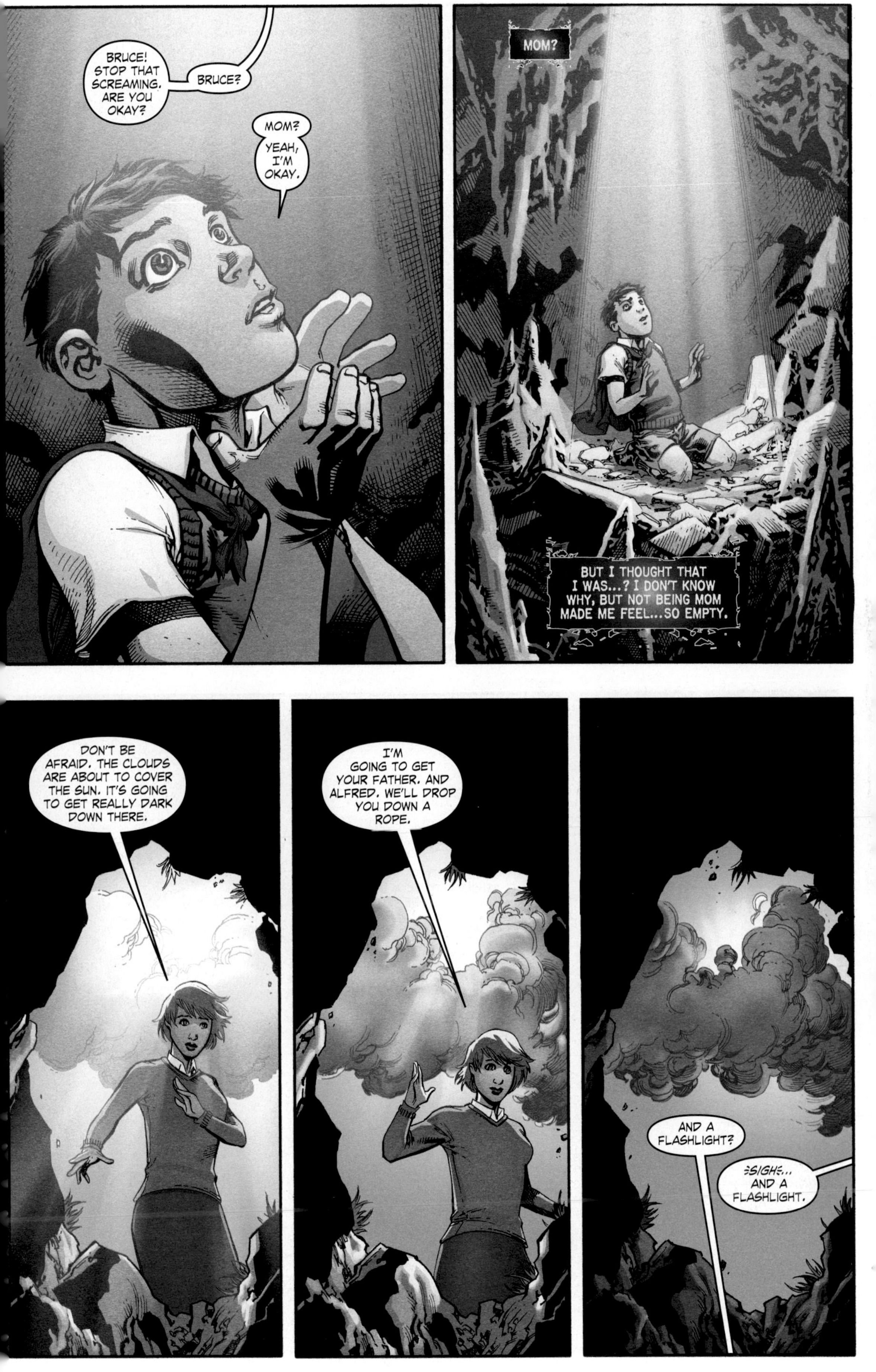
BRUCE?
BRUCE! STOP THAT SCREAMING. ARE YOU OKAY?
MOM? YEAH, I'M OKAY.
MOM?
BUT I THOUGHT THAT I WAS...? I DON'T KNOW WHY, BUT NOT BEING MOM MADE ME FEEL...SO EMPTY.
DON'T BE AFRAID. THE CLOUDS ARE ABOUT TO COVER THE SUN. IT'S GOING TO GET REALLY DARK DOWN THERE.
I'M GOING TO GET YOUR FATHER. AND ALFRED. WE'LL DROP YOU DOWN A ROPE.
AND A FLASHLIGHT?
=SIGH=... AND A FLASHLIGHT.

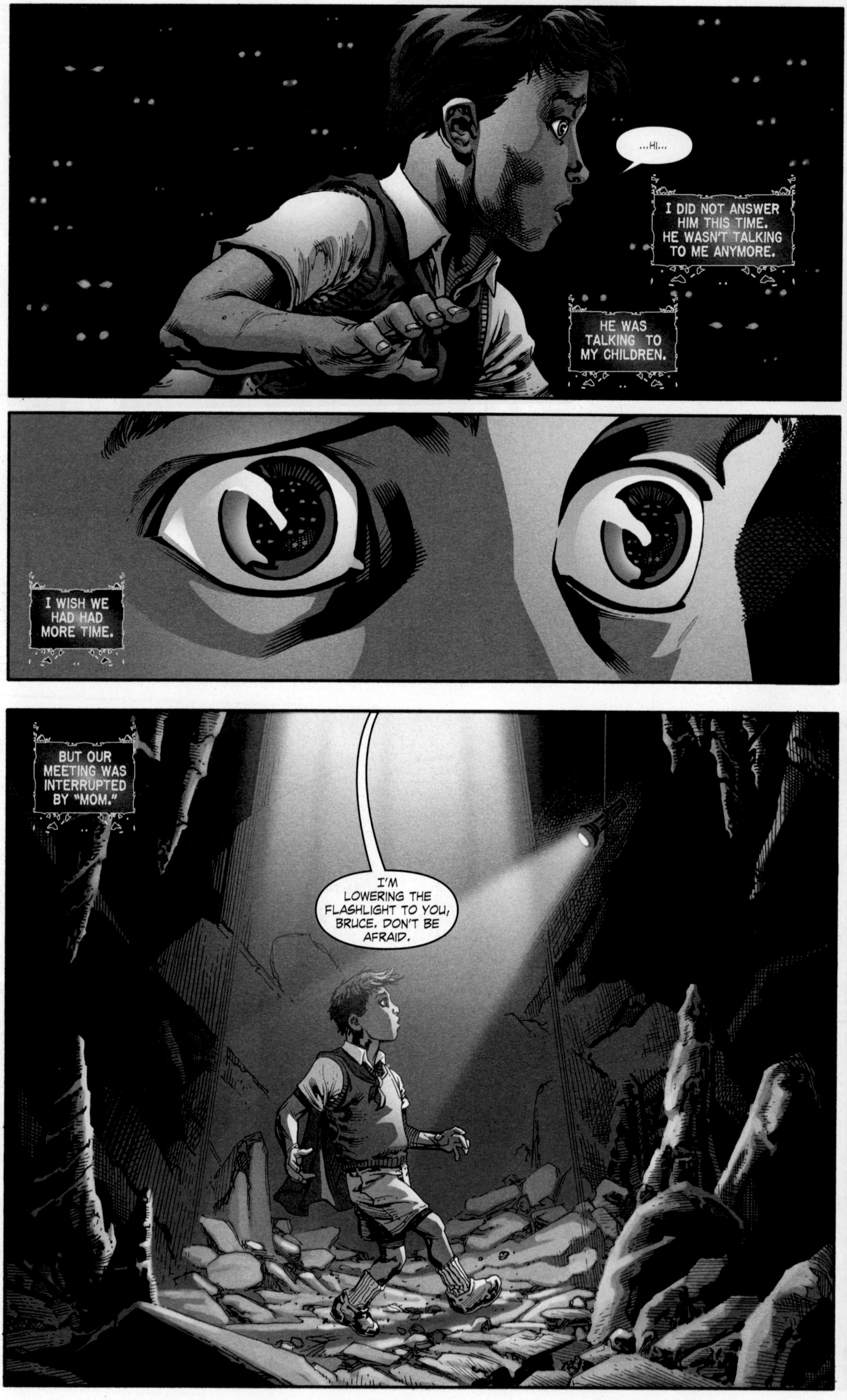
...HI...
I DID NOT ANSWER HIM THIS TIME. HE WASN'T TALKING TO ME ANYMORE.
HE WAS TALKING TO MY CHILDREN.
I WISH WE HAD HAD MORE TIME.
BUT OUR MEETING WAS INTERRUPTED BY "MOM."
I'M LOWERING THE FLASHLIGHT TO YOU, BRUCE. DON'T BE AFRAID.

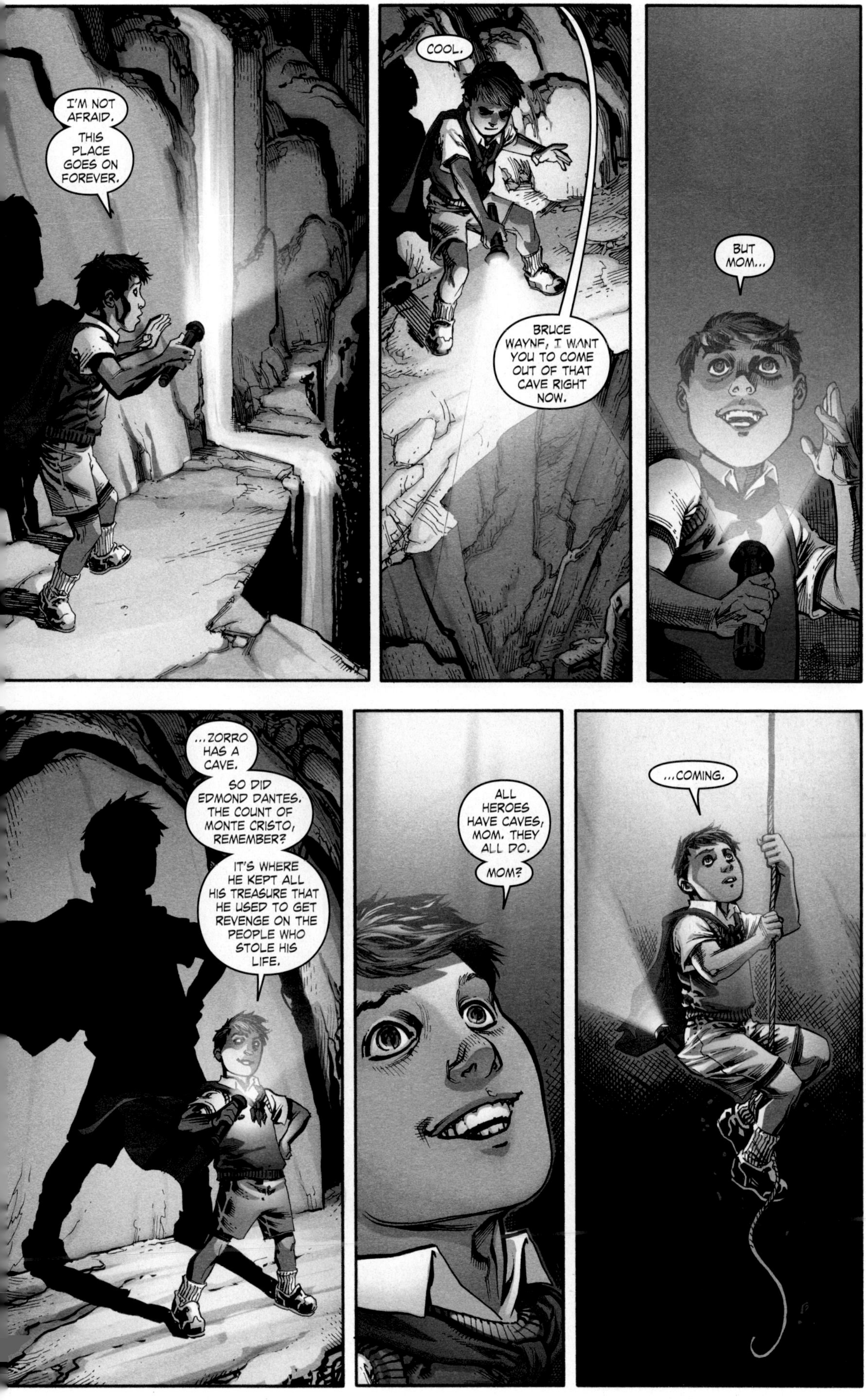
I'M NOT AFRAID.
THIS PLACE GOES ON FOREVER.
COOL.
BRUCE WAYNE, I WANT YOU TO COME OUT OF THAT CAVE RIGHT NOW.
BUT MOM...
...ZORRO HAS A CAVE.
SO DID EDMOND DANTES. THE COUNT OF MONTE CRISTO, REMEMBER?
IT'S WHERE HE KEPT ALL HIS TREASURE THAT HE USED TO GET REVENGE ON THE PEOPLE WHO STOLE HIS LIFE.
ALL HEROES HAVE CAVES, MOM. THEY ALL DO.
MOM?
...COMING.

I DIDN'T SEE HIM AGAIN FOR A LONG TIME AFTER THAT.

AND WHEN HE DID RETURN, HE WASN'T SMILING ANYMORE.

HE WAS SOBBING.

AND IT WAS HE THAT NOW SEEMED EMPTY, AND HOLLOWED.

THERE WAS EVEN A DARKNESS TO HIM THAT HAD NOT BEEN THERE BEFORE.

HIS TEARS FELL LIKE STONES, BUT THEY DID NOT BREAK AS MINE DO. THEY DID NOT SHATTER AND SPREAD LIKE RUBBLE.

THEY WERE THE MOST BEAUTIFUL COLOR.

MOM.

DAD.

THAT'S WHEN I REALIZED THAT BRUCE WAS TRYING TO SPEAK TO ME.

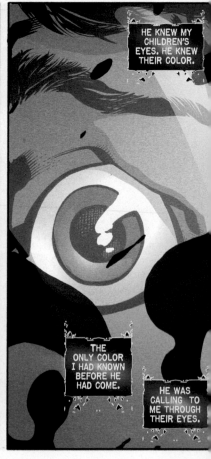

HE KNEW MY CHILDREN'S EYES. HE KNEW THEIR COLOR.

THE ONLY COLOR I HAD KNOWN BEFORE HE HAD COME.

HE WAS CALLING TO ME THROUGH THEIR EYES.

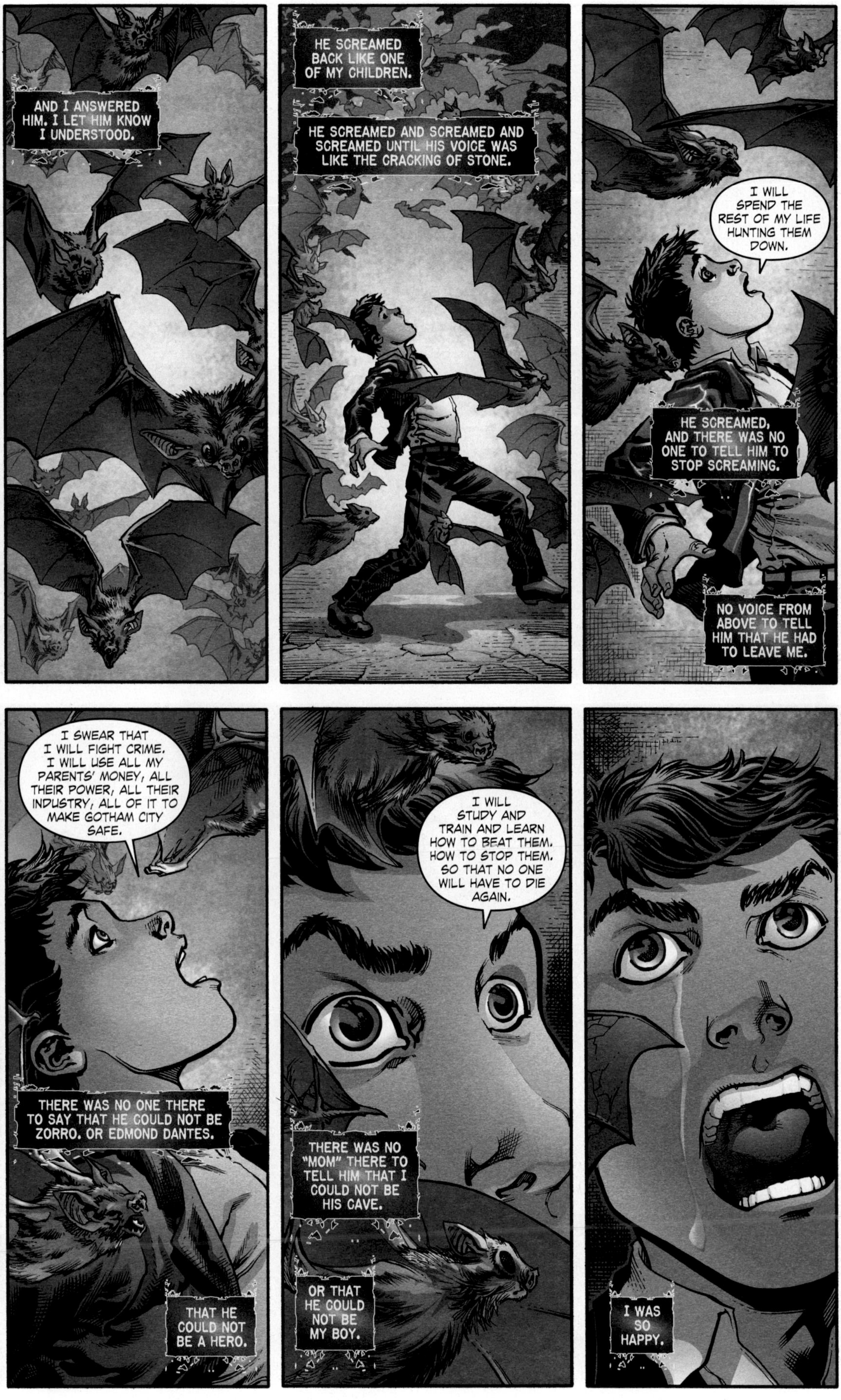
AND I ANSWERED HIM. I LET HIM KNOW I UNDERSTOOD.
HE SCREAMED BACK LIKE ONE OF MY CHILDREN.
HE SCREAMED AND SCREAMED AND SCREAMED UNTIL HIS VOICE WAS LIKE THE CRACKING OF STONE.
I WILL SPEND THE REST OF MY LIFE HUNTING THEM DOWN.
HE SCREAMED, AND THERE WAS NO ONE TO TELL HIM TO STOP SCREAMING.
NO VOICE FROM ABOVE TO TELL HIM THAT HE HAD TO LEAVE ME.
I SWEAR THAT I WILL FIGHT CRIME. I WILL USE ALL MY PARENTS' MONEY, ALL THEIR POWER, ALL THEIR INDUSTRY, ALL OF IT TO MAKE GOTHAM CITY SAFE.
THERE WAS NO ONE THERE TO SAY THAT HE COULD NOT BE ZORRO. OR EDMOND DANTES.
THAT HE COULD NOT BE A HERO.
I WILL STUDY AND TRAIN AND LEARN HOW TO BEAT THEM. HOW TO STOP THEM. SO THAT NO ONE WILL HAVE TO DIE AGAIN.
THERE WAS NO "MOM" THERE TO TELL HIM THAT I COULD NOT BE HIS CAVE.
OR THAT HE COULD NOT BE MY BOY.
I WAS SO HAPPY.

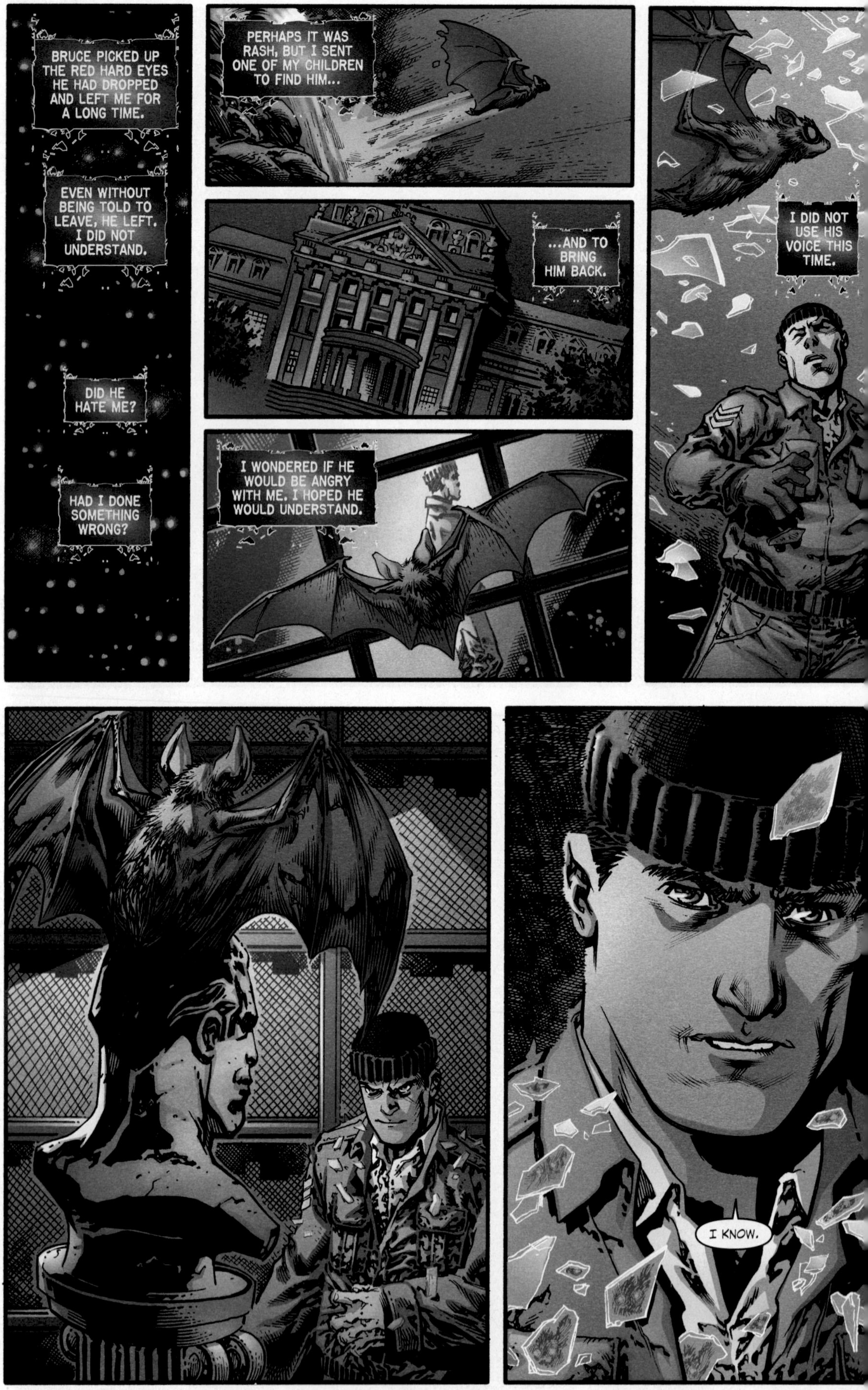
BRUCE PICKED UP THE RED HARD EYES HE HAD DROPPED AND LEFT ME FOR A LONG TIME.
EVEN WITHOUT BEING TOLD TO LEAVE, HE LEFT. I DID NOT UNDERSTAND.
DID HE HATE ME?
HAD I DONE SOMETHING WRONG?
PERHAPS IT WAS RASH, BUT I SENT ONE OF MY CHILDREN TO FIND HIM...
...AND TO BRING HIM BACK.
I WONDERED IF HE WOULD BE ANGRY WITH ME. I HOPED HE WOULD UNDERSTAND.
I DID NOT USE HIS VOICE THIS TIME.
I KNOW.

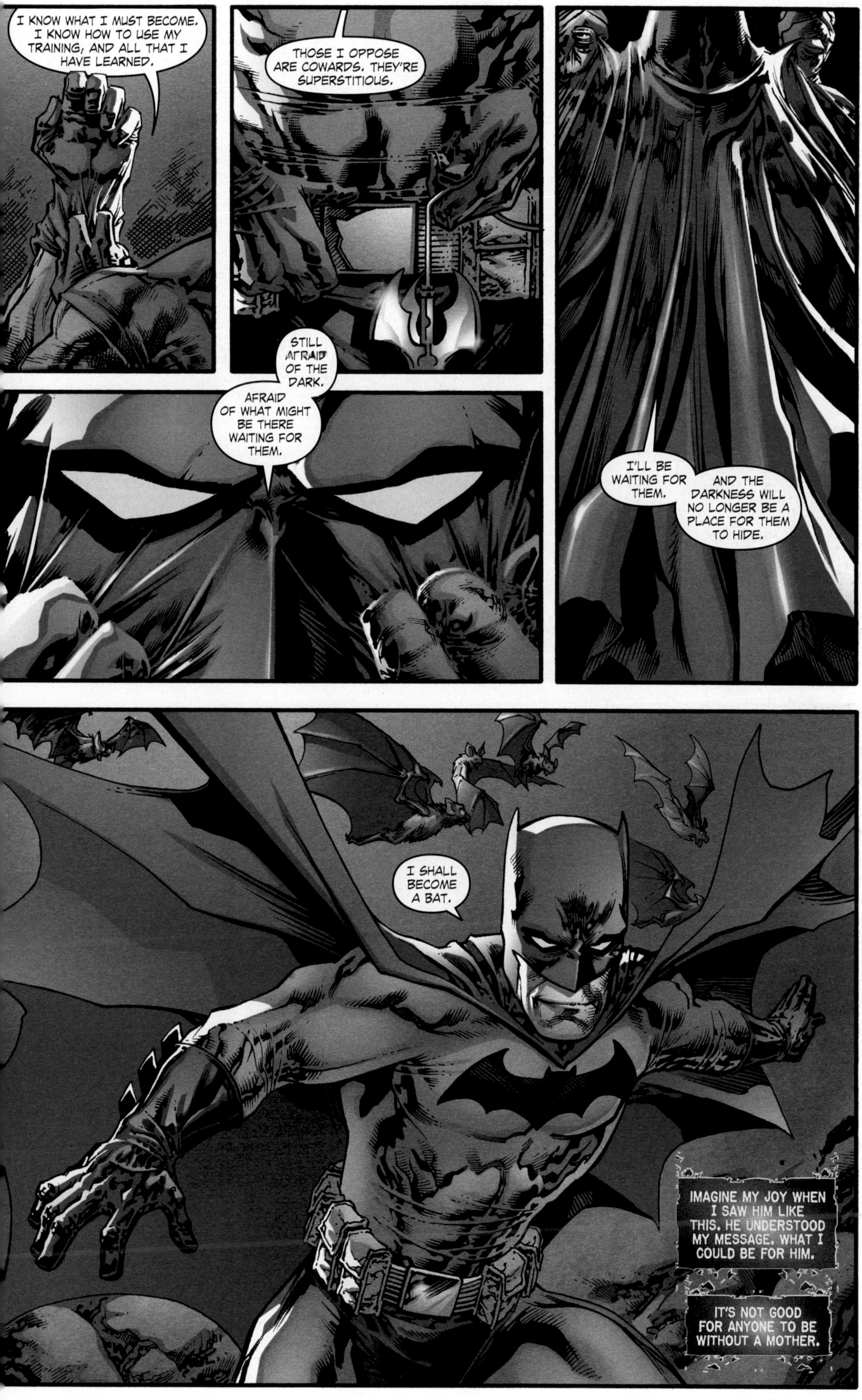
I KNOW WHAT I MUST BECOME. I KNOW HOW TO USE MY TRAINING, AND ALL THAT I HAVE LEARNED.
THOSE I OPPOSE ARE COWARDS. THEY'RE SUPERSTITIOUS.
STILL AFRAID OF THE DARK.
AFRAID OF WHAT MIGHT BE THERE WAITING FOR THEM.
I'LL BE WAITING FOR THEM.
AND THE DARKNESS WILL NO LONGER BE A PLACE FOR THEM TO HIDE.
I SHALL BECOME A BAT.
IMAGINE MY JOY WHEN I SAW HIM LIKE THIS. HE UNDERSTOOD MY MESSAGE. WHAT I COULD BE FOR HIM.
IT'S NOT GOOD FOR ANYONE TO BE WITHOUT A MOTHER.

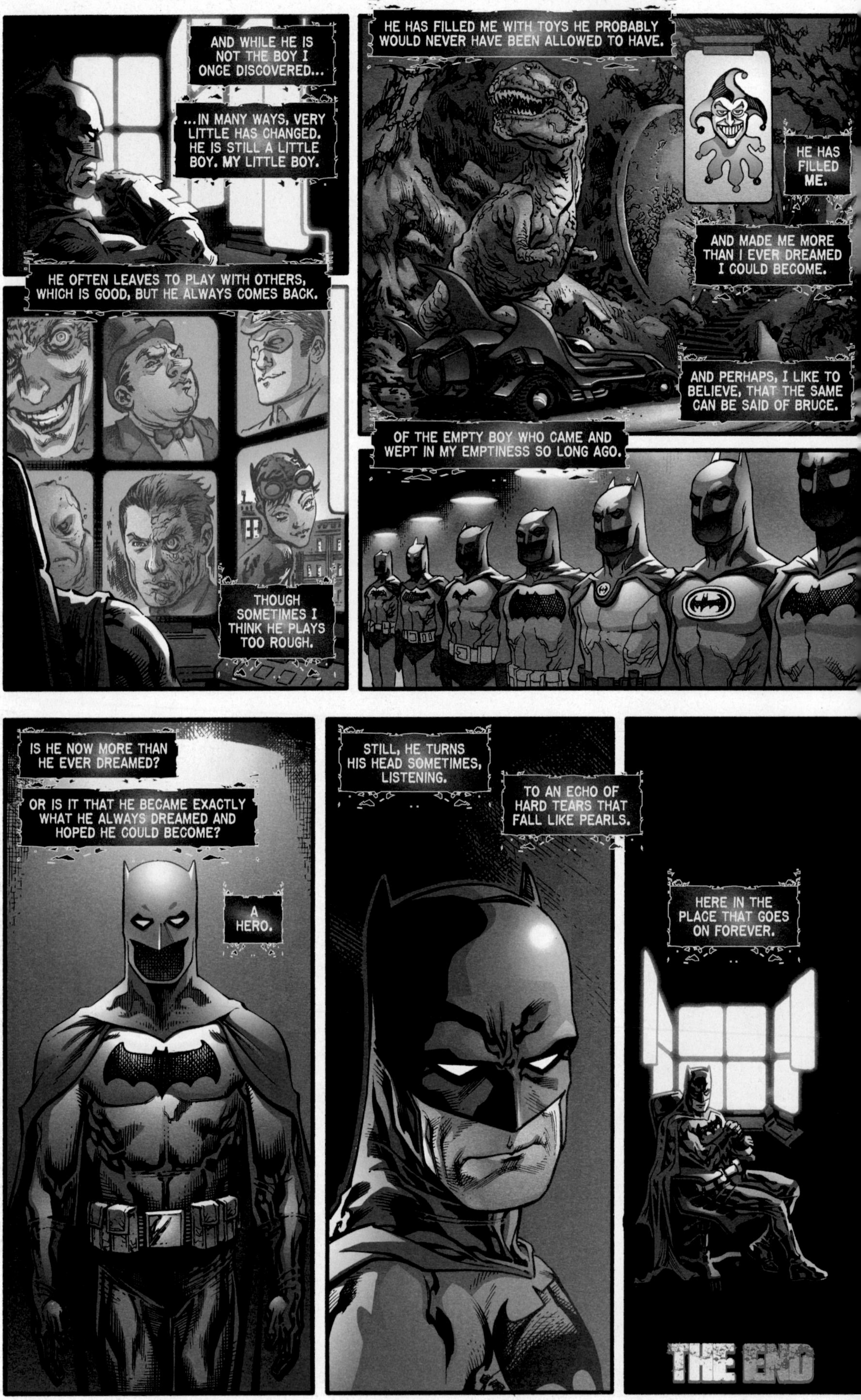
AND WHILE HE IS NOT THE BOY I ONCE DISCOVERED...
...IN MANY WAYS, VERY LITTLE HAS CHANGED. HE IS STILL A LITTLE BOY. MY LITTLE BOY.
HE OFTEN LEAVES TO PLAY WITH OTHERS, WHICH IS GOOD, BUT HE ALWAYS COMES BACK.
THOUGH SOMETIMES I THINK HE PLAYS TOO ROUGH.
HE HAS FILLED ME WITH TOYS HE PROBABLY WOULD NEVER HAVE BEEN ALLOWED TO HAVE.
HE HAS FILLED ME.
AND MADE ME MORE THAN I EVER DREAMED I COULD BECOME.
AND PERHAPS, I LIKE TO BELIEVE, THAT THE SAME CAN BE SAID OF BRUCE.
OF THE EMPTY BOY WHO CAME AND WEPT IN MY EMPTINESS SO LONG AGO.
IS HE NOW MORE THAN HE EVER DREAMED?
OR IS IT THAT HE BECAME EXACTLY WHAT HE ALWAYS DREAMED AND HOPED HE COULD BECOME?
A HERO.
STILL, HE TURNS HIS HEAD SOMETIMES, LISTENING.
TO AN ECHO OF HARD TEARS THAT FALL LIKE PEARLS.
HERE IN THE PLACE THAT GOES ON FOREVER.
THE END

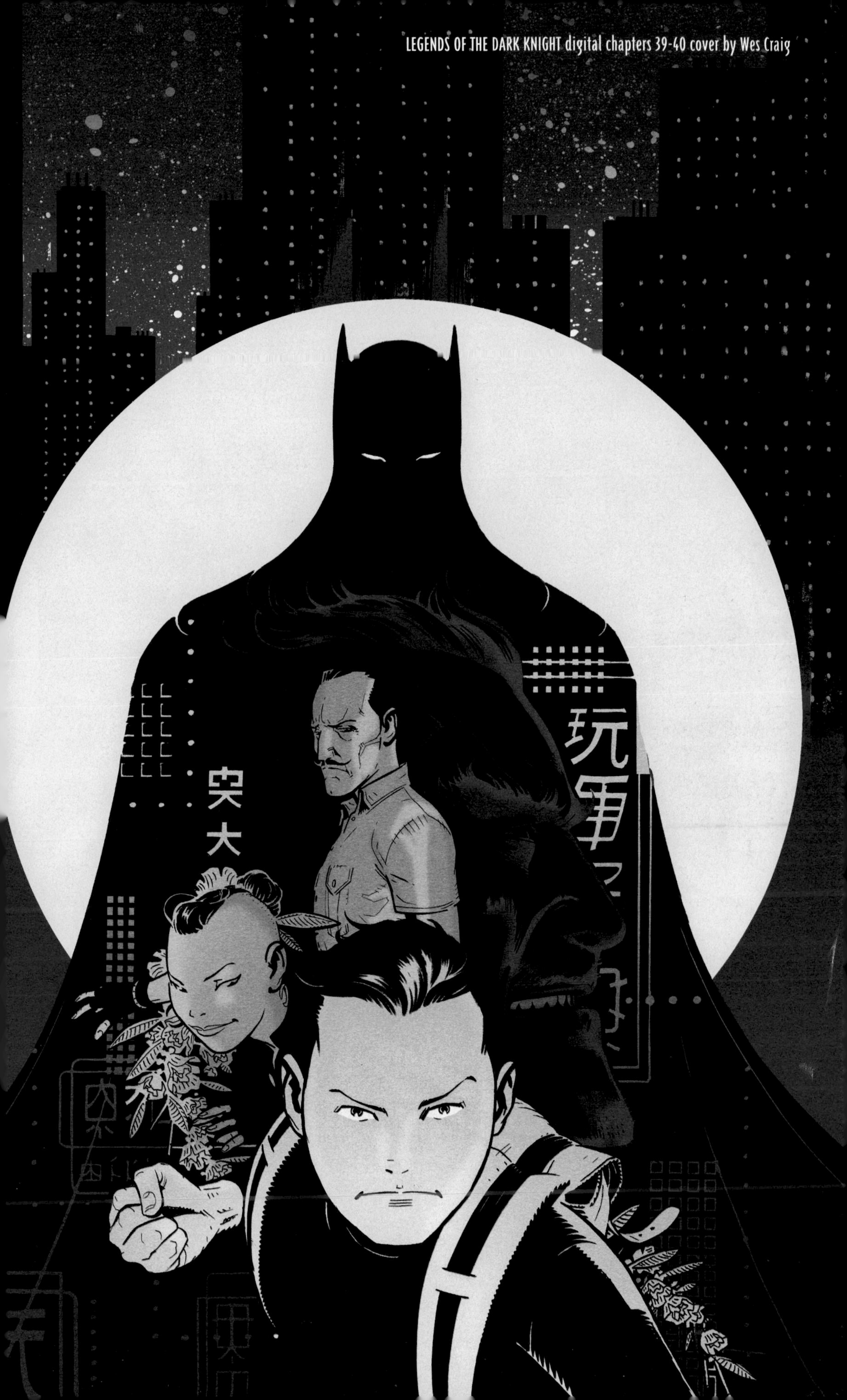

LEGENDS OF THE DARK KNIGHT digital chapters 39-40 cover by Wes Craig

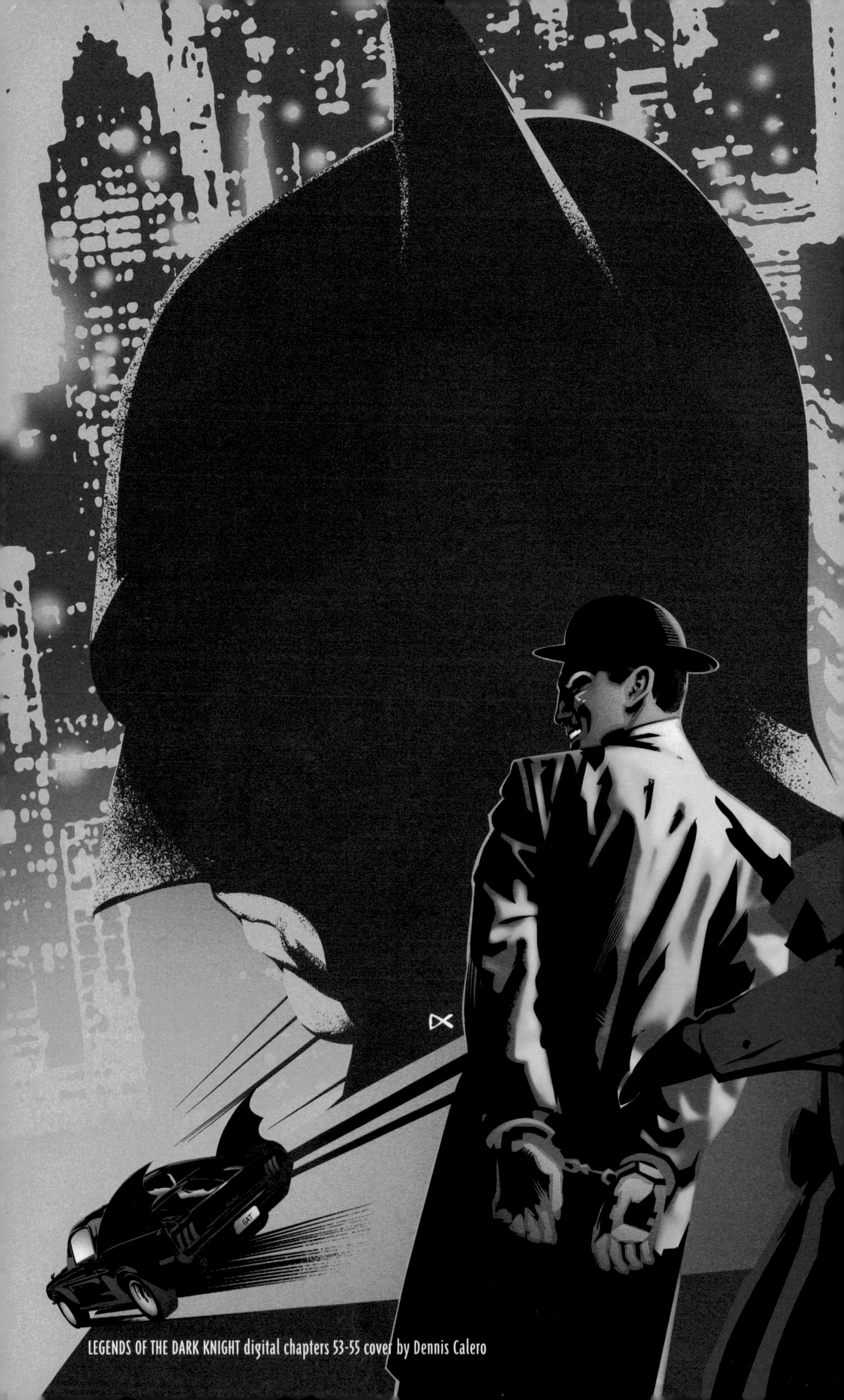

LEGENDS OF THE DARK KNIGHT digital chapters 53-55 cover by Dennis Calero

LEGENDS OF THE DARK KNIGHT digital chapters 56-58 cover by Jason Shawn Alexander

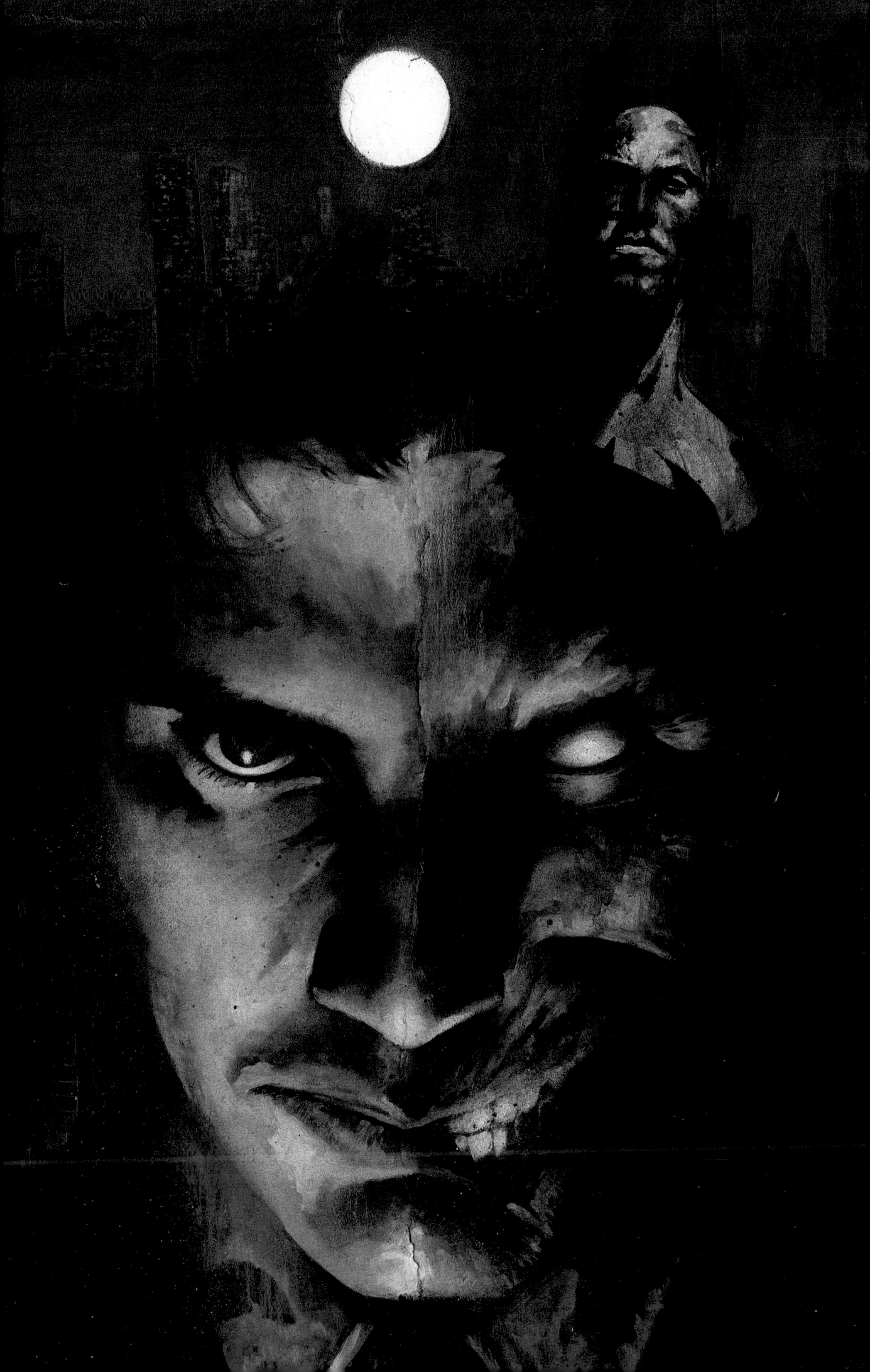

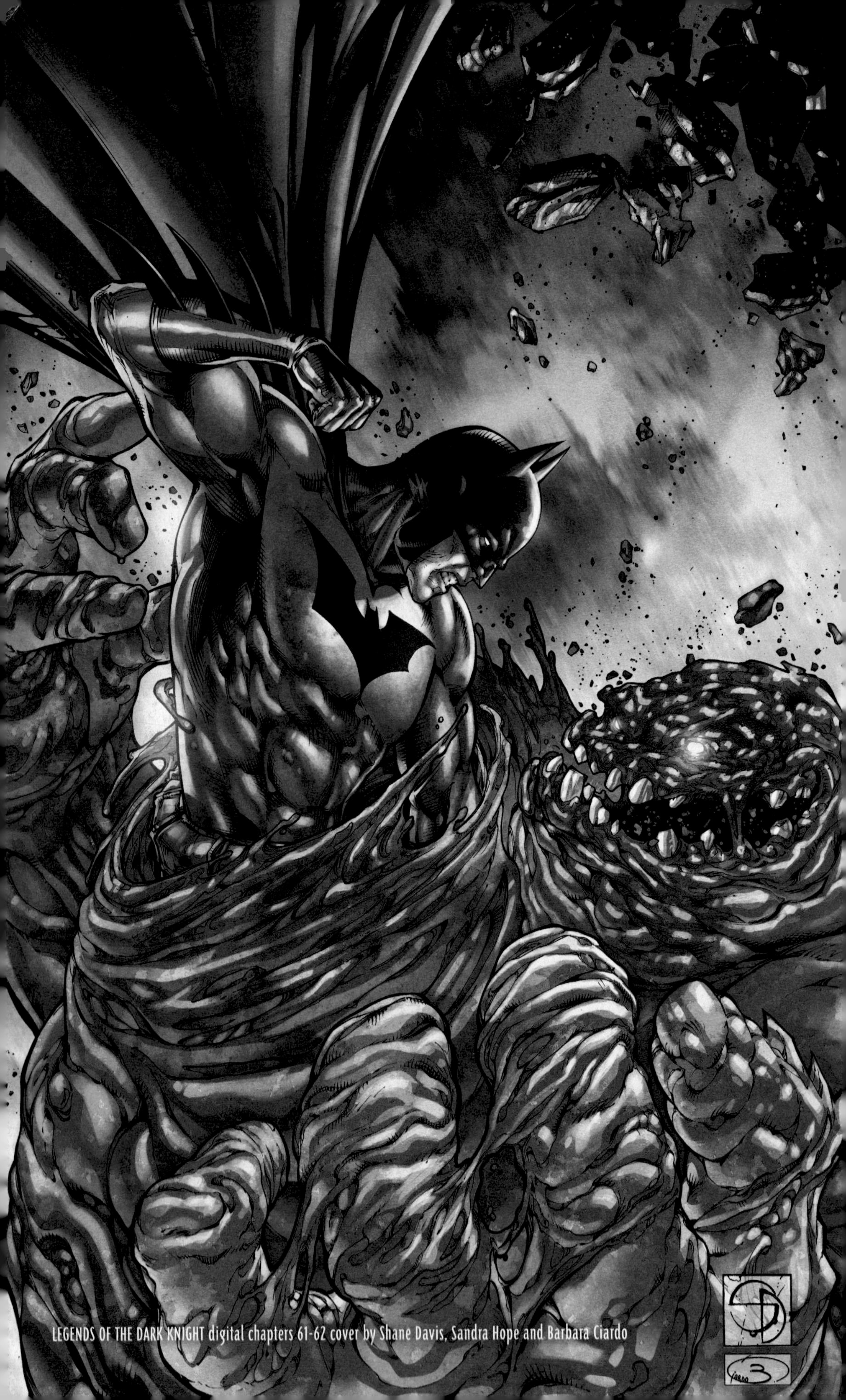

LEGENDS OF THE DARK KNIGHT digital chapters 61-62 cover by Shane Davis, Sandra Hope and Barbara Ciardo

LEGENDS OF THE DARK KNIGHT digital chapters 63-65 cover by Tom Lyle and Thomas Mason

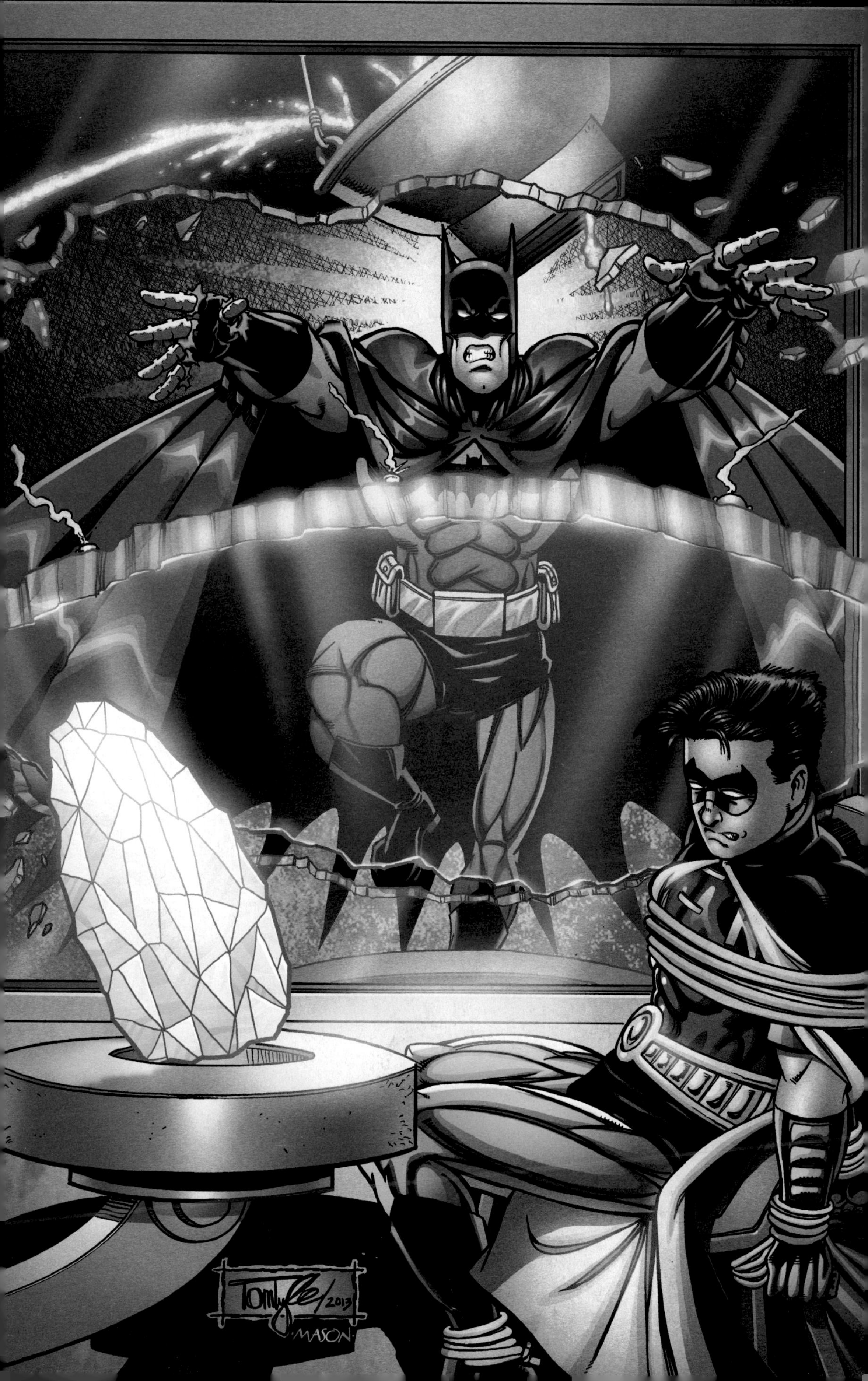

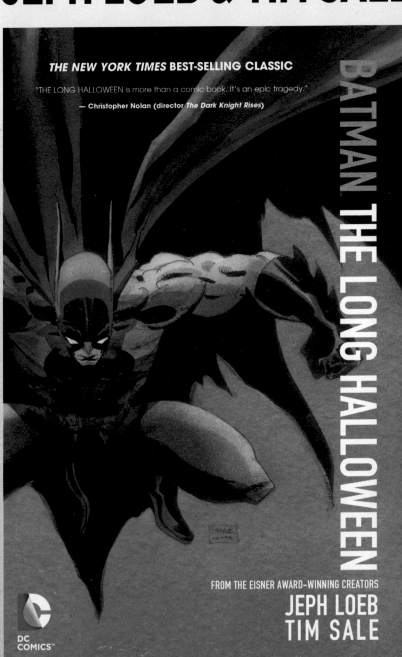